What the Bible teaches

GENESIS

RITCHIE OLD TESTAMENT COMMENTARIES

What the Bible teaches

GENESIS

J. Wesley Ferguson

GENERAL EDITOR   **W.S. STEVELY**

JOHN RITCHIE LTD
CHRISTIAN PUBLICATIONS

ISBN 0 946351 95 3

WHAT THE BIBLE TEACHES
© 2000 John Ritchie Ltd.
40 Beansburn, Kilmarnock, Scotland

Typeset by John Ritchie Ltd.
Printed by The Bath Press, Avon, England.

CONTENTS

MAPS AND CHART

CONTRIBUTOR

WESLEY FERGUSON

Born and brought up in Ireland, Wesley Ferguson graduated from Trinity College, Dublin with an honours degree in Classics. Entering the teaching profession, he taught in various schools in Ireland and England before going out to the Far East to teach in Singapore and then, for a period, in British North Borneo (now Sabah).

Returning to Ireland, he taught Classics and other subjects in Coleraine Academical Institution before being appointed an Inspector of Schools with responsibility for Classics in N. Ireland. He retired from the Inspectorate in 1992. During these years he has been engaged in gospel preaching and Bible teaching in many lands. Since his retirement he has had more time to devote to writing on biblical subjects.

ABBREVIATIONS

AV   Authorised Version, 1611 (known in USA as King James
            Version)

JBL   Journal of Biblical Literature

JSOT   Journal for the Study of the Old Testament

LXX   Septuagint (ancient translation of the Old Testament
            into Greek, often quoted in the New Testament)

NEB   New English Bible, 1970

Newberry   The AV as edited by Thomas Newberry also known as
            "The Englishman's Bible".

NIV   New International Version, 1978

NKJV   New King James Version, 1982

NT   New Testament

OT   Old Testament

REB   Revised English Bible, 1989 (revision of the NEB)

RSV   Revised Standard Version, 1952 (revision of the
            American Standard Version, which was the American
            variant of the RV)

RV   Revised Version, 1885 (published in England, revision
            of the AV)

PREFACE

The publishers have commissioned this Old Testament series of commentaries to complement the completed set of New Testament commentaries issued under the general title "What the Bible Teaches". Together they seek to provide an accessible and useful tool for the study of, and meditation on, Scripture.

While there is no shortage of commentaries currently available on the various books of the Old Testament it was felt that there was no complete series that sought simply to apply the message of Genesis through to Malachi to the concerns of believers today.

The authors of these volumes are not scholars of the original languages and rely on others for guidance on the best modern views of word meanings and similar matters. However all the authors share the conviction that the Bible in its entirety is the Word of God. They believe it to be reliable, accurate and intended "for our learning" (Rom 15.4). This view has been explained further by the Editor in a short series of articles that appeared in "The Believers Magazine", also published by John Ritchie Ltd., in 1999.

The two Testaments fit together so that principles and illustrations from the Old are brought to bear on issues that arise on nearly every page of the New. Knowledge of the Old is therefore an indispensable aid to the proper understanding of the New. In particular the Lord Jesus can be seen in prophecy and picture again and again. He, Himself, as described in the Gospels, is an exemplar of this approach to the Old Testament through His constant reference to people and incidents whose histories are recorded for us and to those prophetic statements that applied to Him.

Given this understanding of the nature and purpose of the Scriptures the main lessons of the books are considered and applied to our circumstances today by authors experienced in preaching and teaching the Word of God.

Since no attempt is being made to produce an academic series the technical apparatus has been kept to a minimum. Where authors have judged it of value attention is drawn to linguistic and other issues. Transliteration, where appropriate, is accompanied by reference to the numerical system devised by Strong to allow the reader without knowledge of the original languages to gain access to the various lexical aids which have adopted this system. The system of transliteration used is that adopted by the Theological Wordbook of the Old Testament

(TWOT), edited by Harris, Archer and Waltke and published by Moody Press, Chicago 1980.

References to Scripture without attribution are taken from the Authorised (King James) Version. Where other translations are quoted the source is given. Measurements given in the Authorised Version have been translated, where appropriate, into their metric equivalents.

Since the commentaries do not necessarily follow a verse-by-verse approach, and to save space and cost, the text of Scripture is not included. It is assumed that all readers have available a copy of the Bible.

The complete Old Testament is expected to be covered in around fifteen to eighteen volumes. These will not appear in the order in which they are found in the Scriptures but simply in order of completion by the authors commissioned for the series.

W.S. STEVELY

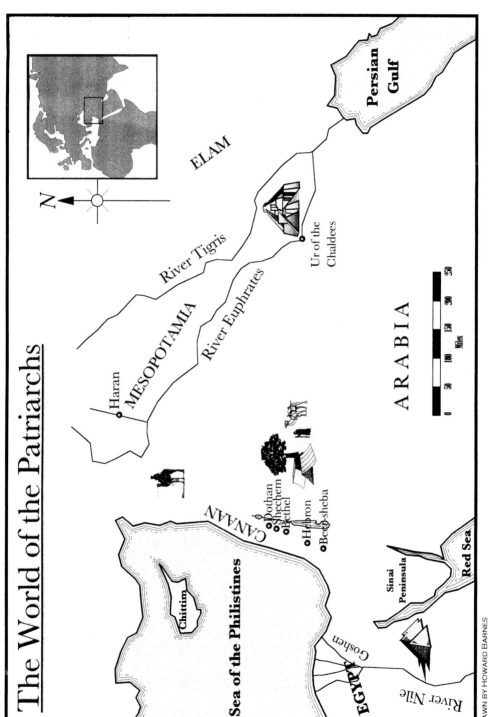

The World of the Patriarchs

Persian Gulf

ELAM

River Tigris

MESOPOTAMIA

River Euphrates

Ur of the Chaldees

Haran

N

ARABIA

Miles

0 50 100 150 200 250

Dothan
Shechem
Bethel
Hebron
Beer-sheba

CANAAN

Sea of the Philistines

Chittim

Goshen

EGYPT

Sinai Peninsula

Red Sea

River Nile

DRAWN BY HOWARD BARNES

BIBLIOGRAPHY

1. *Commentaries*

Atkinson, D. *The Message of Genesis 1-11*. Leicester, England: Inter-Varsity Press, 1990. (Bible Speaks Today Series).
A useful brief outline treatment of the main themes of the introductory chapters.

Baldwin, Joyce G. *The Message of Genesis 12-50*. Leicester, England: Inter-Varsity Press (Bible Speaks Today Series).
Similar to the previous work. Also useful.

Bush, George. *Notes on Genesis*. Minneapolis: James Family Christian Publishers, 1979. (Reprint of the 1860 edition published by Ivison, Phinney & Co., New York).
An old book in a heavy style. Not easy to use.

Cassuto, U. A *Commentary on the Book of Genesis 1-11*. Jerusalem: The Magnes Press, The Hebrew University, Vol. 1 1961, Vol. 2 1964. Translation by I. Abrahams.
A fascinating, detailed work by a learned conservative Jewish scholar.

Davis, John J. *Paradise to Prison, Studies in Genesis*. Grand Rapids: Baker Book House, 1975. Many reprints.
Very useful for its coverage of archeological evidence.

Denton, Michael. *Evolution: A Theory in Crisis*. Bethesda, Maryland: Adler & Adler, 1985.
A molecular biologist, not sympathetic to the idea of creation, describes major problems with evolutionary items and concludes that it is little more than a myth.

Hamilton, Victor P. *The Book of Genesis*. Grand Rapids: Wm. B. Eerdmans Publishing Co., Vol. 1 1990, Vol. 2 1995.
Rich in interesting detail on language and interpretation. Academic style.

Keil, C.F. and Delitzsch, F. *Commentary on the Old Testament: The Pentateuch* (one-volume edition). Peabody, Massachusetts: Hendriksen Publishers, 1989 reprint.
Conservative work by German scholars. Much quotation in Hebrew.

Kidner, Derek. *Genesis, An Introduction and Commentary*. London: Tyndale Press, 1967.
Very compact. Some good, pithy insights. Space limits its coverage.

Leupold, H.C. *Exposition of Genesis* (one-volume edition). London: Evangelical Press, 1972.
Much detail, and loyal to the high view of Scripture. Some very good insights.

Morris, Henry M. *The Genesis Record*. Grand Rapids: Baker Book House, 1976. Many reprints.

Scientific standpoint. Doctrinally sound. Takes the young-earth position regarding creation.

Pfeiffer, Charles F. *The Book of Genesis, A Study Manual.* Grand Rapids: Baker Book House, 1958. (Shield Bible Study Series). Many reprints.
Very brief indeed, but has some good ideas.

Ross, Allen P. *Creation and Blessing, A Guide to the Study and Exposition of the Book of Genesis.* Grand Rapids: Baker Book House, 1988.
Stimulating exercise in the exposition of themes.

Stigers, Harold G. *A Commentary on Genesis.* Grand Rapids: Zondervan Publishing House, 1976.
Useful mainly for its coverage, and application, of archaeological evidence.

Thomas, W.H. Griffith. *Genesis, A Devotional Commentary.* Grand Rapids: Wm. B. Eerdmans Publishing Co., 1946. Many reprints.
Many good chapters on the practical implications of the stories in Genesis.

Wenham, Gordon J. *Genesis: Word Biblical Commentary.* Dallas, Texas: Word Books. Vol. 1 1991, Vol. 2 1994.
The main conservative academic work. Rather heavy on critical analysis for the general reader. Evidence well weighed and judgment balanced.

2. *General*

Abou-Rahme, Farid. *And God Said.* Kilmarnock: John Ritchie Ltd., 1997.
Defence of the scientific accuracy of Scripture. Much on creation and the flood.

Alexander, T. Desmond. *From Paradise to Promised Land.* (Chapters 1-5 in particular). Carlisle: Paternoster Press, 1995.
Up-to-date, scholarly work on the themes of the Pentateuch.

Behe, Michael J. *Darwin's Black Box.* New York: The Free Press, 1996.
A biochemist's exposition of why he doubts the accuracy of Darwinian evolution. Parts are very technical, but they can be omitted. Brilliant communication.

Blocher, Henri. *In the Beginning, The Opening Chapters of Genesis.* Leicester: Inter-Varsity Press, 1984. (Translated by David G. Preston).
Thought provoking, but excessively abstract in its interpretation.

Clark, Robert E.D. *The Universe: Plan or Accident?* (Enlarged edition). Grand Rapids: Zondervan Publishing House, 1961.
Somewhat dated, perhaps, but still stimulating to students of science.

Hitching, Francis. *The Neck of the Giraffe, or Where Darwin Went Wrong.* London: Pan Books, 1982.
A scientist's examination of unanswered queries about evolutionary theories.

Johnson, Phillip E. *Darwin on Trial.* Crowborough, E. Sussex: Monarch Publications, 1994. (First British Edition).

The best examination of the philosophical weaknesses of Darwinism and its offshoots. By an expert in the sifting of legal evidence.

Johnson, Phillip E. *Testing Darwinism, An Easy-to-understand Guide.* Leicester: Inter-varsity Press, 1997.
See previous comment. Guidance on how to stand up to pressure from naturalistic evolutionary advocates.

Kelly, Douglas F. *Creation and Change: Genesis 1.1-2.4 in the Light of Changing Scientific Paradigms.* Fearn, Ross-shire: Mentor, 1997.
An up-to-date work on science and Scripture by a theologian. Takes a young-earth stance.

Milton, Richard. *The Facts of Life: Shattering the Myths of Darwinism.* Corgi Books, 1993 (originally published by Fourth Estate Ltd.)
A journalist's exposition of the gaps and inadequacies in evolutionary science.

Morris, Henry M. and Whitcomb, John C. *The Genesis Flood: the Biblical Record and its Scientific Implications.* Nutley, New York: Presbyterian and Reformed Publishing Co., 1961.
A classic on the flood from the young-earth standpoint.

Ross, Hugh. *Creation and Time: A Biblical and Scientific Perspective on the Creation-date Controversy.* Colorado Springs: NAVPress Publishing Group, 1994.
Evangelical answer by an old-earth scientist to young-earth criticism of him. Often annoyingly defensive.

Schaeffer, Francis A. *Genesis in Time and Space.* Leicester: Inter-Varsity Press, 1972.
Somewhat dated in some matters, but still stimulating on Schaeffer's pet ideas.

Whitcomb, John C. *The World that Perished.* Grand Rapids: Baker Book House, 1973.
Brief outline of the antediluvian world from a young-earth standpoint.

Young, Davis A. *Creation and the Flood.* Grand Rapids: Baker Book House, 1977.
Classic of old-earth interpretation of flood data by an evangelical scientist.

Young E.J. *In the Beginning: Genesis Chapters 1-3 and the Authority of Scripture.* London: Banner of Truth Trust, 1976.
Tightly reasoned examination of the text of these chapters by a sound evangelical.

Young, E.J. *Studies in Genesis 1.* Philadelphia: Presbyterian and Reformed Publishing Co., 1964.
By the author of, and similar to, the previous work.

INTRODUCTION

This commentary is based on the premise that Genesis, along with the other four books of the Pentateuch (the Law), came from the hand of Moses, as the Lord Jesus said (Lk 5.14; 20.37; 24.44). But it will not be taken as merely the word of Moses. The fact that the books of the Bible are all inspired demands that they be taken together, in their totality, as a revelation from God. Thus, neither Genesis, nor any other book in the Bible, can be understood or explained without reference to the rest of the Bible. Many principles which run through both Old and New Testaments are first established in Genesis. For this reason it is often quoted in other books of the Bible as the source of principles established for all God's people. This approach stands in contrast to any idea that human concepts of God evolve from primitive and inadequate notions to more sophisticated theories which are more pleasing to modern people. An evolutionary view of religion demands the continual modifying of beliefs, knowing that they are at best guess work. The practice of the Lord Jesus of going back to what was written and what was laid down at the beginning presupposes that what was recorded in the OT was given by revelation from God and therefore had authority. This position leaves room, of course, for development, but not for correction. There was addition to limited revelation, but never any need to correct wrong ideas, for what was given by revelation in the inspired Scriptures needed no correction.

However, in seeking to argue for the truth of the Genesis account, there is a danger of being sidetracked into controversies (usually about science) which divert attention from the message of the book. On some of the controversial issues Bible-believing scholars differ. Any tendency to use intemperate language, or indulge in intemperate thinking, against those with whom there is a disagreement on matters which are controversial without the integrity or accuracy of Genesis being at stake must be avoided. Thus, since this is an inspired book, by far the highest priority is to study it carefully and reverently, using the tools which are available to discover what lessons God is teaching in it.

In reading some parts of the story modern preconceptions may prompt questions which were not relevant to the author nor intended by the Holy Spirit to be answered by the book. Many "scientific" questions, for instance, are barely relevant because Genesis is written in non-technical language. Had it been written in the technical language of Moses' day it might have become laughably out of date long since. What may seem to be important scientific issues are merely the setting for infinitely more important spiritual questions.

Everywhere in Genesis there is evidence of a plan which focuses on a land and on a people in ways which show God guiding events to fulfil His purpose. The book can be broken down into sections as follows;

Chapters 1-11
These are the foundation on which Genesis, and in some sense the whole Bible, rests. God is seen at work and in absolute control in the world His hands have made. This section also gives an indication that, since mankind became involved in sin, God would need to provide a redeemer.

Chapters 12-25
In this section the focus moves to a single individual, Abram/Abraham, because he is head of a race. Matthew 1 makes it clear to us that this man has special significance as an ancestor of the Christ. These chapters introduce the specific topics of a special line of people descended from Abraham and a special land promised to him by God. They also show Isaac as the spiritual heir of Abraham, rather than his other son Ishmael (Gal 4.22ff).

Chapters 25-28
The story is now told of Isaac and his two sons, Esau and Jacob. This section of the story shows Jacob emerging as the man to inherit from Isaac, but his inheritance is going to come to him only after trial and education.

Chapters 29-36
The importance of Jacob now emerges more fully in these chapters which are devoted to his education in the school of God. They begin to unfold the problems within Jacob's family, for example in the Dinah episode in ch.34.

Chapters 37-50
For the most part these chapters are given to the story of Joseph, and mainly focus on Egypt. A significant part deals with relations between Joseph and his brothers. In this theme an important element is the emergence of Judah as the most prominent of the other brothers and one fitted by divine discipline to lead. The section also deals with the migration of the whole family of Jacob to Egypt.

In the stories of the patriarchs the moral and spiritual lessons demonstrate that a relationship with God involves a person, a community or a race in moral obligations. The book closes with the covenant people, Israel, in Egypt, awaiting a time when they will return to Canaan to take up the land promised them by God, and this theme is continued in the rest of the Pentateuch.

The fact that the story of this special people is set against the background of chs.1-11 is the first indication that this is not just a Jewish story. God is seen unmistakably in Genesis as the God of heaven and earth, Creator of all, Judge of all the earth. The lessons taught in the book have relevance to all of us because we are human. The ultimate meaning of it all depends on the fact that Jesus the Son of God became a man – not only a Jew but equally or more importantly a man. God is not inconsistent. His revelation of Himself in the Old Testament may be added to but it does not need to be corrected, as if it were a stage in the evolution of religious thought. Men's circumstances change, and God reveals more of Himself progressively in Scripture, but He does not have any blind alleys in His revelation. The revelation of Genesis, and also of all the later books, is required if there is to be a rounded view of God. The full revelation of God in our Lord Jesus Christ is, of course, vital, but the Scriptures give a cumulative revelation of which the first layer, as it were, is the book of Genesis. In considering the ways of God with men in Genesis we learn about Him and also about ourselves.

GENESIS 1

Introductory

In commenting on the text of the early chapters of Genesis no special attempt is made to deal extensively with the topics of Creation and Evolution. There are many books devoted to these subjects by writers with expert knowledge of the scientific arguments involved. The Bibliography lists some that may be of help. However the following comments are made by way of introduction.

Creation

The Bible states that the universe and history have a beginning and an end. Everything owes its existence to God, the self-existing Creator. He made it for a purpose, and at the end that purpose will be evident. Those who deny that God is Creator of all usually posit an eternal universe passing through cycles, coming from no original cause and moving to no ultimate goal. These two positions are fundamentally incompatible. For the believer the many questions that can be raised are answered in the words of Hebrews 11.3, "By faith we understand that the worlds were framed by the word of God, so that things which are seen were not made of things which do appear". Scientific theories will wax and wane but faith knows that God's revelation of Himself in Scripture and in Nature will finally be seen to be in complete harmony.

The focus of Genesis quickly moves from the grand view of the universe to God's relationship with mankind. A study of Genesis shows that people who had dealings with God, and were part of His purpose to bless a particular nation, found this a challenging experience. They had a significance because they were within the divine plan, but a relationship with God proved to be demanding. People had moral obligations placed upon them by virtue of their involvement with God. The seeds of these obligations are found in the deeply evocative expression, "breathed into his nostrils the breath of life" (2.7). Such a vital link with a personal Creator is the basis of the belief that the chief end of man is to glorify God and to enjoy Him forever.

Such a view of mankind is in marked contrast to the behaviourist and reductionist position which reduces humanity to the physical building blocks of which bodies are made. C.S. Lewis used to refer to this limited view of mankind as "nothing buttery":– nothing but machines moved by the outside forces of the environment or the inside forces of the chemistry of the genes. On this view nobody can be guilty of anything because he acts under irresistible forces, not having any real choice. Equally, nobody can be credited with any worthy choice or achievement for the same reason. Nothing is better or worse than anything else. Things just exist. Man acts in the existential present and thus proves his existence, but all is meaningless. This is the ultimate despair.

If one is prepared to use reason, and to believe that it is worth while to do so, how eminently reasonable it is to attribute the incredibly complex universe and man's wonderfully, elusively flexible personality to a Mind and Person far greater than all that He has made. God made man in His own image, after His likeness, made him capable of moral choice and able to know the difference between right and wrong. Thus man has the dignity of choosing what is good. Scientific enquiry involves the privilege of examining the wonderful works of God and admitting, what must be obvious, that every new advance in knowledge uncovers new complexities, which a thousand lives would be inadequate fully to investigate.

The fathers of modern European science acknowledged God and set out to examine the world as His handiwork. They saw evidences of design in the universe and were not surprised, for they believed this to be inevitable because God made it. Atheistic scientists today are driven to wonder why, since in their view the universe is the product of blind chance, there are so many evidences of seeming design. For this phenomenon they have no adequate explanation.

Genesis, then, tells the story of God's creative activity, of the orderly cosmos which He created then later broke up by the flood. All of this serves as a background to an account of how He chose a small, obscure family and prepared them for future greatness. In His orderly universe He placed human beings in His own image, gave them responsibility for choosing the good and rejecting the evil, saw them fall, and began the process of preparing them for His greater work, that of redemption and renewal. That chosen family would later be the means, in God's hand, of bringing in the Redeemer. This explains the emphases of Genesis in the story of origins. God was working toward moral and spiritual ends. The Genesis story is not an account of the workings of the physical world, much less of the solar system or the universe. If it were it would be selective, even in its own terms, to the point of being ludicrously inadequate.

What Genesis does do is to lay a foundation for the full revelation of God's purpose as it concerns the human race. It begins to answer basic human questions about destiny:

> Where do we come from?
> Where are we going?
> What does it mean to be human?

Arguably these are the deeper questions, the more important issues. No doubt many surprises will be revealed as more knowledge is gained of the physical world. As science advances, its genuine discoveries will surely confirm Scripture, for the God who made the universe is the God who inspired Scripture. Many confident assertions about the material universe will be stood on their head. And it may not matter significantly when this does happen. It does matter, it matters vitally, that man comes from the hand of God, that He made man for a purpose, that He must therefore be the Judge of mankind. It matters vitally that the early hints of a Saviour for mankind are not mere fancy but a sober revelation of God's purpose. There must always be a clear distinction in the mind between the proper processes of scientific enquiry and the results of divine revelation. Science will advance by refining theories and rejecting what has been shown to lack credibility in the light of new evidence. Sometimes it will go into dead ends and have to retrace its steps. The knowledge of the great spiritual realities has been granted by revelation expressed in the inspired Scriptures. Since it progresses by accumulation, not correction and refinement, there is not the need to jettison items. Care has to be taken to read Scripture to hear what God is saying, not to answer questions which Scripture was never designed to answer. If this is done, there will be no necessity to adjust one's views in the light of "progress" in human thought.

Evolution

The question will arise whether earth's beginnings can be commented on today without seeking to relate the Genesis account to the theory of evolution. Does not that theory contradict the Bible story of creation? This is not a scientific book, but let it be said first of all that the term evolution is used in different ways. The prevailing form which the theory takes at present is naturalistic evolution. This argues for progression from less complex to more complex organisms by chance mutations and survival of the fittest over long periods of time. It insists that this took place without outside intervention. In particular it rules out the possibility that God intervenes. It must, however, be understood that to define evolution like this is to start from a fundamental assumption that is not itself scientific. The atheistic implications of this approach are based on a philosophy, not on scientific evidence. As argued above, there are limits to what questions science can answer.

One very influential principle in the history of modern science is the statement that "the past is the key to the present". Applied to the story of origins, this means that an attempt must be made to argue that the processes which led to the origin of the universe are identical to processes which now operate. If certain processes now take place gradually, it is argued, they took place gradually in the beginning. If this is so then vast periods of time were required to bring about the form of things which exist today. But this assumes the uniformity of the rate of change throughout history, an assumption rather than an ascertained fact. It is generally admitted that some catastrophes have occurred. Very little seems to be known about the impact these may have had on the rate at which change may have taken place.

Again, if the argument stands, one would expect to see less complex organisms now becoming more complex. But there is no evidence of this happening. By contrast, the Bible explains that as the creation progressed in its orderly course it was in response to "God said". For living things this implies that new genetic information came into play because God intervened to make more complex creatures. Moreover, this orthodoxy insists that less orderly physical conditions gave way spontaneously to more orderly. But this is exactly the opposite of what the present teaches. Experience is that order inevitably tends to descend into disorder – the principle of increasing entropy, according to the Second Law of Thermodynamics. One answer given to this is that over long periods of time the process of entropy increase alternates with its opposite, but the evidence for this is lacking. The answer looks like a desperate attempt to get out of an obvious difficulty.

A major difficulty to believing the theory of living things advancing by small changes from lower to higher orders of complexity has been raised. As the structures of organisms are becoming better understood scientists are speaking of the problem of "irreducible complexity", for instance in cell structures. Michael Behe illustrates the problem by a simple but brilliant analogy. He writes of the five basic parts of a mousetrap. Nothing short of all five parts in place and functioning together will produce a device which catches mice. A mousetrap could not have evolved from a simpler device consisting, for example, of just three or four of those parts. This is remarkably like the problem of how molecular assemblies could be the products of evolution from simpler forms. No satisfactory explanation is available to show the steps by which such development could conceivably take place.

Probably most have seen at some time references to what are alleged to be unquestioned examples of evolution. One popular case is that of the peppered moth. It is alleged that changed environmental factors caused the population of this moth in some areas to change from light grey with dark spots to a much darker overall hue. Even if one accepted this, (and there is evidence that the studies on which the claims are based were seriously flawed), further thought on the phenomenon has led many scientists to argue that all that happened was that the darker moths survived in greater numbers. There was simply a shift in the proportions of dark versus light coloured individuals. At the end they were all still peppered moths. Minor changes do take place within species – micro-evolution. What stubbornly refuses to appear is macro-evolution, the change from species to species.

Scientists constantly refer to vast periods of time having passed. The science of dating the older geological periods is surely in its infancy. If not, can such things as the circular reasoning involved in the dating of rocks from the fossils in them and dating the fossils from the rocks in which they appear be accounted for?

This, however, is not the only example of alarming procedures. Other dating methods have produced ridiculous results when applied to organisms whose dates are already known. Even Carbon-14 dating has produced some random results. The examples are well represented in the scientific literature. Some systems do give results which suggest that the time scale is much shorter. The range of diversity is so widespread that more reliable methods must be awaited before much can confidently be asserted about dates.

A vast amount of varied evidence has been accumulating about earth's origins. Yet the subject is so complicated that equally vast amounts remain unknown. Darwin confidently expected that there would soon be evidence to fill in the gaps in the fossil record. He hoped that missing links in the evolutionary chain would be found. This has not happened. Some finds which were hailed as significant proved to be either fakes or hopelessly inaccurately reported. Indeed the absence of intermediate forms in the fossil record has led some scientists to speculate along another line. They have suggested that what they call "punctuated equilibrium" is the answer. By this is meant that long periods of very slow development have been interspersed with short periods of rapid development in which new species arise. The speed of change in these short periods would account, they believe, for the shortage of fossil evidence. No substantial evidence is supplied to explain why such periods of change would occur without outside intervention. The controversy between scientists on this theory has led to what has been called "the Darwin Wars". The one explanation ruled out by their presuppositions is God.

If change occurred by pure chance then it is impossible to replicate it in a laboratory where what happens is structured by the experimenter. The same problem applies to the idea that life arose spontaneously from non-life along the line of changes, which can be induced in the laboratory using the building blocks of living tissue. The fact that some chemicals can be produced under artificial conditions in controlled experiments set up to see if they can be synthesised makes the results rather different from the spontaneous changes suggested by theory.

A final point. The scientific establishment, like most, if not all, establishments, tends to close its ranks against mavericks. Galileo was persecuted, not so much by the religious authorities as such; he was persecuted by the establishment, which included other scientists and their church. Publishers today hesitate to produce what may offend the scientific establishment. Young scientists hesitate to push for a radical review of theories in which establishments have invested vast sums of research money. Yet the cracks are beginning to appear in the evolutionary monolith. Today's orthodoxy may be yesterday's outmoded theory.

Verse 1: God Creating

"In the beginning God created the heaven and the earth."

So begins the divine record, given by a revelation from God. This is not an opinion reached at some point in the evolution of human thinking about God or about the universe. God stands supreme, free and sovereign, outside the creation which He has made. He is ever-existent, dependent on no one and on no cause. He acted in creation because He chose to do so. In the words of Revelation 4.11 (RSV), "Worthy art thou, our Lord and God, to receive glory and honour and power, for thou didst create all things, and by thy will they existed and were created".

While the expression "the heaven and the earth" may safely be taken as a synonym for "the universe", or perhaps for "everything"[†], the focus shifts abruptly in v.2 to earth; and from v.2 onward anything outside the earth is viewed from earth's standpoint.

This sentence in v.1 is not merely the introduction to Genesis, it is the basic foundation on which rests the whole of Scripture. Scripture as a whole is God's revelation to mankind, bringing God within human ken and telling how man can be brought to God. This accounts for both inclusions and omissions in Scripture, and specifically in Genesis. Earth must be central in a story which deals basically with God and His relations with the human race.

The ancient nations who were without this sublime revelation in Scripture, and whose ancestors "did not like to retain God in their knowledge" (Rom 1.28), spoke of many gods, limited by mutual rivalry and by finite powers. Their gods were conceived of as involved in the universe rather than as sovereign over it. Here, by contrast, God is the personal, unoriginated cause of everything, unconstrained by circumstance and unlimited in His power, carrying His purpose forward inexorably to its fulfilment.

This statement deals with a dimension of origins on which science as such has nothing to say; for science deals with processes and the "how" of things, while this statement reveals the ultimate "why". It is appropriate to quote at this point a reference by Sir Peter Medawar (in "The Limits of Science") to "questions that science cannot answer and that no conceivable advance of science would empower it to answer. These are the questions that children ask – the 'ultimate questions' of Karl Popper. I have in mind such questions as:

> How did everything begin?
> What are we all here for?
> What is the point of living?".

Sir Peter could not find God by science, nor could he be sure of God by any other means which he was willing to use, but his analysis of the questions which science cannot answer brings into sharp focus the central concerns of the Bible, questions to which the opening statement must lead if it is heeded.

If it is correct to conclude that this is the emphasis in this verse, and in the Bible as a whole, the importance of Martin Luther's comment on the first article of the creed– "I believe that God has created me" – is evident. Genesis, or indeed the Bible, is not a book which expounds abstract theories to challenge my intelligence; it is a revelation of God and my relationship to Him. Unless it brings me, sooner or later, to Martin Luther's personal response, I am failing, in my reading of it, to listen to the God who speaks in it. Scriptures such as Isaiah 44 and 45 link the truth of God our Creator to His personal interest in us and His work as our Redeemer. In Isaiah 45 God speaks of His rights as Creator (for example in vv.8-13) and also establishes His care as Redeemer (see vv.17 and 21-22). Isaiah 44.21-24 brings the two titles, Creator and Redeemer, together, though in this context the creation in question may well be the establishment of Israel as a nation. As our Creator He faithfully preserves us; as our Redeemer He provides our deliverance from bondage. In both respects we owe all we are and have to Him. This puts everything else in perspective.

Verses 2-5: Darkness and Light

The next four verses show the power of the Creator at work, specifically to create light and separate it from darkness. This distinction was brought about by means of His word, His divine fiat. "For he spake, and it was done, he commanded, and it stood fast" (Ps 33.9). He commanded; it was done; He "saw the light, that it was good" (v.4). Thus the order which is now known begins to emerge on earth. The most basic concept in this process is that of God "speaking". This includes his commands which lead unfailingly to their intended effect, His naming of the things which he has made so as to establish their identity, and perhaps also (in the later stages) the provision of what may be called "genetic information".

Having made a distinction between light and darkness, God gave names to "Day" and "Night".[†] He set an example to His creature, Adam, in this naming process (compare 2.19). In an orderly universe things differ and therefore have different names. This is the basis of the fundamental scientific process of classification. More than that, in view of the symbolic use made in Scripture of "light" to mean "good" and "darkness" to mean "evil" (for example Ephesians 5.8 in NKJV, "For you were once darkness, but now you are light in the Lord. Walk as children of light."), it is the basis of all moral categories also. Genuine moral and spiritual distinctions owe their existence to the fact that God has made them so; thus God is the Judge. The process of creating order continues throughout the six creation days.

But before this orderly distinction of things which differ was established, a series of steps had to be gone through. Initially the earth "was waste and void; and darkness was upon the face of the deep" (RV). In Isaiah we learn (45.18 RV) that "God...formed the earth and made it; he established it, he created it not a waste, he formed it to be inhabited." In the six creation days this progressive, purposeful development of the earth as a habitation for man and the lower creatures of earth is seen. In v.2 the process has just begun, but God's purpose is moving towards its ordered goal which involves appropriate "form" as well as rich diversity ("fulness"). Isaiah's statement clearly refers to the completed work of creation.

Until light was created there was undifferentiated darkness. Until the lower and upper waters were divided and again the lower waters divided from dry land there was an undifferentiated "deep". The description of the Spirit of God, whether considered as an explicit reference to the Holy Spirit or not, "brooding upon" (RV margin) the face of the waters, indicates that there was divine activity to change the state of the earth.

In the NT revelation (Jn 1.3) the Son of God, as the Word of God, is seen as active in the creation: "All things were made by him; and without him was not anything made that was made". Other scriptural references seem to link the Holy Spirit to creative activity, such as Job 33.4: "The Spirit of God hath made me, and the breath of the Almighty hath given me life". Of course, the doctrine of the Trinity had not been articulated in OT times, and indeed is only implicit even in the NT, yet it is difficult to avoid the conclusion that the references to the breath of God, or the spirit of God, are the beginnings of God's revelation of the part played by His Spirit in creation. References such as "through whom also he made the worlds" (Heb 1.2 RV) link Father and Son in the work of creation. All three persons of the Trinity are, therefore, involved in the glorious work of creation.

Verses 6-13: Atmosphere, Sea and Dry Land, Land Plants

On the second day a division is made separating the lower waters on and in the earth from the upper waters "above the firmament". So God makes an atmosphere surrounding earth, enveloped between waters beneath and waters above. The upper waters are sustained in the atmospheric heavens. The establishment of this atmosphere is an essential step towards preparing earth for man and for other creatures.

The appearance of dry land on the third day is brought about by

the gathering together of the lower waters. So a further distinction
is made and the two categories of "seas" and "earth" (or "dry land")
are established. This is in preparation for the earth to bring forth
vegetation. Since man lives on dry land and needs plant life to
sustain him this is another necessary step towards God's final plans
for earth.

With the introduction of this vegetation God has created life; at
this stage just plant life. It is worthy of note that there is, even at
this early stage, repeated emphasis on the fact that each of these
plants produces "after his kind". The amazing variety in nature,
whether of plants or animals, is due to the wisdom of God and His
delight in variety. This is, so to speak, craftsmanship rather than
manufacture.

Throughout these processes there is constant emphasis on the
fact that things happened exactly as God commanded - "and it was
so". At key points in the narrative it is said that God "saw that it was
good". God is working out His purpose, step by step, in a completely
orderly sequence; His acts repeatedly produce distinctions between
things that differ. What He is producing will perfectly express His
own character and perfectly suit His creatures. He is producing
conditions which will make earth habitable, completely suitable for
the human race.

Verses 14-19: Lights in the Sky
Attention has often been drawn to the similarity between the
sequence from the first to the third day and that from the fourth to
the sixth. Light was created on the first day and the heavenly
luminaries were set in place on the fourth. The waters were divided
into the upper and lower reservoirs on the second day and the
waters were filled with creatures on the fifth. Dry land was
established on the third day and the dry land creatures were created
on the sixth day. This has been summarised roughly in this way:
God produced "form" in the first three days, and "fulness" in the
next three.

Light was created on the first day and distinguished, in fact and
in name, from darkness. Now sun, moon and stars are set under
divine authority to "rule" over day and night (compare Ps 136.7-9).
The fact that the creation of light precedes the heavenly bodies in
this account need not present difficulties, but must be seen in the
context of the whole of divine revelation. It is significant that the
Bible ends (Rev 22.5) with a situation in which there is light without
the sun: "And there shall be night no more; and they need no light of
lamp, neither light of sun; for the Lord God shall give them light" (RV).

This Genesis account tells of the orderly placing of light sources for
day and night, for seasons and years; so that they become signs to those

who study them. The numerous references in Scripture to people learning of unusual occurrences, through unusual manifestations in the heavenly lights, make sense only because those lights are so consistent and predictable at normal times. The repeated reference to God's command that they should be for lights, to give light and to divide light from darkness underlines the fact that these are God's creatures performing the function for which He made them. While the believer must avoid the occult, or any aspect of astrology, there is no need to be afraid of the Zodiac or other supposed astrological influences; God is over all the works of His hands, including the celestial bodies - "He made the stars also".

The work of the fourth day expands the truth set out on the first day. Light and darkness are, it is repeated, distinguished. The heavenly bodies through which God gives light on earth are orderly and predictable because they are under God's control. The detail added on the fourth day also develops the idea that earth and heaven are separate places, an idea which will be taken up again in the Babel story in ch.11.

In this narrative little attention is given to the stars. This may be partly because they are much less prominent than the sun and moon as seen from earth. It may also be partly because they were so important in the idolatry of heathen peoples. Throughout the inspired record God is in complete control; sun, moon and stars are His creation set to do His will. The heathens worshipped them as gods. Their religious speculation included accounts of gods and godlings, born of other gods and linked in a disorderly hierarchy of rivalries and struggles for power. Moses' account shows God as supreme, in total control of the light sources through which He marks out days, times, seasons and years. Writers have drawn attention to the fact that in this account of the creation of sun and moon they are not named. The names might have led readers to associate them with the heathen, idolatrous practices. This narrative is couched in terms which are designed to refute idolatry. It is not without significance that now, when many have rejected the knowledge of God as Creator, people are turning increasingly to the old superstitions which are based very often on an outmoded system of pseudo-astronomy. Take God out of His creation and it ultimately ceases to make any sense. If men cease to worship the Creator they begin before long to worship the creature.

Verses 20-23: Living Creatures of Sea and Air

At this point animal life is first introduced. The specific word "created" as distinct from the more general "made", is used here in v.21. It was used in v.1 and will be used again three times in v.27, where God "creates" man in His own image.[†]

It is difficult to escape the conclusion that the Holy Spirit is indicating the importance of the new beginnings which are marked by the first appearance of animal life, then human life. In both contexts (1.21 and 2.7) the phrase "living creature" is used, though in 2.7 this is obscured in the AV by the translation "a living soul". In these verses in ch.1 the "living creatures" include sea creatures and flying creatures.

The exuberance of the creative act is expressed in the reference to the abundance of swarming life in the seas. God's earth will have not only form but also fulness, not only order but rich abundance of life. The sovereign Creator produces wonderful variety and displays also effortless control over the huge creatures found in the sea.[†]

At each completed stage in His work God "saw that it was good" (vv.4, 10, 12, 18, 21, 25). Here for the first time it is also said that "God blessed them" (v.22). The theme of the blessing of God is constantly repeated in Genesis. God creates, provides, preserves, builds, blesses. A contrary force acting against God will be seen in later chapters, but His work will continue and the theme of blessing will emerge strongly at the end of Genesis.

Verses 24-31: Land Animals and Man: The Climax

In v.24 God spoke and land animals were made, each after its kind. So (v.25) God "made" them, and v.25 repeats three times, that each was made after its kind. But v.26 does not continue with a similar wording when it introduces the "making" of man. Instead God is deliberating with Himself: "Let us make man." Man is thus marked out as different from all that has gone before. In the words "Let us make" there may be a hint of the Trinity, but the words do not strictly require such a reference, although they do express plurality.

On each creation day "God said" and a creative result followed. On day three He spoke on a second occasion to make vegetation, creating vegetable life. On day five He spoke a second time to bless His first "living creatures". On day six He spoke five times: creating land animals (v.24), creating man (v.26), blessing man (v.28), bidding man to be fruitful (v.28), giving man permission to eat the plants (v.29) - though it may be possible to combine the last three utterances as comprising the blessing. In this way the inspired record indicates significant new starts in the divine programme.

Man's distinct nature is also expressed in that he is uniquely created "in the image of God", answering uniquely to God among all the creatures on earth, able to respond to God, to communicate with God, to represent God. On this basis God can commit to him dominion (v.28) over the other creatures on land, in the air, in the sea. It is important that this biblical doctrine of the essential dignity of mankind is firmly adhered to. It will emerge in Genesis that the characteristic sin of humans is to aspire to power beyond their earthly status, yet it is also explicit in the book that man was made to have a unique dignity on earth as the only creature made in God's image, after His likeness. The full import of this cannot be comprehended until the NT revelation of the incarnation of the Son of God is given. God will manifest man's dominion when He who is both God and Man rules over a renewed earth, as Hebrews 2 expounds.

It was to man that God communicated His will about eating plants. The animals also had permission, but it was to man, as the creature with God-given authority and able to understand God's will, that God communicated this permission.

One must assume that God made male and female of each kind of living creature, but it is recorded only of man that "male and female created he them". The special activity involved in creating a helpmeet for Adam is described in ch.2, at which point some of the implications of the male-female relationship will be dealt with. God had blessed lower creatures in v.22 in connection with the command to be fertile and multiply; here again, in v.28, God blesses the man and his partner and, as in v.22, the connection is with fertility.

Those who have abandoned belief in a Creator and rejected the biblical account of man as having dominion over earth often fall victim to the false philosophy of pantheism. In this heresy both man and God are absorbed into anonymity and, in effect, are made subservient to something called "Nature", or "All-that-exists". Those who subscribe to this error sometimes refer to "God", in their sense of the term, as "it". Their reason being that to them "God" is a principle or force rather than a personal God. It is essential for believers to hold fast to the dignity of what Scripture teaches about a sovereign God, Creator of all things, and about His creature man, the crown of God's creation.

It is often arrogantly claimed that if there is a God nothing can be known of Him and that, in any case, science has proved that He did not make the world. This leads to people worshipping the creature rather than the Creator. Pantheistic teaching leads to the idea that the universe is permeated with divinity, as indeed mankind is said to be. Then it is asserted that some people are born with a preference for "partners" of the same sex and that this is as normal and natural as being left-handed. Next, the marriage of one man to one woman in a life-long partnership is held to be an intolerable bondage. All of this is based on the initial, flawed presumption that God did not create man, did not establish different roles for different creatures, is not the Judge of mankind and does not see or care what His creatures do.

Genesis 1 presents a picture of a beneficent and wise Creator whose creation is marked by distinctions between kinds of living things, between light and darkness, between the sexes. He has a place for each one in what should be a harmonious, loving and working relationship. If His supremacy is accepted the glory of the honour which He has bestowed upon man as the crown of His creation can be readily understood.

At points where God has completed a phase of creation, it has been recorded that "God saw that it was good". Now that the process has been completed by the creation of man, God "saw everything that He had made, and, behold, it was very good". God's satisfaction is surely expressed in the "behold" as well as the intensifying "very". This was the climax of the six creation days; God had done all things well, and the day is singled out for special attention, for it is the only day of the six in which the definite article, as in "the" sixth day, occurs in Hebrew, though translators often feel that they need to supply it in the other five.

Notes

1 It is common in biblical Hebrew to express the completeness of something by a pair of words naming its extremities, such as "heaven and earth", "good and evil", "big and small". The figure of speech is called merism.

5 The repeated use of "the evening and the morning" is the means employed to signal a series of ordinary twenty-four hour periods during which God was working in extraordinary ways.

21 The verb translated "create" (BARA - 1254) is used only of God's creative activity. In the Genesis creation narrative it is used in 1.1, 21, 27 and 2.3 and 4. These deal with the initial creative act, the creation of the first of animal life, the creation of man and a summary statement of the total work of creation.

21 The AV translates the word TANNINIM (8577) as "whales", but modern translations tend to use such terms as "sea-beasts" and the RV gives "sea-monsters". Again, the variety is said to be due to the work of the Creator, not random mutation; they were created "after their kinds".

GENESIS 2

Verses 1-3: God Ceased from His Work

People speak of the six days of creation, but Scripture includes with them the seventh day as an essential part of the sequence. God must be seen, not just as working in His power as Creator, but also as "ceasing" or "resting" on the seventh day. This is the rest of satisfaction, not weariness. God had not only completed the construction of an orderly universe; He had also filled it with its host of inhabitants. God was so well satisfied that He blessed the seventh day and marked it out as special, "because that in it he had rested from all his work which God created and made". These last three words, "created and made", may be expressed adequately by the translation "creatively made". The Lord Jesus said that "the sabbath was made for man, and not man for the sabbath" (Mk 2.27), and the law of the sabbath in the Ten Commandments was based on God's rest (Ex 20.8-11). It is a fair deduction that God established this seven-day cycle and planned that, for man's good, one day of rest in seven should be observed. This is not to say that there should be a legally enforceable sabbath, but it is perilous to ignore indications of what God has recorded for man's good.

Those who believe in naturalistic evolution look in the processes now observable in nature for the key to the origin of the cosmos. This is based on the assumption that the processes which they believe brought the world into being are still going on. The reference here to God "ceasing" on the seventh day would suggest that the processes (if that word is appropriate) which God used, ceased after the six creation days, for God "ceased (rested) from all his work". It is therefore futile to expect to discover processes strictly analogous to the creative acts of God at work in nature today. It is, of course, true that God has not abandoned His world to look after itself. He sustains it, as, for instance, Psalm 104 explains in such wonderful detail. In that sense He continues to work, as the Lord Jesus said - "My Father worketh even until now" (Jn 5.17 RV). It is the initial work of setting the creation in working order which was complete at the end of the sixth day.

So ends the record of God's initial work of creation, producing an orderly world in which distinctions are made between things which differ because God has made them that way. Each phase of the work is good and the end product very good. Man is the climax, male and female together put in charge of the lower creation. Each part of this creation fits into a harmonious overall pattern, so that the whole is a unity. This pattern and unity were the basis of the confidence of many fathers of modern European science that, when they examined the universe, they would find evidence of the divine plan rather than unpredictable and random data; their confidence seems to have been fully justified on the basis of nature as well as Scripture.

Verses 4-25: Man and Woman in the Garden

The heading, "These are the generations of the heavens and of the earth…", is the first of a series of section headings in Genesis. These provide the main markers in the framework of the book. Since the second of the headings is at 5.1 it is clear that the present section runs to the end of ch.4. Each instance of the phrase "the generations of" deals with the descendants of a person or the sequel to an event. Thus the three chapters in this section deal with what followed the creation of the heavens and the earth – the provision for man in the garden of Eden, his temptation and sin, its bitter results in the loss of Eden, the curse, the sin of Cain, the death of Abel and the birth of Seth to replace him. The expression here, "in the day that" means quite simply "when"; it has no hidden message and provides no clues for the interpretation of ch.1.

Verses 4-7: Man Formed

Before man's creation is recorded, the description of earth's vegetation and the watering of the soil makes it clear that this is a temporary condition set up by God for this early period of earth's history. The "plants" and "herbs" of the field include shrubs and such growing things as grain. The development of these items seems to be delayed until rain and human cultivators are available.

In ch.1 God acts alone, in sovereign omnipotence, to make all things as He pleases. Man is the final and highest creature in all of that sequence. This brief section of ch.2 introduces new ideas about how God wants His world to be. He is referred to here for the first time (and as He always is in the narrative parts until the end of ch.3) as "the Lord God". This indicates that He is seen here not only as God the omnipotent but also as the Lord, in relationship with man His creature. This is particularly appropriate in a context where man's place in the scheme of things is being set forth – "there was not a man to till the ground". God acts as Creator and He makes things grow, but man is intended from the start to be a responsible agent, working to further God's plans for earth. Man is made of dust and made to have close association with the earth as God's agent to care for it. This chapter deals with man's place in the world which God has made and his relations with God his Maker. It supplements the basic facts about man's creation, as given in ch.1, with information about man's responsibility toward God regarding the creation of which he is head.

The chapter has an important message in the context of present-day interest in environmental concerns. Man is made of dust and, in one sense, is of a piece with the world around him. Yet the story of how God made the first man and his wife places mankind on a quite distinct plane from the lower creation. We have a special responsibility for the preservation of the environment, not so much because we are part of it (brother to the ox, as it were), but because God put us here to look after it for Him. We share with the lower creation the fact that we are on earth and owe our life to the Creator. We are distinct in that we have responsibility to God for our exalted position as those with the task of "tilling the ground", to take one of the caring jobs as standing for them all. This is not what is being taught by those influenced by the "new" philosophies which place us beside the other creatures as part of a network of living, interdependent organisms. Such a view takes away our dignity and replaces it with a social contract in which we respect our non-human neighbours as part of a mystical brotherhood in the family of Mother Nature. It is closer to the ancient fertility cults than to the revelation of God our Creator found here in Genesis. Compromise between the two positions is not feasible.

In the meantime God provides a "mist" to water the earth. This word "mist" is variously represented in translations as: mist, streams, moisture, flood, spring-water, fresh water ocean. The essential point is that God provided a basic pre-requisite for fertility, but for the completion of His plans for earth's fertility He will seek man's co-operation. To paraphrase Paul, "Man may plant and water, but God gives the increase" (compare 1 Cor 3.6).

So man is formed of dust (the only creature of whom this is said in Scripture) and becomes a "living creature".[†]

The expression which appears in the AV as "living soul" is identical with that used of animals, in whose case the AV translates it "living creature" (compare 1.21,24; 2.19). But Scripture is careful to record that man is different from the lower creatures, for "God breathed into his nostrils the breath of life", which of course is not said of any lower creature. Man alone has this personal link with God. It may be significant that the phrase "breath of life" used of man here is slightly different in Hebrew from that similarly translated of animals' life (except 7.22, which may not be a real exception). Elihu in Job 33.4,6, already cited in relation to ch.1, seems to have this in mind when he says, "The breath of the Almighty hath given me life", and almost immediately confesses, "I also am formed out of the clay". Luther's personal creed comes back to mind: "I believe that God has created me". The most degraded of men can never be totally like a beast, for he has the possibility of knowing God and responding to Him. The most exalted of men must remember that he is made from dust. A human body reduced to its basic material elements is indistinguishable from the dust of the street. The dust of which we are made reminds us of our creature status; the breath in our nostrils, breathed into us by the Lord God, reminds us of the personal interest which our Creator has taken in man, the crown of His creatures on earth. Thus is set forth the glory of the Lord God, who makes man of dust, breathes into man a life which can be vibrant for Him, and gives man the amazing prospect not only of knowing Him and working for Him here on earth, but also being with Him in glorified form in heaven. God made man in the image and after the likeness of Himself, no doubt in anticipation of the day when He would send His Son forth, born of a woman, to live amongst men as a Man. As a Man the Son of God has gone up in glorious ascension to the highest pinnacle of glory, far beyond all created beings. Men who lose sight of this cannot fail to manifest the spiritual poverty of that loss.

Verses 8-17: The Garden and the Man

This section continues to deal with man as God's agent to care for earth. It is not a chronological account of creation; the chronology is not given here.

The place chosen by God as man's special and privileged home was in an area called Eden. God's special care to provide for man's needs and pleasures is seen in the fact that He placed him in a garden (v.8). God recognised that His choicest creature, made in His image, needs more than food to fill his belly as if he were an ox. He needs what will please his eye, what will satisfy his sense of beauty (v.9a). We ignore at our peril the basic need we possess for beauty. We are aesthetic creatures, able to express noble sentiments in music and song, able to rejoice in colour and form and movement, conscious of harmony in our surroundings.

But man is also a moral creature. He must have choice if he is to arrive at true goodness by choosing God's will for him. If he has no choice to make he is merely an automaton, not a moral agent. Hence God makes the two trees in the centre of the garden. Chapter 3.22 links eating from the tree of life with living forever. Eating from the other tree, of the knowledge of good and evil, leads instantly to death. Man is directly and bluntly forbidden to eat from it. He has equal opportunity to eat from any tree. His choice will make him good or sinful instead of his initial neutral state of innocence.

The tree of the knowledge of good and evil is linked, then, with seeking what is forbidden knowledge. In ch.3.4-5, when the serpent is moving in to clinch the seduction of Eve, he states, "Ye shall not surely die," then adds significantly, "Ye shall be as gods (RV God), knowing good and evil".

So what is forbidden seems to be a desire to have knowledge

beyond one's station as a creature on earth. The interpretation
which best suits this expression, "knowing good and evil", is that
which sets it in a judicial context. A law-court is where decisions
are taken about what is legal or illegal activity - good or evil. What
is offered to man's first parents here is the right to take their own
decision about good and evil, not depending on what God says.
This foreshadows the theme, taken up later, of man needing to
acknowledge that God is in heaven and he is on earth. The idea of
having power through "inside" knowledge appeals to our fallen
condition. In modern times knowledge of the occult remains a key
element in Satan's attack on the human race. "The secret things
belong unto the Lord our God: but those things which are revealed
belong unto us and to our children for ever, that we may do all the
words of this law" (Deut 29.29). Notice how the blessing of God is
connected, not with becoming powerful or impressively clever, but
with conformity to God's will. Contrast with this Lucifer in Isaiah
14.13-14:- "I will ascend into heaven...I will be like the most High".
Satan knew how to use what had been his own downfall.

Man was on probation, needing to be tested to see if he would
do the will of God simply because it was the will of God, not just
because it appealed to him or "felt right". It is worthy of note that
at the end of history, when man's probation is past and the
redeemed have reached their final home, "in the midst of the street
of it...was there the tree of life" (Rev 22.2). God does intend to
have with Him human beings living forever and set free from all
that could harm them. There will be no tree of knowledge of good
and evil, for that probation was in the past and, once in the home
which God has destined for the believer, His people will enjoy what
He has provided, purely by His grace, despite man's failure in the
primeval test.

Verses 10-14 describe four rivers which flow their separate ways
from a common Edenic source. The Pison and Gihon have not been
identified as corresponding to any rivers now known; the Hiddekel
can be identified (compare Dan 10.4) with the Tigris, and the
Euphrates bears its normal name. At least one major cosmic
catastrophe since Genesis 2 (the flood) would make it difficult to
be confident about locating any of the details. Cush (translated
"Ethiopia" in the AV) seems not to be the well-known place in north-
east Africa; one plausible suggestion would identify it with the home
of the Cassites in what would now be called western Iran. No doubt
the details are not part of a geography lesson. They are part of a
description of how the Lord God provided for man, encouraging
him to enjoy so much that would stimulate every legitimate appetite
within the bounds which God established. The mention of four
rivers (four being the number connected with what is worldwide)

suggests that from Eden there is a whole world to be explored; there is wealth and beauty, all speaking of a beneficent Creator.

Meanwhile the man has his work to do in the garden. Work is always part of man's life in God's plan; this theme reaches its final expression in Revelation 22.3 - "His servants shall serve him". Man is made from earth and has links here in Eden with the earth from which he was taken, to care for the garden and preserve it in the condition which God intended; the same two verbs are used in Numbers 3.7-8 of the responsibility of the Levites in tending and keeping the tabernacle in the condition required by God. A place of divinely-given privilege is also a holy place, imposing responsibility on man.[†]

In v.16 God states emphatically Adam's freedom to eat freely from all but one of the trees: "Thou mayest freely eat", literally, "eating thou mayest eat". Then follows the equally emphatic warning against eating from the one forbidden tree: "thou shalt surely die", literally, "dying thou shalt die". This is the first occurrence of the word "die" in Scripture. It is the first hint of this possibility, that all may not continue in this primeval peace and harmony which God has set up. The sentence, "for in the day that thou eatest thereof thou shalt surely die" (v.17), may be taken in three ways:

(1) it may be translated, "for as surely as you eat of it you shall die", but the time expression seems to be more urgent than this;
(2) the translation, "for in the day that thou eatest thereof thou shalt surely be doomed to die/become mortal" seems to be an attempt to rationalise a difficulty rather than to translate;
(3) it seems best to read the phrase as rendered in the AV and the RV and understand that sin brings in a breach between man and God, breaking the harmony and unity noted in the creation story in Genesis 2, thus placing man in a condition called death, that is, spiritual death.

Verses 18-25: A Helper Suitable for the Man

In v.18 a reminder is given that this account of relations between man and the earth, and man and his God, is expanding the narrative of ch.1. In 1.31 God saw all that He had made and, at the close of day six, pronounced it "very good". Here in 2.18 "the Lord God said, 'It is not good that the man should be alone' ". Obviously this pronouncement precedes His summary verdict reported in 1.31.

Attention is being directed here to the importance in the eyes of God of the unit formed by a man and his wife – one flesh. Reading the NT allusions to this, especially Ephesians 5.32 ("I speak concerning Christ and the church") leads to the conclusion that much space is devoted here to the subject of Adam's wife because of its adumbration of the relationship of Christ and His church.

God's answer to man's deficiency was to make for him a helper matching him (or answering to him). Eve would complement Adam. The fact that Eve is to be Adam's helper does not suggest that she is in any way inferior to him, for elsewhere God is represented as His people's helper. Yet it must be said that she is made for him, not he for her (compare 1 Cor 11.9). He has the priority.

There seems no good reason to insist that the forming of the creatures in v.19 to bring them before Adam necessarily occurs after the divine decision of v.18, even if one does not join the NIV in translating "formed: as "had formed". However, the NIV seems to have given the sense required here. These "living creatures" shared that description with Adam, but he was much higher than they were, as is demonstrated in God's bringing them to him "to see what he would call them". This shows man's lordship over all other creatures upon earth. Man shares a created status with the animals, but is given a vastly superior footing before God, for he is made in His image, and holds authority in the world over the animals. Man is God's steward and is responsible before God for the way in which the creatures over which He has given authority are treated. As indicated in the comment on 1.5, God delegates to man the naming process in which He engaged before man was created. Man's naming of the animals is a scientific exercise, recognising that things differ and classifying them accordingly.

By contrast, when God would provide a true partner for man He gave man no part in the process. God must intervene, putting man in a deep sleep. The description cannot but be a reminder of the fact that when a bride was to be provided for the Lord Jesus Christ it was necessary for Him to die. The expression used in v.22 of making the woman – literally, "builded he a woman" – has echoes also in the NT of the church being built. So the woman is built of what is traditionally translated as a "rib" of Adam, and Adam for the first time has someone on earth to whom he can relate and with whom he can enjoy mutual love and loyalty. It is probable that this thought of loyalty is at least a major part of the sense of Adam's exclamation about "bone of my bones, and flesh of my flesh" (compare 2 Sam 5.1).

The clear note of exultation in Adam's enthusiastic reception of Eve should not be missed. Some translators render the "now" of the AV in v.23 as "at last". It does have a place of prominence and emphasis in the verse. Adam's exultation causes him to express his intense feelings in v.23 in poetry. It was God who brought her to Adam, one woman as one man's true complement, so that they would become "one flesh". God made them one in a lifelong partnership, as the editorial comment by the inspired author indicates in v.24: "Therefore shall a man leave his father and his

mother, and shall cleave unto his wife: and they shall be one flesh".
A significant word used here is "cleave", which is used, for example
in Deuteronomy 4.4, of loyalty within a covenant with God.[†]

God brought them together to continue in a lifelong covenant of
mutual loyalty and love. This is the Bible's pattern for marriage and
inevitably is quoted in the NT in this way, for instance in Matthew
19.5. Entering into matrimony brings the awesome responsibility
of a relationship which, the NT teaches, mirrors that of Christ and
the church.

The narrative here has many implications for today, including the
following. First, this pattern marriage, the first in the Bible, is a
reminder that marriage is for life. The "twain shall be one flesh".
The Lord's comment on it in Matthew 19.6 is sobering: "What
therefore God hath joined together, let not man put asunder."

Second, it gives God's answer to quasi-marriages, often called
"meaningful and stable relationships", in which "partners" begin by
professing undying love, but each keeps open the option of simply
walking away from the relationship if it becomes burdensome.

Third, it is a unique relationship, in which the complementary roles
include their sexual partnership. God provides this within a lifelong
marriage. It is part of His plan that man should "be fruitful...and
replenish the earth". Within this marriage bond children are born and
nurtured by their biological parents. Scripture consistently condemns
the perversion of homosexuality as an abomination. It has no point in
common with this scriptural pattern of marriage.

Fourth, this narrative is in marked contrast to the attitudes which
one meets in the war of the sexes. The Genesis 2 pattern is one of
mutual love and respect, each partner complementing the other so
that each is enriched. Glib references to the alleged inadequacies of
the other sex, by people of either sex, are out of place in the light of
this divine pattern. Jokes can so easily reinforce stereotyped images
which blur God's intention. Distraction from a true understanding may
even be created by such things as a declared ambition by feminists to
give women equality with men by ensuring that they have the same
opportunity to engage in immoral liaisons. The only freedom in
marriage is when a man and a woman accept the divine pattern and
find that God's grace is altogether for their good.

In v.25 there is a picture of an innocent state of marital bliss where
there was no thought of anything being withheld from each other.
They were naked and unabashed, happy with each other and with
the provision which God had made for them. This is the last time
that nakedness is mentioned in the Bible without its being
connected with shame or contempt. Modern society ought to think
well of this fact. Fallen humans cannot recapture this state of
innocence; innocent nakedness was the first casualty of the fall (Gen

3.7). So the final verse of ch.2 will be seen as highly significant when considering the story of the consequences of the fall.

Notes

7 The word represented here by "formed" (YATSAR - 3335) is translated "crafted" by Hamilton and "shaped" by Wenham. It would be the normal word to describe the work of a potter or other craftsman. God made the raw materials, formed man of the materials and gave him the unique form of life which he possesses by the divine breath in his nostrils.

15 The word "keep" (SHAMAR - 8104) is used in Genesis 2 and Numbers 3 in the AV. In Genesis 2 the word "dress" (ABAD - 5647), is related to the word "service" (ABODA - 5656), used in Numbers 3 in the phrase "do the service", and in 1 Chronicles 9 and 23 in relation to the "service of the house of the Lord".

24 A vivid commentary on "cleaving" is found in Ruth 1.16. In v.14 of that chapter Ruth, it is said, "clave" to Naomi. Then in vv.16 and 17 she solemnly promised to go wherever Naomi went, to lodge where she lodged, to have Naomi's people as her people, Naomi's God as her God, and finally to die and be buried with Naomi. This is an eloquent "unpacking" of the concept of cleaving.

GENESIS 3

Out of Eden

Verses 1-6: The Temptation and the Fall

The serpent is introduced abruptly. His cleverness (probably a neutral description) is in contrast perhaps to the human innocence as set out in 2.25. It has to be taken that this was a literal snake used by Satan. The importance of this event in Scripture is seen in the frequency with which Satan is hereafter referred to in serpent/dragon character, culminating in his final punishment in Revelation 20. At this stage in Scripture, however, the character of Satan has not yet been developed, and, on the surface, a literal snake addresses Eve. New Testament references such as John 8.44 and 2 Corinthians 11.3 make it clear who the tempter was. It is significant that the creation order has been inverted. Communication and authority should come from God to Adam and Eve, who have authority over beasts which do not talk. Here a beast talks to the woman, who talks to her husband, who acts in such a way that he is afraid to meet God, much less talk to Him.

The serpent shows some knowledge of what God had commanded Adam in 2.16,17, but he distorts the terms of the commandment. Even if the AV rendering, "Ye shall not eat of *every* tree" is followed, this distorts the commandment by ignoring the permission, "Of every tree of the garden thou mayest freely eat". So it highlights the prohibition. But if, as seems probable, it should be translated as, "Ye shall not eat of *any* tree" (RV and others), it becomes an explicit falsification. So far it is phrased as just a question or a suggestion put forth for clarification. This is a ploy still used in seducing the minds of people.

The woman's reply is inadequate however v.1 is translated. She fails to establish the freeness of the permission. "We may eat" should have been "We may *freely* eat". In v.3 she refers to the forbidden tree in terms which could also describe the tree of life, "the tree which is in the midst of the garden", for both of these trees were there (see 2.9). She also adds to the prohibition, "neither shall ye touch it". And finally she fails to express the emphasis on the certainty of judgment in the divine warning, "Thou shalt *surely* die".

Verse 4, however translated, contains Satan's denial of God's warning. It probably means, "Of course you will not die", as the REB has it. These early chapters of Genesis underline the importance of what God says: His word of power in creation and His binding commandment to man. This third chapter shows the importance which Satan places on undermining what God says for he (Satan) "abode not in the truth, because there is no truth in him" (Jn 8.44). By denying what God said in His warning to Adam, Satan also leads Eve on and achieves what is referred to in the other part of Jn 8.44 - "He was a murderer from the beginning".

He continues the process of undermining God's word in v.5, but here he also introduces the insinuation that God's provision for man is really designed to deprive him of something supremely desirable - "ye shall be as gods" (RV God).† This thing which he alleges God is withholding from man is at the heart of the story. Man is God's creature, placed in a privileged position on earth, deriving his knowledge from God. Satan holds out the lure of becoming independent of God, possessing the kind of knowledge which God has, but possessing it without dependence on God. This issue of man's dependence on God is of fundamental importance in Scripture. The best commentary on it is to read of the dependence of the only perfect Man ever to live on earth. He had complete confidence in God and never acted independently of Him.

Eve listened to Satan's slander and, instead of dismissing it or discussing it with her husband, with whom ideally she should have shared everything, she considered the forbidden tree without thought about its forbidden nature. It seemed wholly desirable, to the taste, the eye, the mind. It is a bitter irony that this should be the first scriptural reference to wisdom, a false wisdom. This is far from "the fear of the Lord" which Proverbs links so closely with true wisdom. The power of the temptation may be gauged by the correspondence between the threefold attraction and the analysis in 1 John 2.16: "For all that is in the world, the lust of the flesh, and the lust of the eyes, and the pride of life, is not of the Father, but is of the world".

The story of the temptation has so far been carried forward at a gentle pace, building up to the climax. Then suddenly the narrative is terse and stark: "she took...did eat...gave...and he did eat". About three lines of print in the average Bible tell the basic story of the first act of disobedience.

Adam was "with her" (v.6). Whether or not this means that he was present throughout the preceding dialogue is not entirely clear, but he was with her at this vital point, with her in transgression. They sinned together, as one. This is probably the sense in which Romans 5.12 says that "by one man sin entered into the world". Though they were one in this disobedience it brought about a change in their relationship which marred the hitherto perfect harmony and destroyed the idyllic innocence of their relationship described in 2.25.

Verses 7-8: The Harmony Broken

The result initially is described (v.7) as an opening of their eyes. The tempter had said, "Ye shall be as gods, knowing...". Their eyes were opened and "they knew that they were naked". This was new knowledge indeed, but it brought scant comfort to them. Nakedness had been their condition before but it had not posed a problem -

they "were not ashamed". Now it calls for prompt efforts of self-improvement. Tolerated public nakedness is always a sign of deep-seated decadence in any society, but the first human couple, while sinful, were not decadent.

The sewing of a fig-leaf covering is the beginning of a process which continues to this day when men seek by their own efforts to cover up perceived deficiencies, religious or otherwise. Then, as now, the efforts were futile, for they found it necessary to hide amongst the trees as soon as they heard the Lord coming. The garden remained paradise. God was perfectly at home in it, walking about in it in the coolness of the day. But the man and his wife were out of harmony with God and paradise. Here fear is seen for the first time; the fear that drives men from God is a product of sin. They cannot hide and yet they cannot bear God's presence. When sin's ravages are finally healed, then once more God will dwell among men with equanimity (Rev 21.3) in a fullness not possible in this intervening period.

Verses 9-13: God Investigates

The man and his wife, now sinners, may find it embarrassing to be exposed to God's gaze, but meet Him they must. The initiative for a meeting comes from God. It is always so. He calls to Adam, knowing where he is but requiring him to declare himself. God is not merely man's Judge calling on him to give account (though He is that); He is man's Redeemer starting a process which will lead to a gracious provision and a promise.

At first Adam cannot bring himself to address his sin and speaks of his nakedness, which makes him now feel exposed before God. He admits that he went into hiding from God. God probes his statement and reveals the deeper problem. Today psychologists often worry about people having guilt feelings. The deeper problem is when people are guilty before God, whether they have guilt feelings or not. To that deeper problem God immediately goes with His question, "Hast thou eaten?". He highlights the basis of guilt, the divine prohibition: "I commanded thee that thou shouldest not eat" (v.11).

Adam's reply (v.12) starts with a spontaneous attempt to ensure that Eve is blamed, though the form of this attempt really (but probably unwittingly) places the main blame on God as the one who gave the woman to him. But his explanation falters and peters out in a straight admission, "and I did eat". This establishes Adam's guilt as the main person responsible. Adam was first formed and had a leadership role. It was to him that the original prohibition was given, even before Eve was formed. It was he who had the primary responsibility to obey it.

God turns then to Eve, requiring her to give account. She correctly states that the serpent beguiled her, but she also ends her statement, "and I did eat". This leaves the serpent, the prime mover in the transgression, to face God. But he had not been on probation as man had. He is not asked to give account.

Before looking at the curse on the serpent it is appropriate here to attempt to assess the enormity of the rift which had appeared. Man had been placed in a position of rule over the animals and the temptation had stood this hierarchy on its head, with a talking serpent leading the woman. So a wedge was driven between man and beast. To man was given authority to name the beasts as a token of his authority over them, but also as an exercise of his unique power among earth's creatures, the power of speech. A talking serpent overturned that order of creation. A woman had been made as complement, companion and helper to the first man. She had acted independently, seduced by a lower creature acting out of its sphere. It attracted her to an act which she hoped would raise her above her divinely given sphere. In acting independently of her husband she reversed their roles. Accusation and evasion by man and wife further marred the harmony between them. This is indeed the fall to outdo all other failures.

Verses 14-19: God Passes Sentence

God simply declares to the serpent, "Because thou hast done this…". His guilt is clear. He alone of the three involved is cursed. But this cursing is a new word in the vocabulary of Scripture. It provides the counterpoint to the Genesis theme of blessing. The animal which was conspicuous for its cleverness is now conspicuous for its being cursed. It is now appropriate that it crawls on its belly. Humiliation is its lot, expressed as eating the dust. One may compare the language with that of Micah 7.17, where of humiliated nations it is said, "They shall lick the dust like a serpent". In Isaiah 65 millennial peace is graphically described, with harmony restored among animals. Then abruptly, "and dust shall be the serpent's meat" (65.25). There is no alleviation of the judgment on Satan, though men will be redeemed. For men redeemed it will in the end be gloriously true that there shall be no more curse (Rev 22.3), but Satan is outside of this hope. Theories about the physical appearance or mode of locomotion of the serpent before the fall are almost entirely speculation.

Verse 15 serves as a transition from God's cursing of the serpent to his sentence on the woman. God declares as part of the curse that the serpent and his progeny will be at constant enmity with the woman and hers, to their own destruction. But the curse is deliberately so phrased as to draw attention to the curse on this serpent individually: "*thy* head" and "*thou* shalt bruise". This is intended to be seen as the forecast of Satan's doom, which is inseparably linked with the seed of the woman in the more particular sense of the One who would be in the unique sense Son of Man. Kidner puts it neatly, "Jesus as the last Adam summed up mankind in Himself". After the event of the virgin birth of the Lord Jesus, the appropriateness of the expression "the woman's seed" is made evident. In this context it is relevant to note that early in the NT (Mt 4.1-11) the Lord Jesus was tempted by the devil and overcame him, in contrast to this defeat of Eve. The Second Man brings in a new hope and a new order of human, this time victorious, living. Our hope depends entirely on our link with the Second Man.

The bruising of the serpent's head represents for the believer his final defeat. New Testament references bear this out. Romans 16.20 contains the promise: "And the God of peace shall bruise Satan under your feet shortly". Revelation 20.2-3 (RV) also tells of the coming of an angel, "And he laid hold on the dragon, the old serpent, which is the Devil and Satan, and bound him for a thousand years, and cast him into the abyss, and shut it, and sealed it over him, that he should deceive the nations no more...". Then, finally, Revelation 20.10 tells how "the devil that deceived them was cast into the lake of fire and brimstone".

In the same way, there is, in the bruised heel of the woman's seed, a clear reference to the sufferings of Christ in His victory over Satan. Satan's doom must be seen in the context of Genesis as linked with hope for mankind brought in by His own suffering through One descended from Eve.

Sin has brought new sorrowful dimensions into all aspects of life. There is still joy in the birth of a baby, joy that new life has been given. Psalm 113.9 is apposite here: "He maketh the barren woman to keep house, and to be a joyful mother of children". What God declares in v.16 is that He will greatly increase the pains associated with child-bearing. "Thy sorrow and thy conception" should be understood as "thy pains in child-bearing". In itself the statement, "thy desire shall be to thy husband", hardly constitutes a cause for sorrow or fear. If, when taken in conjunction with the following "he shall rule over thee", it becomes a divine threat, a connection must be sought between the two statements which justifies that. The most obvious way is to see this pronouncement as declaring an aspect of the war of the sexes, which arises because of the fall. Woman's sexual attraction to her husband is her most potent weapon, but very often it leads to a situation in which he turns it back upon her and uses her desire to dominate her. On both sides this is a distortion of God's intention that mutual attraction and love should lead to close harmony and mutual support. Throughout this section there is the strong feeling that what might so easily have been blessing and joy is, by sin, distorted into sorrow and pain. Where the relationship between man and his wife might have been one of consistent mutual attraction and support it can so easily become one of mutual selfish exploitation.

God's sentence upon Adam seems to reflect the fact that Adam personally had been forbidden to eat, yet he had eaten. Note the frequency of "eat" in vv.17-19. There is no mistaking the heavy emphasis on "I commanded thee" in v.17. Chapter 2 set out the close link between man and soil in a divinely given harmony. Here the stark pronouncement is, "Cursed is the ground for thy sake". Man is not cursed as the serpent was, but his main occupation in tending the earth brings him up against a bitter curse. What had been rewarding work in harmony with God and the soil becomes bitter toil. Man would continue the work which God had given him to do, but he would have to do it in very different conditions from those in which he had originally worked, battling now against adverse circumstances. This parallels closely the judgment on the woman, that the God-given role of child-bearer would become for her an experience of greater pain, due to the now fallen nature of the man and woman. The phrase "all the days of thy life" reminds Adam that his life span is now limited. Man's close links with the soil are restated, but with the ominous addition, "till thou return unto the ground...unto dust shalt thou return" (v.19). If our preferred interpretation of 2.17 is followed, this goes beyond the initial judgment, "in the day that thou eatest thereof thou shalt surely die". That was an instantaneous, spiritual death; this is the inevitable, sooner or later, physical death, the end of man's life on earth.

Man's sentence also includes reference to hitherto unmentioned plants, namely, thorns and thistles. These are now part of the difficulty to be faced by man. The plants will be outside the garden, as man will. Another new factor in a familiar setting is the reference to sweat. Adam was no stranger to work, but work will now be toilsome. This whole context brings instantly to mind the sufferings of Christ, with Gethsemane's sweat (Lk 22.44) and the crown of thorns (Mt 27.29), before He was "brought...into the dust of death" (Ps 22.15). Adam was made from dust and returns full cycle to dust. Flesh has no future but dust.

Verses 20-21: Hope through Grace

At this point the narrative records, seemingly abruptly, that Adam called his wife Eve (Life), as being, the inspired writer adds, "mother of all living". This serves to point forward to a future for mankind despite the ravages of sin. It is a note of hope, however Adam intended it.

Such hope is enhanced in the description of God's care for His creatures in providing coats of skin to cover their nakedness. They had been able to provide for themselves only inadequate coverings in which they dared not meet God. Proper clothing, it is being stressed, is an essential thing for human beings now that they are fallen. It is a healthy exercise for those who are fond of dressing well to consider that the basic purpose of clothing is to cover shame. It is difficult to avoid the feeling that once again there is here a secondary hint of the need that sinful people should depend on God to provide them with a proper standing before Him, as it were a coat, the wearing of which removes the need to hide from the presence of God. These coats are an indication of their sin but also of God's ability and willingness to address the problem. Before their fall they could be in God's presence naked and unabashed; now He required that they be clothed as a sign of their fallen condition, but, by the same token, as a sign of His grace.

Verses 22-24: Expelled from Paradise

The precise meaning of God's expression about man becoming "as one of us" (v.22) is disputed. One suggestion is that it means "like God or angels". A reference in 2 Samuel 14.17,20 is sometimes quoted in support of this interpretation, but the expression, "an angel of God", found in those verses in the AV, may be better read as *the* angel of God", an oblique way of saying God. In any case one might hesitate to accept an interpretation in which God and His creatures, albeit heavenly creatures, are classed together like this. A second interpretation is to see in the verse a hint at the doctrine of the Trinity. On balance this is preferable.

Whichever way one takes this phrase, man is represented as being in a forbidden state as to his knowledge. It is best to take this as saying that man has decided to declare his independence of God as the source of his knowledge. In the ultimate sense all true knowledge, as well as all wisdom, finds its source in God. To presume to be independent in this respect is a fundamental form of sin.

Some take it that the tree of knowledge of good and evil produced a fruit which in itself conferred enlightenment of some kind. Whether this is true or not, it does appear from v.22 that the tree of life produced fruit which prolonged life indefinitely. Now a sinless man in whom was no seed of physical corruption might do this happily, but a sinner, in whom corruption had already begun its work, would do it at his peril. The issue is sharply presented in an ancient heathen Greek myth, in which immortality was granted to a mortal man called Tithonus, so that he might marry the goddess of the dawn. She soon tired of him as he withered and shrank, for she had omitted to ask for perpetual youth to accompany his immortality. The myth goes on to tell how he became a cicada, chirping endlessly.

God acted in judgment when He drove man out of the garden. Unending life on earth as a sinful man (therefore spiritually dead), experiencing progressive corruption, was not what a merciful Creator had in mind for man. Man outside the garden was to come back to earth, from any dreams of divine status, "to till the ground from whence he was taken". At the entrance to the garden, (compare the orientation of both tabernacle and temple), on its eastern side, God placed the cherubim. Their function was "to keep the way of the tree of life"; that is, to guard against unauthorised approach to it. Note has already been taken of echoes between the description of the garden of Eden and those of the tabernacle and temple. The cherubim, so prominent in them, are another reminder that fallen people have no place in the presence of a holy God except as God opens a way for them. What a fall! That he who had been given responsibility to "dress and keep" (2.15) the garden is now excluded by the cherubim who "keep" (3.24) the way of the tree of life! The revolving/whirling sword and accompanying flame/flashing reminds us of God's making "his ministers a flaming fire" (Ps 104.4). Access to the tree of life will once again be granted to some of our race in the final victory of the gracious plan of God (Rev 2.7; 22.2,14,19 RV). Until then man is outside, barred from the privileges enjoyed inside the garden, facing the curse of a broken law, but not forgotten by God.

From this point Adam and Eve feature in the narrative only in relation to their progeny. The way is being prepared for the later stages of Genesis, when the issue of progeny will be prominent in the setting up of the twelve tribes of God's chosen people Israel. The importance of genealogy will emerge when it is seen that the story of Abraham and his descendants is a preparation for one pre-eminent theme, the seed of Abraham who is also seed of the woman and is our Redeemer. This accounts adequately for the fact that chronology is relatively unimportant in Scripture, while genealogy is so prominent, especially at the start of both the Old and New Testaments.

Notes

5 The Hebrew ELOHIM (430) is ambiguous here as in some other contexts in Scripture. It may be simply the plural word for "God", as in many places, referring to the true God and singular in meaning though plural in form. On the other hand it may be a simple plural, "gods", in which case the serpent would be saying that divine privileges would belong to mankind if they declared their independence of God.

GENESIS 4

Verses 1-8: Two Offerings and a Murder

The theme of progeny, introduced already, is developed in this chapter. The first human child is born and named Cain. Eve makes a comment on the name and links it with the verb "acquired" – this seems the most likely translation of the name, though there is support also for "brought into being" (REB). We are not, in any case, committed to interpreting Cain in the way she suggests.[†]

Scholars are not agreed on what she meant. The fact that she does not say "a baby", but "a man", may be explained by her excitement at the extension of the human family, an important event when there have so far been only two of them. Perhaps one should not build too much on this detail in view of the similar use in John 16.21: "A woman when she is in travail hath sorrow, because her hour is come: but as soon as she is delivered of the child, she remembereth no more the anguish, for joy that a man is born into the world". The translation of "from the Lord" causes problems, but it should probably read "with the help of the Lord" (RV). She has been promised progeny and the Lord has made good His promise, it appears.

By contrast, the birth of Abel is announced very briefly (v.2), as a matter of fact. If his name means, as it seems to, "Breath", or "Weakness", it is a negative or else prophetic name in view of the brief and abruptly ended life as recorded in this chapter. Abel was a keeper of sheep, the first in a usually honourable line of shepherds in Scripture. It is noticeable, for instance, that many of the patriarchs were shepherds, tending their sheep and living in tents away from the corruption of city life. David also exemplifies the virtues of a man who proved God while he tended his father's sheep, was exalted to the throne and filled the role of shepherd-king with distinction. He protected his people, provided for their needs, led them by example, and became the prototype of his greater Son. David also gave the vision of ideal shepherd care in his precious psalm on the Lord as his Shepherd. It may be profitable, then, to see in this context some spiritual significance in Abel's occupation.

Cain was a tiller of the ground, toiling against the effects of the curse. From the produce he brought an offering to the Lord. This is not said to have been firstfruits, which might have been expected. The concept of firstfruits was not unknown, it appears, for Abel brought "firstlings" (v.4). The Lord did not view Cain's offering with favour. How the favour of the Lord might have been expressed is not revealed, but at any rate Cain knew that it had not been granted.

Abel by contrast brought the pick of the firstlings of the flock. The Lord received his offering with approval. Hebrews 11.4 records that Abel offered by faith. The most obvious sense of this would be that he followed divine directions for approach offerings. So, says Hebrews 11.4, "he had witness borne to him that he was righteous, God bearing witness in respect of his gifts" (RV), and he heads the list of the people of faith in that great chapter. Sin had put a distance between men and God, and the first man of whom it is recorded that he knew God's favour was a man who, by faith, found the way of approach to God. Significantly, Hebrews 11 speaks of his being shown by God to be righteous.

Cain's reaction to his refusal tells us something about the spirit in which he approached. He thought that God must accept his offering and he showed fury and surliness when it was rejected. It may be possible to argue that God's rejection of the offering was due to Cain's attitude in bringing it. One notices that the wording is "Cain and…his offering" (v.5), just as it had been "Abel and…his offering" (v.4). But it may be false to distinguish between the attitude of the offerer and the nature of the offering. The nature of the offering reflects the attitude of the offerer. Moreover, it is clear that some sort of guidance had been given by God, whether directly or through Adam and Eve. It is reasonable to believe that Abel's blood offering was more acceptable than a cereal offering, as having been prescribed by God, but this is not made completely clear in the Genesis account. The Levitical offerings did include both cereal and blood offerings.

Verse 7 is extremely difficult to interpret with any degree of confidence. "If thou doest well" may refer to Cain's life in general or to his offering. "Shalt thou not be accepted?" is variously translated. Some render "forgiven" for "accepted". Some translate the whole clause as, "You hold your head up", presumably in confidence of acceptance. Most render "sin lieth" as "sin croucheth" (that is, like a demon or a wild beast). In the AV the end of the verse would naturally refer to Abel, the words "his" and "him" having no other obvious person to refer to. Some scholars, (for example, Ronald Knox) argue for this interpretation. On balance, however, it is best perhaps to read it something like this: "If you do well, will you not be accepted? And if you do not do well, sin crouches at the door. Its urge is towards you, but you must master it". This rendering (which involves a number of insoluble grammatical problems) presupposes an interpretation along the following lines: "If your offering is a proper one, will it not be acceptable on your behalf? But if you offer unacceptably you are exposed to the threat of sin's destructive power. Sin's lying-in-wait has you as its prey, but you can still have the victory over it if your attitude changes and you make an acceptable offering". The debate on this verse is far from over, it would appear.

Verse 8 also contains a verbal oddity. It opens with the incomplete statement, "And Cain told Abel his brother…" (RV). The Septuagint reads, "And Cain said to Abel his brother, 'Let us go out into the field/plain' ". If this is a correct reading then a clause has dropped out of the Hebrew manuscripts because it had an ending similar to the next clause. This is the solution followed in the REB, NIV and other versions; it is also noted in the RV margin. This text would lead smoothly into the account of the murder, but it is difficult to be sure that it is correct.

Cain and Abel are together, then, in the open plain, away from the likelihood of anyone else intervening (Deut 22.25-27 provides a useful comment on the situation). The only narrative given about the activities of the two men has been the record of their occupation and their approach to God. Now they are on their own and paradise seems far away, for it is stated without preamble that Cain "rose up against Abel his brother and slew him". This is the fruit of sin. Its first expression was an act which was sinful in that it directly disobeyed God's explicit commandment.

Verses 9-15: Divine Retribution
This act is against "his brother". When Adam sinned God came asking him, "Where art thou?". Here the question is, "Where is Abel thy brother?". It is a reasonable assumption that, as in the question to Adam, God was asking this to provide an opportunity for Cain to confess. God certainly knew exactly where Abel's body was. All men's sins call forth a question from God after the pattern of one or other of these questions. Cain expressed what was in his heart when he murdered Abel, "because his own works were evil, and his brother's righteous" (1 Jn 3.12). So both sides of God's law have been broken: man has disobeyed God and murdered his brother. One vital truth is stressed in this story: the man whom Cain killed was his own brother. Human sin starts with turning away from God, but it never stops there. He who is at variance with his Maker will not treat his fellow-man properly. In Romans 1 Paul gives a record of human sin as manifested in the general state of affairs in the Gentile world of his day. The first step was to refuse to acknowledge God as God, but the end of the process was moral perversion and the dreadful catalogue of mainly violent sins listed in Romans 1.29-31.

Cain's response to God's question shows an attitude far advanced in sin beyond either Adam's or Eve's in their initial interrogation by God. He immediately lies: "I know not". His question, "Am I my brother's keeper?", suggests contempt for Abel, who was a "keeper of sheep". God's sad question, "What hast thou done?", is almost exactly like His question to Eve in 3.13. It does not ask for information but rather expresses deep sorrow. The references to Abel as Cain's brother climax chillingly with the repeated expression, "thy brother's blood". This is the first mention of blood in Scripture and how tragic that it must be a brother's blood, shed in hatred! Blood shed cries to God for just vengeance. Cain has given his brother's blood to the ground to drink, but even from the ground it cries for justice, for it was "the blood of righteous Abel" (Mt 23.35), the first man to die and also the first martyr for righteousness' sake. How reassuring to read of One whose blood "speaketh better things than that of Abel" (Heb 12.24)! Abel's blood cried out against righteousness violated, while Christ's blood speaks of righteous redemption and remission for the guilty.

Cain has polluted the ground with his brother's blood and he must be cursed from the ground by experiencing specially grudging response

from it when he tills it. Cain is the first man to be cursed. When he
wanders as a vagabond/vagrant it is not that he prefers the nomadic
Bedouin way of life, but that he is restless, perhaps afraid, probably
looking for something better than the meagre crops which he can wring
from a hostile soil.

Once again, there is a contrast between the silence of Adam and Eve
when sentenced and the protest of Cain: "My punishment is greater than
I can bear". This is probably the best rendering of the words. Cain shows
some insight in his realisation that his sin takes him away from God's
presence (compare v.16 with his statement in v.14). He is unrepentant and
must experience the truth that sin separates men from God. The language
is strongly reminiscent of the charge by Isaiah against Israel: "…your
iniquities have separated between you and your God, and your sins have
hid his face from you…For your hands are defiled with blood…" (59.2-3).

But then Cain, anticipating a future time when the family has increased
beyond its then present level, continues (v.14b): "and it shall come to pass,
that whosoever findeth me shall slay me" (RV). God corrects him, for human
life is not to be subject to summary justice meted out by individuals. He
promises Cain that any who, as it were, "take the law into their own hands"
against him will be punished sevenfold; that is, with the utmost rigour. It
should be emphasised here that the idea of vendetta, in which a kinsman
has responsibility to execute vengeance on a shedder of blood, is very far
from what is described. God will protect Cain from summary vengeance
and take a grave view of any such practice. As a token of this divine
protection Cain is to receive a mark.[†]

This will brand him as a sinner, granted, but it will guarantee him divine
protection. The position is a little like God providing coats of skin for
Adam and Eve, showing that they were sinners but that God had a care for
them notwithstanding. It is surely justifiable to believe that God's protection
would also grant him space to repent, something that he shows, so far, no
inclination to do.

Verses 16-24: Cain's Family

Cain, then, leaves the place where God is present to those who submit
to Him. His dwelling-place is Nod (Wandering). His family begins with the
birth of Enoch, and the first city in Scripture is built. The early cities in
Genesis are generally connected with sin and rebellion against God; man's
attempt to achieve security by his own efforts, when only God can give
true security. As the text stands this city called Enoch was built by Cain,
probably to show his determination to have some fixed location associated
with his family. This would accord with his calling it Enoch after his son.
Wenham comments that a slight emendation of the text would make Enoch
the builder, and the name of the city would then be Irad, after Enoch's
son, but there is no manuscript support for this, attractive as it may be on
other grounds.

The first of the line of Cain about whom there is any elaboration is Lamech. Significantly he is the seventh from Adam on this side of the family, for seven is a number which constantly crops up (along with its multiples) in biblical genealogies (compare Mt 1.17). There are also many other occurrences of groups of seven in this section of Genesis, for the narrative contains many intricate examples of patterned structures. Lamech is the first man recorded as having more than one wife, but then only one wife has been mentioned so far except Eve, and none is named except Lamech's two. It may be that this bigamy is recorded to indicate departure from the original order of monogamy, but the point is not made explicitly in the narrative. Certainly, when we come to the NT teaching on marriage the Lord Jesus refers to the original creation of a single pair, two made one flesh and not to be severed (Mt 19.4-6).

Many names are given in vv.20-22 of Cain's gifted family and descendants and their varied life-styles and achievements. They were successful as builders, as artists and craftsmen, as technologists and musicians, and marked by energy and initiative. If they were alive today they would win awards in many fields of human endeavour. Nothing, however, indicates any interest on their part in calling upon the name of the Lord. Their achievements are recorded, not to suggest that achievements are spiritually undesirable, but to show that they are not enough in themselves. This is seen in the fact that Lamech was not morally a better man because he was a technologically advanced man. He composed a kind of hymn (v.23), in praise of his own violent self-promotion. This seems to have been his intention in gloating over his over-reaction to wrongs. God's law would never countenance such a policy. Indeed it was to correct such excesses that the law of "an eye for an eye" (the *lex talionis*) was given (Ex 21.24). The implication of v.24 is that God may avenge Cain sevenfold but Lamech can avenge himself much more effectively and ruthlessly. Lamech stands firmly in the line of men who feel no need of God because, they believe, they can fend for themselves without His help.

Verses 25-26: Abel Replaced

After this display of braggadocio, v.25 comes in so quietly that there is a sudden realisation of having moved into a very different sphere of life. The family of Cain has been left for a gentler air. It is immediately noticed that Eve starts her explanation of the naming of her new son with "God". The Creator is being given His proper respect. When Cain was born she had begun her statement with "I…". She lays the responsibility for Abel's death again at Cain's door, simply but clearly. Seth is to be the start of a new line and that point is made by the record in v.26 where his son's name is given. This is sufficient to indicate that a new beginning has been made.

The most significant item in this short passage on Seth and his line is the simple record, "then began men to call upon the name of the Lord". Cain and his line declared their independence of God. In the context of

Seth's family, men sought through worship to have a relationship with God. Isaiah 64.7 has an interesting expression linked with calling upon God's name. After the charge that "there is none that calleth upon thy name", the prophet adds, "that stirreth up himself to take hold of thee". Here at last, after the record of Cain's family, is hope in that men are stirring themselves to lay hold of God. Isaiah provides an apt comment on Seth's family, or at least some of them.

This ends the section of Genesis described in 2.4 as "the generations of the heavens and of the earth". It has included the most exalted view of humanity as God intended man to be. It contains the solemn account of the fall from that place of privilege, but it contains also reassurance in that God always tempers judgment with mercy. The final note is one of hope, for some men at least have begun to call upon the name of the Lord. The tension between people with faith and those without it will continue throughout Scripture. So also will the tension between the themes of blessing and cursing. God has not abandoned sinful man, but man's lot, whether blessing or cursing, must depend on his response to God's commands and God's grace.

Notes

1 There are many examples in Genesis, as elsewhere in Scripture, of ideas suggested by names. Many of these are plays on the sound of the names rather than what one would normally think of as "meanings". Some of these will be highlighted in this commentary, but others will be passed over.

15 Many have speculated on what the mark may have been. Scripture gives no hint, so the speculation has ranged very widely. Much of it, however, is based on the idea that the mark was some kind of brand to show Cain as accursed. This represents God as merely vindictive, whereas it is clear that the mark, whatever it was, was designed to protect Cain.

GENESIS 5

Chapter 5.1 – 6.8 The Line from Seth to Noah

Introductory

This section, down to 6.8, is headed "the book of the generations of Adam" and, as normal in Genesis, deals with Adam's descendants during his life or after his death. It deals with Adam's descendants of the line of Seth, Cain's line having been considered in the previous section. It is noteworthy that in the case of Cain's line there are some details of the names and achievements of his descendants but it is not as complete a genealogy as this section. Here the pattern is generally to state the age of each person when he became father of the next person on the list, and then to give his age at death. The reason for the extra detail here is that this is the line in which God has particular interest. This line will lead to Noah, through whom God will preserve the human race. This is the line which will reach on into the future of the nation of Israel and the coming Messiah.

Chapter 5, verses 1-2: Creation Recapitulated

First of all, however, there is a recapitulation of the original creation of man. There is a reminder of God's high view of man's place in His creation – "in the likeness of God". Then the complementary sexes, male and female, are mentioned again (v.2), appropriately in a section consisting mainly of a line of descendants. The note of hope at the end of ch.4 is repeated in this reminder that God "blessed them".

Verses 3-24: Seth to Enoch

It is useful to consider the implications of v.3 for the method being used in this genealogy. While ages are given, the intention is not so much to establish chronology as to map out the descent of notable figures in the dealings of God with men. Thus Adam clearly had at least two sons before Seth was born and his daughters remain nameless (v.4), their place in the chronology unspecified. The people mentioned are included because they are essential to the continuity of the line. On the face of it, v.3 makes it appear (if ch.4 is ignored) that Seth was Adam's first son, which is not the case. This should make us wary of dogmatic statements about whether others mentioned here were the eldest. They may have been included simply because they were the fathers of those in the genealogical succession.

The detail about Seth, that he was begotten in Adam's "own likeness, after his image", must surely be read along with the message of hope implied in v.1. God's original plan for man will not be defeated by the irruption of sin. The image of God is evidently transmitted beyond the first man who bore it.

Perhaps this is the place to raise the question of the great age of these early men when they became fathers and also when they died. Traditions of longevity among early humans exist also in ancient non-biblical sources, some of which (such as those from Sumeria) include figures vastly greater than those in Genesis. It can only be taken that early humans did, for reasons unknown , live very much longer than people now do. It may be idle to speculate why. The reduction of life-expectancy as the biblical record proceeds is not a steady decline but a series of steps. Ancient translations of the OT (such as the Greek Septuagint) give figures at this stage in Genesis which are higher than those in the Hebrew manuscripts which are the basis of the AV. The figures in these ancient translations raise seemingly insuperable problems due to the fixed point of the flood.

There is no record of how many children Adam and Eve had. If Adam's longevity is a sign of his physical superiority to modern man perhaps they had a very large family, but that is just not known. What is known is that God gave Adam and Eve a son called Seth, through whom He preserved a line to carry forward His plans for mankind. It is also repeated with chilling regularity in the chapter, that each of these very aged men died. These are the first recorded deaths except the one violent death narrated in ch.4 and a second violent death celebrated in Lamech's song. (It is surely correct to take 4.23 to refer to the same victim twice through the Hebrew poetic convention of parallelism).

The pattern of information is almost identical down through the generations. Then comes Enoch, the seventh from Adam (compare Jude 14), and the pattern is modified. Enoch's period on earth was very much shorter than any of the others in the list. He also fathered Methuselah at an earlier age than the others fathered their named sons, 65 years as compared with, for example, Methuselah's age of 187 when he fathered Lamech. But the striking departure from the standard wording comes in the statement about Enoch's life after the birth of Methuselah. Instead of the usual statement that he "lived", in Enoch's case it says that he "walked with God".

The subject of this section is, as has been said, the line of Seth, down to Noah. It is exclusively a record of the one man in each generation who carried the line forward until Noah was born. Enoch was the seventh man in the line, a significant number in genealogies. Of him it is recorded that he walked with God, as it is also recorded of Noah (6.9), the tenth and last in this line. Walking is a common biblical word for the habitual behaviour of a person. Walking with God indicates a habit of living in the consciousness of responsibility to God and communion with God. The Septuagint renders it "pleased God", which underlies the commentary on this verse in Hebrews 11.5, "before his translation he had this testimony, that he pleased God". It is worthy of note that the author of Hebrews connects this kind of life with the realisation that God "is a rewarder of them that diligently seek him". One's mind goes back immediately to Genesis 4.26 and the companion reference in Isaiah.

Probably this statement is made about Enoch at this point in preparation for the end of his life on earth. It is not said that he died, and the comments of Scripture on this give clear guidance as to its import. The Septuagint gave an early lead in the interpretation of the passage. Its rendering of the words "he was not" expanded it to "he was not found". The Septuagint is again the version quoted in Hebrews 11.5.

In itself the accompanying statement, "for God took him", is ambiguous and could be an oblique reference to his death. When, however, it is compared with the story of Elijah's glorious assumption to heaven in 2 Kings 2 the meaning is clear.[†]

That identical terms should be used of the departure of these two godly men from earth confirms the general agreement that they were exceptions to the rule that all die. God has given a vignette prefiguring the great event when, in a rapidly deteriorating moral climate, He will remove the godly from earth before acting in fearful judgment in preparation for the reign of Christ. When the church has been taken away to be with the Lord, as 1 Thessalonians 4.16-17 teaches, the Day of the Lord with its severe judgments will begin (compare 2 Thessalonians 2.2-4 (RV) and 2.8) in preparation for the setting up of Messiah's kingdom. It is the hope of each living believer today that the Lord may descend from heaven and take us away to be with Himself without our even having to die. To those who, like Enoch, enjoy a walk in the consciousness of God's nearness the prospect is particularly precious.

Verses 25-32: Methuselah to Noah

Children take pleasure in remembering odd factual details and are always pleased to recite the name of Methuselah as the oldest man recorded in Scripture and 969 years as his age at death. Even the number 969 looks pleasing in its symmetry. Mature reflection on the ways of God still causes pleasure in contemplating how long this man lived, for his death was to herald the coming of the flood. God is slow to anger, giving men ample space to repent.

The birth of Noah provides another departure from the pattern in this genealogy (5.29). His father, Lamech, commented on the name he was giving to his son. If Lamech believed that Noah would bring to earth a time of quiet and rest the subsequent history of the early years of Noah's life must have surprised him. Lamech's comments do serve to repeat the theme of toil and curse resulting from sin. Noah would be the one through whom God would bring in hope and promise, but only after cosmic upheaval and not until years after Lamech's death.

The final verse of ch.5 is by way of rounding off the genealogical part of this section. It marks out the age of 500 years as a significant point in Noah's life. The verse can hardly be understood as stating that the three sons were triplets, all born that year. (For comment on the order in which the boys were born see at ch.10.21). Possibly the best interpretation is that his eldest was born that year, the others subsequently. The chronology is secondary to the genealogy, as usual in Scripture.

Notes

24 In both this verse in Genesis and the 2 Kings 2 references the Hebrew word for "take away" is (LAQAH - 3947).

GENESIS 6

Verse 1-4: Corruption Sets In

Chapter 6 opens with a time indicator which moves the story of Seth's line forward towards the point where only Noah's family survives of that line or indeed of any line. It introduces the episode in which the "sons of God", attracted by beautiful women ("daughters of men"), "took them wives of all that they chose" (RV). This episode is a notable crux for commentators.

The first problem relates to the identity of the sons of God. Elsewhere in the OT, where sons of God are mentioned like this, without explanation, they are angelic beings of some kind. It is assumed here that readers will understand what kind of persons these are. One would expect, then, that the title would be used in its normal way. Many commentators, however, find it difficult to accept that angels, though fallen, would experience sexual attraction. Interpretations, with few exceptions, fall into three broad groups:

(i) The sons of God were angels or similar beings, in rebellion against God in seeking a place outside of their proper sphere by cohabiting with earthly women. Those who hold this view appeal to references such as Jude 6 (RV) which refers to "angels which kept not their own principality, but left their proper habitation". Some details of that context may not support this interpretation as strongly as they are alleged to do by those of this persuasion. The strength of this view is that it presents a picture of monstrous procreation of a kind which might well be expected to call for a drastic removal of the results. The contention that the fact that angels "neither marry, nor are given in marriage" (Mk 12.25) refutes this position hardly holds, for unions such as are envisaged here are monstrous for the very reason that they are totally against the true nature of angelic life. A significant tendency can be seen here for mortals to aspire beyond their earth-bound relationship in seeking links with imposing "spiritual" partners.

(ii) A second view is that the sons of God are men of Seth's line drawn aside to marry women of the Cainites. This view runs into a problem in that the title "sons of God" does not, without explanation, imply Seth's line. Indeed, many argue that the vast majority of them soon degenerated to become virtually indistinguishable from Cainites. The interpretation in this present commentary at 4.26 may be a slight counter-argument to this claim of radical degeneration. A greater problem for this interpretation is the fact that it is even less probable that the title "daughters of men/Adam" would refer, without explanation, exclusively to female Cainites. If it is accepted that there was a predominantly godly line, then their seeking intermarriage with women of an ungodly line would be reprehensible. Would it, however, be sufficiently grave to lead to God's wiping out mankind? The picture of society divided as this view presupposes is not sufficiently clear-cut to give strong credibility to this interpretation. It must, however, be granted that one can more easily conceive of human males, rather than fallen angels, being attracted to human females.

(iii) The third main view also presupposes that the sons of God are human. Its proponents understand them to be men of kingly or princely status. In support of this it is argued that David's son is described in 2 Samuel 7.14 as God's son and again God addresses a Davidic king in Psalm 2.7 as "my son". Again, Psalm 82.6,7 (RV) reads, in an address to rulers in Israel, "I said, 'Ye are gods, And all of you sons of the Most High.' Nevertheless ye shall die like men, And fall like one of the princes". Yet nowhere does Scripture simply refer, without explanation, to sons of God when kings are intended, unless it is here in Genesis 6. Moreover, if the daughters of men here are commoners, what is so spectacular about the marriages? There is nothing in the language of these verses in Genesis 6 to suggest that these women were being exploited and forced into harems. And if a relatively small group of men transgressed like this, would God respond by wiping out mankind? There may, granted, be an answer to this last point in, for instance, the pestilence which God sent on Israel because of David's sin on one occasion (2 Sam 24).

Each of these lines of explanation runs into some kind of difficulty, but, on balance, some form of the first interpretation seems to fit the context best. Briefly, it takes the title, "sons of God", in its usual sense, it presents a monstrous intrusion into human society, it fits into the following picture of open rebellion against God calling for His judgment and for the cleansing of human society from this pollution.

There are problems again in 6.3. The line of interpretation which fits the context best is to understand "My spirit" as "My breath", as in 2.7 ("the breath of life"). The verb "strive with" (DIN - 1777) is difficult because of its rarity. It was understood by ancient translators as "abide/remain in" and many modern scholars have come to agree with this translation. This would indicate God's intention to take back from mankind, by the judgment of the flood, the life He gave them. God continues by referring to the fact that man is "flesh". This would suggest that God has decided to act in judgment in a situation in which men are behaving as if they were not mere mortals dependent on God.

Yet once again, in declaring that He must act in judgment, God gives man a sign of His mercy; "his days shall be an hundred and twenty years". This is interpreted generally in one of two ways:

(i) Some understand it to indicate God's intention to shorten human lives to, say, a norm of 120 years. This would not fit in very closely with the pattern of shorter lives given in Genesis in the time immediately after the flood. Yet one does find later a few people who had life-spans of about this length–for example, Moses. In ancient non-biblical writers there are some references to peoples who had life-spans of about 120 years. The Greek historian Herodotus remarks that Ethiopians often lived to about this age and that Egyptians tended to live to about 110 years.

(ii) Others take it to refer to a period of which, to use the language of 1 Peter 3.20, "the longsuffering of God waited in the days of Noah". God is never in a hurry to pour out His wrath. He is slow to anger, as Scripture consistently maintains. This interpretation seems preferable.

Commentators have further problems in 6.4. The word translated in the AV as "giants" occurs in only two places in the OT, here and at Numbers 13.33. The RV accepts defeat and leaves it untranslated as "the Nephilim". The word may mean something like "fallen ones". In Numbers the spies from Israel saw Nephilim in Canaan and beside them felt themselves to be tiny. Ancient translators, in Greek and Latin, understood the name, as the AV does, to mean giants. The run of the passage suggests that the Nephilim are to be identified with the "mighty men...men of renown" of 6.4, though this is not absolutely sure. If these are the same and are the result of the unions described in 6.2 and 6.4, there might be, in the nature of that union, a possible cause for their exceptional qualities. This again leads towards interpretations of the whole context which see interference from powerful beings outside humanity. The title "men of renown" is literally "men of name", and it may be appropriate to note the fact that later in Genesis (chs.11-12) a contrast is drawn between the ungodly, who seek to make a name for themselves, and the godly Abram, whose name God would make great. These "men of name" would inevitably be self-made men. The spirit is the spirit of Lamech (4.23-24), of Nimrod and of the men who will be in open, worldwide rebellion against God when the Lord Jesus descends to put down rebellion and set up His kingdom (2 Thess 1.7-10).

The expression in 6.4, "and also after that", can hardly mean after that but before the flood. The most straightforward way to take it is that Numbers 13.33 shows the result of a later assault by the powers of darkness on the human race. If this is the correct interpretation it is no surprise that that attack is focused on Canaan, the land which God was giving to His people. It might also provide a reason for the strict instructions about destroying the inhabitants and, especially, about avoiding at all costs any intermarriage with them.

Verses 5-8: God Resolves to Destroy Human Life

This final part of the section marks the end of this phase of the line of Seth. Wickedness has increased greatly on the earth, evidently overwhelming people of whatever family, with one exception, namely that of Noah. The core of the problem is exposed in 6.5, "the heart". As usual in Scripture, this is not so much a reference to the affections or emotions as to the intentions, motivations and will. People's minds were filled with evil and this moved them to plan and carry out evil projects. The picture is one of constant occupation with evil. How similar conditions were then to those in the present!

God's reaction is stated in forceful language. He cannot be complacent when people have perverted all that was planned by God for them. His desire is to bless, but their behaviour demands that, in accordance with His holiness, He act in judgment. So instead of blessing He punishes. This is expressed as God repenting that He made man, and is due to His deep indignation at what people were doing (vv.5-7). He takes no delight in the death of the wicked: "As I live, saith the Lord God, I have no pleasure in the death of the wicked; but that the wicked turn from his way and live" (Ezek 33.11). He never created any man with his damnation in view. Yet His holy character demands that He damn the unrepentant wicked person.

A moving sidelight is thrown on this period by the Lord Jesus in Luke 17.26-27. He describes the typical preoccupations of the antedeluvians in these words: "They did eat, they drank, they married wives, they were given in marriage, until the day that Noah entered into the ark, and the flood came, and destroyed them all". In other words, a situation which deeply moved the heart of God with sorrow and indignation was seen by the people on earth as perfectly normal. Everything went on as usual. Warnings of doom were seen by them as the product of a sick mind. This could hardly be more relevant for modern times. Those who profess the name of Christ cannot afford to allow themselves to accept tacitly the values of a society which treats God as at best irrelevant. The sobering aspect of the Lord's summary of the attitudes of the antedeluvians is that He mentions simply that they were occupied with the affairs of daily life as if they thought that life was going to last indefinitely. The believers' most telling testimony today is in their ability to live above the sensuality and materialism of society, and in their use of material prosperity without being enslaved to it.

The language of God in 6.7 is unmistakable: "I will destroy man whom I have created from the face of the earth…". This can hardly be understood as a local or regional disaster. It is judgment on mankind as such. The other details, about animals being destroyed, are commentary on the main text, which is the destruction of mankind. If this be the case, then surely God is defeated? No; judgment and mercy go together. Once again God upholds His own holiness and righteousness without forsaking His mercy. "But Noah found grace (favour) in the eyes of the Lord". This brings the story of this section up to Noah, the tenth from Adam and the end of an era, and once again the story of mounting human sin is set against a background of divine mercy and grace. There is hope, but no thanks to man. The next section will deal with "the generations of Noah" and relate the story of judgment and a new beginning with Noah. This eighth verse is the link.

Chapter 6, verses 9-22: The Flood Announced and Preparation Made

Introductory
This is the first phase in a main section under the usual kind of heading–
"the generations of". The section continues down to the end of ch.9 and
contains the story of Noah and his family through the flood and after it. It
establishes the background which anticipates the prominence to be given
later to the Semites, the descendants of Shem. It also opens up the way
for the development of the theme of Canaan as a place opposed to God
and His people, but at this stage personified in Noah's son Ham and Ham's
son Canaan.

The main part, down to the end of ch.8 tells of the end of the antediluvian
world under the judgment of God. It continues the theme of the grace
and mercy of God which spares some people to carry forward the record
of God's blessing and sovereign grace. After the flood there are references
which tell of prosperity to be enjoyed by the Semites. There will, at the
same time, be a tension between the positive response of Noah to God's
dealings and his failure to do God's will fully. God's grace may spare men,
but they remain tainted and handicapped by sin.

Verses 9-12: Noah and His Contemporaries: A Contrast
Noah is the focus of attention in v.9. He is depicted as a man of godly
integrity. His uprightness is set "among his contemporaries". It seems that
"perfect in his generations" would be best rendered as "blameless among
his contemporaries". His uprightness is in contrast to their corruption.
His acknowledgment of God is in contrast to their living for the present
without a thought of God. He has the testimony, with Enoch his great-
grandfather, as one who "walked with God". He has three sons, on whom
attention will focus in most of this section.

The background is dark. People have turned their backs on God and, as
inevitably happens in such circumstances, have taken to venting their
hatred on each other. The key words in vv.11-12 are "corrupt" and "earth".
The picture of society is dreadful in its perversion of all that God originally
intended for man, and the consequences for earth as well as man are dire.
Corruption in relation to God expresses the spiritual ruin which underlies,
and inevitably leads to, moral collapse. Men who hate God come to hate
each other. Hence the accompaniment of corruption is violence, for men
who have no reverence for God will sooner or later show scant reverence
for other men made in His image. Verse 12 shows movingly how God *saw*
the corruption, a reminder that initially He had, by contrast, seen what He
had just made and declared it "very good". All the world is affected by the
ruin of mankind in general.

Verses 13-22: The Ark Ordered and Built
God announced to Noah His intention to put an end to "all flesh". God's

opening words to Noah in v.13 may best be understood as meaning, "I have decided to bring all flesh (humanity) to an end". All animals, however, must also perish, for they are linked with mankind. It may be that the animals are included in "all flesh", as they may perhaps be later in the section, but the facts are not affected by the translation. Both men and beasts must die. God's reason for this decision is the worldwide violence. No doubt these conditions are to be traced back to the unholy alliances in vv.1-2, but God's judgment fell on mankind at large on account of the wickedness described in vv.5, 11 and 12. Their destruction would involve the overthrow of the habitable state of the earth, so that the order and fruitfulness and amenities which people had enjoyed would be disrupted. This is tersely described in 2 Peter 3.6: "the world that then was, being overflowed with water, perished".

The instructions for the building of this first recorded floating vessel are very sparse. Dimensions are given in general terms, but the precise shape is not described. It is not known, for instance, what exactly the cross-section of the ark looked like, or whether it had a keel. The light sources are not clearly specified, nor is there any real description of the roof. One translation of v.16 opens, "You are to make a roof for the ark, giving it a fall of one cubit when complete..." (REB), but this understanding of the words is not generally agreed. What is certain is that God provided Noah with enough information to make an ark which would survive the flood.

The ark seems to have had only one door (v.16). Gopher wood (v.14) is mentioned only here in Scripture. It is surmised that it was some kind of cedar or other conifer. The word "rooms" (AV) in v.14 is an odd word (QEN - 7064), normally rendered "nests". It can be taken that it is used here with an extended meaning, but that meaning is not certain. Without changing the Hebrew consonant text, but giving it a different set of vowels from the usual ones, it can be understood, and is now usually understood, to mean "reeds". This might describe a vessel with a timber structure, with reeds woven into it in some way, and the whole structure covered inside and out with bitumen ("pitch"), but the picture is far from clear. Some commentators retain the interpretation that the structure was entirely of timber, with "rooms" (rather than "reeds") and "caulking" inside and out. All things considered, this may be the best suggestion.

The biblical cubit is not always the same length, but the general overall length of the ark was probably 140 metres, the breadth 25 metres and the height 15 metres (v.15). The word "window" (AV) in v.16 (TSOHAR - 6672) is variously understood. It is not the same word as in 8.6 (HALLON - 2474). Its interpretation is affected to some extent by how the instruction in v.16, "in a cubit shalt thou finish it above" (AV) can be interpreted. If the word TSOHAR is taken to mean "roof", the instruction can mean that a cubit's space should be left between the top of the walls and the roof. Many oriental buildings even today have this arrangement for ventilation. The precise meaning of the verse, however, is far from clear.

The arrangement in three decks (v.16) would give a reasonable average height of about 4.5 metres for each deck. This, along with many other aspects, is in marked contrast to fantastic details contained in non-biblical versions of a great flood narrative.

In v.17 there occurs the first explicit mention of a flood as the means of destruction. The word for flood here (MABBUL - 3999) occurs in the OT only in the Genesis flood narrative and in Psalm 29.10: "The Lord sat as king at the Flood; Yea, the Lord sitteth as king for ever" (RV). God is in full control, as the repeated "I, even I" indicates. The dignity of this record is in marked contrast to ancient Babylonian fantasy about a great flood. The explanatory clause, "and every thing that is in the earth shall die", perhaps indicates that in this context "all flesh" includes the animals, but the clause may also be understood as an addition to the statement about all flesh. Presumably fish and other sea creatures are excluded, as there are no directions for their rescue.

The phrases such as "all flesh", "under heaven", "every thing that is in the earth" seem deliberately designed to make it unmistakably clear that a worldwide flood is intended. The debate about whether this is inconceivable rages in scientific and pseudo-scientific circles. Many of the problems raised in objection to the physical feasibility of a worldwide flood arise from preconceived ideas about such things as the formation and age of mountain chains. Similar debate rages around the question of whether there are evidences of such a global catastrophe. Here again preconceived ideas affect what any particular scientist will accept as possible evidence. Theories of dating, for example, are so wildly irreconcilable that there does not at present appear to be even a basis for real debate. Details of these arguments can be examined in a range of books which the scientifically minded may consult. Some titles are included in the bibliography to this commentary.

A new fact is revealed in v.18 about Noah's relationship with God. Here we find the first biblical reference to a covenant.[†] God has committed Himself to Noah's preservation and welfare. In a book which develops God's special covenant relationship with Israel this is a most significant seed concept. This covenant is with Noah, but it includes his wife, their sons and the sons' wives.

Noah is to take into the ark two of each type of animal, male and female. Creation was orderly, "after his kind", and now the rescue follows the same orderly pattern. Sin may lead to the destruction of order in society, but God still has not forsaken the orderliness which marked His first creatorial activity, and He will yet restore the orderly arrangement of animals, each after its kind, in the new world which will emerge after the flood. Interestingly, this is the first time that mention has been made in Genesis of male and female in referring to animals. This is a record of survival measures, and breeding pairs must survive. Hence the repeated phrase in vv.19-20, "to keep them alive". The record is realistic in details, such as the instruction to provide "food that is eaten" for the different types of animals and for the humans. The collection of the animals does not present Noah with an impossible task, for the animals would "come" to him (v.20).

The simplicity of v.22 is eloquent. In ch.3 Adam failed to obey the single prohibition given him by God. So sin entered. Noah, the righteous man, in complete contrast, obeys in all details the substantial task entrusted to him, "according to all that God commanded him". So a basis is laid for the new world which will emerge from the flood.

The account is brief and simple. In reality this was a prolonged period of time when "the longsuffering of God waited in the days of Noah, while the ark was a preparing" (1 Pet 3.20). The conclusion that it was during this period especially that Noah was "a preacher of righteousness" cannot be avoided. He had no message of invitation for others, only of judgment. But his message of judgment met no response of repentance such as Jonah's similar message (albeit a more urgent one in terms of time-scale) met in Nineveh. People simply ignored his words and his even more eloquent craftmanship. They were too busy ensuring that life went on as normally as was possible amid the growing collapse of social order. They had no reason in the events within living memory for believing that life would not go on as it had done in their father's time. No doubt they said things like, "Since the fathers fell asleep, all things continue as they were from the beginning of the creation" (2 Pet 3.4). The one thing which they overlooked or did not know was that God had warned Noah "of things not seen as yet" (Heb 11.7). Hebrews 11 says that it was by Noah's obedience in preparing the ark that "he condemned the world". It comes as no surprise that this testimony was so long extended, during the laborious work of constructing the ark. God is slow to act in judgment. Yet even after so long a time the record of the Lord Jesus is that they, "knew not until the flood came, and took them all away" (Mt 24.39). Living in days which bear an unnerving similarity to the days of Noah one cannot fail to read the challenge in the record of this great man of God with his single-minded devotion to the task given him by God. Ark-building made him an oddity in a corrupt society which lived for the visible, tangible things. There are lessons to learn from him.

Notes

18 The basic concept of the covenant relationship between God and His people as set out in Scripture contains a number of parts. It involves the great truth that God is pleased to commit Himself to undertaking the cause of His covenant people. They in turn are therefore responsible to be faithful to Him, to the exclusion of false gods, and also in righteous, holy living. They are also responsible to be faithful to each other in loving, considerate behaviour. The concept which deals with this complex of obligations accepted by God and men in the covenant is contained in the Hebrew word HESED (2616,2617), translated in various ways, but most commonly appearing as "mercy" in the AV.

GENESIS 7

Verses 1-5: God Invites Noah into Safety

Whether v.1 is read as, "Come thou…" or, "Go thou…", the sense remains substantially the same, and translators do not agree on which verb to use. God has given instructions to Noah for the preparation of a place of safety, Noah has obeyed fully and now the time has come for him to enter. God refers back to the righteousness which had distinguished Noah from the vast majority of his contemporaries. He will be the link with future generations of human beings. Here again God's judgment is tempered with mercy. Noah's family will also be saved, presumably because Noah is head of the house and his influence has saved them from the excesses of wickedness which were prevalent. Verse 1 declares that God is a God of judgment, "seeing" people as they are. This is the principle set out in Proverbs 15.3: "The eyes of the Lord are in every place, beholding the evil and the good". Verses 2-3 spell out the distinction to be made between clean and unclean animals as Noah preserves specimens of each kind. They are preserved in pairs for future breeding (v.3). The distinction between clean and unclean was formalised in the law of Moses for purposes of offering and for human consumption, but there is no problem in accepting that, long before the days of Moses, God had already made clear the distinction to early men before the flood. If clean animals are to be used for sacrifice after the flood they will need to be preserved in greater numbers.

Verse 4 gives the timescale of God's plan of destruction. He gives seven days for the final stage of preparation. Forty days of rain will follow and the result will be the annihilation of life outside the ark. Thus Noah is briefed about the final preparation. His response is as would be expected; he follows instructions implicitly, "according to all that the Lord commanded him".

Verses 6-16: The Rescue Operation Completed

A hundred years had passed since Noah, as recorded in 5.32, became a father. His three sons had married but there were no grandchildren. Eight people, then, four men and four women, entered the ark. They were accompanied by the pairs of animals, as God had decreed, male and female. All was orderly, and all was ordered by God, as in the creation, according to their kinds. At the end of the seven days mentioned by God in v.4 the flood came.

This summary in vv.6-9 is followed by a more detailed analysis in vv.10-16. Firstly, in v.11, the precise date is given. The times during this period are recorded in detail in 7.11 – 8.14, according to an exact, symmetrical pattern. The flood began on the 17th day of the second month in Noah's 600th year (7.11). The earth dried and he was able to leave the ark on the 27th day of the second month in his 601st year (8.14). The duration of the event was, therefore, a solar year of 365 days. However, it is interesting to note the literary construction used to give a palistrophic arrangement of the time periods involved. They overlap and should not be added as if they could give the sum total. They are (in days) 7, 7, 40, 150, 150, 40, 7 and 7. The references showing this are 7.4,10,17,24; 8.3,6,10 and 12. All seemed at the time to be a complete destruction of the orderly creation which God had made, but all was completely under His control, as is suggested by the perfectly symmetrical series of days.

Then in v.11, in addition to torrential rain ("the windows of heaven were opened"), water was released from beneath, for "the springs of the great deep burst out" (REB). This was not just the first rain mentioned in Scripture; it was a cosmic upheaval involving the distortion of the earth's crust to release underground water in vast quantities. At creation God had separated the upper and lower reservoirs of water. At the flood He released them in one horrendous cataclysm. Similarly, in creation God had gathered the waters on earth together in one place (1.9), separating them from dry land, but now He releases the water to overwhelm everything. An important feature of the flood is that God broke up the order which He had created. This process was perfectly controlled, but it was none the less catastrophic. This torrential rain continued for 40 days, a key number in Scripture, connected especially with testing (compare the 40 years during which God tested Israel in the wilderness wanderings, or, by contrast, the 40 days during which the Lord Jesus fasted in the wilderness, "led by the Spirit in the wilderness during forty days, being tempted of the devil" (Lk 4.1-2, RV).

Verses 13-16 repeat in greater detail the identity of the occupants of the ark. All were possessors of the breath of life, which God was withdrawing from all other living creatures on earth. The expression "all flesh" may be seen as an indication of their dependency on God, creatures on earth, made by His hand. They enter the ark according to their kinds, for God is always orderly in His actions. Creation has not been a total failure, for its order continues as He acts in judgment. His mercy in judgment is indicated by His measures to preserve within those in the ark "the breath of life". God is able to save and to destroy. "And the Lord shut him in". How dreadful the destruction of a rebel civilisation! How secure the objects of God's mercy, "shut in" by His hand in the place of safety! Those whose salvation He undertakes cannot be snatched from the secure place in which He shuts them.

Verses 17-24: The Waters Prevail

Verse 17 stresses that "the flood was forty days upon the earth", a repetition of v.10. But here the emphasis is on its impact on the ark. Though the waters "increased" the ark was not overwhelmed, for the waters bore it up "above the earth". Earth was overwhelmed, but the ark was above it all. Verse 18 intensifies the record of judgment with waters which "increased greatly", but the ark was "upon the face of the waters". Verse 19 repeats the liturgy, with the waters prevailing "exceedingly" upon the earth – one of six references in this section to the flood being "upon the earth". In this verse the added fact is that "all the high hills, that were under the whole heaven, were covered". As if this were not enough v.20 adds that above the mountain tops the water was fifteen cubits deep. This must mean that the water level was fifteen cubits above the highest peak of the mountains. So the waters "prevailed"; (note the repetition of the word "prevail" in vv.18,19,20,24). And outside the ark? The impact was felt by creatures of all orders from the flying to the creeping, and not least (though last mentioned) mankind. All were overwhelmed, for all were "upon the earth" (v.21). The expression used in v.22 is not "the breath of life" simply, as it was in v.15, but the more elaborate "the breath of the spirit of life" (RV), recalling the time when God breathed into man's nostrils the breath of life (2.7). The verse would appear to refer only to mankind.

The theme of v.23 is how God destroyed, or, to translate the word as it is given elsewhere, "blotted out" (MACHA - 4229) man and beast, all who were "upon the face of the ground". This is the word used in Psalm 69.28 when David prays of the wicked, "Let them be blotted out of the book of life" (RV). On a happier note, it is the word used in Isaiah 43.25, "I, even I, am he that blotteth out thy transgressions for mine own sake, and will not remember thy sins". God is able to save and to destroy. As Peter has it 2 Pet 2.5 (RV), He "spared not the ancient world, but preserved Noah with seven others".

"And Noah only was left, and they that were with him in the ark" (v.23, RV). The form of this statement may suggest that they were saved because of their association with Noah. But saved they were. And what a contrast between "on the earth" and "in the ark", a contrast between destruction and salvation! In judgment God remembers mercy. Upon the earth, there was only water which "prevailed" 150 days. It is almost as if there were a reversion to the primeval darkness "upon the face of the deep". The worldwide nature of this judgment may be compared with the repeated references in Revelation to the judgments to be poured out upon them "that dwell upon the earth". Mankind will be divided then, as at the flood, into earth-dwellers and those saved by God.

GENESIS 8

The Flood Recedes and Life Returns to Earth

The processes recorded in ch.8 are the reverse of those in ch.7 where there was an irresistible, overwhelming expansion of the destructive power of the flood until all was desolation and life on earth had disappeared. Only in the ark was life preserved, for it rode high above the earth, on top of the water. In ch.8 the flood steadily ebbs until land is once more revealed, then dry, then walked on by living creatures again.

Verses 1-4: The Flood Decreases, the Ark Rests

This section is opened with a gleam of hope. God has not lost control of destructive cosmic forces. There were, of course, indications of this divine control, but now it becomes more clearly evident. "God remembered Noah" is the first occurrence of this idiom, repeated for instance in 19.29 where God "remembered Abraham, and sent Lot out" of Sodom in its overthrow.[†] It is the inspired comment by Moses on the relationship between God and Noah. The flood destroyed mankind who had turned away from God, but God took knowledge of Noah and his family for blessing and salvation. The ark was the first sign of this care of God for Noah. Now, in reversing the destructive advance of the flood, God once again shows His care for him.

Associated with Noah in this manifestation of divine care is the world of living things. Man was the head of all creation on earth originally. He remains the head of the recreated earth, if it can be called that. The living things in the ark were "with Noah". He was the focus of God's concern.

When the primeval darkness was "upon the face of the deep" (1.2) God acted, for "the Spirit of God moved (hovered) upon the face of the waters". Now God "made a wind (the same word as "Spirit" in 1.2) to pass over the earth". However such references to divine activity are understood, they are recorded to show God in action, and this is the message of Scripture. God is there and He is not silent. Debate about "natural forces" or "supernatural agency" often misses the mark, for it often presupposes the idea that nature - and some will write "Nature" as if to deify it - normally functions without God, according to its own "laws". Such an idea misrepresents the laws of nature. They are merely a systematic description of what happens in nature. It must be remembered that it happens because God is pleased to act in an orderly and predictable manner unless He has good reason to change His mode of operation for special purposes. There is no need to worry about "naturalistic" explanations of divine interventions, for with God there is no dichotomy between nature and supernature. God is in control.

So the waters assuaged. The sources of the flood, whether celestial or subterranean, were closed (v.2). Verses 2-3 reverse the process by which the flood had prevailed. The first indication that this has happened is that the ark rested on the mountains of Ararat, showing that the depth of water above the mountains was now insufficient for the ark to float over them. The location of this area is vague. The ark grounded (v.4) somewhere in the general area of mountains in Armenia. From a biblical perspective the play on words between "rested" and "Noah" is perhaps as significant as the name of the mountain area where the ark rested.[†]

Verses 5-14: Waiting for the Time to Leave the Ark

This is a narrative of fact, not a fantasy, and the waters receded steadily (v.5), but without magical sleight of hand, for over two months more, before the general run of mountains were visible. Step by step the world was returning to something of its antediluvian order.

Noah became active again in v.6, starting the sequence of activity which would enable him to decide when it was time to vacate the ark. He opened the window (not the same word as the AV "window" in 6.16) to send out a raven. The raven survived outside the ark until the waters had dried up, but it did not return. Then he sent out a dove, and this time the purpose of its sending is made explicit, "to see if the waters were abated...". But the dove found no "rest" (another play on Noah's name) and returned to the ark because of the general prevalence of the flood. There is a graphic little touch in the narrative as Noah "put forth his hand, and took her, and brought her in unto him into the ark" (RV).

Verse 10 may imply that Noah waited seven days after he sent the raven before he sent the first dove, for it says that he "stayed yet *other seven* days" (v.12). The same dove was sent again, and again she returned in the evening with proof that the waters had abated. She bore an olive leaf. A third time, after a further seven days, she was sent out and did not return. It must surely be an intentional feature in this phase of the narrative that rest and seven-day cycles of waiting are interwoven. The seven-day cycle of work and rest was familiar to all readers. The fact that the dove had brought back an olive leaf is also pregnant with associations. Normal life in Israel was dependent on the inhabitants having, among other plants, their fruiting olive trees. Life was returning gradually to normal.

On the first day of a new year (v.13) Noah removed the covering of the ark. Almost nothing has been previously mentioned about the covering, but it was at any rate possible for Noah to remove it. He then saw for the first time that the ground was dry, but he waited some weeks before the earth was ready for its inhabitants (v.14).

Verses 15-19: The Ark Vacated

The exodus from the ark was timed by God. Noah went out at God's command. He had obeyed explicit, detailed commands to the letter. God now gives him further similarly detailed commands. This again underlines the fact that God, who was in control throughout the flood, brings out of the ark all the people who went in - "thou, and thy wife, and thy sons, and thy sons' wives with thee". God is able to save all those to whose salvation He pledges Himself.

The command to bring forth with him all the various kinds of creatures is framed in terms which again point forward to the establishment of normal life on earth: "that they may breed abundantly in the earth, and be fruitful, and multiply upon the earth". Once again everything was done as God commanded. God's original creative plan for the earth to be inhabited by humans and various kinds of animals has not been frustrated, even though He destroyed virtually all earth's inhabitants. There emerges from the ark a full range of animals, classified as before into their kinds, along with all the people who went in. God is now ready to make a new beginning.

Verses 20-22: A New Start

The antediluvian world was no more. Peter wrote (2 Pet 3.6) of water, "whereby the world that then was, being overflowed with water, perished", and placed that destruction alongside the future destruction of our world by fire.

A new start was being made, and it was made auspiciously, for Noah built an altar, the first altar to be mentioned in Scripture. Abel's sacrifice presupposes an altar on which it was offered, but this altar of Noah's is the first explicitly mentioned.

This was a great sacrifice, with victims from every clean type of beast and fowl. One must assume that this is the first reason why creatures are classified in Scripture as clean or unclean, to make the point that only the best is good enough to give to God, or more accurately, that only what is clean is acceptable to God. The nature of the sacrifice is also given, for it was a burnt offering. In other words, Noah was giving to God a voluntary offering which was wholly for God. But burnt offerings did make atonement for the offerer, for Leviticus 1.4 says, "it shall be accepted for him to make atonement for him".

God took knowledge of Noah's offering, for "He smelled a savour of rest" (v.21 Newberry margin). Once again, that word "rest" is brought in with symbolic force. It was accepted not only for Noah, but also for the world at the head of which Noah now stood. God promised, then, not to place any further curses than He had already placed on the ground. This is followed by the clause, "*for* the imagination of man's heart is evil" and so on. This may be a short way of saying something like this: "I will not add further curses on the ground, *for*, though such curses are well deserved by men whose imagination is evil, this sacrifice enables me to be merciful". If it does mean this, "for" virtually means "though", as it is taken in a number of modern translations. The point is made in any case that God has not lowered His standards.

At least it can be said that the ordered creation has been re-established, and that the turmoil and cataclysm of the flood has been hushed. Verse 22 lists those seasons which make up the rhythms of the agricultural year.

Seedtime in early spring (February to April) is followed by harvest (May to early June). The cold season (January to early February) contrasts with the heat (September to October). Summer (mid-June to August) when the harvest is past contrasts with winter (November to December) when all is bare. Day and night are the odd pair in this sequence. They relate more to the physical need for nightly rest than to the longer rhythms of the seasons. God has once again declared that He is for mankind, His creatures, ready to bless and richly provide, requiring that humanity, through His bounty, be fruitful and prosperous (v.17).

Notes

1 The Hebrew ZAKAR (2142) is very common in the OT with this connotation of action which shows care. Its emphasis is on God's willingness to involve Himself in ensuring the welfare of His people.

4 The Hebrew verb for "rest" has the root NUACH (5117) echoing Noah's name. In v.9 the dove "found no rest", and there the Hebrew noun for "rest" is MANOACH (4494). This is a theme on which the passage rings the changes to establish a message.

GENESIS 9

God's Covenant Established and Future Races Forecast

Verses 1-7: God's Blessing for Future Life and Man's Responsibility

The flood has purged the earth. Noah has offered sacrifice to God. God is able once again, as in 1.28, to pronounce blessing in anticipation of fruitfulness and copious progeny. Noah and his sons are to fill the earth, again as in 1.28. The theme of fruitfulness and multiplying recurs in Exodus 1.7. It must surely be significant that in that passage Moses takes up this theme as preparations begin for the establishment of Israel as a nation. Even here in Genesis the emphasis rapidly shifts from nations to the special nation in God's plan for mankind.

Once again, while humans and animals of all kinds enjoy life from God, mankind is set apart as the one creature whose "fear" is upon all the others. Mankind is specially privileged, but this special status also involves special responsibility for the lesser creatures. God Himself has absolute power, yet He always considers His creatures' needs. In Psalm 104 the psalmist refers to the manifold forms of living things, all nurtured by God. Then he concludes, "These wait all upon thee; that thou mayest give them their meat in due season. That thou givest them they gather; thou openest thine hand, they are filled with good. Thou hidest thy face, they are troubled; thou takest away their breath, they die, and return to their dust" (vv.27-29). In the same way, He expects man, made in His image, to exercise authority with what it pleases us to call "humanity". So, in Proverbs 12.10, "A righteous man regardeth the life of his beast: but the tender mercies of the wicked are cruel". It is not by accident that the biblical figure of a king is characteristically a shepherd, a man who leads and guides but also feeds and protects. The Epistle of James (3.7) speaks of man's ability to train and control all kinds of animals. Training is more effective when it is gentle but firm than when it is oppressive and harsh.

At the beginning God had given the various growing plants to Adam for food. The language of 1.29 is so general that in theory it would include plants which humans cannot eat. So here, when to plants are added animals of all kinds, it seems at first glance that there are no exceptions to the animals which will feature in human diet. Since, however, a difference has already been made between clean and unclean, it may well be that only clean animals are included in what is provided for food.

The restriction in v.4, taken in the context of other Scriptures, is best understood as meaning that when the animal has been killed its blood should be allowed to drain from the flesh as it was later decreed it should in the Levitical offerings. Blood was the vehicle of life in animals as in humans. That life was given to them by God as to man. Therefore it merits the greatest respect by man.

But human blood is the vehicle of a form of life much higher than that of animals which are eaten. Human life is of an order which gains its distinctive value from being made in the image of God, and being made for eternity. There is a great solemnity in the description of God's decision to destroy all humanity by the flood. The wanton destruction of human life is an act which God views with the upmost repugnance. This is expressed in v.5 by the fact that even an animal which took human life was held responsible. But when a man takes his fellow-man's life this is far more serious, for the man he kills is his "brother". Both killer and killed are made in the image of God. It is an unspeakably horrible situation that one of them should kill the other. People who reject the scriptural teaching that God is Creator, and has made the human race uniquely in His image, cannot hope to understand what the Bible says about the sanctity of human life. Verse 5 solemnly ends with God's warning, "at the hand of every man's brother will I require the life of man". Human laws may ignore this but God has not devalued human life as many countries are seeking to devalue it.

This respect for fellow-humans is stated here in its most fundemental aspect, that of respect for human life. The principle, however, is more broadly applicable. James in his epistle (3.9) shows that it is inconsistent to bless God, our Father, and with the same tongue to curse "men, which are made after the similitude of God". Murder is merely the logical extension of hatred and a host of other sinful ways of treating and thinking about one's fellows. What makes these things especially unacceptable to God is that all are valuable to God in a way unique to the human species.

Verse 6 should therefore be examined against this background. There is a possibility that "by man shall his blood be shed" could be translated as, "for that man shall his blood be shed". This would leave open the question of who would or should shed it. Should it be left to God to avenge the blood of the slain person? It seems much more appropriate to continue the theme of v.5, which laid down the principle that the blood-shedder is responsible to God his Creator for taking human life. The rendering of the AV should therefore be retained. In Numbers 35.33 it is laid down that bloodshed pollutes the land. In that same chapter, v.31 decrees that no ransom should be accepted for the life of a murder: "he shall be surely put to death". God established human government to execute judgment and uphold order. This verse shows how God sees this principle in action with reference to murder. The reference to "his brother" in v.5 harks back to Cain's slaying of Abel, though at that point the responsibility devolved here to human government had not yet been established. Cain's murder of Abel was the prototype of the slaying which is the subject of v.6.

If the full solemnity of the verse is grasped there are a number of implications. The death penalty here is not primarily a deterrent but rather a statement of the unique value of human life before God. The murderer should have considered this before he committed this capital offence. Equally those to whom the administration is entrusted should weigh the implications carefully before acquitting or condemning a person on a capital charge, for his life is also sacred. If police forces or law courts or juries are so corrupt that the evidence is not reliable or not properly sifted, then justice in these cases cannot be done and human government must collapse into anarchy.

In Numbers 35 God established in Israel cities of refuge to which someone who had unintentionally killed another person could flee for safety. This provision maintained the solemnity of the violent killing of a human being. Because human life is sacred even inadvertent killing of any person must be treated as of great import. On the other hand the provision also ensured that a distinction be made between an accident like this and deliberate, intentional killing for which no city of refuge existed.

Much of what is written currently about crime and punishment, particularly in connection with murder, shows an attitude of near despair. It is often assumed that mistakes will be common. It is also assumed that the aim is merely to try to deter others from committing the same crimes. If the execution of justice does not deter others, the argument runs, then why bother? This is a council of despair and a denial of the basic principles of justice. The person who has committed the crime is found guilty if the evidence shows, beyond reasonable doubt, that he is guilty. If he is found guilty his punishment should reflect the seriousness of his crime. In the case of murder this verse in Genesis says that his crime is of unparalleled seriousness and merits a capital sentence. This decree lays down the basic principle; whether there are cases in which it might be appropriate to exercise mercy is a matter not dealt with here, but such mercy is not necessarily excluded.

But the emphasis in the passage is on the future. God therefore repeats (v.7) the blessed command which looks forward to a peopled earth enjoying the bounty of God. Man, then, has his responsibility to move out to people the earth, to tame and care for the animal creation, to tend the plant life and to execute justice.

Verses 8-17: God's Covenant with Mankind and All Living Things

In v.1 God's blessing was upon "Noah and his sons". Here in v.8 His communication is likewise with Noah and his sons. The emphasis is shifting from the one man who found favour with God to the generations which will succeed him. So God's covenant is not with Noah personally but with him and his family and their descendants after them. The AV "you" in v.9 is, of course, plural. In ch.6 God spoke of His covenant with Noah in relation to Noah's entry into the ark. Now that Noah and his sons have emerged from the ark to begin a new age, God speaks again and commits Himself to preserving man and beast from the possibility of ever suffering destruction by a worldwide flood. During the flood God was always in control. Now He assures Noah and his family that He controls the vast reservoirs of water and can assure that no flood will destroy the earth (v.11). God does not will it so and it will not happen. The phrase is again repeated, that the living creatures are "with you". God's prime concern is man, His highest creature, and lower creatures benefit from their association with man. So His covenant is with the animals as well as man (v.12).

The bow in the cloud is a good example of how God condescends to man's limited understanding by providing simple reminders of His undertakings and His care. His covenant with mankind and the lesser creatures is the guarantee that, when natural disasters strike, God is still in control over all His universe. The rainbow is the symbol which He chose to represent this undertaking never again to destroy the world with a flood. While this is the first rainbow mentioned in Scripture it is not safe to assume that there were no rainbows before the flood. Such reasoning would impose a burdensome chain of implications which would be far-reaching. The important message here is that God once again declares Himself to be in control of His universe, that He has established His ability to destroy and to save, and that He has given His word that such a flood will not recur. The repeated emphasis is on His covenant with the earth and all that lives on it. Once again it is stressed that in judgment God remembers mercy.

Verses 18-27: A Preview of Noah's Descendants
This portion properly speaking starts a new section. The story of the flood has been closed on the positive promise that it will not be repeated. Now begins the story of the generations after Noah. As so often in Scripture, a story about a man serves to set the scene for the kind of people his descendants will turn out to be.

The three sons who entered the ark with Noah also emerged with him. Their names are again repeated here. It is not accidental that the pregnant statement is made (v.18) about a descendant of Ham while no comment for the moment is made about any descendant of Shem or Japeth, or for that matter of any other descendant of Ham. Canaan in Scripture is linked with the fact that God decided to destroy a civilisation whose wickedness called down His judgment (compare 15.16; Deut 9.4-5, for example). The occupation of Canaan by Israel was intended to be accompanied by the annihilation of a thoroughly corrupt and depraved race. That race is linked here with Ham through Canaan his son.

The universality of the flood is again presupposed in the statement in v.19 that the descendants of Noah's three sons overspread the whole earth, or perhaps we should catch the later echo better if we translated "they were scattered over the whole earth". The verb (NAPATS – 5310) is related to the word used in 11.9 where God acted in judgment at Babel and we read, "and from thence did the Lord scatter them abroad upon the face of the earth". Thus we are prepared for the later story of nations as they impinge upon the developing story of God's plans.

There is some debate about how to translate v.20. A literal rendering

gives something like: "Noah, the man of the land, was the first to plant a
vineyard" (Wenham). The words "was the first to" would strictly be
translated as "began to". It would not be factually accurate to say that Noah
was the first tiller of the earth, for Cain must have tilled the earth to produce
the materials for his offering. The integrity of the biblical narrative requires
the rejection of such a translation as "Noah, who was the first tiller of the
soil, planted a vineyard" (REB). If the phrase "man of the land" is taken to
mean "farmer", that fits in well enough into Wenham's translation. Cassuto
understands "man of the land" as "master of the earth" in the sense,
apparently, that Noah was the head of the human race in this new earth
after the flood. Taking Wenham's translation as substantially accurate the
verse can be read as saying that Noah was the first person to cultivate the
vine.

The vine is an essential part of biblical scenery. In times of peace men
grew their olives and figs and grapes. Thus Micah (4.4), after his familiar
reference to beating swords into ploughshares and spears into
pruninghooks, says, "But they shall sit every man under his vine and under
his fig tree; and none shall make them afraid". Wine itself in Scripture is
often seen as that which "maketh glad the heart of man" (Ps 104.15). The
other face of wine, as a "mocker", as a snare to those who would have
ambitions to please God, is also very common in Scripture. It is sobering
to see that, in this first reference to a vineyard and to wine, it is the ugly
side which is emphasised. The vineyard and the wine were morally neutral,
but Noah, despite his upright character, was the first recorded example of
drunkenness. In his defence, presumably he had no experience of the
danger of drunkenness. Yet it must be remembered that the Bible frequently
denounces it, and later examples in Genesis will show the seductive and
destructive power of wine.

Chapter 3 showed (v.7) a sense of shame at one's nakedness as the first
effect of the fall. Here Noah, a righteous man, is naked but unconscious
for the moment that he is in a shameful condition. Ham, who came upon
him in this condition, is significantly called here the "father of Canaan",
for the Canaanites were to become notorious for their immorality and
excess. Ham's reaction to the situation showed an utter lack of respect for
his father. Nakedness is viewed in Scripture as a matter of deep shame. So
when Hanun of the Ammonites wanted to show his rejection of David's
overtures of peace he declared his contempt of the envoys by shaving off
half of their beards and cutting their garments short at the buttocks (2
Sam 10.1-4). In that context it is recorded: "the men were greatly ashamed".
Similarly in the prophets the horrors of captivity include the shame of
being paraded naked by the conqueror. But that a man should fail to cover
his own father's nakedness was virtually unthinkable. Ham went even
further, for he went out and told his brothers about it.

Shem and Japheth were understandably ashamed of their brother's
scandalous behaviour. Their covering of their father was carried out in a

way which expressed their respect for him, their abhorrence of Ham's behaviour, and their determination to remedy the disastrous situation. The story provides an illustration of what might be involved in obedience to the Fifth Commandment, "Honour thy father and thy mother: that thy days may be long upon the land which the Lord thy God giveth thee" (Ex 20.12). Many autobiographical writings nowadays provide eloquent examples of a lack of such respect for parents and other relatives. It almost seems as if the inclusion of shameful deeds increases sales.

The story began with Noah's action in drinking and becoming drunken. It continued with Ham's shameful reaction to the situation and his brothers' commendable remedy. Now it ends on the pathetic note: "And Noah awoke from his wine". It is common nowadays to speak of alcohol and other means as "removing inhibitions", as if this were merely a clinical observation by a psychologist. The fact of the matter is that they remove the sense of shame which is rightly felt in the normal course of events when shameful things are said or done. But there comes a time when alcohol ceases to remove that sense of shame, and, when the person who indulged "wakes up" and is told what he or she has done, the sense of shame can be crushing.

Noah's sense of outrage against Ham leads to his brief prophetic pronouncements on the descendants of his sons. For an Israelite the descendants who were most repugnant were the descendants of Ham's son Canaan. Hence the curse pronounced on that line is directed at the son Canaan rather than Ham who was guilty of the original misdemeanour. This is the first time in Scripture that a human being has pronounced a curse. If there was euphoria in welcoming the fresh start after the flood, with its promise of fruitfulness and prosperity, this episode has abruptly dispelled that feeling. Man is still sinful and races will emerge whose whole lives tend away from God into ways of gross spiritual darkness and immoral excess. God will draw a nation to Himself, but there must be a clear distinction morally between them and the depraved nations of men. The moral degradation of Canaan is to be reflected in their servitude to the races springing from Shem and Japheth.

The race of Shem receives a brief blessing, set against the servitude of Canaan to them. The fact that only in this blessing is the title "the Lord God" used may give some indication of the covenant relationship which will exist between the Semites (starting with Abraham) and God. The blessing of God is also called down on Japheth. It is to be expressed in Japheth's being "enlarged" (the verb is a play on "Japheth"). The sense of the expression "dwell in the tents of Shem" is not completely clear, but it probably refers to situations in which Gentiles of the line of Japheth ally themselves with Shem as the more powerful force in the alliance. Canaan will know servitude to Japheth as to Shem. This poetic pronouncement by Noah on the descendants of his sons bears a resemblance to other poems or prophecies by men of God, usually uttered shortly before their death. There are examples in Genesis in chs. 27 (Isaac blessing Jacob and

Esau) and 49 (Jacob's prophecy on his sons), as well as in Deuteronomy 33 (Moses blessing the tribes).

Verses 28-29: A Summary

Verses 28-29 serve as an end-piece to this section. They sum up the years of Noah, as was done of so many others in ch.5. Noah, last survivor of the men whose actions before the flood were recorded, is dead. The antediluvian emphasis on individuals is about to give way to analysis of how nations emerge from families. Verses 22-27 of this chapter begin that process. The end of Genesis will show the people of God's choice on the verge of the time when they will become a nation rather than an extended family.

GENESIS 10

Nations Descended from Noah

Introductory

The genealogies which occupy this chapter display a strange mixture of named individuals, towns and countries. There are, of course, three main lines - Japheth, Ham and Shem. Each of these is opened with a formal heading (vv.2, 6, 22) and has a formal end-piece (vv.5, 20, 31). The whole chapter is rounded off with a further end-piece (v.32). These end-pieces refer to families, languages, lands and nations. The chapter, then, is far from being a genealogy of specific families in terms of individuals and their offspring. It is rather a framework for looking at how, over a period of some generations, nations arose which would impact in some way on God's chosen people descended from Abraham. The references to languages make it clear that chs.10 and 11 are not chronologically in sequence, for we find the origin of language diversity expounded in ch.11 but taken for granted as an established fact in ch.10. The arrangement of the two chapters as they stand leaves the Babel story as the end of a section on "the generations of the sons of Noah" (10.1 - 11.9). When ch.11 continues (v.10) with a differently slanted account of "the generations of the sons of Shem" it leads in smoothly to "the generations of Terah (11.27 - 25.11), and Abram in particular. Thus the end of ch.11 will be a watershed in Genesis, where the broader themes are left behind and God is seen working with a people called out of a largely estranged world to be His special interest.

Verse 1

The heading in 10.1 covers the section down to 11.9, moving forward swiftly from events just after the flood and preparing for the call of Abram. The closing verse of ch.10 draws a line under the three sections of Noah's descendants and contains a significant reference: "and by these were the nations divided in the earth after the flood". Implicit in this phrasing is the fact that these three sections constituted the population of the world at that time.

Verses 2-5: Japheth's Line

Most of the names are those of peoples, although the precise identity of many of them is a matter for debate. Such information or hints as can be gathered from other sources locate many in the general area from the upper Tigris and Euphrates across through Asia Minor and South Russia to Cyprus, Greece and possibly Carthage in North Africa. These are, broadly, Gentile peoples other than those immediately impinging on Israel or south of it. Much of the identification remains somewhat speculative. Among the more generally agreed identifications are Madai as the Medes, Javan as Greece or specifically Ionian Greeks, Kittim as Cyprus or part of it. The reference to the "isles" in v.5 is perhaps the "coastlands" of the Gentiles.

Verses 6-20: Ham's Line

This is given in much greater detail than Japheth's line. One good reason for this is the fact that Israel had much closer dealings with these peoples. Many of them would appear to be located in or around Arabia, Yemen, Assyria, Mesopotamia, Egypt, Phonenician territories close to Israel, and the promised land itself. Among clearer identifications are Cush as Ethiopia (probably the area now called Nubia), Sheba in south-west Arabia, the Mesopotamian and Assyrian locations associated with Nimrod, Pathrusim as Pathros in Upper Egypt, Caphtorim as Cretans (whether in Crete or possibly in south-west Canaan) and the peoples of the land of Canaan.

The record is interrupted, or so it seems, by an account of the evil but heroic figure of Nimrod. He is presented as someone who made a mark as an outstanding champion ("began to be a mighty one"). Indeed he became a byword as an outstanding hunter. "Wherefore it is said" introduces an editorial comment, in this case the quotation of a traditional expression: "Even as Nimrod the mighty hunter before the Lord". His political might is reflected in the reference to his "kingdom" and to "a great city", probably to be understood as referring back to Nineveh. There are echoes in this Nimrod story of the antediluvian line of Cain and in particular the sinister but powerful Lamech. The biblical picture is consistent, that some men become great in their own sight and that of their fellows by their own prowess, but these are not the men whom God takes into His plans and conspicuously blesses. They are too independent, too proud, to be blessed by God. If v.11 is understood to say that "he went forth into Assyria" (RV), this serves to explain the inclusion of Assyrian place names such as Nineveh. This translation must be considered very probable.

Special attention is paid to the descendants of Canaan. Their occupation of the land which God gave to Abraham and his seed is explanation enough for the prominence given to them. This also accounts for the record in detail of the area controlled by them (v.19). This is substantially the promised land.

Verses 21-31: Shem's Line

As usual in Genesis, the most significant line of descent is given last and the significant aspects of it emerge as it unfolds. In this case the special importance of Shem for the Genesis narrative is marked first by the extra statement in the introduction in v.21, linking Shem to Eber, the ancestor of Abram. This is reinforced by the second genealogy, in ch.11, in which the link is made between Shem and Abram himself.

But first a detail in v.21. Scholars are not agreed whether the correct translation is, as in the AV, "Shem ... the brother of Japheth the elder", or, as in the RV, "Shem ... the elder brother of Japheth". The order in which the brothers are named is Shem, Ham and Japheth, but that does not necessarily indicate that Shem was the eldest and Japheth the youngest. Ham appears from the language of 9.24 to have been the youngest. The

RV rendering of v.21 reads more naturally than the AV and one is probably justified in taking it as accurate. This will involve explaining the chronology behind 11.10. If this rendering of v.21 is correct this is one of the very few instances in which God took up the line of the eldest to make a significant move towards His purposed goals.

In v.22 the names of five sons of Shem are given. Then four sons of his son Aram are listed, but nothing more is said of this branch of Shem's family. Instead there is given the name of one son of Arphaxad, namely Shelah, then Shelah's son Eber, then Eber's two sons Peleg and Joktan. Joktan's thirteen sons are listed, and the area where they lived is described (v.30). But this once again is a case of giving a genealogical dead end before dealing shortly after, in greater detail, with the significant branch of the family. In this case that branch is the one through Eber. It will feature in the more detailed genealogy in ch.11.

One further point calls for comment. In v.25 it is said of Peleg: "for in his days was the earth divided". In view of the vivid narrative of events at Babel which follows almost immediately it is best to take this as a reference to the scattering of the nations at Babel when their language was confused.

The genealogy of Shem is rounded off at this point in the usual formal way by v.31. It is worth noting the characteristic feature of the genealogies in ch.10, that families, tongues, lands and nations are specified. The interest lies in the peopling of areas of the world in what may be called "spheres of influence" more than in any strict chronological account of genetic inheritance.

Verse 32: The Families of Noah

Verse 32 is the end-piece for the whole chapter, rounding off the comprehensive survey of the significant national and family traditions descending from the family of one man, Noah. The reference in the verse to nations being "divided" continues the theme of the earth being peopled by scattered nations, as expounded in ch.11.

GENESIS 11

A. Verses 1-9   Rebellion at Babel
B. Verses 10-32   Shem to Abram

A. Verses 1-9: Rebellion at Babel

Chapter 10 has consistently raised the subject of separate nations, living in various areas, with their own identities and speaking different languages. This is what one might expect in view of the divine command to be fruitful and multiply and fill the earth, in view also of the diversity of languages which confronted even the first readers of Genesis. These nine verses in ch.11 provide a new insight into the subject of the diversity of races and languages.

On the face of it the first section of this story, in vv.1-4, would sound positive and encouraging if this were only a secular story. There was harmony among the people. They understood each other and co-operated with each other (v.1). They acted prudently, it seemed, in seeking and finding a fertile area in which to settle (v.2). They made good use of the technology available to them in developing building techniques which would enable them to use local materials. Incidentally, archaeologists' finds confirm that ancient buildings in this area, made in the way described here, were extremely durable. The bitumen (AV "slime") which is found locally in Mesopotamia provided a most appropriate binding agent for the bricks. The bricks were seemingly not just sun-dried, but baked thoroughly (literally, "burned to a burning), presumably in some sort of kiln-like system (v.3). They planned their mega-project with due regard to the work which needed to be done and the benefits to be reaped from it (v.4), and seem to have been united in purpose, well organised and well prepared.

However, v.5 dispels any euphoria one may have been feeling. It becomes clear that the Lord had been left out. But He was interested, as He is interested in all that concerns the welfare of His creatures. He is not just "God", the infinite, possibly inscrutable, Creator; He is also "the Lord", who made human beings to have relationship with Himself. Human projects must end in disaster if He is left out. The problem is that if men leave Him out they may begin to believe, as they plan their super-developments, that they are in some sense gods. So the Lord interested Himself ("came down", in the vivid language of this vivid story) in what "the children of men" were building. The builders were only men, whatever pretensions to independence they may have cherished. This verse is the pivot around which the story turns. From this point on it becomes more and more clear that, far from being a glorious and unqualified success, this project was impious and an unqualified disaster from start to finish. It is probable that the text implies God's contempt for the pride of the builders in the fact that He "came down" to see the tower, though its head was supposed to be "in the heavens".

Verses 6-7 answer vv.3-4 in close detail. It is beyond the scope of the present commentary to attempt to analyse in depth how the language of the two sections uses echoes and inversions of sounds in the Hebrew words and phrases employed. Men's plans are turned on their head by God, and the Hebrew wording subtly represents this. What had seemed wisdom is shown to have been folly. So v.6 resumes the theme of unity and harmony. It shows that the building of a city with a tower as its focus is not the end of the project; it is only the start - "this they *begin* to do" for they will not be satisfied with a mere building project. It is not by chance that the word "have imagined" (ZAMAM - 2161) is used by God. It is the same word as that used in Psalm 37.12: "The wicked *plotteth* against the just". The building programme is part of a much more ambitious scheme. God will not allow men to continue with sin and folly indefinitely. Here as in Eden they must be stopped (see 3.22). This account of the wrath of God overturning men's ambitious schemes is reminiscent of the description in Romans 1 of how God reveals the folly of men who seek to ignore His glory as Creator. A prominent aspect of the Romans 1 description is the list of words which show men unable to agree or co-operate with each other (vv.29-31).

As men have jumped into action with "Go to", or more colloquially, "Come on", so God in v.7 is equally ready with the same expression to give His response. Men had communicated effectively with each other but had failed to communicate with God. They had been able to speak effectively and hear accurately, but they had failed to ask God about this project or to listen to what He might say. So He brings their communication to each other into confusion, for if men will not bring God into their counsels they soon lose the ability to communicate with each other. There cannot be fulfilment in social life without God being involved as the centre and pivot of everything. This is as true of modern attempts to create super-states as it was at Babel.

They had planned to build a city. City-builders in Genesis up to this point have not been men of God. The tower which would be its focal feature would have "its head in the heavens" (YLT). This may be the kind of idiom used in Deuteronomy 1.28 where the cities of Canaan are described as "great and walled up to heaven". On the other hand, it accords well with the independence of God which these people have manifested if we see the expression as an indication of their self-sufficiency and arrogance.

The climax of their project outline was the key to their motivation in the whole scheme: "let us make us a name". These people were marked by the same spirit as Lamech before them, a spirit of self-sufficiency and self-aggrandisement. It is in keeping with the way language is used in this story that the expression they use, "a name", is the same in Hebrew as the name of the line of descent from Noah which God was going to take up, namely

"Shem". God had His Shem, they would make their own "shem" great. We remember also that in the antediluvian rebellion there were involved "men of name" ("of renown" as the AV puts it).

Their fear was that they would be nonentities if they were scattered. So they would build a secure identity in a fixed location and the glory of that magnificent achievement would be theirs. And of their kingdom there would be no end!

But God confused their speech. Communication broke down. Unity was shattered and they were scattered. This brings us back to the account in ch.10 of how mankind spread into different areas, with distinct racial or national identities and separate languages. The dream of a single, strong, self-sufficient state died, for a time at least - "they left off to build the city".

They had planned to make themselves a name. But the name which they left for posterity to remember and consider was Babel. This may mean "The gate of God (or the god)", but to Jewish (and other) readers it recalls the meaningless "babble" of people whose language communicates nothing of meaning or sense. The inspired comment is, "because the Lord did there confound (BALAL - 1101) the language of all the earth" (v.9). The repetition of the phrase "all the earth" falls heavily on the ear at this stage. God's plan was to people all the earth and His plan could not be thwarted.

So much for the story as it stands in Genesis 11.1-9. It is necessary, however, to take account also of the link with the vignette of Nimrod in 10.8-12. It was noticed there that his achievements included the statement, "And the beginning (or prime) of his kingdom was Babel". This prominent figure was the kind of person one would expect to find connected with a project like Babel. He had the outstanding energy, the heroic stature, the organising flair, and the independence of spirit, needed for such a grandiose project. Further, when taken in the context of later biblical references to Babylon, the theme of human pride and rebellion against God begun here can be seen as the seed-bed of an important scriptural tradition. Babylon was the source of the complex tradition of idolatry which would later provide the focus for human rebellion. When God gave a worldwide kingdom to Nebuchadnezzar his response was to swell with pride: "Is not this great Babylon, that I have built?" (Dan 4.30). This was the kingdom which God used to punish His people, but the men of Babylon used the victory to glorify themselves and their gods. When finally human power and rebellion are humbled by God as envisioned in the book of Revelation their fall is seen as the fall of Babylon: "Babylon is fallen, is fallen, that great city..." (14.8). The great false system set up against God and His heavenly Jerusalem is in that same book seen as "Babylon the Great, the mother of harlots and abominations of the earth" (17.5).

In the context of Scripture as a whole, then, this short passage is of seminal significance. It represents one of the most outstanding examples of human rebellion, a declaration by humans of their independence of

God. It is of a piece with Satan's pride which will not own his status as a creature, and with Adam's determination to decide for himself what was good or evil. It called forth an inevitable response from God, for He will not give His glory to another. Men thought they could decide where to live in security, using careful planning and co-operation to glorify self and avoid the anonymity of being scattered. They would make their name glorious, but God confused their language and their name in Scripture is the Babble of confusion.

Verses 10-32: Shem to Abram

Strictly speaking this part of the chapter consists of a complete section, vv.10-26, comprising "the generations of Shem", and the start of a new section, "the generations of Terah", extending from 11.27 to 25.11.

(i) First, then, the genealogy of Shem down to Terah. This reverts to the strict formula used in ch.5, where the father's age at the birth of his son is given, followed by the extent of his life after that and the unvarying statement at the end that he "begat sons and daughters". The genealogy has few distinctive details and calls for only a few comments.

The age of Shem at the birth of Arphaxad is given as 100, "two years after the flood". Taken in conjunction with 5.32 this would suggest that Shem was not the eldest son and that he was born two (or three?) years after Japheth, which would determine the interpretation of 10.21. It is likely, however, that round figures are being given in this case - 100 years and 500 years.

The ages of men in this genealogy are lower than those in ch.5, and they tend to decline as the list progresses. Thus the first four, from Shem to Eber, range from 600 years to 433. The next five, from Peleg to Terah, range from 239 to 148 if the reading of the Hebrew text followed by the AV in v.32 is followed. The age of the men at the birth of the named son drops suddenly from one hundred years (Shem) to thirty-five (Arphaxad) and remains at around that age except in the case of Terah, who was seventy when his son was born. So almost all of these postdiluvians became fathers at a much earlier age than the antediluvians did, a significant factor in a period during which God wanted men to repeople the earth.

The birth of Terah's sons gives rise to the same phenomenon as with Noah's sons in 5.32. It can probably be assumed that they were not triplets and that the facts have been foreshortened by the three names being given at the time of the birth of the eldest. One question arising from this will be dealt with at v.32.

(ii) Verses 27-32 take the genealogy of Terah down to Abram and beyond, but it rapidly becomes clear that the interest focuses on Abram. Terah's three sons are given consistently in the same order - Abram, Nahor and Haran. Haran is quickly disposed of. He was father of Lot and he died in Ur during Terah's lifetime. Lot will feature in later incidents, usually serving as a contrast to Abram, who was renamed Abraham during Lot's life. Abram married Sarai and Nahor married his own niece, Milcah. The two marriages are important in the later narrative.

The incompleteness of the genealogies can be seen if the line of descent of the Semites in 10.21-31 is compared with this chapter. In ch.10 Peleg, fourth in line from Shem, has no descendants listed, yet here he is ancestor of Abram:

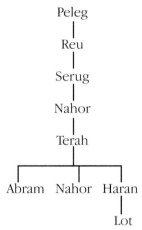

The change of tempo in the narrative is marked by the comment, "But Sarai was barren; she had no child". This opens one of the main themes of the Book of Genesis, the theme of descendants, "a seed" for Abram in fulfilment of divine promise. The barren wife is also a frequent theme in Genesis and indeed in later books of the Bible. The line of Nahor is left undeveloped at this point, but it will re-emerge in ch.24 when a bride is being found for Isaac, Abram's son. Events are being dealt with here in greater detail when they are of spiritual significance for the story. Individuals who are major figures in the record are engaged in significant experiences which are told in great detail as principles of living for God are being established.

Verse 31 introduces an event of momentous importance, the migration of the family of Terah from Ur to Haran. The verse says that they "went forth ... to go into the land of Canaan", then leaves unexplained the fact that they stopped short at Haran, where they "dwelt". This migration will be important for the story of the family because it introduces the subject of their dwelling in places in which God took particular interest, the final destination being the land which would be promised to Abram. The initiative to leave Ur seems, on the surface, to have been Terah's. He "took" Abram and the others. It seems clear enough from Joshua 24.2 that Terah was an idolater, serving other gods. It is also clear that God appeared to Abram in Ur, as Stephen says in Acts 7.2: "The God of glory appeared unto our father Abraham, when he was in Mesopotamia, before he dwelt in Haran". This would refer to the event described Genesis in 12.1. Putting the different elements together it can be concluded that the initial plan to leave Ur was in the heart of Abram. His father Terah and some of the family fell in with his plan and Terah led them as far as Haran.

Stephen said in Acts 7.4 that Abraham left Haran "when his father was dead". Throughout the chapter Stephen shows an ability to recall details of OT stories accurately. It seems likely, therefore, that he would get this fact correct. If so, what text did he read in Genesis 11.32 - 12.4, for 12.4 says that "Abram was seventy and five years old when he departed out of Haran"? But if Abram was born 135 years before Terah died, and if Terah died before Abram left Haran, Abram was at least 135 when he left Haran.

If Abram was much younger than his oldest brother, whom one assumes to have been Haran, and if we rationalise the dates by this supposition, then Terah was 130 when Abram was born, which seems highly unlikely in view of the special point made of how wonderful it was that God enabled Abram to become a father at 100 years old.

It does not seem satisfactory to "spiritualise" Stephen's reference to Terah being dead. This solution would take Stephen to mean that when Terah refused to go on to Canaan Abram rejected him and counted him as dead. The solution is very strained.

A tentative suggestion is to follow a reading given by the Samaritan Pentateuch, which gives 145 years instead of 205 in 11.32. Philo the Jewish writer also reads 145 years in this verse. A number can easily be miscopied in manuscripts. This would be the simplest solution but must for the time being remain merely a suggestion.

At any rate the final verses of ch.11 close the subject of Abram's ancestry in the context of the nations which would later impinge upon him and his descendants. In a sense all of chs.1-11 are introduction. They introduce Abraham, from whom is descended the race which is of greatest importance to God and men, for from it came the Lord Jesus Christ. The first eleven chapters serve as an introduction to Genesis but also to the whole Bible. Among other important lessons to be learnt from them is the fact that the OT cannot be read simply as a book about the religious experience of one race, the Jews. These chapters set the story of Israel in the context of the whole world, indeed the whole universe, and declare that God is the God of all creation, with sovereign rights over all. In wonderful grace He takes knowledge of individuals and makes Himself known to them. This is a very, very different thing from the now popular idea of the evolution of the concept of God in humanly devised religion. There is no neutral ground between the two positions.

GENESIS 12

Introduction

Strictly speaking this is a part of a section beginning at 11.27 and continuing down to 25.11, under the heading "the generations of Terah". It has been noted, however, that the move from Ur was presented in 11.31 as under Terah and the narrative there merely listed the main figures in the family who went to Haran. This in effect creates a tension between their expressed intention "to go into the land of Canaan" and the final record in 11.32, that "Terah died in Haran". The story from the broader standpoint of Genesis starts with Abram, not Terah, and it starts in Ur, as 15.7 makes clear: "I am the Lord that brought thee out of Ur of the Chaldees". It can be taken, then, that ch.12 starts the substantive narrative of the divine origin of the chosen people, called out of Ur through God's call to Abram. Here for the first time Abram becomes an initiator of action, as distinct from a group or family member under Terah. Interest in this section, down to 25.11, will centre on Abram (later renamed Abraham) and his son Isaac as being fathers of the chosen people. They are patriarchal figures, carrying responsibility, in some sense, for the future destiny of their people.

Verses 1-9: Abram's Journey from Ur to the Negev

A new beginning is signalled in v.1 by the statement that the Lord spoke to Abram. This is not merely tribal migration or the unfolding of shifting social patterns. God took an initiative, without which there would be no story. This incident seems to have been the basis for Stephen's assertion in Acts 7.2: "The God of glory appeared unto our father Abraham ...". Abram responded in faith. That is, when God spoke and gave a command Abram trusted God and therefore obeyed. It was not a leap in the dark; it was a step along with God.

The command was to leave country, kindred, father's house. Ur was idolatrous and God was going to establish a people who would have no other gods beside Him. Terah does not feature in this narrative, presumably because while he was active in the journey from Ur to Haran he was not acting in faith and probably remained an idolater.

The conviction that this is God's first dealing with Abram is confirmed by a structural detail in the narrative of Abram's faith. Here at the outset God spoke of "a land that I will show thee". When Abram's faith reached its strongest point, in 22.2, God once again directed him to "one of the mountains which I will tell thee of". These two episodes bracket the story of Abram's journey of faith with God. The same faith stepped out on two difficult journeys, confident that it was safe to travel with God. Humanly speaking the journeys were both folly, but God is real and Abram's faith could trust Him when he could not understand.

Abram set out, then, for a land unknown to him. He received for his faith a promise (v.2) that God would make of him a great nation. This theme, of a nation in a land under God, is an essential part of the fabric of Genesis and indeed of much of Scripture. Abram did not live to see it fulfilled, but he will see it fulfilled in a future day.

Another promise was that God would bless him - this theme of divine blessing runs through Genesis. Whether the final clause of v.2 is translated as "thou shalt be a blessing" or as "be thou a blessing" it amounts to the same thing. God had no plans to make one man or one nation an object of His blessing merely to show His love for them. His plan was to bless them so that they would be the channel of blessing for others. The principle is found, for example, in Psalm 67, where the opening and closing sections pray for God's blessing and confidently expect it, but closely linked with this is the confidence that He will bless the nations through Israel. It is still the case that if God's blessing is enjoyed, it is with a view to communicating that blessing to others. God loved the world as really then as He does now. So His final purpose for blessing Abram was that "in thee shall all families of the earth be blessed" (v.3). Praise God, this shall indeed happen when Christ bestows blessing on a renewed earth as He is beginning to do in this age of grace in the case of people who respond to the gospel.[†]

We must not miss the promise in v.2, that God would make Abram's name great. Previous mention has been made of "men of renown", literally "men of name" (6.4). Some individuals have been self-proclaimed as great men. Lamech boasted of his prowess and Nimrod became a legendary hero. But this is altogether different. This man's name is not just a short-term sensation. This is greatness in the divine scale of assessment. The people of God today are happy to agree with Paul that Abraham is "the father of all them that believe" (Rom 4.11). It is a small thing that today Muslims, Jews and Christians call their sons after Abraham across the nations of the world. God's assessment goes beyond even that scale of greatness. By contrast, the men in 11.4 who feared obscurity, and tried to make a name by establishing a great city, have disappeared and left no name except Confusion.

On the interpretation which we are following, some foreshortening of events occurs at v.4: "Abram departed [from Ur], as the Lord had spoken unto him; and Lot went with him [whether from Ur or Haran]: and Abram was seventy and five years old when he departed out of Haran". The actual final completion of the journey is described in v.5, which lists in brief the people who went on the stage of the migration from Haran to Canaan. The constant reference to Sarai, Abram's wife (as in v.5), is a feature of this part of Genesis. She plays a vital part in the story if Abram is to have descendants, but she is barren. This sets up a tension in the narrative. Lot is also constantly mentioned in this section of Genesis. But he is always a follower. He has no vision of God and hears no word from God, as far as the narrative reveals. Both Lot and Sarai, for different reasons, will be important in the succeeding chapters, but for the moment their presence is established by unobtrusive repetition.

In v.5 Abram is also beginning to emerge as a man of some wealth, which will be a significant matter before long. Lot, too, had evidently accumulated wealth in Haran. "The souls that they had gotten in Haran" would appear to be people who had become attached to them, presumably as employees and dependants. Is it reading too much into this to suggest that some at least had learned to trust the one true God through their contact with Abram?

There is a note of satisfying finality in the end of v.5: "and into the land of Canaan they came". What follows is a process of setting foot on the land in its length, from the North, through the centrally located Shechem (v.6), as far as Bethel/Ai (v.8) and finally the South (the Negev).

In his journey through the land, Shechem was the place which at this stage had the most significance for Abram. He camped evidently at a tree which was a landmark. It appears in the AV as the "plain" of Moreh, but scholars are agreed that it should be translated as either "terebinth" or "oak", at any rate as a tree. He was an outsider in a land already occupied by the Canaanites (v.6). The place at Shechem acquired a memorable part in his story because here the Lord appeared to him, another instance of God taking an initiative to make Himself known. The words spoken by God to Abram once again combine an implicit promise of descendants ("thy seed") and an explicit promise of the land as their possession. Abram is again marked out as a man of faith, for he signalled his acceptance of God's promise by building an altar, on which, presumably, he offered sacrifice. When he moved on to a site between Bethel and Ai he again pitched his camp and again built an altar. In his journeys Abram left no lasting memorial to his visits except the altars which he had built.

At last God is, it seems, building a new family, later to become a race, as His representatives on earth. They will know and worship Him, He will bless them and give them territory. The special relationship between God and Israel is inextricably linked to their possession of the promised land. All seems set for prosperity and a wonderful, inspiring success story. Then comes the episode, in vv.10-20, which puts all in hazard again.

Verses 10-20: Abram Goes Down to Egypt

"And there was a famine in the land". This is a recurring motif in OT stories of times when God's people were based in Canaan. It was a country in which they depended on God for fertility of the land. It is described in Deuteronomy 11.11-12 as "a land of hills and valleys, and drinketh water of the rain of heaven: a land which the Lord thy God careth for". So God's people would need to learn to trust Him. When they were in Egypt, during their sojourn and captivity there, it was different (Deut 11.10): "the land of Egypt, from whence ye came out, where thou sowedst thy seed, and wateredst it with thy foot, as a garden of herbs". In Egypt people were in control of the water supply by irrigation - watering with the foot. Now God would test Abram's faith as later He tested many others.

The failure of Abram's faith is startlingly abrupt. He went down to Egypt to sojourn there. It is a painful process to recall the record in Hebrews 11.9 of his faith: "By faith he sojourned in the land of promise". Here he sojourned in Egypt because of the lack of his faith. It is not surprising, then, to read that he began to be afraid when he was in Egypt. When faith wanes fear intrudes into the experience of God's people. His fear arose from the fact that Sarai was so beautiful that he thought he would be murdered by men who desired her and who considered him an obstacle to their designs. His plan was to arrange with her that they should represent her as his sister. Evidently he thought that anybody desiring her would enter into marriage negotiations with Abram for her hand. These negotiations could be prolonged, and they were not planning to stay very long. There was some justification for his expectation that her beauty would be noticed. What he had not counted on was that Pharaoh's courtiers would notice it, and Pharaoh did not need to engage in prolonged marriage negotiations with anyone: "the woman was taken into Pharaoh's house" (v.15) - as briefly and simply as that. Abram, having apparently lost Sarai, now suffered the embarrassment of receiving lavish gifts in exchange, including valuable novelties like camels. The situation had become bafflingly complex, and Abram had no answer to his problems.

But God had an answer: "And the Lord plagued Pharaoh and his house" (v.17). The story is not about a hero called Abram, as is already obvious. It is about God dealing providentially to further His own plans, and Pharaoh with all his power is not outside the range of God's providence. So divine intervention begins a process of undoing the knots. From v.17 to v.20 there is a constant emphasis on the word "wife". This is the point at issue. In later chapters God will glorify Himself by giving Abram a son by Sarah. Now He glorifies Himself by securing her release. Pharaoh could demand that Sarai be added to his household, but he could not demand things from God when God intervened.

Pharaoh's angry interview of a silent Abram makes painful reading. He had a right to be angry. Was not his household plagued? His rapid-fire questions leave no room for Abram to answer, even if he had been disposed to do so. The final indignity comes in the abrupt "now therefore", introducing his sentence on this troublesome foreign visitor. Abram was in effect driven out of the country. Sadly he was driven out as Adam was driven out of Eden - the same word (SHALACH - 7971) is used, "sent him away" (compare 3.23, "sent him forth"). What an indignity for the man who believed God! It will be a delight to read how Jacob as an old man, after the refining and maturing process of God's grace, was brought into the presence of Pharaoh "and Jacob blessed Pharaoh" (47.7,10). What a contrast!

As to the wealth which Abram received from Pharaoh, it may be seen as an instance of God providentially overruling circumstances. It is dubious exegesis to say that the dispute in ch.13 would never have occurred had Abram and Lot not been enriched in Egypt. After all there is no evidence of Pharaoh enriching Lot, and there was plenty of room in Canaan for both Abram and Lot, as Abram himself implies in 13.9 ("Is not the whole land before thee?").

Notes

3 This interpretation fits the context better than the other, which is equally possible on linguistic grounds. This would translate: "in thee shall the families of the earth bless themselves". This would mean that people would pray or wish to be blessed "as Abram is blessed", using his blessing as a standard to be sought after. Blessing would at any rate flow to those who blessed Abram. The corollary is that cursing would light on those who cursed him.

GENESIS 13

Abram and Lot Separate

Verses 1-13: The Dispute and its Resolution

In ch.12 Abram's departure from the path of faith was introduced abruptly: "and Abram went down into Egypt to sojourn there" (v.10). That departure is now past history, for this verse records that "Abram went up out of Egypt ...". The end of ch.13 will confirm the feeling that events are moving forward once more towards the goal which God had in mind.

A practical lesson from the episode in Egypt is that our departure from a path of faith always has some consequences for others, particularly for those who depend on us. This is obvious here as it affected Sarai. She went down with Abram, she suffered the humiliation involved in events there, and now she came back with Abram. The story, however, does not end there for Sarai, for there will be later repercussions of the sojourn in Egypt.

Likewise, Lot went down to Egypt with Abram. He had consistently been a follower. At the time of Abram's descent to Egypt it was not mentioned that Lot was with him. It is almost as if it can be taken for granted that Lot follows Abram. Here it is noted that he came back up with Abram as far as the Negev, the south of the promised land. Lot is highlighted here, because he is about to be used as a contrast to Abram and he is about to take a crucial decision which will be to his irrecoverable loss.

Another detail in preparation for the following story is the mention that "Abram was very rich" (v.2). Much of this wealth was gained in Egypt, though an inference may be drawn at 12.5 that he was already quite wealthy before he went to Egypt. Abram is nowhere criticised in Scripture for being wealthy and it is rash to pass too sweeping a judgment on him for it here. One must admit that there may possibly be some significance in the echo between 13.2 and 12.10. The famine which led to his going down to Egypt was described in the earlier passage as "grievous" (literally "heavy") and here Abram is said to be "very rich" (literally "very heavy"). This leaves the possibility of a suggestion that his wealth was a weight upon him at this point. Yet if this is the case the theme is not openly developed in the chapter, which ends with Abram back in harmony with the will of God, enjoying fellowship with God and receiving confirmation and expansion of earlier promises.

His wealth is described in terms which give prominence to cattle, which incidentally includes sheep and other "small cattle". This is no surprise, for he was a tent-dweller and his wealth reflected his life-style. Verse 3 is in harmony with this emphasis. It is assumed that he will journey, as a man who kept flocks and herds would do. The journey has, however, a spiritual dimension which is the principal interest. It was a retracing of his steps to the place where tent and altar had been prominent in his life. Recovery of lost ground, in the spiritual sense, involves going back to principles which have been lost. Abram returned to his pilgrim life and to his fellowship with, and worship of, God. He was returning, spiritually, to what had been true of him "at the first" - note the phrases in vv.3-4. Whatever other associations Bethel/Ai may have had, for Abram this was "the place of the altar". There were no altars in this sense in Egypt and there was no mention of Abram "calling on the name of the Lord" there. Abram has come home.

Superficially, Lot shared the return with Abram, though his movements are never recorded as having centred on the altar, nor is he said to have called on the name of the Lord. He had flocks, herds and tents, as Abram had. And thus the problem arose. The emphasis in the record (v.6) is on the difficulty of their dwelling together with their vast flocks and herds. It is worth commenting that neither Abram or Lot is blamed for the dissension. Indeed it was their herdsmen who quarrelled. The problem of obtaining water for such vast numbers of animals was aggravated by the fact that the Canaanites and Perizzites were in possession of the land (v.7).

Is this comment perhaps drawing attention to the possibility that strife between Abram and Lot would leave them more vulnerable to attacks from their enemies? Certainly it is true that strife between the godly of all ages leaves them exposed to attacks from others who are hostile to their faith. In purely practical terms, the local tribes would be competing with these newcomers for limited water supplies (compare 26.19-20). If Abram and Lot were at loggerheads they would not be able to unite in staking a claim to their share.

Abram's reaction was not just to rationalise the handling of the problem in terms of how to feed and water the cattle. He probed below this mundane level to find the deeper principle. Very simply, brothers should not quarrel. In the broader sense they were brothers, though of course in the narrower sense they were uncle and nephew. There is an echo here of the principle which God identified in 4.9: "Where is thy brother?". The sin of Cain was seen as especially heinous in the fact that it was his brother whom he slew. Abram was not grasping or rigid in his dealings with his "brother", but when occasion demanded, as in ch.14, he proved a formidable opponent to those who attacked his kinsman.

Abram had always been the leader and Lot the follower. It might have been reasonable that the senior partner should have first option. It is not completely certain from the evidence that Abram was the older man, though what evidence there is seems to point that way. But Abram was not only the senior man in taking initiatives or in being the older. He was also the more spiritual and mature. Hence he took a spiritual lead in solving the problem. Interpersonal relations are not handled by God's people merely on a level of managing situations to avoid conflict. The spiritual solution involves putting a higher value on spiritual values and spiritual possessions than on material gain or status. Abram's yielding first choice to Lot marks Abram as the greater man. The principle of greatness being signalled by humility and generosity is not only a NT truth. Phillipians 2 is in harmony with Genesis 13.

Lot was quite ready to accept the solution offered. He chose on the basis of what he could see. But so did Eve in 3.6 when she disobeyed God. Lot's problem was that he could not see far enough. What he saw was the well-watered plain of Jordan, so beautiful that it conjured up visions of the Garden of Eden. It would have stood out in the landscape because of its fertility, for it enjoyed the benefits of human industry in its extensive irrigation works. The area on which his attention centred extended as far as Zoar. It was not only fertile as Egypt was, but it also owed its fertility to irrigation as Egypt did. This fact is noteworthy in view of the contrast, noted above at 12.10, between the watering of Egypt and Canaan. Lot had recent memories of the security and prosperity of Egypt, where men managed their water-supply by their energy and initiative. It is sobering to reflect that Lot had this experience of Egypt because he followed Abram there. Even good men can lead others into situations which will produce spiritual weakness.

Reservations might be expressed about the fact that the area Lot chose owed its fertility to irrigation rather than to God's direct provision. Yet it must be admitted that it was extremely beautiful, perhaps an obvious choice, one might say. The difficulty lay mainly in Lot's basis for choice. He had never had a record of listening for God's direction. Here he simply chose (v.11) and that was the end of the matter. But it was far from being the end of the story for Lot; in v.10 there is inserted the chilling clause, "before the Lord destroyed Sodom and Gomorrah". It becomes apparent that Lot's choice was a fateful choice, for Sodom has become a byword. Moses also knew, and he drops this clause into the story to put the Edenic scene in perspective. Lot was short-sighted, spiritually myopic. He thought first and last about material prosperity. It is well to consider his mistake in the light of Paul's solemn warning: "They that desire to be rich fall into a temptation and a snare and many foolish and hurtful lusts, such as drown men in destruction and perdition" (1 Tim 6.9, RV). Lot escaped with his life but his family were "drowned".

The story of Lot's choosing ends ominously with, "and Lot journeyed east", away from God's blessing. As if to underline the contrast, v.12 restates carefully where Abram and Lot dwelt now that they were separated. Spiritual and unspiritual people can have only limited fellowship because their "dwellings", spiritually speaking, are apart.

So Lot "moved his tent as far as Sodom" (v.12, RV). A marker is put down (v.13) at the end of this episode to prepare the reader for later events: "But the men of Sodom were wicked and sinners before the Lord exceedingly". In comparison with sinners in general they were wicked sinners, and even then the Spirit of God adds the final heavy underlining - "exceedingly". Lot's vision did not take this fact in. This was not a case of a man going there as a righteous man (which Lot was, as Peter states in 2 Pet 2.8) to testify or even to help the sinners. If it had been such a case, no doubt God would have preserved him and his family, and Lot would have been careful to act in ways calculated to preserve his own testimony and his family's morals. He was righteous, says

Peter, and he was grieved by the lasciviousness of his neighbours, but he had mixed motives which had doomed his testimony and his family's most vital spiritual and moral interests. His choice of Sodom was the first step in a steady decline into disaster.

Verses 14-18: God's Promise to Abram Confirmed

Though Lot had chosen the most prosperous area he could see, Abram was not left to make do with substandard land. Nor did he have to console himself with the thought that he would get enough to enable him to survive. Now that Lot had gone, God had something to say to the man who, knowing that God had made promises, had been prepared to let another take prior choice.

God's first words to Abram are a direct echo of the story of Lot's choice: "Lift up now thine eyes" (v.14). Confronted with the panorama of the land Lot "lifted up his eyes" (v.10) and chose. Now God says, in effect, "see now what I have chosen for you, Abram". Lot journeyed east (v.11), but Abram is bidden to look in every direction, for all will be his. It will be his because God has given it to him, not because he has chosen shrewdly, or even manipulated Lot's choice. And it will not be a temporary possession as Lot's would. God gave a territory east of the Dead Sea to the children of Lot for a possession, outside of the land altogether (Deut 2.9). By contrast, Abram's territory was given to him and his seed "for ever" (v.15).

At this point in the story Abram stood with his barren wife and saw the fertile plain where Lot had gone to settle. Lot would be prosperous, and, apparently, his wife was not barren as Sarai was. What, if anything, had Abram gained by his generosity and meekness? He had gained immeasurably. He had a word from God confirming earlier promises and adding to them. God would make his descendants, to whom this whole land would be given, as innumerable as the grains of dust on the earth. This is the refrain of this part of Genesis - land and descendants. Abram would not live to see either promise finally fulfilled - how could he? - but he had good long-distance vision, by contrast with Lot. He could never see the final fulfilment during his lifetime because the promises will come to finality only in Christ. But the people of faith do not expect to balance their accounts in the short term.

Meanwhile, Abram could "walk through the land in the length of it and the breadth of it" (v.17) and know for certain that he and his descendants would possess it. Perhaps the best commentary on the situation is Hebrews 11.1: "Faith gives substance to our hopes and convinces us of realities we do not see" (REB). This short episode in which God reassures Abram ends with the familiar emphasis. Abram still had his tent - so too had Lot, but he will soon "progress" beyond that. Abram still had a location like that at Moreh - by the oaks/terebinths (RV) of Mamre, in Hebron. He built an altar there, once more the most permanent aspect of his sojourn. Abram had returned fully to his vision and his mission.

GENESIS 14

Abram Rescues Lot and Meets Melchizedeck

Introduction

This chapter at first sight sits oddly in its context. The link is firstly with the story of Lot's decline begun in ch.13. The chapter is also in some ways a fitting prelude to the more detailed catalogue of the peoples of Canaan at the end of ch.15. Chapter 14 shows four oriental peoples in league against five other peoples in or near Canaan. The orientals held control until they overran Sodom and Gomorrah. Then, since Lot was captured, Abram became involved, but Abram also had a treaty with the Amorites and the Amorites had also been overrun. Hence Abram's intervention was inevitable. The sequel to the military action is the most interesting part of the chapter in the setting of the whole Bible, for it brings in the remarkable figure of Melchizedeck.

Verses 1-12: Four Eastern Kings Put Down a Rebellion

These twelve verses are basically background information for the story which concerns us in Genesis. The four kings were heads of tribes which lived in areas whose approximate location can be identified, though almost nothing is known about any of the kings in the story. Their kingdoms may not have been particularly large or powerful, but the confederation of the four made a formidable power bloc. Shinar is the old name in Scripture for Babylonia, at this time a much less prominent place than later. Ellasar was possibly around the region marked in NT maps as Cappadocia. Elam was in south-west Persia, fairly close to Babylonia. Tidal is described as king of "nations" (AV) or "Goiim" (RV), who are tentatively identified as Hittites from Anatolia (in the area now called Asia Minor).

These four confederates subdued the local kings in the Dead Sea area - Sodom, Gomorrah, Admah, Zeboiim and Bela. After twelve years of subjection they rebelled in the thirteenth year and the following year the four kings set out on a punitive expedition.

The scope of the expedition was extensive. The first place they subdued was Ashteroth-Karnaim (which may actually have been two neighbouring places), lying to the east of the northern tip of the Sea of Galilee. The Rephaim who were defeated there reappear in the story of the later occupation of Canaan by the Israelites after the Exodus from Egypt. They were feared because of their exceptional stature. The second place subdued was Ham, lying south-east from the southern end of the Sea of Galilee. Shaveh-Kiriathaim, which fell next, was east of the northern part of the Dead Sea. The conquest of the Horites of the Mount Seir area took the victorious orientals south as far as the Gulf of Aqaba, as it is now called. Verse 7 means that they turned northwards again, heading towards the

Negev. Their first conquest there was En-mishpat, that is Kadesh, which is significant for us as having been the southern boundary marker of the promised land.

At this point the five local kings from the area around the Vale of Siddim, south of the Dead Sea, mustered their troops against the invaders. The slime pits mentioned in v.10 were bitumen deposits. The verb which describes the king of Sodom and Gomorrah as "falling" there may mean that they "hid" there. This appears to be the simplest understanding of the incident. At any rate those two kings survived though their goods were plundered and their people carried off. The fact that Lot was among these captives arouses the attention. It is particularly interesting to read that he "dwelt in Sodom". He had ceased, it would seem, to be a sojourning alien and had become a resident of the city. This can only spell a further step on his downward course. The invasion put an end to the illusion that security and prosperity were to be found in making common cause with the citizens of these wicked cities. The foolishness of his choice is becoming increasingly obvious, and when he was carried off so were his family. Departure from God must have a harmful impact on loved ones. Sometimes decisions are taken in the hope that they will provide greater security for one's family, but if God is left out of the decisions those who are supposed to benefit are usually harmed.

Verses 13-16: Abram to the Rescue

One escapee made his way to Abram to report on the defeat. Abram is oddly described in v.13 as "the Hebrew", "the man from the other side" as the Septuagint translates it. The description is odd because it was usually applied to Israelites by outsiders rather than, as here, by other Israelites. An interesting detail about Abram here is the addition to the information about where he was living. It had already been stated that he dwelt by the oaks of Mamre, the Amorite. The new information consists of the names of Mamre's brothers, Eshcol and Aner, and the fact that they were allies of Abram. It seems as if the Spirit of God, while recording the fact that Abram had honourable treaties with his neighbours, is careful to insist that he remained separate from all the Canaanites, an outsider by virtue of his different way of life.

Abram's response was prompt. He mustered his trained men, his retainers, specially trusted men as having been all their lives in his service. It is not surprising that a man with substantial wealth in the form of cattle, and living in territory mainly controlled by alien and potentially hostile people, would have his own security force. Most of the armed forces one would be likely to meet would have been similar private forces or else marauding parties from other areas.

The oriental force which had done so much damage must have been some sort of marauding army which fought quick battles and moved on. They had already turned north from El-paran and were heading for home through Canaan. Abram pursued them northwards to Dan on the northern frontier, made a two-pronged surprise attack by night and drove them in disarray to the area north of Damascus. This means that he followed them and drove them out of Canaan. He recovered all the plundered property, Lot and his goods, and the rest of the captives taken from Sodom. Abram thus brought blessing to those among whom he lived by his practical help when they were in need. It must be carefully noted that he also delivered Lot. Lot might seem to many to have been the shrewder man when he chose such a "desirable" area in which to settle, and Abram might have seemed to be making a tactical error in giving Lot first choice. But Abram was counting on God to make good His promise, and his awareness of a spiritual dimension did not make him an idealistic dreamer, unable to manage his affairs. In this situation, where his brother Lot was in need Abram was prompt to do what needed to be done, relying on God to provide the circumstances which would give him the victory. Melchizedek confirms that this is exactly what God did.

Verses 17-24: Abram Discriminates Between Two Offers

Abram returned south with his spoils and delivered captives. The king of Sodom came out to meet him near Salem, if it can be taken that the King's Dale in v.17 is the same as the place of the same name in 2 Samuel 18.18. It seems likely to be the same in view of the sudden twist which the story takes at this point. It seemed as if Abram were about to be offered some alliance by the king of Sodom, but there was an intervention by the king of Salem. This king, Melchizedek, appears abruptly in the story, forestalls the approach of Sodom and presents us with one of the most intriguing episodes in Genesis.[†]

Melchizedek has importance beyond what is told in this very brief narrative. In the first place, he was both king of Salem and priest of God Most High (El Elyon), Creator of heaven and earth. He has of course significance because he is the first priest mentioned in Scripture. Most of the scriptural references to priests are within the sphere of the family of Aaron, the first high priest in Israel. It is all the more interesting, therefore, to see that the first priest mentioned is not of that family and, unlike any of that family, is also a king. The best explanation of this phenomenon in the context of the Bible as a whole is to see in this story foreshadowings of the high-priestly glory of our Lord Jesus Christ.

The narrative should probably be taken to imply that he made a covenant with Abram in sharing a feast of bread and wine with him. As priest he also blessed Abram in the name of God Most High. It is best to take "possessor" in v.19 (AV) in its more basic sense of "creator".

The blessing attributes Abram's victory to the fact that God delivered his enemies into his hand. So Abram was encouraged and strengthened by this mysterious figure. Abram was not slow to acknowledge that

Melchizedek was higher than himself. He gave him a tenth part of all, presumably meaning "of all the booty". This is the first instance in Scripture of a tithe being paid. By paying it Abram owned his allegiance to God Most High. Later payments of tithes are by people who accept the claims of God, though in some instances they are paid for the support of those who serve God at His sanctuary (Num 18.24). It is instructive that at the end of the OT, in Malachi, blessing is promised to those who pay the tithes owed to God (3.10) and it is solemnly urged that a curse rests on Israel because of tithes which have not been paid (3.9).

Melchizedek disappears from this narrative as suddenly as he appeared. He becomes of special interest because he reappears abruptly in Psalm 110. Israel recognised this as a messianic psalm and in it, among the other glories attributed to Messiah, is the statement (v.4), "Thou art a priest for ever after the order of Melchizedek". Thus the abrupt appearance of this king-priest, without genealogy or record of death, is made a pattern of perpetual priesthood. He is next encountered in Hebrews 5.6, where Psalm 110.4 is quoted and the reference is made explicit to our Lord Jesus Christ. The writer of the Hebrew Epistle explains that Melchizedek, in the unique description of him as priest without genealogy or recorded death, being "made like unto the Son of God; abideth a priest continually" (Heb 7.3). It is well to "consider how great this man was" (Heb 7.4) and to delight in the timely and full provision which God made for Abram at a crucial time of danger when about to be approached with an offer by the king of Sodom. We are irresistibly reminded of the exhortation to us Christians in a passage in Hebrews which deals with the ministry of our Great High Priest: "Let us therefore come boldly unto the throne of grace, that we may obtain mercy, and find grace to help in time of need" (4.16). The timeliness of the ministry of Melchizedek is underlined by the fact that the king of Sodom is announced to be on his way to meet Abram before it is revealed that another would arrive first to make an offer which would make Abram safe against the seduction of Sodom. We little realise how often we have been delivered from temptation by timely interventions in our circumstances by the One who, though exalted in heaven, is "touched with the feeling of our infirmities" and active on our behalf.

It is worth commenting on the fact that, while God's purpose which is being set forth in His Word centres on Abram as the ancestor of our Lord Jesus Christ, God did have others who were His servants and whose lives went largely unrecorded in Scripture. Incidentally, the Melchizedeck episode underlines again the great Genesis theme of blessing. The blessing and the tithe response are followed immediately by a contrasting approach made to Abram by the king of Sodom.

After the heartening story of Melchizedek's timely intervention, there is a sudden return to the king of Sodom who had set out to meet Abram. Now he makes his bid for a relationship with Abram. Let Abram take the booty while the king of Sodom recovers his people. Commentators point to his abruptness and the fact that his first thought is "Give!". In any case, as victor Abram had the right to retain both booty and people.

Abram's response raises the encounter onto a different level. He says, "I swear by uplifted hand to the Lord ... that I will not take ...". The king of Sodom was occupied with the horizontal relationships. Abram, strengthened by Melchizedek's ministry, adjusts horizontal relationships by his relationship with the Lord. He can therefore with an easy mind let Sodom have its people, but he has obligations to his own men and his allies. His own men are entitled to what might be called subsistence allowance, while his allies are entitled to their fair share of the spoils. For himself he will retain nothing so that there will be no suggestion that Sodom has enriched him. One assumes, then, that Sodom did receive a share of the spoils, to which strictly it had no right. But Abram had gone to battle in the first instance not to gain spoil but to deliver Lot and presumably also his own allies. Abram had been made rich by God and he had shown once again, as he did in ch.13, that God meant more to him than present earthly gain. Men of God still learn lessons from Abram in this regard.

Notes

18 Hebrews 7 makes much of the features of this man as given in Genesis: (i) he was King of Salem, that is King of Peace; (ii) he was King of Righteousness, the meaning of his name, Melchizedek; (iii) he was priest of God Most High. In all of these things, says the writer of Hebrews, the record is designed to remind us of Christ.

GENESIS 15

God's Promise to Abram Sealed in a Covenant

Verses 1-6: Abram Receives and Believes God's Promise of Seed

Since God spoke to Abram in 12.1 the themes of descendants and land have never been far from the centre of interest in his story. In some sense Abram underlined his claim to the land again in ch.14 when he pursued the invading forces of the Chedorlaomer confederacy from south of the land to Dan, the northern frontier, and even beyond Damascus. It was emphasised there, in the words of Melchizedek, that God "delivered thine enemies into thy hand".

It was after these things that God revealed Himself in a special way to Abram. The wording is that "the word of the Lord came unto Abram in a vision" (v.1), an unusual form of words which recalls the kind of language used of God's revelations to His prophets. Perhaps Abram needed encouragement after his victory, for the invaders had shown themselves well equipped for wide-scale marauding and a force which might well return on a revenge expedition. At any rate God's salutation was, "Fear not, Abram". It was his awareness of who God was which had stood him in good stead in 14.22 when he swore to the king of Sodom by "the Lord, God Most High, Creator of heaven and earth" (NIV) that he would take nothing from Sodom. On that occasion God was his shield. Now, as the subject of descendants is about to arise, he needs to be reminded of his special relationship with God, for not only is God his shield, there is also the question of his reward. Hence the addition: "thy reward shall be exceeding great" (RV margin).

But then Abram raised the question of not just descendants or seed in general, but, specifically, even one son to succeed him. The broader question of innumerable descendants must be tackled at this point where he had not even one son. What was the point of whatever God gave him if all was going to be fruitless because Abram would "go" - that is, "go hence (die)" - without a son (v.2)? By default his heir would be Eliezer, a man of Damascus, who was his faithful servant, born in his house. His words almost have the ring of accusation or at least indignation: "Behold, to me thou hast given no seed" (v.3). Abram needed some firm reassurance, hence "the word of the Lord came unto him" (v.4). That word was unmistakable in its import, that Eliezer would not be his heir. Abram would have a son. It must be remembered here that Sarai was barren and at this stage there was no explicit promise of her bearing a son. That matter is left in abeyance for the moment.

In ch.13, when Lot had separated from Abram, God had said to Abram, "Lift up now thine eyes, and look" (13.14) at the land which God would give him. Now the other main concern, that of descendants, is handled in similar fashion: "Look now toward heaven, and tell the stars, ... So shall thy seed be" (v.5). God concentrated Abram's gaze in each instance on something that would fix His promise in Abram's mind. In ch.13 the point at issue was the land, and the reference to innumerable descendants (13.16) passed almost without comment. Here in ch.15 Abram's concern was that he had not even one son to carry on his name. The promise of innumerable descendants was therefore repeated, with vivid illustration in the starry heavens, and "he believed in the Lord" (v.6). The emphasis, as on more than one former occasion, is on the relationship between Abram and God.

The incident is marked as of special moment by the description of God's response: "he counted it to him for righteousness" (v.6). Abram had had faith in God before this, for instance when he was called in Ur, obeyed and went out, not knowing where he went (see Heb 11.8). In James' Epistle this verse in 15.6 is referred to in connection with the supreme test of Abraham's faith in Genesis 22, when he offered up Isaac (Jas 2.21-23). His faith was something which persisted through his life from Ur onwards. God accounted his faith-obedience as righteousness. If a child was to be born of Sarai it would be a case of life being brought from a dead thing, for she was barren. That feature of the promise is as yet only hinted at, but it will become a central element of Abraham's faith at its highest point in ch.22. Paul makes much of this aspect of justifying faith in Romans 4.24,25, where he characterises it as believing "on him that raised up Jesus our Lord from the dead, who was delivered for our offences, and was raised again for our justification". The principle of faith being counted for righteousness has far-reaching implications in the dealings of God with mankind. Paul refers to this principle in Romans after he has shown that, regardless of ethnic or religious origins, men are all undeserving, all bereft of hope that their own merits will please God, all left standing silent before God's verdict of guilty. Nothing can be demanded from God as of right, but He delights to enrich those who trust in Him. He is their shield and their reward is very great.

Verses 7-21: God's Covenant that the Land Will all be Abram's

God took Abram's mind back to the time when He brought him up out of Ur. He had had a purpose in doing this, to give him the land of Canaan for an inheritance. This is rather like the way in which, later on, God repeatedly reminded Israel of how He had brought them up out of Egypt to bring them into a land which He had given to them. Such reminders are valuable to people of faith. God does not take people up, raise their hopes, give them promises and then leave them stranded. Those who trust Him will never be ashamed. That is to say, they will never have to admit that their trust in God was a mistake because He could not make good His promises.

But at this point Abram needed a sign that it was indeed the purpose of God to give him the land, a sign that he had not somehow previously been mistaken in his understanding of God's promise. God's response was to prescribe a complex ritual through which he would ratify His covenant regarding possession of the land. There is some debate about aspects of the meaning of the ritual. Certainly it bears a substantial resemblance to oath-taking rituals in confirming covenants. The dividing of the victims provided a path to be trodden between the pieces by the party or parties binding themselves by an oath. In this case it is to be noted that only God went between the pieces of the divided victims. This was not a two-sided agreement by parties entering into mutual obligations. It was an acceptance by God of sole responsibility for the covenant - a matter of promise, not conditional on Abram's fulfilment of terms imposed upon him, and is consistent with many aspects of God's relationship with Abram. The keyword often is "promise". This is in contrast with the Sinai covenant, where Israel entered into undertakings which they could not sustain.

The setting of the events at this covenant ceremony is sombre. The path to the fulfilment of the covenant by which Abram would receive the land would not be easy or short. First, there were the birds of prey which swooped down (v.11) on the victims as if to interrupt the covenant. Abram drove them away as he had driven away the kings from the East in ch.14. A factor in the possession of the land which God gave him would always be the predatory interest of surrounding powerful nations, the unclean birds of prey. It was Abram's responsibility, by God's help, to drive them away.

Then followed a sunset scene: Abram experienced a deep sleep in which he felt a prolonged or repeated sense of horror and profound gloom (v.12). This was the prelude to a divine revelation of the trials through which Abram's descendants must pass in exile and bondage for 400 years (v.13). The note of promise in v.14 must not be missed, for God would judge their oppressors and bring them back out of bondage with great wealth. Meanwhile Abram would die at a ripe old age in peace. The period of four generations (v.16) which would elapse before the exiles would return must correspond to the 400 years, taken as four lifetimes. The periods are given in round figures, not as a strict chronology. The exodus from bondage would coincide with the point at which God decided that the Canaanite inhabitants (here referred to in a general way as the Amorites) had gone so far in their evil that judgment could no longer be withheld (v.16). God is a God of judgment, and when the time is ripe He will execute judgment in perfect accord with His holy character. His persecuted people must know that He will not act before "the iniquity of the Amorites [or whoever else defies Him] is full".

The dark scene became darker still. God passed between the pieces of the severed victims as a smoking pot, as a flaming torch. Commentators rightly compare this with the awesome manifestations of God's presence at Sinai - smoke and fire and dreadful gloom (Ex 19). God was about to make a covenant with Abram regarding possession of the land. Such a relationship with God can never be a thing which we can take casually. This was to Abram an experience of unforgettable awe, for God was pledging Himself with full solemnity to grant specified territories to him and his descendants. God's anger is indeed a fearful thing, but so too is His coming in grace when we understand the tremendous privilege we have. Privilege demands holiness.

Legal documents which give title of a specified property to a specified individual always identify the property precisely. So here God gives the bounds of the land as the Euphrates and the river of Egypt. The river of Egypt is best taken as equivalent to the "brook" of Egypt, namely Wadi el-Arish, to give it its usual modern name. Ten tribes in Canaan are listed, ten tribes which would be in occupation of the land which God had given to Abram and his descendants. This presupposes a process of dispossessing them, which would only be feasible if God gave His people victory. Such victory involved their being in relationship with Him. In ch.14 it was Abram who drove out the eastern forces, while Lot, righteous man though he was, was merely a captive set free when God worked through Abram. It has been rightly pointed out that God made it clear to Abram in ch.15 that He could be trusted. Equally the chapter shows that those whom God champions are people whose confidence is in Him. God remains unchanging, and unconditional promises made by Him are sure of fulfilment. It is for His people, of whatever age, to ensure that He is given the trust which is appropriate. Abram "believed in the Lord; and he counted it to him for righteousness".

GENESIS 16

Sarai Contrives a Solution to Her Barrenness

Verses 1-6: Sarai Gives Hagar to Abram: Conflict and Flight

The next few chapters, with the exception of the Sodom episode, are taken up with the question of a son for Abram in fulfilment of God's promise. The repetition in the opening part of this chapter of the phrase "Sarai Abram's wife" serves to draw attention again to the long-endured pain of barrenness. Abram's early experience of the promised land was of famine, and now it seems that the persisting theme in relation to the promised seed is barrenness.

Almost immediately, however, a tension is set up by the reference to Sarai's handmaid, her personal servant, called Hagar. Although Hagar had lowly status, as a foreigner and a lady's handmaid, her name is given. This serves as a token of her future importance, for she was to become the mother of races descended from Abram.

Her Egyptian origin is stated. It seems safe to assume that she was acquired while Sarai was in Egypt with Abram. If so, this is yet another legacy from that sad episode, though evidently quite a few years have gone by since the return (v.3). Not that Hagar is blamed for the events that follow, for she had no part in the arrangements which were Sarai's idea throughout.

Sarai began her proposal to Abram well, with the acknowledgement that it is God who gives or withholds offspring, a theme familiar throughout Scripture. Her proposal was also in line with what was practised widely in the ancient Middle East if a woman did not bear children to her husband. It was common practice for the husband to have intercourse with his wife's handmaid to produce a child for his wife. Her intention was that Hagar (whom, incidentally, she never mentions by name throughout the story, as if she has refused to acknowledge her as a person) should bear a child which would be reckoned as Sarai's. This is a kind of surrogate arrangement. It will emerge as the story develops that the plan went badly wrong for Sarai. Initially, indeed, all seemed to go well, for Abram "hearkened to the voice of Sarai". On second thoughts, however, there is cause to wonder if it did go well. This same expression was used once before, in 3.17, of Adam hearkening to Eve's voice. The echo is clearly deliberate. In ch.3 Eve's initiative was against God's command and Adam's welfare. Adam was led by Eve, instead of leading her. Abram was equally mistaken in refusing, as he did throughout this episode, to take a responsible lead. The echoes of ch.3 continue in the sequence: "she took" ... "she gave" ... "and he". There the commodity handed over was the forbidden fruit; here it is Hagar. The inspired writer quickly shifts the emphasis when he says that Sarai gave her to Abram her husband "to be his wife". Before too much blame is placed on Sarai, however, it must be remembered that Abram had used Sarai in Egypt as a means to his own safety in that plan which misfired and ended in Abram virtually handing her over to Pharaoh. Using people for selfish ends can be a risky business.

"And he went in unto Hagar, and she conceived" (v.4). What had cost Sarai years of fruitless anguish and pain came so easily and readily to Hagar. Sarai had to learn that God would fulfil His purposes in ways which declare unmistakably that He controlled events. He would not open closed doors or closed wombs until the time came when human resources had run out. Hagar's success in conceiving did not prove that God was blessing the arrangement.

Hagar's reaction to the knowledge that she was pregnant was understandable. The great legislator in this period, Hammurabi, laid down regulations for what should happen in cases like this if the handmaid misbehaved by claiming equality with her mistress. Hagar's reaction was reasonable enough. Was she not also Abram's wife, like Sarai? And had she not conceived a child by Abram, unlike Sarai? Hammurabi's legislation showed a shrewd understanding of human nature in that it anticipated the likelihood that a handmaid in these circumstances might well forget her legal standing.

Sarai, equally understandably, felt that she had been badly treated. The idea that Abram should father a child by Hagar was hers in the first instance. Yet she could hardly have been expected to look with equanimity on a rival who could conceive a child so easily. Her language is rather extreme as seen by the force of the expression rendered "my wrong" (v.5). It amounts to saying, "the violence done to me" - Hagar's ease of conception was felt by her as a blow from Abram. "I have given (her)," said she, "into *thy* bosom ...; the Lord judge between me and thee".

Having been led by his wife into a situation which could not solve the problem which it addressed, Abram now sought to avoid accepting responsibility by saying that there was really no problem, for Hagar was Sarai's handmaid and she had complete discretion as to how she treated her (v.6). What Abram did not say was that in accepting Hagar he had implicitly accepted moral responsibility for her as "his wife". Sarai needed no encouragement. She ill-treated Hagar, who fled from her. Strictly speaking, Hagar had no legal right to flee, yet one can sympathise with her in her flight.

Verses 7-14: Hagar Has Dealings with the Lord

Hagar's flight may well have provided Sarai with some alleviation of her bitter distress. Sarai had arranged Hagar's union with Abram and it might for the moment seem that she had now, by her treatment of Hagar, managed a solution to the destruction of her relationship with Hagar by removing her. But this is primarily a story of God's dealings with Abram and his descendants, and God was not satisfied to abandon Hagar now that she was pregnant by Abram. Thus, "the angel of the Lord found her".

It is beyond the scope of this commentary to attempt a detailed analysis of the very significant phrase which occurs here for the first time in Scripture - "the angel of the Lord", or, as it sometimes appears, "the angel of God". This is also the first occurrence of the actual word "angel". Suffice it to say that in the scenes where the expression occurs, God communicates with someone and a man usually appears to the person. This one who appears is identified as "the angel of God" or "the angel of the Lord".[†]

At some point in the scene "the angel" speaks as if he were God, though in his communication he may also give a message as if he were God's messenger. The persons to whom he appears often are aware of having seen God. What surprises them is not that they have seen God, but that they have survived the experience. Since "the angel" comes with a revelation from God, yet himself speaks as God, the traditional view that these are appearances of God (theophanies) is attractive. Once again incidents are occurring which prefigure later revelation of the three Persons of the Trinity. God is revealed in His Son, even before incarnation.

God's grace to Hagar is seen in this encounter. Here, as in ch.21, the encounter takes place by a source of water. When Abram and Sarai could not supply what Hagar needed, or did not care to supply it, God did care and did provide.

Shur, to which she fled, has usually been located by scholars between Kadesh-Barnea and the border of Egypt. Hagar seems to have been on her way back home to Egypt, but her thoughts were not God's thoughts. She was carrying Abram's son and the place to be occupied by her descendants was in the plan of God, not in the anonymity of her former status in Egypt.

She was accosted by a stranger who knew her name and status. Of course people did meet strangers at wells, for everyone needed what the well supplied. But it was startling when such a stranger proved to know far more about one than one had thought possible (compare Jn 4.29). The mode of address by the angel to her in v.8 reminded her that she was Sarai's handmaid. Her failure to keep this in mind had led to strife with Sarai which had occasioned her flight. Since she was Sarai's handmaid she must account for her movements. Why was she here? Where had she come from? Where was she going? Her reply amounts to an admission that she was a deserter fleeing from her mistress. She was therefore instructed to return to her responsibilities in submission to Sarai. There may be some point in the shift of expression from Abram's "in thy hand" (v.6) to God's "under her hands" (v.9). It seems that obeying God was not going to be easy for Hagar.

Then follows a gracious promise to her of innumerable descendants, just as had been given to Abram. The pronouncement, "Behold, thou art with child", marks this as a solemn declaration by God. (She already knew quite clearly that she was with child.) Moreover, her unborn child would be a son; this she did not know. As in other similar divine declarations before the birth of special children, the name was prescribed by God.

The child was to be called Ishmael - "God has heard" - for God had heard, and, by implication, taken note of her sufferings at the hand of Sarai. As to her son's character, he would be "a wild-ass man". The wild ass in Scripture is portrayed as uncontrollable and independent (Job 39.5-8, for example). He would be noble in a way, yet so proud as to be in constant conflict with others (v.12). The AV rendering of the end of v.12 does not match the context. The sense is better represented by "he shall dwell opposite all his brothers" (Wenham) or, more freely, "he will set himself against all his brethren" (Stigers). In short, he and his descendants would be fiercely independent and warlike nomads. It was a fitting promise for a child whose very conception caused a storm of contention. The history of his Arab descendants is likewise a story of a proud people with a tradition of disputes.

Hagar's honest reaction (v.8) to this divine encounter suggests that she had learnt much in her mistress's house. Her ready understanding of what was happening is impressive. It is remarkable in a book which develops the roots and early history of the Israelites that this foreign bondwoman is seen in direct contact with the God of Israel, here seen as the God who hears. Her reaction at the end of the encounter was to exclaim that He was indeed also the God who sees. This was for her a place of vision. Her explanation of her name for God, "the God who sees", gives problems to translators. These arise from the combination of two ideas in the episode: vision and provision. Possible translations include, "Truly here I have seen him who looks after me?" (Wenham – note the query), or, "I have now seen the One who sees me" (NIV). Hence, says the editorial comment, the well is called "The well of the living one who sees". God's seeing is the prelude to God's providing. Probably it is best to cut the knot by accepting the rendering given by Wenham: "…him who looks after me". Hagar had reason to be satisfied that day, even though she was about to set out on the journey back to Sarai, for she had had contact with Someone who could provide when her mistress and Abram were far away. What happened when she returned is not made known, for God does not include details in the inspired narrative just to satisfy the reader's curiosity, however justified it may be felt to be. It is interesting that there is no further mention of the family conflict for many years in the Genesis account, until Isaac was weaned (21.8-14) and Ishmael became the initiator of trouble which led to his expulsion with Hagar from Abram's home.

Verses 15-16: Ishmael Born

The record of Ishmael's birth takes no account of Sarai's scheme that the baby should be treated as hers. This was the son of Hagar and Abram, and Sarai is omitted from the narrative. Hagar has been instructed, "Thou … shalt call his name Ishmael", and here it is recorded that "Abram called his son's name, which Hagar bare, Ishmael". Abram fully accepted his responsibility towards Hagar at this point. One wonders what were the feelings of this godly man of eighty-six years as he called his firstborn son Ishmael - "God has heard" - and pondered on the fulfilment of God's promise and his own burning desire for descendants. The three-fold repetition in these two verses of "Hagar bare" serves to set the issue of Abram's descendants in bold relief. The oracular forecast of what kind of man Ishmael will be is not reassuring if one looks for a fulfilment of God's promise in *this* child. Had Abram, even at this late stage, begun to long, "O that Ishmael might live before thee!" (17.18)? However, there is no place for Ishmael in the mainstream of divine purpose which is being followed in Scripture. The line of Ishmael is a cul-de-sac as far as the promised seed is concerned.

Notes

7 In addition to this passage the angel of the Lord (God) appeared again to Hagar in ch.21; He spoke to Abraham in 22.11; He appeared to Moses in the burning bush in Exodus 3.2; He visited Gideon in Judges 6.12, but in v.16 it is "the Lord" who spoke to him; He appeared to Manoah and his wife in Judges 13.3, but in v.22 Manoah says, "We have seen God".

GENESIS 17

Introductory

An important feature of this chapter, and one which is often pointed out, is the amount of space devoted to what God has said. In what God said, great prominence is given to His promises within the covenant. The restatement of the covenant defines the promises more precisely and is marked by a change of name for both Abram and Sarai.

Verses 1-8: Promises and Responsibility within the Covenant

It is first of all indicated that thirteen years had passed since Ishmael's birth at the end of ch.16. If Abram had been planning to recognise Ishmael as heir to the promises he must have been feeling that some kind of act of recognition might soon be appropriate.

After these thirteen years had passed over in silence God appeared to Abram and we hear Him address Abram abruptly: "I am God Almighty" (NIV). This is a translation of "El Shaddai", one of the important biblical titles of God (found mainly in Genesis and Job), variously translated by modern scholars, but the ancient Greek translators, for instance, render it "God Almighty" or "God the Sufficient One". This seems appropriate in connection with God giving fertility to perpetuate the covenant family.

God is all-sufficient, and He does condescend to enter into relationship with His creatures, but they are expected to exercise their God-given power of moral choice and walk with the integrity which is appropriate in those so privileged. Abram's integrity would not be the basis of the covenant, but it was expected of him. We recall that Noah was the other man described in Genesis as "perfect" (TAMIM - 8549), and God made a covenant with him. Walking before God, as here, and walking with God, as Enoch (5.22) and Noah (6.9) did, are kindred ideas and indeed the Septuagint rendered them both in the same way as "be pleasing to God".

After exhorting Abram to walk before Him, God went on to give covenant promise of fruitfulness. Abram's response was one of worshipful prostration. This was followed by more detailed promises in relation to the covenant. A prominent feature of these is the specification of the things which God would do for Abram. For example, God would make him fruitful, the father of many nations. When Abram's son would be born it would be obvious that it was God who had made this possible, for in all this story it is God's doing and God's giving which is emphasised. There is a progression, too, in the promises: Abram would have many descendants (v.2), he would be father of many nations (v.4), and his descendants would include kings (v.6). His name must now be changed to signal that he had entered upon a new phase of his journey with God, a phase represented in the name Abraham, the form of which has echoes of the word meaning Father of Nations.

Once again the Hebrew habit of playing with the sound of names is met. This is the first time anyone's name has been changed in this way in Genesis to mark a key point in their life. It re-occurs almost immediately in Sarai and later on, for example, in Jacob. The same phenomenon is also seen, it should be observed, in the NT, in the case of Simon, surnamed Peter, and perhaps also Saul ("who also is called Paul" (Acts 13.9)).

Not only was the covenant with Abraham and his descendants, but it was to be "throughout their generations for an everlasting covenant" (v.7, RV). In other words, the covenant had no limits. Formal agreements in the ancient world, when they were to operate without time limits, were often phrased like this. Above and beyond material and territorial blessings which belonged to the covenant was the vital matter, "to be a God unto thee, and to thy seed after thee". However much the fact that God was the prime mover in establishing this covenant is valued and stressed, the promise that God would be their God has the inevitable corollary that they would be His people. God would be faithful in His covenant and He expected them to be faithful also.

The view taken above in ch.15 was that at that point God swore, in the ritual performed there, to a covenant with Abram. A different view merits consideration.[†]

According to this view chs.15 and 17 signify God's promise of a covenant with Abram, and Abram's acceptance of the promise and his obligations in relation to the covenant. Chapter 22 then sees Abraham receive God's oath and enter finally into the covenant on that basis. In ch.22 Abraham showed conclusively (see 22.12) that he was fully committed to the will of God and the promise was ratified by God's oath (22.16). On balance it seems preferable to see God restating His covenant and defining the terms in greater detail as the relationship between Him and Abraham matured. The ceremony in ch.15 does seem to represent God entering upon a ritual rather than a verbal oath and so sealing a covenant (15.18) with Abram. A reference such as Psalm 89.3 shows (in the common Hebrew feature of repetition with variation) oath and covenant in close association as in Genesis 15.18. The verse in Psalm 89 reads: "I have made a covenant with my chosen, I have sworn unto David my servant". This same Psalm also illustrates how God considers His covenant established under oath as being inviolable. The psalmist relates how God entered into an everlasting covenant with David, yet conditions in his own day seem to belie God's promises. God had said that He would not break His covenant, nor alter what He had spoken (Ps 89.34), yet He would punish unfaithfulness by David's children (vv.30-32). In other words, God required integrity in those who were in covenant relationship with Him, He would punish those who were unfaithful with temporary eclipse of the covenant, but He would be faithful to His promises to David's line. This seems to sum up the tension between an unconditional covenant and the requirement that those in a covenant with God must show integrity. God's punishment of those in covenant relationship with Him is itself a proof of His faithfulness to the covenant: judgment must begin at the house of God.

Just before the end of His promises God mentions for the first time that the name of the land promised to Abraham is Canaan. This was understood but it has now been made explicit. Characteristically of this stage of the promises it is an *everlasting* possession. Verse 8 ends the details of God's covenant undertakings with the central issue: "I will be their God". The verses which follow will set out Abraham's obligations under the covenant.

Verses 9-14: The Sign of the Covenant: Circumcision
The concept of human responsibility in this covenant made by God with Abraham and his seed accounts for many of the details given in this chapter. In v.7 God said He would establish an everlasting covenant with them. The corollary of this is given in v.9, that they should keep it throughout their generations. The permanent obligation on them to observe the terms of the covenant is repeated several times in the chapter.

The sign of the acceptance of this obligation was the rite of circumcision, which, it is emphasised, would be permanently a mark "in your flesh" (v.13) of the everlasting covenant. It would serve to remind them always that they were God's holy people, bound to His service by covenant, and in this sense would be a sign. Paul refers in Romans 4.11-12 to the circumcision of Abraham as "a seal of the righteousness of the faith which he had while he was in uncircumcision" (RV). In other words, it was a sign which declared the already existing relationship between Abraham and God, a relationship based on his faith.

Circumcision was fairly common among ancient peoples in the area. Some of the nations, notably the Philistines, were indeed stigmatised in Israel as "the uncirumcised", but many of the surrounding races did practise circumcision. In this present study the meaning of the rite to the heathen nations who practised it is not a particular concern. Given the context in which it was prescribed by God as the sign of the covenant, however, an attempt must be made to assess its probable meaning for Abraham and his people.

In the first place, those who would claim to be of the same people as Abraham must practise it. In other words, it was an indication of the people's commitment to obey God's command to Abraham. It was also a command in connection with God's promise of a line of descendants for Abraham. Hence it is probably not incidental that it was performed on the male member associated with procreation. The continuation of

Abraham's line was to be in association with God, within the covenant between God and Abraham. The cutting off of the foreskin may be also taken as a symbol of the commitment of Abraham's people to eliminate moral and religious unfaithfulness within the covenant. The heathens practised religion in which immorality, in the form of temple prostitution, was an essential part of the ritual. Abraham and his descendants had no part in religion which was divorced from morality.

It is noteworthy that the rite included the whole community, bond and free. One assumes that it was taken for granted that the females were included in the covenant relationship, in that God viewed man and wife as one. Every male slave, born in the house or bought with money (v.13), must also be circumcised, for they were part of the community. Its inclusiveness may also perhaps be seen in that it was applied to newborn sons. This indicates that it was not, as in some other societies, a rite of puberty or test of manliness. If the cycle of seven-day weeks was already established, the rite being performed on the baby's eighth day (v.12) would symbolise a new beginning in the community of God.

The practice of circumcision was an essential element in the covenant relationship between God and Abraham's people. This was true to the extent that any person not circumcised must be "cut off from his people". Initially this must refer to the first introduction of the rite, for thereafter the responsibility lay on the father or the head of the household. Is it implied that a man who failed to circumcise his son should suffer this penalty? The incident in Exodus 4.24 when God would have killed Moses for failing to circumcise his son would suggest as much.

There is debate about what precisely is meant by "shall be cut off". Did it mean that the individual would be excluded from society, with the possible thought that he would be left to God to punish? Or did it mean that he must be executed? Similar pronouncements on other requirements, for example in Leviticus 17.8-10; 26.17, suggest that the penalty was to be death, whether inflicted by the community or by God's intervention.

Verses 15-22: Sarah to have a Son called Isaac, Covenant Heir

In vv.4-7 God linked the changing of Abram's name to Abraham with the promise of descendants and the establishment of the covenant. Sarai now must also have her name changed to Sarah to mark the imminence of her bearing the son of promise. At long last, after all the anguish and bitterness and false starts, Sarah would have a son. The blessing of God in this matter is strongly stressed (v.16), for in bearing this son she would become mother of nations, and indeed of kings. The theme which has already been noted, of God specially blessing those whom He brings into the mainstream of His plan, is restated here. Reading Genesis against the background of all Scripture, glimpses can be seen here of God's choice of David as king and also glimpses of Christ Himself. Remember that in Matthew 1.2-16 the kingly line of Jesus which begins with "Abraham begat Isaac" continues with "Jesse begat David" and climaxes with "Mary, of whom was born Jesus, who is called Christ". So all those references to Sarai being barren were positive reminders, not just of pain and disappointment, but of the fact that God often allows faith to reach a total impasse before He reveals that He has the answer. He has had His people's highest good in mind from the very start.

If God had opened Sarah's womb many years before, both she and Abraham would have been pleased and no doubt grateful. But now (v.17), as Abraham lay prostrate in worship before God, his mind was tossed about with emotions. His laughter can hardly have been due to sheer incredulity or, on the other hand, to sheer joy. He "considered his own body now as good as dead ... and the deadness of Sarah's womb" (Rom 4.19, RV). It may be saying too much to claim that at this stage "he wavered not through unbelief, but waxed strong through faith, giving glory to God" (Rom 4.20, RV). He had certainly reached the state of confidence when his faith was tested in ch.22, but this sudden revelation, when all hope of a son by Sarah was gone, was an overwhelming experience which threw him into turmoil.

In this crisis he did what is so often done when presuppositions have been overturned. He fell back on the familiar, on the second best which he had come to assume was God's best for him. His words are the first recorded request addressed to God in prayer: "Oh that Ishmael might live before thee!" (v.18). In the period of thirteen years during which he had had Ishmael growing up in his home Abraham had come to assume that the promise of descendants depended on Ishmael. But Ishmael was not born of promise, he was "born after the flesh" (Gal 4.23), a product of human efforts to help God out of a supposed difficulty. This theme will be played out a number of times in subsequent episodes of the story of God's people in Genesis and many later books. The life of faith can only be lived when the people of faith act in faith.

God did not condescend to argue with Abraham. First, the promise was explicit and unmistakable: "Nay, but Sarah thy wife shall bear thee a son" (v.19, RV). This son was to be one of a select group in Scripture whose names were prescribed by God before their birth. Moreover, his name, "Isaac - He laughs", would declare the inadequacy of Abraham who laughed in response to the divine promise, and Sarah who would laugh within herself (18.12) when she overheard the promise repeated. Later they might well laugh for joy that God had brought a living heir out of "dead" parents. It was with this Isaac that God would establish His covenant after Abraham, and this everlasting covenant would also be with Isaac's descendants. All of this was as clear and precise as it could be, but the finality of the revelation is underlined by the promise that Isaac would be born in just one year's time (v.21). An with that breath-taking finale the series of divine communications in the chapter ends abruptly (v.22).

But before the end of His promises about Isaac God condescended to answer Abraham's prayer about Ishmael, for, as Ishmael's name ("God has heard") suggests, God does hear: "And as for Ishmael, I have heard thee" (v.20). Here for the first time God declared of Ishmael, "I have blessed him". He also repeated His promise to Hagar that Ishmael would have many descendants (16.10). More specifically Ishmael would beget twelve princes (compare 25.12-16) and from him a great nation would spring. Thus far God would go in answer to Abraham's desire for Ishmael, but there would be no covenant relationship for the son of Hagar and the promises of God which had stimulated Abraham's progressing faith would be fulfilled through the line of Isaac, not Ishmael.

Verses 23-27 : Circumcision Instituted

Abraham lost no time in obeying the command to circumcise. "In the selfsame day" he circumcised Ishmael, his homeborn servants and his purchased slaves. Prompt obedience was Abraham's normal response (compare 22.3, "early in the morning"), and this despite his advanced years (v.24). Ishmael, who seems to have had a close bond of affection with Abraham, also submitted to the rite at thirteen years of age, on the same day as Abraham did. Abraham's obedience was not only prompt but also complete. Yet the males circumcised that day did not include the one through whom the promises of God would be carried forward within the covenant signified in circumcision. He was yet to be born.

Notes

7 See T.D.Alexander in JSOT, No.25, 1983, art. "Genesis 22 and the Covenant of Circumcision".

GENESIS 18

Abraham Considers God's Omnipotence and Justice

Verses 1-15: Is Anything Too Hard for the Lord?

Abraham's amazing experiences with God in this chapter began simply enough. He was sitting in his tent doorway in the noonday heat, when he saw three men standing near by. In a rural setting like this, as he sat in the doorway of his tent, we might have expected him to see them while they were some little way off. The fact that their coming took him by surprise may point to the fact that they were no normal visitors. His reaction was prompt and spontaneous. The duties of an honourable man were clear in the matter of hospitality, and those of a man of God were even clearer. This sacred duty of hospitality was unquestioned throughout the ancient world. The NT exhortation in Hebrews 13.2 would have occasioned no surprise: "Be not forgetful to entertain strangers". There is no suggestion at this point that Abraham was not merely extending to them the hospitality he felt was due to strangers. The politeness was an indication of Abraham's character, not of the exalted status which he was later to learn belonged to the visitors.

Comment has often been made on the picture of haste and activity in vv.2-8. Running was not a common activity among the old. It was normally the place of the young servant to be seen running. But when hospitality was involved even old Abraham must run to meet the men and show elaborate respect by the depth of his bow in welcoming them. He seems to have addressed the one who stood out as a leader. "My Lord" and "thy servant" are terms of proper courtesy. Hospitality must be seen to be the privilege of the host. Travellers in the noonday heat require first "a little water" to wash their feet and then a place to relax in the shade. Then they can have "a morsel of bread". This would describe any kind of meal, for the guest must be made to feel that the hospitality being offered was no trouble to the host. The response from the strangers was in a very low key, but they consented readily enough to accept the hospitality.

At this point Sarah is brought into the action. Interestingly, the last time Sarah was directly involved in the story of Genesis was when she dealt harshly with Hagar and Hagar fled (16.6). Here she was ordered to get fine flour, knead it and make bread "quickly". Until the end of this episode (v.15) she is never prominent but always near, on the fringes of the activity, but at the centre of the interest. Abraham himself "ran" to the herd, fetched a choice calf and gave it to a servant to prepare. The pace of the story is sustained by the economy with which it is told here. The meal was then served, complete with milk and a kind of yogurt (CHEMA - 2529). This last item, usually translated in the AV as "butter", was, and is, a standard part of bedouin diet (compare Judg 5.25). The haste and preparation were complete and Abraham was now free to stand by his guests as they ate.

In all this opening part of the chapter Abraham took the lead as a good host. Everything must be done, and done quickly, to oblige and welcome the guests. Everything was in Abraham's hands and reflected his status as an honourable man, and a righteous man who exercised willing and generous hospitality. All that the guests had said was, "So do, as thou hast said" (v.5).

Suddenly, at v.9, without warning, the pace changes as the initiative passes from Abraham to his guests. Though Sarah was active she was not visible, which was what would be expected when strangers were being entertained. Their question, "Where is Sarah thy wife?" made it clear that she was the centre of their interest and that they were not chance visitors, for they knew her name. His reply, prefaced by "Behold" (v.9), shows his surprise, perhaps his apprehension. Of course she was in the tent, but what was their interest in her? And how did they know her name? And if they knew her name, surely they knew perfectly well also where she was? The reader has been alerted by the narrator (v.1) to expect a theophany, but Abraham had not been prepared. It was a good thing that he had carried out his host's duties so generously, for he was "entertaining angels unawares" (Heb 13.2). More than that, in providing generously for visitors whom he thought to be men, he was honouring the Lord Himself.

There may be hints in the words used earlier that these visitors might be more than they seemed to be. In v.10 the words spoken made it clear to Abraham that this was a divine visit. The narrative technique underlines this aspect of the incident by changing from what "they" said to what "he", and then "the Lord", said. First there was a promise to return "next year" (v.10), or perhaps "this time next year", for this does seem to be the best rendering of what the AV translates as "according to the time of life". Then the promise, "Sarah thy wife shall have a son". On the previous occasion when this had been promised Sarah had not been actively involved in the divine visit. Abraham had fallen on his face and laughed (17.17). Here Sarah was listening in the inner compartment of the tent. The narrator brings the tension in the situation to the fore by the explanation of v.11, that both Abraham and Sarah were old and that she had passed the menopause; "was past age" as Hebrews 11.11 puts it. The situation is reminiscent of Luke 1.18-19, where Zechariah and the angel Gabriel discuss the promise earlier given by Gabriel that Elizabeth his wife would bear him a son (Lk 1.13). Zechariah understandably protests, "I am an old man", and Gabriel, equally understandably in view of who he is, replies, "I am Gabriel, that stand in the presence of God".

In this case the reaction to the promise was Sarah's. Abraham had already received this promise in 17.19. Now Sarah also must face it. At first exposure to the promise of imminent pregnancy her spontaneous feeling was that this was unreal. Hence she laughed within herself, a laugh of incredulity, not scorn. She thought that there were two good reasons why there must be some mistake: first, she was too old to have pleasure in conceiving, and second, Abraham was too old to beget a son. It is interesting that there is a NT reference to this speech of Sarah to herself. Peter (1 Pet 3.6) cites Sarah as an example of a holy woman of old who was subject to her husband, obeying him and "calling him lord". This is the one context in which Sarah called Abraham, "lord". Evidently the context in which she used the term did not shock Peter into excluding her from the class of "holy women".

Sarah still remained outside the discussion, which was now a one-sided conversation between the Lord and Abraham. In fact Abraham did not speak, in this section, after v.9! Sarah must face the reality which overleaps the bounds of normal reality. Hence the question by the Lord to Abraham, "Wherefore did Sarah laugh?". Sarah had the same problem as Zechariah in Luke 1. She looked at normal earthly factors of possibility and impossibility. Zechariah had said, "I am an old man". But God had intervened, so the boundaries of possibility had been radically redrawn. God is the One who "calleth those things which be not as though they were" (Rom 4.17). At this point the Lord asked the rhetorical question, "Is any thing too hard for the Lord?". To which the answer, of course, must be, "Obviously not - if you put it like that". Up to this point it does not seem that either Abraham or Sarah had realised that this was *the* question which must be asked. It is not by accident that this principle is repeated by the angel in the matter of the pregnancy of Zechariah's wife Elizabeth in Luke 1.37: "For with God nothing shall be impossible", even if the verse in Luke 1 is taken more literally with the RV, "For no word from God shall be void of power". This principle is the theme of this section of Genesis 18.

When the principle has been enunciated, so again is given the divine promise of a son for Sarah in the next year. Sarah's denial at this point may have been based on the false assumption that a laugh inside is not a laugh because nobody hears it. God heard it. He knew that her denial was prompted by fear. His blunt rebuke ends the conversation and concludes this topic for the time being. And still Abraham was silent.

Verses 16-33: Shall Not the Judge of All the Earth Do Right?

The signal that the topic was at an end came when the three men rose to leave Abraham. Then abruptly it is recorded that they "looked toward Sodom" (v.16). It can be readily understood why the Lord appeared to Abraham and gave the promise to challenge Sarah, but what business could the visitors have with Sodom? Nothing good has so far been said of it, and it has been tersely condemned - "But the men of Sodom were wicked and sinners before the Lord exceedingly" (13.13). Lot's commitment to it had done him no good and appears to have made little change in Sodom either.

Abraham, courteous as ever, began to walk with them on the first steps of their journey, presumably toward Sodom. It seems almost as if Abraham were reluctant to part from his heavenly guests. Then follows an amazing rhetorical question from the Lord: "Shall I hide from Abraham that thing which I do?". Later in the OT, Amos (3.7) would establish the truth that God takes His prophets into His confidence, but the prophetic office as such has not yet been established. Nevertheless, three times in Scripture Abraham is described as God's friend (2 Chr 20.7; Is 41.8 and Jas 2.23), firstly by Jehoshaphat, then by God Himself, then (as a quotation) by James. James associates the description with the fact that Abraham believed God and it was reckoned to him for righteousness. James also insists that Abraham could be seen to believe God because of what he did, citing the ultimate test of the patriarch's faith in Genesis 22 for proof. But the question from God here remains an amazing example of divine grace. An important element in this section is going to be Abraham's intercession for Sodom, and it is obvious that his mind is on Lot in Sodom. God's heart anticipates the movements of Abraham's heart when Sodom must be overthrown - "What of Lot?".

God's first articulated thought in relation to telling Abraham is about the greatness which He had destined for his descendants and the blessing to flow out to the world from him. This is elaborated in the statement that God had "known him", more accurately rendered "chosen him" (NIV), for that is the import of the word in this kind of context. God's purpose in choosing Abraham is then set out, that Abraham should so guide his children and household that they would "do justice and judgment" (v.19), and so God's promises to Abraham would be fulfilled. It is still consistent to view the covenant as unconditional, in spite of the wording here, if we read the covenant as it is explained in Psalm 89 in relation to David. But so far Abraham had not been addressed in vv.17-19.

The first words spoken to Abraham, in v.20, introduce the burden of the second part of the chapter, adumbrated in the clause in v.16, "looked toward Sodom". The problem starts with the grievousness of the sin of Sodom and Gomorrah, still unspecified. As a result of their sin a "cry" had gone up to God. After man's expulsion from Eden a cry had gone up to God from the ground, from Abel's blood. Heaven "heard" the result of that first murder. Here heaven "heard" the outcome of Sodom and Gomorrah's sin, whether a cry from victims or simply a discord from a society out of harmony with God. The message is simple, that when a society is out of harmony with God because of sin, He takes note. Without this understanding there is no secure basis for morality. It was this understanding of the concern of God for sin which led Joseph to refuse the advances of Potiphar's wife. He might well have been confident that if he had co-operated with her in her evil proposal she would never speak to her husband about it, but Joseph lived before God, not Potiphar: "how then can I do this great wickedness, and sin against God?" (39.9).

God would not, indeed could not, remain aloof. He must deal with this sin. In this sense He would "come down". In Exodus 3.8 He came down to deliver. Here He would come down to punish, that is if the sin had reached the stage of demanding exemplary punishment. He would not judge by hearsay ("I will go down"), and He would not act prematurely ("whether they have done *altogether*..."). Before the flood He left Noah to preach righteousness during the long years during which the ark was being prepared. He is slow to anger, but when their sin had reached a critical height of heinousness, when it was "altogether" as reported in the cry of it, His holy character demanded action. His judgment is as inflexible when it is ripe as it is unhurried up to that point. The principle remains solemnly true: "The Lord is not slack concerning his promise, as some men count slackness; but is longsuffering to us-ward, not willing that any should perish, but that all should come to repentance" (2 Pet 3.9).

The logical reading of the initial story of three visitors (v.2), then the Lord speaking (v.13), then "the men" going toward Sodom (v.22), then "the two angels (coming) to Sodom" (19.1, RV), prompts the interpretation that the Lord appeared with two angels, and that the two angels went on to Sodom while Abraham "stood yet before the Lord" (v.22).

Abraham's intercession is an amazing account of the frankness of a man who knew God and felt that it was inconceivable that God could act unjustly. The expression in v.23, that Abraham "drew near", prepares the way for his pleading on behalf of any righteous people who might be in Sodom. The problem in Abraham's mind was, "How can God, who is just, destroy the righteous with the wicked?". In the early part of the chapter he had faced the difficulty of how God, confronted by a physical "impossibility", could fulfil His promises. He learned there that God is omnipotent. Here he grapples with a problem of how God, who by definition is just (being Judge of all), could destroy the wicked in their city where righteous people also lived. Abraham knew Lot to be righteous and his pleas were on Lot's behalf, therefore his pleading ignored Gommorah and focused on Sodom where Lot lived. He would learn here that God is right in His judgments, not merely righteous in theory.

Abraham's attempts to negotiate with God were based on the assumption that all those in the city would perish if God destroyed the city. He began with a plea based on an assumed righteous quota of fifty in Sodom. He laboured the point that it was surely unthinkable that God would destroy those fifty. His peroration is eloquent: "Shall not the judge of all the earth do judgment?". This translation is an attempt to show the echo of the subject, "the judge" (SHAPAT - 8199), in the object, "judgment" (MISHPAT - 4941). A judge's task is to distinguish the righteous/innocent from the wicked/guilty. Abraham is here pleading that it would be out of character for God, who is Judge of all, and who expects human judges to make such distinctions between innocent and guilty, to fail Himself to make the distinction in Sodom by destroying them without distinction.

God agreed to Abraham's proposal to spare the city for the sake of fifty righteous. But Abraham still had no peace of mind that there would be as many righteous as this number in Sodom so as to justify Lot's salvation. He knew enough of the character of God, and of the Sodomites, to try again. Yet he could not presume. He knew himself to be a mere man on earth, mere dust (v.27). Yet plead he must. Down came the target to forty-five, then forty (vv.28-29). Then, apologetically ("let not the Lord be angry, and I will speak"), he negotiated for thirty, then twenty (vv.30-31). Finally, with even greater timidity he pleaded "but this once" for the city to be spared for the sake of ten. Again, as in each previous plea, God agreed to Abraham's figure. Abraham had pleaded with God because he knew God, and on the basis of what he knew of God. Some aspects of his pleading recall Moses' pleading on behalf of rebellious Israel in Numbers 14.13-19. Moses pleaded on the basis of God's past dealings and character, and God answered Moses "according to (Moses') word". In a sense God agreed here to Abraham's word, but it was good for Lot that He did not act according to Abraham's word.

Abraham knew God, and therefore pleaded with Him. God also knew Abraham, and Abraham had said "yet but this once". Therefore, as soon as He had answered this last plea He "went his way", for Abraham was a man of his word and he had said his last word. "And Abraham returned unto his place" (v.33). One wonders what was in his mind. It was surely not possible that there were fewer than ten righteous in Sodom after Lot had stayed there for years? Yet how could one be confident when everyone knew what Sodom was like?

God was not in difficulty, even if Abraham thought He was. Abraham had overlooked the possibility which was uppermost in God's mind. The time had come for Sodom to be overthrown, along with its neighbours. Their "iniquity was full" (compare 15.16). God's judgment would not be turned aside. Equally certainly He would not slay the righteous with the wicked - Abraham's prayer had indeed been heard (compare 19.29 "God remembered Abraham"). He would answer the intention of Abraham's prayer while acting in a way which seemed to deny the request. Lot has been a means of drawing attention to the outstanding spiritual greatness of Abraham, even though it was by contrast. The covenant promises will be fulfilled and Abraham's dealings with God will add to his spiritual stature. By contrast, the final record of Lot's degradation, after the overthrow of the cities of the plain, will spell out in greater detail the cost of compromise, both to Lot and to his family.

GENESIS 19

The Overthrow of Sodom and its Sequel

Verses 1-3: Lot Entertains Two Angels

Chapters 18.16-33 and 19 form one closely knit story. This action commenced with Abraham's three angelic visitors in the afternoon looking toward Sodom (18.16). Now, in 19.1, the "two angels" reached Sodom. It has already been noted that only two angels went on ahead, for "Abraham stood yet before the Lord" (18.22). The accounts of how Abraham and Lot received the heavenly visitors have some similarities but some telling differences. For instance, when the visitors arrived Abraham was sitting in the doorway of his tent. Lot likewise was sitting in the gateway. The difference is that Lot sat in the gate of Sodom, seemingly an honoured resident in a stronghold of evil and corruption. Abraham, on the other hand, sat at the place which spoke of his separateness from corrupt society, his tent. Lot's welcome was very like Abraham's, a deep bow to express proper courtesy.

Lot's invitation to the visitors to spend the night was inevitable because they arrived "at even". The courtesies were impeccable and as one would expect. In fact there is a long-standing tradition which links the ancient verdict of Lot's righteousness with his ready welcome of the heavenly visitors. This was a tradition in ancient Israel long before Peter in his epistle (2 Pet 2.7,8) described him as righteous. The suggestion that Lot invited the guests in to spend the night because he was embarrassed at the realisation that otherwise they would not be safe in Sodom, seems strained and unnecessary.

Their reluctance to accept the invitation does give cause for uneasiness. They had evidently felt no qualms about accepting Abraham's invitation to dinner, and that can hardly be put down to the demands of courtesy. Lot's vehement insistence that they must stay with him is a sign of his genuine desire to be a good host. They had a meal with him, including unleavened bread because this could be produced quickly. No mention is made of the other members of Lot's household. This contrasts with the involvement of Sarah in catering for the guests' needs in the previous chapter. But Sarah was of central importance in ch.18 because of the message brought by the angels, quite apart from the issue of hospitality. Lot's wife is anonymous and has no part in the covenant or purpose of God in Genesis.

Verses 4-9: A Night Assault on Lot's Home

The news that Lot had visitors had spread quickly, for a large and representative crowd of men (old and young) arrived "before they lay down". The men of Sodom had a high degree of unanimity in their devotion to evil, for it has been made clear that there were not ten righteous people in the city. Their demand was peremptory and explicit. To them these visitors were men and could be exploited.

Their demand was inexcusable according to the norms of ancient society, not to speak of what God would expect. Hospitality was viewed as a sacred responsibility, and Lot had hospitably received the visitors. Therefore the men of Sodom were in breach of hospitality in demanding that the guests be handed over. Secondly, their demand involved that, whether the guests consented or not, they should submit to the sexual demands of the men of the city (v.5). This was not acceptable in any nation in that area in the ancient world, and certainly not in Israel. It is denounced in Jude 7 as "going after strange flesh", that is men lusting after men, for that is what they thought the visitors were.†

Thirdly, their demand, backed up by force of numbers with its threat of violence, was a breach of civilised behaviour. It also violated standards which would later be enshrined in the law of Moses, that foreign visitors should be treated with consideration and respect, and that provision should be made for their needs (Ex 22.21; 23.9; Lev 19.10).

Lot's attempt to negotiate with his fellow-townsmen was at least brave, even though it was a forlorn hope. He went out to them and shut the door to protect his visitors. There is an irony in his anxiety to protect them in view of what happened afterwards. He had the courage to describe what the men of Sodom were doing as wickedness. His suggested compromise comes as a great revelation of the undermining of his moral integrity by the atmosphere in Sodom. It is difficult to imagine how even a weak man, as Lot was, could suggest handing over his two still virgin daughters to that mob, to do with them what "is good in your eyes" (v.8). Lot had evidently not considered the powerful impact of the surrounding moral corruption when he chose to live in Sodom, but this evil which he proposed was his initiative and his alone.

His neighbours were not impressed by his suggestion. They were more interested in the men than in his daughters. If he would not hand the men over they would take him instead and repay his arrogance in full. He had come in as a mere sojourner and now wanted to play the judge, telling them what was wicked! Once again an insight is given into the contrast between the divine interest in protecting aliens ("strangers" in AV) and the Sodomites' total disregard for this principle. It seemed at this point that Lot was incapable of protecting his guests and in great personal danger of molestation or even death.

The scene has been set for the destruction of the city. Should one attribute God's decision to destroy it to any one factor rather than the others? Was it their violence which moved Him? Or their oppression of the strangers? Or their homosexuality? Or the list of things mentioned by the Lord Jesus (Lk 17.28): "they did eat, they drank, they bought, they sold, they planted, they builded"? But all of these things were unexceptionable, surely. Why then did He list them? Because the people were occupied with the affairs of daily life and gave no thought to God. They had eliminated God from their calculations and had no thought that their life was a gift from God, or that they were answerable to God. They "did not like to retain God in their knowledge" (Rom 1.28). The contempt for the weak, the rejection of normal hospitality, the violent denial of others' human rights and, in particular, their perverted sexual practices, all declared their estrangement from their Creator. Their sins had mounted up to heaven and their iniquity was now full, demanding prompt divine intervention. It is sobering to reflect on this in the present day, when so much in society, in the "global village", is reminiscent of the days of Lot and Noah.

Verses 10-16: Rescue by the Angels

Lot's good intentions as host and his best efforts as mediator had failed. He was marooned outside his own barred door, faced by an undisciplined mob with violence and rape in their hearts. Then, very simply, "the men put forth their hand, and pulled Lot into the house to them, and shut to the door". The sentence contains at least two echoes of Noah's story, when Noah brought the dove back in (8.9) and when God shut Noah into the ark (7.16). God was not in difficulties and Lot did not need to sacrifice his daughters, even if they had been acceptable to the mob.

The angels "smote the men that were at the door of the house with blindness". This was a supernatural intervention, possibly through a blinding light, as the word for "blindness" (SANWER - 5575) may suggest (compare 2 Kings 6.18, where the same word is used). The Sodomites' inability to find the door argues that their minds were blinded or confused as well as, or rather than, their eyes. The narrative leaves them stupidly, persistently, groping for the door they could not find. God had shut the door and they could not open it. Lot could not fail to detect at this point the heavenly nature of his visitors.

The angels turned their attention then to the reason for their coming to Lot. They were there to rescue him and as many of his family as could be rescued. This was God's answer to Abraham's worry. The righteous could be delivered (2 Pet 2.7) though the judgment must fall. The principle is the same as at the flood (2 Pet 2.5), that God would not forget the righteous and would deliver them, but He must also destroy the persistently impenitent. The Scriptures go forward in human history to a future day when the call will go out, "Come out of her, my people ... for her sins have reached unto heaven, and God hath remembered her iniquities" (Rev 18.4-5). This will usher in His judgment on a society which has congratulated itself on its prosperity and has deliberately refused to acknowledge God. It is interesting that at the flood God is said to have remembered Noah, here He is said to have remembered Abraham when He saved Lot, but in Revelation 18 He is said to have remembered the iniquities of those being judged. God does not lose control, even though men may panic at times and may wish to help Him out.

The angels spelt out to Lot what was going to happen, why God was intervening and the reason why He must act now (v.13). The details of how many were in Lot's family are not certain. He had a wife, certainly, and two daughters whom he described as virgins. There were also "sons-in-law", but it seems best to follow the translation "which were to marry his daughters" (v.14, RV margin). This would leave possibly just two daughters of Lot, as yet unmarried, probably quite young though having at least reached puberty. Lot, then, turned his attention to his prospective sons-in-law, warning them that the Lord was about to destroy the city. Their incredulity may be attributed to the evil which was so deeply ingrained in the Sodomites, "old and young", the moral blindness, or deafness, which was endemic in the city. One has, however, an uneasy feeling that Lot had so compromised his witness for God and righteousness that when he warned them they found it difficult to take him seriously. Ungodly people, find it difficult to believe a man who, for instance, gives his whole energy to money-making or career-building and then tells them that he is waiting for the Son of God from heaven. Many of us have some personal unease as we read the story of the reaction of these young men to Lot's warning.

If the young men would not listen they could not be saved. Morning dawned and the angels were ready to do their day's work promptly, now that the time for action had come. At first they urged Lot to hurry and take his wife and two daughters out of the city - "lest thou be consumed in the punishment (RV margin) of the city" (v.15). But despite what he had suffered in Sodom, Lot found it hard to act decisively and obey. He "lingered". It is a sobering fact that the only people who left Sodom that day before judgment fell were pulled out by angelic hands - two angels with four hands pulling out four reluctant people, an illustration indeed of divine mercy. This mercy was focused particularly on Lot, as the end of v.16 shows. It was for Lot particularly that Abraham was praying.

Verses 17-29: Reactions to the Divine Intervention
Once out of the city Lot and his family were urged to escape for their lives without turning back or stopping anywhere on the plain. The only refuge from the consuming judgment was the hills. One of the angels had assumed the speaking role (v.17) and to him Lot addressed his appeal. In brief he argued that, while he appreciated that his life had been saved, it was not safe to flee to the hills for fear of some unspecified danger there. He who had not been afraid to linger on in Sodom after an angelic warning was now afraid to obey an angelic command to escape! Lot's reaction contrasts strongly with Noah's detailed obedience to all that God had told him to do so as to escape the flood. Lot had an

alternative suggestion, an insignificant city called Zoar which God could easily spare and so accommodate Lot's wishes. When, amazingly, God agreed to his proposal it must be suspected that the reason lies in v.29 - "God remembered Abraham, and sent Lot out". At any rate, whether to the hills or to Zoar, Lot must flee with all speed. God is slow to anger, but when the time comes for judgment He can act with awesome dispatch. So Lot entered Zoar just as the sun rose (v.23).

Forthwith the divine fury, fire and brimstone, fell on Sodom and Gomorrah. The record leaves no room for ambiguity - "He overthrew those cities, and all the plain, and all the inhabitants of the cities, and that which grew upon the ground" (v.25). The comprehensive catalogue of destruction is another reminder of the description of the flood overwhelming everything and everyone on earth. This was divine judgment in action to destroy a society which had reached the point of no return in its corruption.

God had been very patient and kind towards Lot despite Lot's reluctance to escape. If only the story could have ended there! But the rescue was not complete as far as the family was concerned. An angel's hand could pull Lot's wife out of Sodom, but Sodom was still in her heart. Reluctant though he was to leave, there is no suggestion in the narrative that Lot wanted to go back. His wife, whose origins and name are alike unknown, had no place in the future of Lot and his people. Her heart was in Sodom, she disobeyed the direct command, "Look not behind thee" (v.17), and she became a cautionary figure, to point a moral - "Remember Lot's wife!" (Lk 17.32). What physical process is involved in her becoming a pillar of salt is uncertain, but she perished and remains a monument to what happens to those who, even on the threshhold of divine judgment, resist divine grace.

What of Abraham while this was happening? There is a touching hint of his feelings in the description of his rising up early in the morning. He was not a man to relax and take things easy when he had an exercise before God for a relative in mortal danger. He took his stand "where he stood before the Lord" (v.27). That is, he went back to the spot where he pleaded with God for Sodom the previous day. He looked out over Sodom and its surroundings and saw, from all the area, smoke, "as the smoke of a furnace". There ends the reference to what Abraham did, but immediately the reason is given for God's great patience with Lot - "God remembered Abraham, and sent Lot out of the midst of the overthrow ..." (v.29). During the flood God "remembered Noah" (8.1) and the flood began to subside. Here God "remembered Abraham" and saved Lot. It was well for Lot that he had a "brother" who had power with God. If only there was more of that power to-day, what might not be accomplished in the saving of friends?

Verses 30-38: Lot's Final Humiliation and Loss

Lot had declined God's command to flee to the hills on the ground that it was not safe to do so. Yet here he was, still afraid in Zoar where God had allowed him to go instead (v.30), and fleeing to the hills. His loss of all material well-being is symbolised in his dwelling in a cave. One wonders what was going on in the minds of his daughters as they saw him, always previously indecisive, now totally demoralised, having lost all. Moreover, they had lost their mother in circumstances which should have sobered anyone with any vestige of the fear of God in them.

The minds of the daughters had recovered from the recent solemn events and turned to consider their situation. The world they had known had vanished literally in smoke, and with it had gone the promise of marriage to husbands already chosen for them. Their father was old and without confidence, in no fit state to negotiate a marriage for them, even if he had had opportunity. Their solution to this problem has features of what might be expected in Sodom. They were accustomed to a society in which the weak could expect no respect or pity. Now their father, in his weakness and confusion, would become the father of their children. They knew that what they had in mind would not meet with his approval, so they must make him drunk so that he would not have to be a conscious agent in their plan. They were confident that they could make him drunk. What previous experience had they of the effects of excessive drinking? Had Lot taught them of the dangers of it? It is not an accident that this second reference in Genesis to drinking alcohol is once more linked with a scene of shame and sexual impropriety, not to put it more strongly.

Lot was not aware of what was going on during, or even after, the shameful incestuous unions. Undoubtedly he knew or guessed about it later on, but Scripture draws a veil over the later days of Lot. Meanwhile he was being used by his daughters for their own purposes, just as he had purposed to use them in Sodom for his plan to save his guests. In neither case is there a suggestion that the person(s) being used would be consulted. Did they even know, after their life in Sodom, that incest was sinful in the sight of God?

The plan was put into effect on successive nights. First the elder, then the younger, lay with Lot and conceived. So easy was this devious plan to produce offspring for themselves. The daughters were the planners and agents of it all. They went far, far further in dishonouring their father than Ham went when he inadvertently saw Noah lying drunkenly naked. Their dishonouring of Lot was premeditated and required active implementation. And throughout it all Lot lay unconscious of how they were using him. Here ends the story of the man who walked and dwelt for many years with Abraham the friend of God. He made bad choices, set wrong priorities, married a wife who brought him no blessing, and lost all. He was "saved; yet so as by fire" (1 Cor 3.15).

The story has at least one purpose in the scheme of Scripture. It establishes why the Moabites and Ammonites had the relations which they had with Israel, for the older daughter bore Moab and the younger Ben-ammi, ancestors of the Moabites and Ammonites. God acknowledged the place of Lot's descendants and granted them territory, as described in Deuteronomy 2.9,19. So Israel was not to "distress" Moab or Ammon, because they were occupying the territory which God had given them.

Notes

5 Homosexual acts between consenting adult males were allowed in the countries around Israel. If there was no consent such acts were forbidden. In Israel the law of Moses was to stipulate that homosexual acts, whether by consent or not, were strictly forbidden because they were "an abomination" to the Lord (Lev 18.22; 20.13). The conclusion drawn by some commentators, that such acts are an abomination because they pervert the original order in creation, is inescapable. See especially Wenham's article, "The OT Attitude to Homosexuality" in Expository Times vol. 102, pages 359-363.

GENESIS 20

Sarah Denied and Abimelech Troubled

Verses 1-18

Early in his experiences with God in the land of promise Abraham had been tested by famine (12.10-20) and sought a solution in Egypt. His fears had led him to deny that Sarah was his wife. Serious results followed for the Pharaoh and consequent embarrassment for Abraham. Yet he emerged from that experience materially enriched.

During his period of supporting Lot, Abraham had maintained a consistently high level of commitment to the life to which God had called him. Now Lot has been phased out of the story and immediately it is recorded that Abraham went on a journey which took him away from the places on which his special dealings with God were focused - Shechem, Bethel and Hebron. He journeyed toward the Negev and dwelt between Kadesh and Shur. That is to say, he went to the far corners of the land and into the territory between the land and Egypt. Gerar, where he settled, was evidently on the border of the land. No reason is given for his going so far from where he had known the blessing of God, and so near places where his deceit had led to his humiliation.

His decision to lie again about Sarah is not explained just yet, but later he said he was afraid (v.11). He had scarcely ground to fear that men would be stricken by Sarah's beauty, for she was well past the age when men might desire her as they had done thirty years before. Why then did Abimelech take her to his palace? A suggestion which merits consideration is that the wealth of Abraham and the possibility of a profitable marriage alliance moved him. This might be a good commercial transaction.

At any rate God could not accept the arrangement. He came to Abimelech in a dream at night, as He did on a number of occasions in the Pentateuch to others, both inside the covenant community and outside it. The message to Abimelech was blunt: he was as good as dead because he had taken another man's wife. Abimelech did not know what the reader of the story knows, that Sarah was soon to become the mother of a son called Isaac, the son of promise, through whom the covenant blessings would be carried on. It seems that the promises are in danger of being caught up in an unsavoury marital tangle. But immediately (v.4) reassurance is given, for Abimelech had not lain with her. This is an assurance of vital significance, for there must be no question about the true paternity of the son of promise.

Abimelech's alarm seems at first to be excessive. Why should he fear for the whole nation? The answer must be that he believed that kings by their evil deeds brought down divine judgment on their whole nation. He pleaded that his people had done no wrong, that "he himself", namely Abraham, had told Abimelech lies, that Sarah had confirmed what Abraham had told him, so Abimelech had acted in integrity and innocence. God's word, as well as Abimelech's, testifies that there had been no sexual contact between Abimelech and Sarah. The promised seed has no slur on his paternity.

God had intervened to save Abimelech from unwittingly committing a serious sin. This meant that he must act at once to restore Sarah to her husband, however questionable Abraham's conduct had been. Interestingly, the emphasis in God's words to Abimelech was on the fact that Abraham was a prophet who would pray for him, for his forgiveness. This is the first mention of a prophet in Scripture; it is also the first occurrence of the word "pray" (PALAL - 6419), though prayer has been referred to under other terms. Abraham's role in the Sodom incident had been as intercessor, and his intercession was based on the fact that God had revealed to him the truth about Sodom and its impending overthrow. Abraham's intercession for Abimelech would be effective only if Sarah were restored. God's covenants and His gifts to His servants do not depend on those servants being above reproach. In Scripture it is the righteous man who "falleth seven times, and riseth up again" (Prov 24.16). By contrast the wicked lives in habitual sin.

God would uphold the covenant with Abraham and preserve the line of descent through Sarah above reproach. Abimelech must accept that Abraham and Sarah were under divine protection. Psalm 105.14 says, "Yea, he [God] reproved kings for their sakes". Abimelech's life and the lives of his family depended on his response to Abraham and Sarah.

His response was prompt. He "rose early in the morning". This idiom describes a prompt, whole-hearted response, a determination to see the thing through. It was used even of God, in Jeremiah 7.13,25 for example, when He was assuring Israel of how thoroughly He had warned them. Not only Abimelech but also his servants were afraid.

Abraham was called and Abimelech remonstrated with him. Abraham said he had been afraid because they were godless people. Evidently he underestimated their fear of God, their willingness to believe God. It is then disclosed that Sarah was indeed his half-sister. Granted, but she was his wife and he had told a whole lie. It is difficult to see that the reason for the deceit given in ch.12 to the Pharaoh was still valid, whatever Abraham said.

Once again God overruled His servant's failure and Abimelech gave lavish presents to Abraham to express his repentance that he had inadvertently threatened the sanctity of Abraham's marriage. It is worth repeating here that this episode is dealt with in detail of a kind which prevents the possibility of any slur on the paternity of Isaac.

Abimelech was impressed by Abraham's standing with the God who speaks and reveals secrets. He would be happy for Abraham to stay anywhere he liked in Abimelech's land. Moreover, he explained to Sarah that he was giving a gift of 1000 shekels of silver to her "brother" as compensation. This very lavish sum would "cover the eyes"; that is, it would make a statement that Sarah's position as Abraham's wife had not been compromised. The final clause of v.16 which the AV translates, "thus she was reproved", should be rendered, "you are vindicated". This clarifies the meaning of the covering of the eyes in the same verse. Abimelech's response had been prompt and generous, yet he was resentful of Abraham's deceit, for it is noticeable that he spoke to Sarah of Abraham as her "brother", which was the crux of the deception.

The final note in this episode rings oddly in one's ears. Abraham has played a deceitful and unnecessary trick on a man who in some sense feared God. Abimelech's reaction has been righteous, generous and God-fearing. Then it is recorded that Abraham prayed to God for Abimelech and his wife and the people. Failing Abraham certainly was, but he was a prophet and he was in covenant relationship with God. So God healed Abimelech, his wife and his maidservants, who had been rendered barren because of the false position into which they had been tricked. This is an example, perhaps, of how the king's sin, whether deliberately or unwittingly committed, affected his people in general. The comment in v.18, that "the Lord had fast closed up all the wombs...", underlines once again that Jehovah is not seen as a tribal or national god, He is God the Creator, Giver of life, to be honoured by people of all races.

The final phrase in the chapter has almost a note of triumph in it, after all the unsavoury dealings of Abraham. After all the contingencies Sarah is "Abraham's wife", not just a half-wife!

GENESIS 21

Isaac Born, Ishmael Cast Out, Covenant with Abimelech

Verses 1-7: Isaac Born: The Promise Fulfilled At Last

Since he was first called by God out of Ur one of Abraham's main pre-occupations was that God's promise of descendants should be fulfilled. Sarah had initiated the resort of getting a son by her handmaid and Abraham had become attached to Ishmael and had evidently become willing to accept that he was the promised son. Then God informed him that this was not the case, that the promised son would be Sarah's and would be called Isaac. As the years passed this seemed more and more obviously impossible. Firstly, Sarah passed the menopause, and secondly, Abraham was past the stage of being physically able to father children. Then, in ch.18, they were both confronted by a message from heavenly messengers that they were about to become father and mother of a son. The Lord's answer to their incredulity was, "Is any thing too hard for the Lord?". The child's birth would be humanly unthinkable - unless it was brought about by divine intervention. God, who gives life and who gives new life in all its forms, season after season and generation after generation, can turn back the biological clock if He pleases. "And the Lord visited Sarah as he had said". This episode clarifies why Scripture records how so many barren women became mothers of men who had special places in the plan of God. Examples, among others, are: the wife of Manoah, mother of Samson, in Judges 13.2-3; Hannah, mother of Samuel, in 1 Samuel 1.2,5; and Elizabeth, mother of John the Baptist, in Luke 1.7. God was declaring that He was at work and that He was able to fulfil all His promises without human subterfuges or short-cuts. "Is any thing too hard for the Lord?".

God had intervened in the physical condition of both Abraham and Sarah, and Sarah conceived and bore Abraham a son. In vv.1-7 the language, seemingly repetitive, is designed to underline the fact of this miraculous event, a son born to Abraham, with no doubt about his paternity, and to Sarah, with no need for a surrogate mother.

Abraham, as has been seen, was normally prompt to obey. According to God's instructions (17.19) the son was called Isaac, and according to the same instructions (17.12) Abraham circumcised him on the eighth day. Again, the wonder of divine enabling is spelt out in the statement that Abraham was 100 years old when his son Isaac was born to him. The emphasis here is entirely on Abraham's obedience in response to God's intervention.

By contrast, in Sarah's response to the situation we are given a vignette which deals with emotions. This is true however we translate v.6. One version has Sarah declare that the people will laugh at her because God has made her an object of amusement or possibly even ridicule.[†]

More probable is the interpretation adopted by the AV which has her exult in the fact that God's intervention has caused her to laugh in harmony with Isaac's name. Not only that, but she is confident that all the people will laugh in joyful surprise with her that at last her pain and reproach are past and joy has come. Who would ever have thought, she says, that Abraham would receive news that Sarah was breast-feeding her own offspring, whom she had borne to Abraham, and him so old? This reads well in the context and the details fit in more easily than in the alternative interpretations. At last the flood-gates of Sarah's maternal fulfilment have opened. The mood is euphoric.

Verses 8-21: Ishmael Cast Out

The next phase of the story opens with a bland statement that "the child grew". Euphoria was beautiful when Sarah held her new-born son at her breast, but there came a time for him to be weaned. The purpose of God moves forward. Weaning was usually celebrated with great festivity. It probably occurred when Isaac was as much as, say, three years old, for he was a special son, to be treated with extra care.

The occasion of the weaning feast brought in the first note of harshness. Nothing has been heard of Ishmael since he was circumcised when he was thirteen years old and Abraham was ninety-nine. At that time Abraham had hoped and prayed that Ishmael might have a place in God's plans (17.18). God had rejected the request and promised a son by Sarah who would enjoy covenant relationship with God. Then He promised future blessing and greatness for Ishmael, outside the covenant. Now, at the weaning feast Sarah saw Hagar's son, who was also Abraham's son, "mocking".†

Sarah's demand to Abraham was cold and peremptory. The inspired writer (v.9) gave Hagar's name, but Sarah could not bring herself to call her by name. She was "this bondwoman". Nor could she bear to name Ishmael; he was "her son", the bondwoman's son. Sarah's thinking had reached a crucial point. It was a matter of inheritance and she was determined that all would be Isaac's; Ishmael must be disinherited, a mere bondwoman's son. Earlier Sarah "took Hagar her maid ... and gave her to her husband Abram to be his wife" (16.3). But times had changed. Isaac had been born and Sarah was determined now, because of what had just happened at the weaning feast, that Ishmael should have nothing.

Abraham's reaction to Sarah's demand was hostile. He had not seen the incident and anyway he was fond of Ishmael, who had always, it appears, fitted into Abraham's own plans very well. But Ishmael was also growing, was almost a full-grown man. Perhaps Abraham had not been so exuberant in his welcome of Isaac as Sarah had been. At any rate there is no record of his rejoicing at Isaac's birth. Had he really been fully reconciled to the rejection of Ishmael by God in favour of Isaac? When v.11 refers to Abraham's thought for "his son" there is no doubt which son is meant; it is Ishmael. At an intellectual level Abraham had accepted that the promises would be fulfilled in Sarah's son, and therefore he accepted in theory that Ishmael must be displaced, but his heart still grieved for the loss of Ishmael. We do tend to be like this. We know the theology of situations, we accept that the will of God is best, but when we face the emotional reality of the knowledge we find it hard to part with the cherished objects of our affection. Besides, Ishmael seems to have been a manly lad, and he would probably soon have been bringing home the results of his archer's skills. Abraham might even have come to relish his son's venison, as Isaac later relished Esau's!

But that day, when Sarah spoke, what filled Abraham's mind was the pain of renunciation if he gave in to her. (In the next chapter Abraham was going to have the greater test of whether he would be willing to give up Isaac, the son of promise.) It was a good thing that God once again intervened to tell him that, unlike a former occasion on which he had acted unwisely in listening to Sarah (16.2) to take Hagar, this time he was right to accept her demand to put Hagar away. Paul must have had this in mind when he wrote in Galatians 4.30, "Nevertheless, what saith the scripture? 'Cast out the bondwoman and her son: for the son of the bondwoman shall not be heir with the son of the freewoman' ". He could quote Sarah's words almost verbatim as what "the scripture saith" because God endorsed the rejection of Ishmael as heir to the promises. Furthermore God spoke as Sarah had done, avoiding Hagar's or Ishmael's name, as if to endorse Sarah's judgment. Abraham was reminded that his descendants, within the covenant that is, would be traced through Isaac. He was reminded also that Ishmael was not going to be forgotten by God, for God would make a nation of him.

Again, as on other occasions (compare especially 22.3), Abraham responded promptly, however much it cost his emotions. He rose early in the morning, in whole-hearted determination to do the will of God fully. The task might be unpleasant, but he would do a full day's work for God. The supplies given to Hagar and her son are told in basic outline. It is almost beyond belief that he gave her just bread and water. But bread and water were basic requirements, and Abraham gave them what they needed for the present. A skin (that is the meaning of "bottle" in the AV) of water would hold probably about fifteen litres of water. While Abraham obeyed whole-heartedly, his emotions may be expressed in the little detail, "putting it on her shoulder", a gentle token of his genuine care for Hagar. She shows up in this chapter as a woman who knew God and loved her child dearly. Why should Abraham not make the parting with signs of care and affection? He gave her also the child - this must be the meaning, not that he put the boy of sixteen years on her shoulder. And he sent her away. Ishmael at this point leaves the story of the covenant dealings of God with Abraham and his descendants.

So Hagar departed and wandered blindly in the wilderness. She had no goal to her walking, no promised land and no relatives in, say, Haran. She had not managed to join a caravan of travellers as people in her position would normally have tried to do. God was going to have dealings with her in grace and she would encounter Him in the depths of her need. It was inevitable that the supply of food given to her by Abraham would fail, and fail it did. Human resources were at zero.

She set her son down - "cast" is too vigorous a word - under a shrub, and withdrew far enough not to hear his whimpers. She was sure he must die, for she had understandably forgotten God's promises (16.12). It is not stated at this point whether she prayed or he cried. However, she wept out loud and it can be inferred that he did also, for God heard his voice (v.17). Divine compassion, and divine ability to make good the promises to Abraham and Hagar, moved into action. The angel of God called to her from heaven.

The question, "What aileth thee, Hagar?", served to call her attention, but required no answer. It also established who was calling her, for in this desert only God knew her name. God knew exactly where Ishmael was - "God hath heard the voice of the lad where he is", for God had undertaken to take care of Ishmael's future. Human resources had failed her, but she should not fear (v.17), for God had seen and heard and come to deliver. This is a wonderful story, in a book which deals with God working in Abraham's family through Isaac. God had accepted what was perhaps a harsh demand by Sarah, but He is still the God of pity and He had accepted that Abraham's second-best solution for barrenness would be looked after.

Hagar was encouraged, then, to take the collapsing lad by the hand and set him on his feet (v.18), for God had great plans for him - He would "make him a great nation". This was a greatness to be made by God. The God who could provide could also give the eyesight to see the provision. Now Hagar had been at the end of her resources, for she had thought only of what Abraham had provided. But the well was there all along, even as Ishmael lay apparently dying of thirst. How did they come in their blind wandering to this precise spot where there was water? God's eye was upon them from the time that Abraham with aching heart sent them away. She could fill the bottle and both had plenty to drink. She need not doubt God again. Abraham could only give her a skin of water for their journey, but God could direct her aimless wandering to a well. "And God was with the lad; and he grew, and dwelt in the wilderness, and became an archer". God not only gave him water when he was destitute. He also gave him the faculties which enabled him to develop the skills to become self-supporting in the desert. The wilderness would hold no terrors for him. His mother, faithful to him as ever, sought a wife for him among her own people in Egypt. She was not one of the chosen people, nor in the full sense was he, but she did for him what seemed best to her. This finishes the record of Ishmael in Scripture but for the genealogical footnote in 25.12-18. In effect he had been written out of the record to leave room for the main theme of Isaac.

Verses 22-34: Abraham's Covenant with Abimelech

Abimelech's approach, with his army commander, to Abraham was occasioned by their noticing that God was with him in all that he did. They were inviting Abraham to enter into a covenant with them (compare v.23 with v.32). Abraham's prosperity under the good hand of God was such that his neighbours sought his friendship. He entered a covenant from a position of strength. The principle is the same as in Zechariah 8.23, where future prosperity for the Jews takes the form of attracting Gentiles of all nations: their exclamation is, "We will go with you: for we have heard that God is with you".

The proposed covenant would apply also to the generations to come. Abimelech could plead his own kindness to Abraham in the past and he drew attention to the fact that Abraham was a sojourner in the land. Abraham accepted the terms, said, "I will swear", and Abimelech had his covenant. Yet there was, throughout the negotiations, an air of wariness between them; they were never entirely at ease together.

Abraham raised just one problem, the problem of a well which servants of Abimelech had forcibly taken from him. Abimelech protested that the thing was done without his knowledge, implying that it would not have been done with his consent. Abraham accepted his assurance and sealed the reconciliation with a gift of sheep and oxen, which also sealed the formal entry into the covenant. Incidentally, it is never said that the well about which Abraham had complained was actually returned to him by Abimelech.

In addition to the gift of sheep and oxen Abraham set apart seven ewe lambs conspicuously, thus arousing Abimelech's curiosity. What did they mean? Abraham's response was that they were a gift to Abimelech and also a witness that "this well" (v.30) was Abraham's, for he had dug it and there would be no question about ownership of it. Thus he named the well Beersheba, the Well of Seven. The name also suggests the meaning, the Well of the Oath, in celebration of the covenant between the two men. So Abimelech departed.

The story of the sending away of Hagar and Ishmael came to its climax at a well. This incident of the establishment of the covenant between Abraham and Abimelech likewise centred on a well. The scene is being set for the emergence of Isaac as the next great figure in Genesis, for, as Abraham was characteristically an altar-builder, Isaac was a well-digger.

Abraham considered the well with Abimelech significant, for he planted a memorial tamarisk tree (RV) in Beersheba (v.33) and "called there on the name of the Lord". Thus Abraham in some sense sanctified this southern end of the land. He called on the Lord under the title of "the Everlasting God" (El Olam), the third title he had used since he set out on his travels. In 14.22 he swore by God Most High (El Elyon); in 17.1 God revealed Himself to him as God Almighty (El Shaddai); now Abraham celebrates this covenant by calling on the Everlasting God. He still had no permanent home, even in the land. He still dwelt in a tent, but he had a lasting portion in God, the Everlasting God, whose presence with him sustained and enriched him long after the "permanent" things, on which other people, such as Lot, set their hearts, had slipped away into oblivion.

Notes

6 On the second occasion when "laugh" is used, the Hebrew word is TSACHAQ (6711), which is ambiguous, being used for laughter due to merriment or scorn. It is ideally suited to the Hebrew practice of word-play, which is prominent in this passage; compare "mocking" in v.9.

9 The Hebrew text has the verb "mocking" (TSACHAQ - 6711) without an object or complement. The verb may mean simply "playing". The Septuagint expands it, "playing with Isaac". The verb is related to the noun "Isaac", a typical Hebrew play on words. It is best to follow the AV here. It explains best how Sarah was so deeply moved as to demand the expulsion of Hagar and Ishmael.

GENESIS 22

The Sacrifice of Isaac and a Hint of His Future

Introductory

This chapter is the climax of the story of Abraham's life of faith. In it he faces the supreme test and emerges victorious. It contains echoes of his initial act of faith in leaving Ur and setting out for Canaan. It also has hints of future dealings which God will have with Abraham's people. From a christian perspective it has strong foreshadowings of Calvary. In Jewish and christian writings it is the part most frequently dealt with of all the life of Abraham. This may be due in part to its remarkable narrative structure, but it is also, and mainly, because of its theological message. No story with a theological burden was ever so far removed from dry-as-dust or book-lined-library treatment. It is vibrant with life and with human experience of a God who can be known and also relied upon in life's deepest crises.

Verses 1-2: God Puts Abraham to the Supreme Test

The opening words, "after these things", especially when read along with 21.34, "many days", suggest that there had been a lapse of perhaps quite a few years since Isaac was weaned. Guesses of Isaac's age in ch.22 - and they are only guesses - vary greatly, from an incredible thirty-seven years to a small fraction of that age. He seems at least to have been able to go on an extended journey and to have carried timber up a mountain side. He was no child in our modern sense of child. There may even be a hint that his age was comparable to Ishmael's when he was driven out, for in the two stories (21.17, compare 22.5,12) Ishmael and then Isaac are referred to as "the lad".

The story is the record of how God "tested" Abraham and showed that he feared God (vv.12,16), making manifest "all that was in his heart" (compare 2 Chr 32.31 in reference to Hezekiah). The opening is paced slowly, one might also say hesitantly, as if the enormity of what God was asking of Abraham must be approached gently. God called Abraham by name and he responded to show he was listening: "Here am I" (RV). This has the effect of drawing the reader's special attention to what follows.

God's words begin gently and can be rendered, "Please take...". But the sentence is weighty with dreadful import concerning "thy son, thy dear son, whom thou lovest, Isaac". Abraham by this time had only one son left, for he had, at God's command, cast out his dear Ishmael. Years had passed by and now his dear son was Isaac, doubly so because all the promises were vested in him, apart from the natural affection which had developed in those years.

Abraham had to face the test of "taking" his son and every word in the opening moves closer to his heart, climaxing in "Isaac", the last word of the description. He was to "take himself" into the region of Moriah. The verb (HALAK - 3212) is the one God had used in 12.1, "Get thee out ..." of Ur. Even the sequence of "thy country, and…thy kindred and…thy father's house" is echoed in the series of references here, ending in "Isaac". What began with that first call upon his faith was reaching its climax in this last call upon it. The place name Moriah is paraphrased by some (see Knox's translation, for example) as "Clear Vision". In Moriah he was to "offer him there for a burnt offering" - a horrendous demand by any standard. The reader has been warned in v.1 that this was God's test for Abraham's faith, but discovers, a few verses later, that all worked out well. Abraham however had only this painfully slow opening and dreadful demand, without explanation. Did he remember the echo of 12.1 in the "Take yourself to the region", or in "one of the mountains which I will tell thee of" the parallel in 12.1, "unto a land that I will show thee"?

Nothing like this had been asked of him before. When he left his country, he had God's promise of a land. When he was called upon to sacrifice Isaac he was being asked to sacrifice the son in whom God's promises were stored up, without any promise restated to support his faith. How could this be right? And who had ever heard of God asking for human sacrifice? Molech perhaps, but not God. Only a careful, clear-headed consideration of his own path with God could ever have guided Abraham through this nightmarish moment. Could God bring life out of death? Yes, He had done so in giving him Isaac when he was as good as dead and Sarah's womb was dead (compare Rom 4.19).

The place name Moriah occurs in Scripture in only one other reference, 2 Chronicles 3.1, where it is the site of the temple built by Solomon. If, as seems probable, the places are identical then this was going to be a place of sacrifice in later history. And Abraham was being asked to offer up a burnt offering, the offering which was wholly for God, the offering in which the offerer, in effect, said to God, "All that I am I give to Thee in my proper substitute, this victim". If Abraham could rise to this challenge this event would indeed lead to "clear vision", the vision of man upon earth owing everything to his Creator and prepared to give back everything to Him in worship. This is not something which takes place merely as a theory in a person's head; it is as practical and as costly as it can possibly be.

Verses 3-10: Abraham's Obedience

"And Abraham rose up early in the morning" – the customary response of Abraham to God's demands. It had cost him much, as when he had to part with Ishmael, but never so much as now, when what had at last seemed clear risked being clouded over again. His preparations were methodical: an ass for carrying equipment, two servants to help, split wood for the offering, and in the middle of the list "Isaac his son". He might busy himself with the preparations, but always in the centre of the situation was "Isaac his son". True worship can never be merely a matter of methodical processes; it always involves looking at things, however dear they may be, against the claims of God and then saying, "Yes", to God. So he "rose up, and went unto the place of which God had told him".

A three-day journey gave him ample time for reflection. He must not be allowed to obey God on the strength of a surge of adrenalin. He needed time to consider, to reckon, to weigh up relevant factors. There are many instances in the OT of people who had three days in which to face up to their decisions, and the experience was often sobering. Israel went three days into the wilderness, found no water, found bitter water at Marah, then saw the waters "healed" by God's power (Ex 15.22-26). Similarly, when they were approaching Jordan in their journey to Canaan, they stayed for three days before the final approach to Jordan to prove the power of God to open a way through for them (Josh 3.2). On their journey, then, Abraham had three days in which to reflect on this latest and greatest proof of God's power and care. Hebrews 11.19 says that he reckoned "that God is able to raise up, even from the dead" (RV). He had seen God's power to bring life out of death, but this was a step further, God's power to raise dead people.

The third day brought the moment of truth when Abraham "lifted up his eyes", always an indication in Genesis of a significant looking (compare 13.10,14; 18.2; 24.63). What he saw was the "place". It was time for this most sacred moment in Abraham's dealings with God to be arranged as between God and himself, with only Isaac present. He instructed the young men to stay there with the ass. He and Isaac would "go yonder and worship, and come again" (v.5). This is the first reference in Scripture to worship in the strict sense - 18.2 is not quite comparable. Abraham was prepared to give God his dearest possession, his son. It seems, though, that he was by now trusting in God to do the humanly impossible and grant him to return safely with Isaac - hence the words "and come again" quoted above. This interpretation gives more cohesion to the story than, for instance, a suggestion that Abraham was saying what he believed to be inaccurate, if it is assumed that he did not believe Isaac would come back.

The moment had come for Isaac to begin to feel his part in the event. He must bear the wood on which he would be laid on the altar. Commentators understandably feel here echoes of the story of the Lord Jesus when He "bearing his cross went forth" (Jn 19.17) to be crucified. Abraham himself accepted the burden of the flint - which appears to be what is meant by the "fire" - and the knife. They must have been heavy in the old man's hands. "And they went both of them together". In the reference to what Isaac carried there may be a hint that he also was a volunteer in this sacrifice, ignorant though he evidently was at this point of what was to happen.

No mention thus far of any word from Isaac. But then comes the only recorded conversion between Abraham and Isaac at any stage of their life together. The conversation developed slowly and hesitantly, like the one between God and Abraham in vv.1-2. First a polite, "My father", answered by, "Here am I, my son". Isaac could see the obvious lack of a victim if they were going to make a burnt offering. His question, "Where is the lamb?" marks one of the great moments in OT foreshadowings of the Lamb of God. Abraham's answer was literally correct and sounds confident enough. God would provide for Himself the lamb. "So they went both of them together". No other words recorded. Was it a silent journey, two men busy with their own thoughts?

"And they came to the place…". "And Abraham built an altar there", an exercise of which he had had good experience, but never in circumstances like these. Next he laid the wood in order on the altar. This must be done in proper order, for it was for God. Psalm 5.3 (RSV) is a comment on this: "O Lord … in the morning I prepare a sacrifice for thee, and watch". The verb there rendered "prepare" (ARAK - 6186) is the word normally used in the Levitical offerings for setting all in order in a sacrifice (compare Lev 1.8,12), and it is the word used here in Genesis. Abraham was determined to do the will of God carefully and fully.

Then we read, "and bound Isaac his son, and laid him on the altar upon the wood". Never in the history of Israel was such an offering ever laid on God's altar. This is what Abraham was prepared to do because he believed God. So says James (2.21-23) - "faith wrought with his works, and by works was faith made perfect". And what of Isaac? There is nothing about what he said or did. He presumably submitted without being told by his father what was in his mind about God raising him from the dead. Heaven was silent. "And Abraham stretched forth his hand, and took the knife to slay his son" (v.10), as a man might slay a lamb. What devotion to God's word and God's goodness! To all intents Abraham obeyed and offered up Isaac, as Hebrews 11.17 says: "By faith Abraham, when he was tried, offered up Isaac".

Verses 11-19: God Intervenes and Confirms His Covenant Promises

The verse in Hebrews 11 goes on (RV): "yea, he that had gladly received the promises was offering up his only begotten son". The word "was offering up" indicates that he was prevented from completing the action. It was never completed, for heaven's response to the obediently lifted knife was swift and urgent. This is one of those great occasions when God called men by name with the urgency of a double call. Abraham as so often was quick to respond, "Here am I". God's message to him was to do "the lad" no harm; the point had been fully established: "for now I know that thou fearest God". God of course knew it all along, but Abraham had to prove it. Now God knew it experientially. Faith must be "made perfect", as James would say, by works. This was the supreme test of faith, and Abraham's faith had stood the test. His faith caused him to view God with fitting reverence, here called "fear".

God's words in v.12 are wonderful: "thou hast not withheld thy son, thine only son, from me". The Septuagint renders this: "for my sake thou hast not spared thy beloved son". The mind goes to Romans 8.32: "He that spared not his own Son, but delivered him up for us all, how shall he not with him also freely give us all things?". Is it too much to read in this incident in Genesis 22 a faith and devotion which moved the heart of God as He looked forward to what was already an established purpose, that He would show His wonderful grace by not sparing His own Son? Paul's adaptation of the words from Genesis suggests that he sees Genesis as a picture of God giving His Son. God understood how Abraham felt, in the sense that He had already purposed to give His Son for us.

Once again "Abraham lifted up his eyes" (v.13). This was the place of clear vision indeed. He saw "behind him a ram caught in a thicket by his horns". Often at moments of crisis the answer to the problem is within reach, but there has to be a turning round to become aware of it. God had provided a ram for a burnt offering. It was securely caught, held by its strongest feature, its horns. It was also held in a way which put no blemish on it, not held by a part which would tear and bruise. God's provision is always of perfect quality.

Isaac need not die, for God had provided a ram for a burnt offering instead of him. Abraham acted promptly in taking and offering it. What he had said had proved correct and God's provision had been seen. The story, which had suggested the perfect harmony of Father and Son as our Lord Jesus went to the place of sacrifice, now suddenly provides a vivid picture of a substitutionary sacrifice, a ram instead of Isaac. Here at Moriah, where later generations would come to worship God through victims which would die instead of them at the temple, the principle of substitutionary sacrifice was vividly portrayed. But further, it was near this same place that God provided finally a perfect, unblemished, substitutionary Sacrifice. Small wonder that this chapter has been the subject of much writing and the cause of much worship by Christians.

Abraham's response to this remarkable provision by God, which had vindicated his faith, was to name the place Jehovah-jireh, "the Lord will provide/see" (v.14). It was a place of vision and of God's provision. The two ideas are interlocked in the verse. The place came to be recognised as most important, a sacred site, honoured by a traditional saying, "In the mount of the Lord it shall be provided/seen". This title, Jehovah-jireh, is the first of a number of notable instances which honour the Lord by giving Him a title compounded of His name (Jehovah) and an association which His people wish to commemorate.

God had not finished yet. He called again to Abraham out of heaven and swore an oath to him. God acts in sovereign freedom, but He responds to His people's faith-obedience. Abraham had "done this thing", not withholding his son, his only son, and God expressed His appreciation by repeating the covenant undertaking. This was the climax of God's promises first given in their basic form in ch.12. Now God was going to bless Abraham abundantly - this is the meaning of "in blessing I will bless thee". God does not need to swear to us. Men swear to give their words greater weight and certainty, so they swear by One greater than themselves who is absolutely trustworthy. God would show the certainty of His covenant with Abraham, so He swore, for Abraham's sake, by His own name, the highest authority by which one can swear. As Hebrews 6.13,14 puts it, "Because he could swear by no greater, he sware by himself, saying, 'Surely blessing I will bless thee'". God would also multiply Abraham's descendants abundantly to become as innumerable as the stars of heaven, or as the grains of sand on the sea shore. Moreover, his descendants would occupy their enemies' strongholds and rule over them. In his descendants would all the nations of the earth be blessed. God always intended that a nation which He conspicuously blessed would be a vehicle for divine blessing to other nations. This has never happened through Israel as it should have done. There is, however, reason to rejoice that in a future day God will bless all the nations through Him who is Abraham's seed. Then Israel will be the head of the nations and not the tail (Deut 28.13), for through Christ's rule they will fulfil God's purpose in choosing them to be a blessing. God's purpose was free and unconditional, but, through His grace made effective in Abraham, it will be seen to be in harmony with Abraham's faith-obedience.

So Abraham and his young men returned to Beer-sheba and he dwelt there. Oddly, no mention is made of how Isaac reacted to all of this, or of what he felt or said after that one exchange as "they went both of them together". The story is a story of Abraham's faith being tested and found genuine, not a human-interest story of people's feelings. The modern press would major on Isaac's feelings, but God's Word is different.

Questions have sometimes been asked about where Sarah was during the events of this chapter, or how much, if anything, she knew of the command of God. The fantastic stories which the Jewish writers in particular have woven around Sarah's absence from the story should demonstrate the futility of such speculation. It is the story of the testing of Abraham's faith and Sarah is not involved.

Verses 20-24: A Hint for Isaac's Future

It seems irrelevant at first that at this point, after the triumph of Abraham's faith and before Sarah's death, there should be this note about the family of Nahor, Abraham's brother, of whom nothing has been heard for so long. Milcah had borne him eight sons. His concubine, Reumah, had borne him four sons. One of his sons, Bethuel, had a daughter called Rebekah. Rebekah is the only girl mentioned in this genealogical note. She had eleven uncles, all included, and her father, but she is the only girl listed. Her inclusion is obviously in preparation for Isaac's story. Now there is mention of his future wife set in her family context. Immediately following this note (23.1-2) is the account of Sarah's death and burial, and, in 24.67, Isaac "brought her [Rebekah] into his mother Sarah's tent, and took Rebekah, ... and Isaac was comforted after his mother's death".

GENESIS 23

Verses 1-2: Sarah's Death

Sarah had established a noteworthy record by giving birth to her only child when she was long past the age at which, humanly speaking, she could conceive. God was at work to establish that He was willing and able to make good all His promises. Now Sarah was dead, almost forty years later. She had had a long and eventful life, reaching what was considered as a good old age of 120 years, and an extra seven years for good measure. She was, says Peter (1Pet 3.5-6), one of the holy women of old, wife of the man who had so long before received the promises. But her death and burial, as will be seen, were not recorded in Scripture just because, or even mainly because, she was such a great woman.

She died in Kiriath-arba, which was the older name of Hebron. This was an area connected with many of Abraham's most memorable experiences with God, for it was near to Mamre (compare, for example, 13.18, where Abraham built an altar at Mamre, in Hebron). Sarah belongs to the story of God's dealings with Abraham in promises and the covenant relating to land and posterity. Hence the note that Kiriath-arba was "in the land of Canaan". Her story in Genesis began in 11.31 at her leaving Ur with her husband. Some of their kin had been left at Ur, and some had stayed at Haran, but Sarah went on with Abraham to the promised land. Now she was to be buried there. Ur and Haran were in the past; the present and the future were linked with Canaan.

Abraham had many memories of Sarah, some of them no doubt sobering as he could recall his own failures. But prominent in the story of this chapter is his sorrow at his loss of Sarah after so many years of marriage. This is the first mention in Genesis of a man weeping. Hagar wept (21.16) when she was in distress for her son as she went with him in banishment from the land. Abraham's sorrow for Sarah was deep, but the narrative places the events connected with Sarah's death firmly in the land and in a context in which possession of the land is to the fore. Sarah's name disappears from the story until the brief mention of her funeral in v.19.

Verses 3-20: Abraham Buys a Field in Canaan

During the negotiations in this narrative Sarah is only referred to indirectly, for example as "my dead", or "thy dead". The story of the transaction is symbolic in its import. Sarah died in the land and would be buried in it. God had promised the land to Abraham and his descendants. How then would he obtain a place to bury Sarah? He must buy it, for he did not own even one field yet.

He turned, then, from his weeping "before his dead", rose up (v.3, compare v.7) and addressed the business in hand. He approached "the children of Heth", that is the Hittites. He was, he told them, only a resident alien, which is probably the significance of the expression "a stranger and a sojourner with you" (v.4). His request was to purchase a burying-place. That he wanted to purchase it is made clear by his expression, "a possession of". This would be the first property owned by him in Canaan, purchased to "bury his dead out of his sight". No previous burials were recorded in Genesis; only Abraham had received God's promise (15.15) that he himself would be "buried in a good old age". This burial serves to carry forward the transition from Abraham to Isaac, but it also, perhaps more importantly, carries forward the theme of possessing the land. It seems that there should be no surprise if God begins very slowly the process of fulfilling His promises of innumerable descendants and a land for a possession.

The narrative of the transaction is best read as a detailed account of a formal contract drawn up with due courtesy. An important feature of this business etiquette is its obliqueness. So the Hittites politely remonstrated that Abraham was not really just a resident alien but on the contrary "a mighty prince", or literally, "a prince of God". It may be that the phrase "among us", which they added to the "mighty prince", was a courteous modification of Abraham's phrase "with you" - he was almost one of themselves, they were suggesting.

Their first suggestion, while generously couched, does less than offer to sell him a burying-place. He could have the very best place (v.6), whichever he chose, none would deny it to him, but there was no offer to sell it to him. Attention has sometimes been drawn to the repeated "bury thy dead" in v.6, coming at the end of the polite sentences, as if reminding him that they were well aware that he really did need urgently to come to some agreement.

Abraham was determined to carry the negotiation forward. His rising up (v.7) suggests that he was about to make a formal proposal. Attention is drawn to the fact that he was negotiating with "the people of the land", and, in view of the promises of his future possession of the land, this was going to be a most important symbolic purchase. But if they could be courteous, so, very properly, could Abraham, so he bowed to them and pressed his proposal. Let them put his case to Ephron, son of Zohar, that he agree to Abraham's purchase "for the full price" (v.9, RV) of "the cave of Machpelah, ... in the end of his field". He needed only a corner of Ephron's property to purchase. He was pressing that it was a purchase he was seeking.

Most translators agree with the RV that v.10 should be translated, "Now Ephron was sitting in the midst of the children of Heth". In other words, he was present throughout this exchange of oblique courtesies and he now carried on the same style of negotiation. His answer, however oblique, was a proper offer, for it was given "in the audience/hearing of the children of Heth", that is it was given among witnesses and therefore could be a basis for a contract. There were witnesses - "all that went in at the gate of his city". Interpreters differ as to whether this expression indicates local rulers or all who happened to be passing. The former seems to fit the context better.

The repeated use of "Hear us/me" (vv.6, 8, 11) is emphasised when a formal bid is being made. The style is similar to the complicated negotiations which used to take place in market places during buying and selling. Ephron's proposal was that Abraham should take the field along with the cave, the audible agreement to be witnessed by the bystanders.[†]

His proposal was framed in terms of "giving" the property, so he still had not agreed to sell it. His use of the verb "give" did not, of course, mean that he was seriously intending to give it to Abraham as a gift. It should be understood as his polite way of avoiding the mention of a price. This is a Middle Eastern tradition in some places even today.

Abraham expressed his positive reaction to this proposal by bowing, even though he had not intended to buy the whole field. He carried the negotiation another stage forward by saying aloud in the presence of witnesses that he would pay the price of the field. In other words he invited Ephron to name his price.

Ephron, still courteous, declared that a piece of land worth a mere 400 shekels should not cause any problems between them. It does seem, when compared with other land deals (for example, 2 Sam 24.24 and Jer 32.9), that the price was high, but Abraham needed the burying-place urgently and market forces were as real in those days as now. Ephron had not, strictly speaking, asked for 400 shekels as the price. He had hinted that that was his price and that they need not quarrel about such a small thing.

That it was seen as Ephron's asking price is borne out in v.16: "And Abraham hearkened unto Ephron; and Abraham weighed to Ephron the silver, which he had named in the audience of the sons of Heth, four hundred shekels of silver ... ". Ephron had formally asked for four hundred shekels before witnesses and Abraham weighed out the amount, "current money with the merchants"; that is, "according to the weight current among the merchants" (NIV). It is remarkable that there was no bargaining, beyond the question of how much Abraham should buy - the cave or the field as well as the cave in it. Certainly the narrative insists that Abraham became, by any reasonable criterion, the legal owner of the field with the cave.

Verse 17 sets out in detail what was included in the sale. It reads rather like an estate agent's detailed description of a property. Verses 17 and 18 also say that this property so described was "made sure unto Abraham", that is became his legally, "for a possession", for he bought it and did not just acquire burial rights. It was legally a binding contract, as having been entered into in the presence of witnesses (v.18). These verses show the importance being given to this purchase by Abraham of even a small part of the land of Canaan. God had said that He would give all of it to him and his descendants. This was the first step towards that end. Happily he and his descendants will not have to buy it piece by piece at prices like that charged to Abraham!

Verse 19 restates the details of the burial, as if to underline its symbolic importance. Sarah belongs to the initial stage of God's plan for Abraham's people. She was dead and Abraham was making a formal statement that his people's future lay in this land. There was no thought of going back to Haran or Ur, or aside to Egypt. The same issue will be taken up again, notably in the arrangement for Joseph's bones (50.25). The Hittites had formally accepted that Abraham had acquired legal ownership of a field and all in it in their territory and according to their customs regarding ownership (v.20). This same field features in later chapters for the burials of Abraham, Isaac, Rebekah, Jacob, and Leah (49.31). The use of this burial place in this way declared a continuity of hope in the promises of God to Abraham. It was an act of faith repeated at a number of stages. This was an issue of much greater moment in the chapter than the exposure of Abraham's feelings at the loss of his beloved wife of so many years. This is salvation-history not human-interest tales.

Notes

11 Some scholars have suggested that the purchase of the field would make Abraham legally liable to charges which he would have avoided if he could have purchased the cave alone. Others have challenged whether the legal provisions which are referred to applied in this society at this time. It is, however, an interesting and possibly correct interpretation. It would show Ephron as driving a really shrewd and hard bargain.

GENESIS 24

A Bride for Isaac

Verses 1-9: Abraham Makes His Servant Swear to Seek a Bride

Again, the statement is made that Abraham was old, and is repeated here because he is seen preparing for Isaac's future. This is central to the major theme of innumerable descendants for Abraham through Isaac. If this were merely a human arrangement it would be inexplicable that the subject had not arisen before Isaac was almost 40 years old (25.20). God's entire lack of haste in the story of Abraham and his descendants is remarkable and consistent. Even in modern times, perhaps particularly in modern times, there is the need to learn the frequent necessity of waiting inexplicably long periods for God's time to intervene.

In view of Abraham's advanced age he was about to set his house in order before he would die. He had experienced divine answers to many questions and had received many promised blessings. It was time to make arrangements for future descendants by finding an appropriate bride for Isaac. Accordingly he called his senior servant, evidently Eliezer of Damascus (compare 15.2) though he is not named in this chapter.

The task given to the servant was so momentous that it must be marked by a solemn oath taken by the servant that he would fulfil his mission faithfully. He must put his hand under Abraham's thigh to swear. That is, he must swear on the solemn importance of the procreative process. He swore by the Lord, God of heaven and God of earth, but the oath concerned matters in the realm of procreation; hence the oath with hand on the organ of procreation. The oath was that he would never take for Isaac a wife who was a Canaanite. This prohibition undoubtedly looks forward to the time when "the iniquity of the Amorites" would be "full" and God would command their elimination (Gen 15.16; compare 1 Kings 21.26). He must go to Abraham's own people for a bride. The servant's reaction (v.5) shows him to be a man with a proper sense of responsibility. It is better not to vow than to vow and not perform it (Eccl 5.5). He would not bind himself by an oath to do something if it would be impossible to perform it - if, for example, the woman would be unwilling to follow him to Canaan. In that case, he was asking, would the oath compel him to take Isaac to her in Mesopotamia (v.5)? Abraham's answer confirms what is already known, that the promises of God to Abraham's people are inseparably linked with the land. Therefore Isaac must not go back to Mesopotamia. Abraham recalled that he had God's word and God's oath that Canaan would belong to him and his descendants. In this confidence Abraham was sending his servant, knowing that God would "send his angel" to prepare the way. If, however, the woman refused to come, the oath would not bind the servant. The terms having been clarified in this way, the servant took the required oath and was ready to depart on his mission.

It is easy to see why Abraham would not want a Canaanite wife for Isaac. It is not altogether clear why he wanted simply a woman from the area around Haran, regardless of her religion or family. The area will later be called Paddan-aram (28.2); here in v.10 it is called Aram-naharaim (translated in the AV as Mesopotamia), which means "Aram of the two rivers". The bride would at least be Semitic. In the providence of God she was of their own kin.

Verses 10-28: The Servant Goes and Meets Rebekah at the Well

The servant was suitably equipped as the emissary of a wealthy man on an important mission. Ten camels were needed for transport, for betrothal demanded that gifts be given which represented the wealth and status of the suitor. The possession of ten camels on a mission like this indicated considerable wealth, for camels were still not very common. The status of the suitor was of much greater importance to the bride than that she should know anything about him. The servant's journey took him to the city of Nahor - recalling that old genealogy of Nahor at 22.20-24. Abraham's faith was vindicated: the angel of God had guided him (v.7).

In this section of the story the scene has shifted from Canaan to Aram-naharaim. The story has taken a great leap, ignoring the long journey and giving the setting for the meeting between the servant and the bride-to-be. Thus he is found making the camels kneel outside the city by the well at the time of evening when the women go out to draw water. Even this brief sketch portrays a settled, orderly society, predictable in its movements and depending on each group in society fulfilling its obligations.

The servant knew that this might well be the crucial moment of his journey. Whether he had previously prayed is not told, but he did pray now to the Lord, the God of his master Abraham. He asked for success in his mission that day, and by praying for God to "keep faith with" (or "show kindness to") Abraham, he placed the prayer firmly within the ambit of God's covenant relationship with Abraham. He evidently understood at least one vital issue in prayer, that the ground of requests to God is, at the deepest level, the character of God. It is the principle recognised by Abraham when he cried, "Shall not the Judge of all the earth do right?" (18.25).

This man had a very clear perception of his role as servant, so he provides lessons in serving God. The servant must understand clearly what his master's will is and make sure that he does it. There must be no room for mistakes; hence this man's prayer contains sharp descriptions and precise requests. He meant business and required for his peace of mind answers which would be unmistakable. If we pray to God in reality we can afford to speak to Him clearly and later on, perhaps much later, we shall know that God has said, "Yes", or, "No". If we are content to "say prayers" we shall probably ask in general terms, expect no specific answers and have no means anyway of recognising answers from heaven. The servant's graphic descriptions are characteristic of the man. As befitted a servant he had a good memory for detail, as will be seen later in the chapter.

The substance of his prayer, then, was that, as the women came to draw water, he would ask a damsel to let down her pitcher and give him a drink, she would do so and would also offer to water the ten camels. It was hardly a random way of identifying the right girl, for her offer to water ten camels would indicate her willingness to do hard work as well as her hospitable spirit. It was a very shrewd test of a suitable wife for Isaac. So he would know that God was fulfilling covenant promises to Abraham in the response of the girl.

Again, as in v.10, the action moves swiftly. "Before he had done speaking" Rebekah came out. Her name has appeared only once before, in 22.23 in the genealogy of Nahor's descendants. This identification is repeated here in v.15. Her lineage is given before her appearance or character are described. Both of these are quickly established, for she was very beautiful and a chaste virgin.

She went down to the spring and came up again. He politely made his request, according to plan. The action at this point is very rapid, for he was eager to do his master's will and Rebekah was eager to show hospitality. He "ran" to meet her and she "hasted, and let down her pitcher". Her alacrity matches that of her great relative Abraham when he entertained angels unawares (18.2-8). Her courtesy was impeccable and extended, as he had prayed it would, even to the ten camels. She would continue to draw "until they have done drinking" (v.19). As she poured out one pitcher she "ran" to fill it again, until she had done as she promised. Meanwhile he watched silently (AV "wondering at her held his peace") to see if this was, so quickly, the answer to his prayer.

As the task was completed he was satisfied that this was indeed so. He gave her a gold ring weighing half a shekel, and two gold bracelets weighing ten shekels, asked her whose daughter she was and enquired about lodgings. She gave him the names of her father, her paternal grandmother and her grandfather, but the servant still did not know her own name. She assured him that it would be no problem for them to accommodate him.

His response was to bow and worship the Lord and pray, presumably out loud. He acknowledged God's "faithful lovingkindness" (AV "mercy and truth") to his master Abraham in that He had guided him to the house of a relative of his master. Abraham had said that God would guide him and He had indeed done so. Rebekah stood listening and promptly ran and reported at home all that had happened (v.28).

Verses 29-49: The Servant, Welcomed by Laban, Explains His Mission

Rebekah's father was Bethuel, but for reasons nowhere explained he does not feature at this point in the story. In v.28 she ran to her mother's house. Here in v.29 her brother Laban appears as the moving force in the household. His eagerness to entertain the servant was not less than Rebekah's. In view of the subsequent history of Laban careful note should be taken of his motivation in v.30; when he saw the valuable gifts which Rebekah had received he was moved with hospitable emotions. He ran to the well and found the man waiting there with the camels. His greeting, "thou blessed of the Lord", would suggest that he had not been instructed in the principle of laying hands suddenly on no man. In fact, he was more concerned with laying hands on the valuable gifts than on the man. His assurance that he had "prepared the house, and room for the camels" can hardly be taken literally, for he had been in such a hurry to run to the well that he had scarcely had time to make any preparations. These first impressions of Laban's shrewdness will be fully justified later.

The arrival at the house was followed by the necessary chores of unloading the camels and feeding them, then washing the feet of the travellers. By this time some food had been prepared and all seemed set for the servant to be assured of his welcome and - who knows? - maybe made less vigilant than he should be. This servant had not been chosen for his mission without good reason. No doubt the food was enticing, but his master's business came first. He would not eat until he had told his mission. Laban was shrewd enough to know that he must accept this, and his crisp, "Speak on", is in marked contrast to his earlier verbose welcome.

The story which the servant told is broadly familiar from the earlier chapters. It is a thorough resumé of the background to his present mission, the precise terms used by Abraham in giving him his task, and the response which his proposal required from his host and Rebekah. Firstly, he was present with authority from his master Abraham. His description (v.35) of Abraham's greatness and wealth, based on God's blessing, is a reminder of the terms which God had used when He called Abraham originally (12.2-3). God had made his name great, had blessed him with wealth. The present mission was a step towards the fulfilling of God's promise of innumerable progeny and a great nation to spring from Abraham. With admirable economy the servant described how Isaac was the only son of his mother's old age and the sole heir to all his father's great wealth. This part of the situation must not be clouded over by any verbiage.

The mention of Abraham's son (who incidentally remains anonymous in the servant's account) prepares the way for the heart of the message - a wife for this wealthy heir. The servant was so sure of having been guided by God that he focused on the "kindred and…father's house" part of Abraham's more general instruction that he should go "unto my country and to my kindred" (v.4). He ventured to add a clause to what Abraham had said: "The Lord, before whom I walk…". The servant was painting a picture of a father who was a man of God, a true picture, but not exactly in words which Abraham had used. Laban and the family could scarcely miss the implication about God guiding him (v.40). If there was going to be an obstacle, he suggested, it would be set up by the family of Rebekah - "if they give her not to thee" (v.41, RV).

He related the details of his prayer at the well and its immediate answer, item by item. On one point commentators argue that the servant reversed the order of events. In the narrative of the meeting with Rebekah and his gift of gold to her (v.22) the gift preceded the questions about whose daughter she was. In his retelling, the question about whose daughter she was (v.47) preceded his putting "the ring upon her nose, and the bracelets upon her hands" (RV). Perhaps when he discovered who she was he put on her the gifts which he had already given into her hands. Nothing of any great import can be based on this detail.

After he had told his story he concluded with an account of how he had worshipped the Lord who had guided him to his master's kinsman. The Lord had acted with covenant kindness. All that remained was for Rebekah's kinsfolk to act towards their kinsman Abraham with matching kindness. If they refused he would have to go to some other family. The servant had made his case as strongly as he could, for he was sure that the Lord had guided him "in the right way".

Verses 50-61: Mission Accomplished, the Servant Leaves with Rebekah

The agreement of Rebekah's family to the servant's proposal brings the only appearance of Bethuel, her father, in the whole story. He must have been very old or completely incapable of leading in family matters. It is noticeable that the agreement came from "Laban and Bethuel", in that order. They agreed that the Lord was at work in the servant's mission and had made His will known. They were therefore not in a position to take any decision which was independent of the Lord's. This interpretation of "bad or good" is almost exactly parallel to that suggested for "good and evil" in 2.9. So Rebekah was free to go to be the wife of Abraham's son. The matter had been settled without any mention of Isaac's name or character, only his financial position. It had also been settled without reference to Rebekah's wishes. Later she would have a decision to take about timing, but on this basic question she was not consulted.

The servant could only respond once again by worshipping the Lord for prospering his mission. Now he was free to bestow on Rebekah the full splendour of his master's gifts - silver, gold, clothing. There must be no stinting on the bride-money, for Abraham was a great man and greatly blessed by the Lord. Rebekah's family also received the costly gifts which they rightly expected - and interestingly, once more, her brother and mother are mentioned, but not her father.

Only then did the servant think of supper. One could easily have forgotten that he had not eaten yet. And so to bed. Next morning his first thought was to be on the road back to Abraham, for his task was not yet completely done. But the family, having agreed to a profitable match for Rebekah, were not willing to be in a hurry to let her go. After all, the deal had been struck and the gifts had been given! So they pleaded that she be allowed to stay for "ten days or so" (NIV). They had agreed to the match on the basis that the Lord had made His will known in the matter. Now (v.56) the servant took that same line as justification for his haste, for the Lord had prospered his way and would doubtless expect him to complete his task with all due dispatch. But the family were not content this time to accept that the Lord was at work. They wanted a decision from Rebekah, perhaps hoping that she would plead to stay for some time. The timing of her departure was the only matter on which she had a choice.

If they had hoped that her loyalty to them would lead her to delay her departure as long as possible, they were to be disappointed. The question to her was simple and direct: would she go with Abraham's servant? Her reply was equally to the point: "I will go". So she was sent away, together with her nurse. She went with her family's blessing. They wished that she would have vast numbers of descendants (literally, "thousands of ten-thousands") who would be victorious over their enemies. This harmonises with God's promises to Abraham (compare, for example, 22.17). It is revealed at this point that she had slave girls, presumably as Sarah had owned Hagar, and presumably part of her dowry.

Verses 62-67: Rebekah Comes to Isaac

The servant's return journey is of no greater interest to the inspired narrator than the outward journey had been. The scene shifts abruptly to Isaac, in Canaan, at Beer-lahai-roi, in the Negev, going out into the field in the evening to meditate. As he went he "lifted up his eyes", another of those highly significant looks which are marked by that expression. The large group of camels must have been a striking sight, and there can have been little doubt in his mind that this was the returning servant.

The importance of their meeting is signalled by the statement that Rebekah too "lifted up her eyes" and saw Isaac. She dismounted and asked the servant who the man was who was coming to meet them. His reply confirmed what she had probably hoped. "It is my master". Interestingly, Abraham was frequently referred to in the earlier part of the narrative as his master, but, with the return of the servant with Rebekah, Isaac becomes the prominent figure in the story and is referred to as "my master". Proper modesty must be observed, so Rebekah veiled herself to meet her future husband.

The servant reported back to Isaac on how he had fulfilled his mission. Sarah was dead and Abraham ceases to be the main male figure in the story. So Isaac brought Rebekah into his mother's tent, married her and loved her. It is not known how much the servant had told Rebekah about Isaac during the journey. She may have a good deal of information, but it is of no interest to the inspired narrator. Isaac had been told by the servant about the fulfilment of the mission, so he presumably knew how she had measured up to the test at the well and that she had responded willingly to leave home without undue delay. They were a normal couple by the standards of their culture, married by others' choice and learning after marriage to love each other. Thus "Isaac was comforted after his mother's death" (v.67). This statement effectively closes the Abraham-Sarah phase of the story, to open the Isaac-Rebekah phase. As Rebekah is seen taking a high profile in their home, there is perhaps a reflection of the home in which she was brought up, where Bethuel emerges in the story as a cipher and Rebekah and her mother relate to Laban, the organising man.

The story of Abraham's sending his senior servant to get a bride for Isaac has often been seen as providing a picture of Christ's bride being sought from among the Gentiles through the work of the Holy Spirit. This is an interesting exercise, but it is at least as important to locate the story in the wider record of God's dealings with Abraham's seed in the developing covenant relationship.

GENESIS 25

A. Abraham's Death and Ishmael's Genealogy
B. Rebekah's Twin Sons

A. Verses 1-18: Abraham's Death and Ishmael's Genealogy

Verses 1-11: Abraham's Other Wife, and His Death

The account in the first six verses of Abraham's other marriage is a kind of footnote to his life. He has already ceased to be the focus of attention in the main narrative, but he is one of the very great men in the Bible and there are a few facts that must be told in this footnote.

His second wife, Keturah, is mentioned in 1 Chronicles 1.32, where she is described as his concubine. This suggests that she was taken as a second-class wife while Sarah was still alive. It has already been noted that the narrative is not always meant to be chronological.

Why then does the mention of Keturah and her offspring occur here? Abraham had been told by God that he would be the father of many nations (17.5). So far the story has been confined to his two sons, Ishmael outside the covenant, and Isaac the son of promise and heir to the covenant. At this point, when the last details about Abraham are being given, his other sons by his concubine Keturah are mentioned. As with Hagar (16.3) the title given here to Keturah is "wife". Not only are the names of his six sons by Keturah provided, but in the case of Jokshan and Midian their descendants are also recorded.

The descendants of Keturah have names which connect them with different areas of Arabia, Mesopotamia and Syria. This accords with the statement in v.6 that Abraham sent them away eastwards, out of Isaac's way, as he had previously sent Ishmael. Abraham gave them gifts, for it was not God's intention that they should inherit alongside Isaac. They were thus acknowledged as sons of Abraham, but in a secondary sense as far as inheritance was concerned. They were founders of other nations but outside the scope of the story of salvation. So was fulfilled the promise to Abraham that he would be father of many nations.

But Isaac was different. Abraham, we read, "gave all that he had unto Isaac". This was a matter of inheritance, not just a gift, and God had decreed that Isaac was the one who would carry on, not only the physical line of Abraham, but also the spiritual line. The faith of Abraham would be replicated in Isaac, who would continue the covenant relationship and the link with the land. The others were sons, but were sent away to the east, out of the ambit of the covenant.

It remains now to record Abraham's death, at 175 years. Once again, the narrative is not in chronological order. Abraham was 100 years old when Isaac was born (21.5) and Isaac was forty years old when he married Rebekah (25.20). Isaac was sixty years old when Esau and Jacob were born

(25.26). This means that Abraham in fact lived long enough to see Esau and Jacob in their teens. Abraham, however, ceases to feature in the story after Isaac's marriage, because the focus is on Isaac from that point on.

The record of Abraham's death takes careful account of his exceptional spiritual greatness. At his death he was not only an old man, but he was also "full of years". Knox's translation is somewhat free, but it catches the sense: "He died content in late old age, his tale of years complete". He had finished his course, had kept faith with the Lord within the covenant and was now passing on in Canaan, where the Lord had placed him. His work was faithfully done and he could be content.

Abraham, then, "was gathered to his people". This might at first sight seem to refer to burial in a family burial place. But Abraham was not so buried, and his burial is recorded separately in the next verse. Moreover, three other people in Scripture are said to have been gathered to their people though they were not buried in an ancestral tomb - Ishmael, Moses and Aaron. Moses is a particularly interesting case (compare Deut 32.50; 34.6), for "no man knoweth of his sepulchre unto this day". Obviously the people of God were confident of a continuity beyond death, of personal survival, even if they had no precise theology to back it up. What a privilege it is to be found standing in "our Saviour Jesus Christ, who hath abolished death, and brought life and immortality to light through the gospel" (2 Tim 1.10)! The answers are now available to so many questions to which the people of God had no clear guidance before our Lord Jesus rose victorious from the tomb.

At Abraham's burial Isaac and Ishmael are seen collaborating in the ceremony, the only occasion on which this seems to have happened. Both had a right to be there and a responsibility to honour one who had been a good father to them. God takes note of such occasions. The burial took place where Abraham had purchased land to bury Sarah, the only land that he owned in Canaan. The closing statement in v.11, that "God blessed his son Isaac; and Isaac dwelt by the well Lahai-roi", is an indication that he inherited the role of Abraham, dwelling in the land. Incidentally, once again Isaac is associated with a well, for its name means "The well of the Living One who sees me".

Verses 12-18: The Genealogy of Ishmael

These seven verses constitute "the generations of Ishmael", an interlude between sections of the main story. In 21.20-21 Moses records how Ishmael grew up and was married away from the promised land and the covenant people. After that there is no mention of him until he joined Isaac at his father's funeral. The account of the acceleration of the ripening purpose of God will occupy the next part of Genesis. First it is necessary to remove Ishmael from the narrative by giving a brief genealogy which will effectively draw a line under his story.

First he is recorded again as Abraham's son, born to him by Hagar, who is described as "the Egyptian", then as "Sarah's handmaid". Ishmael's is unmistakably a second-class line: he is not the heir to the promises. He lived a long life of 137 years, and "was gathered unto his people". He had twelve sons, an interesting contrast with Isaac, who had only two (compare 21.18 regarding Ishmael's numerous descendants).

The descendants of Ishmael were nomadic, living in villages and "encampments" (v.16, RV). One of his sons was Kedar and various Scriptures refer to the tents for which Kedar (the place) was famous, the black bedouin tents made from goat's hair as referred to in Song of Solomon 1.5: "I am black, but comely, ... as the tents of Kedar". This accords well with the summary of Ishmael's life-style given in 21.20. Those of his sons whose names can be linked with tribes can be located broadly in northern Arabia. While nomadic, they appear to have had organisation, so that they had a "prince" over each "nation" or "tribal group" (v.16).

The summary in v.18 of the extensive area where they dwelt may reflect their nomadic way of life. It stretched from Shur, south-west from Canaan and on the borders of Egypt; included Havilah, which appears to have been in south-west Arabia; and took in Ashur, south-east from Canaan. This interpretation is based on translating v.18 along these lines: "They dwelt from Havilah to Shur, which is opposite Egypt approaching Ashur. Opposite all his brothers he settled" (Wenham). Once again there is a hint of the tension between Ishmaelites and their neighbours.

B. Verses 19-34: Rebekah's Twin Sons

Introduction to the Generations of Isaac (25.19 - 35.29)

The section entitled "the generations of Isaac" formally starts here, and, as expected, deals mainly with the family and descendants of the person named, Isaac. At 11.27 began the section on the generations of Terah, in which the main character was Abraham. That section ended at 25.11. The very short section entitled "the generations of Ishmael" starts at 25.12 and deals with the later fortunes of his descendants. Here in 25.19 the generations of Isaac begin and will last until 35.29, which records the death of Isaac. The main subject of the section, however, is God's education of Jacob.

Verses 19-20: Isaac's Marriage

This is a summary of the basic data about Isaac's birth and marriage. Both of these are set down formally. A point of some significance is the fact that Rebekah is described not only as daughter of Bethuel the Aramean (RV margin) but also as sister of Laban the Aramean (RV margin). Laban is being brought to notice because he will feature prominently in the Jacob story. This brief introduction, then, forms a link between the facts gleaned in the previous chapter and the section which is now being opened.

Verses 21-26: Two Sons for Isaac and Rebekah

By this time some of God's promises to Abraham were being fulfilled, or indeed had already been fulfilled. He had been blessed with great wealth, he had reached the promised land and purchased a token field to which he had legal title. He had descendants through Ishmael outside the covenant, and also through his concubine Keturah, but again outside the covenant. In the covenant community Abraham himself was still alive, he had his son Isaac and Isaac's wife Rebekah. And so the total remained during the twenty-year wait between Isaac's wedding and the birth of Rebekah's only children, twin sons.

Human arrangements were of no avail; only God gave offspring. And Rebekah was barren. Isaac acknowledged his dependance on God for the offspring which would fulfil God's promises of descendants. No mention is made of when he prayed, but it might be expected that he would do so when it first became evident that Rebekah was barren. If so he had to wait a weary time for the answer. However, what is recorded in Genesis is that his prayer was heard, rather than that it was a long time before it was heard. Piety is no guarantee that God will answer every petition quickly.

The clash of interest in the inheritance, between Hagar's son Ishmael and Sarah's son Isaac, was something which could be easily understood. After all, the union with Hagar had been a way contrived by Sarah to help God out of a difficulty which He did not really have, and anyway Hagar was a bondmaid. In the case of Isaac's heir there was no link with a bondmaid. Rebekah was at last pregnant by Isaac and there could be no problem about inheritance or a place in the covenant - surely not?

But the account contains a sharp change of tone: "And the Lord was intreated of him (responded to his entreaty), and Rebekah his wife conceived"; then, abruptly, "And the children struggled together within her" (vv.21-22). The verb "struggled" sets the scene for much strife in the chapters which follow. Even though the unborn children were twins, of one father and mother, a difference was going to emerge between them. Rebekah was puzzled. Why had God, after these twenty anxious years, granted her conception, only to allow a difficult pregnancy? This appears to be the general meaning of the enigmatic question: "If it be so, why am I thus?" She felt that the violent struggle going on in her womb was a portent of trouble, and she was alarmed. She did the proper thing by asking the Lord about it.

The Lord's answer is one of great importance for an understanding of His ways. She must understand that she was not going to be simply a mother of her husband's children. She was going to be the mother of two nations through the twins. The people descended from the first to be born would serve those from the second. God's power and grace have already been seen in His dealings with Abraham and his family. Here His sovereign choice is introduced. In the lives of Esau and Jacob features are seen which would indicate reasons for God's dealings with them. Here God declares His intentions for the future of the nations descended from twins as yet unborn: the people descended from the elder would serve those descended from the younger. God's choice is the only reason needed for the difference in the destinies of the two peoples. Verse 23 is quoted by Paul in Romans 9.10-12 in this sense: "but when Rebekah also had conceived by one, even by our father Isaac; (For the children being not yet born, neither having done any good or evil, that the purpose of God according to election might stand, not of works, but of him that calleth;) it was said unto her, The elder shall serve the younger". All of which is Paul's commentary on the destinies of the twins' descendants as nations.

The first to be born, then, was an unprepossessing baby, "reddish" and hairy. Neither of these features would be desired by a mother in her new baby. The redness may have been in the hair with which he was covered. It is not possible here to attempt to grapple with the multi-layered Hebrew puns in the description and the naming. Suffice it to say that the ideas of redness and hairiness encompass the name of Esau, his people Edom and their place Mount Seir.

The second son was born clutching his brother's heel. This action of course is highly symbolical of Jacob's grasping what Esau might have expected to have. So they called him Jacob, for his name sounds rather like the word for "heel" (AQEB - 6119); the word "heel" is also connected in Hebrew with a verb "to supplant, or follow closely" (AQAB - 6117). The name Jacob, in its longer form Jacobel, would mean "God protects him". The play on names is typical of Hebrew. This little incident at his birth establishes the main characteristic of Jacob especially in his earlier life - his struggle to be one move ahead of others.

The tradition of a vulnerable heel has been encountered already in the reference to the seed of the woman in ch.3. It recurs here in the birth-story of Jacob and Esau. It resurfaces, interestingly, in ancient Greek legend, in the story of the hero Achilles, who was said to be invulnerable except in his heel. Obviously this tradition caught the imagination of the ancient world.

Verses 27-34: Esau Sells Jacob His Birthright

The preparation for the next crucial incident is very terse: "And the boys grew". The struggle in the womb was going to develop and sharpen into competition between the boys and bitter conflict which would drive them apart by many miles. So, from slight beginnings, the influences and relationships which are experienced when young may develop into things which will exert an irresistible compulsion on adult life.

The description of Esau's appearance in v.25 may have been designed to hint at what kind of man he would be. He attained great skill in hunting and loved the open-air life. Jacob, by contrast, was a quiet man, more at home among the tents than in the hunt. There is some disagreement about the word which appears in the AV at v.27 as "plain" (TAM - 8535), but there seems no good reason to depart from translations such as "quiet".

The saga of strains and stresses in family life continues. Isaac himself makes little impact, and the story has to be read carefully and his motives probed to get any picture of the man. He was passive, or at least submissive, during the incident when he was to be sacrificed. He was even passive in the choice of a wife. His wife Rebekah, on the other hand, always appears active and decisive. However, at this point it is disclosed that they were both guilty of a dangerous favouritism. Isaac loved Esau because he had a taste for the game which Esau brought home from the hunt. There is no clue as to what he thought of Esau as a person or what kind of relationship existed between them as people. The basis for his partial love seems flimsy. Rebekah loved Jacob, and no reason of any kind is given for this. Perhaps he was easier to manage, or more helpful, or perhaps she remembered the divine word, "the elder shall serve the younger".

The occasion for the first open rift between the young men was simple. Jacob was making a stew. In came Esau from the field, exhausted with his active pursuits. He saw the stew and politely, but urgently, asked for it. Its red colour seems to have appealed to him, for he repeats the word "red" (ADOM - 122) in his request. The inspired record links the colour red here with the name of his descendants, the Edomites. Jacob's reply was a contrast to Esau's spontaneous outburst of enthusiasm for food. He dispensed with politeness: "First (or perhaps "Immediately") sell me your birthright". He had obviously been meditating on a deal of this kind and had his proposal ready to formulate. Esau, driven by appetite, and by his own account ready to die of hunger or exhaustion, reasoned that a dying man would have little use for a birthright. What he needed was food! Jacob immediately came back with a brusque: "Swear to me immediately!". His cold, calculated ruthlessness is chilling. He is grabbing Esau's heel. The swearing of an oath declares that this deal is binding and permanent.

As so often in Genesis stories when people were unwittingly taking momentous decisions Esau's capitulation is described baldly and flatly: "and he sware unto him: and he sold his birthright unto Jacob" (v.33). He received the lentil stew, ate and drank and rose up and went his way. To him it was a simple thing of little importance. But there is no doubt about the importance of the incident to God and His inspired penman: "thus Esau despised his birthright". It would have given him a place of honour among God's people, but he thought nothing of that. It would probably have given him a double portion of the inheritance, but his vision was too short to see so far ahead. It was linked with the blessing of God, for God was committed to bless the line of Abraham and Isaac, but he had no thought of such things. It is often in the everyday things that the believer manifests where priorities lie and how real, or unreal, spiritual pretensions are. Esau lost out that day, not just because of an appetite for stew, but because he had little appetite for what God set before His people as goals.

We are not asked to prefer either Esau or Jacob. Esau is written off in Hebrews 12.16 as a profane (or godless) person, who for one morsel of food sold his own birthright. His casual attitude to his privileges cannot be condoned. Yet, in some ways, he can be less forbidding than his calculating, grasping brother. God had purposed in any case to give the priority to Jacob, even if he had not cheated Esau. So in the end it is in Jacob that the story of divine purpose is carried forward. After all, the story tells how God fulfilled His purpose through His sovereign grace and mercy, in spite of the failures and sins of those who were in covenant relationship with Him. Whether we like Jacob or not he did desire the birthright and the blessing of God. It will be instructive to see whether we need to adjust our early impressions of Jacob as we see later what changes God's education of him produces. Incidently, Esau is not the last person in the OT who, though oldest in the family, did not live up to his privileged birth (compare 49.3-4). Perhaps we need to learn at times that God is more interested in educating us than in pandering to the pride we may feel in our privileges. Anything we have that is worth having, He has given it to us. Anything we are that is of value to God, He has made us by His grace. "As it is written, He that glorieth, let him glory in the Lord" (1 Cor 1.31).

GENESIS 26

Verses 1-5: Isaac Directed to Gerar in Famine

The mention of a famine "beside the first famine that was in the days of Abraham" serves to link this story with that of Abraham going down to Egypt in a famine (12.10). In this chapter Isaac repeated Abraham's failure during that visit, in disowning his wife. A deliberate comparison is drawn also with Abraham's repetition of the failure when he later lied about Sarah in Gerar.[†]

When Abraham went down to Egypt it was not said explicitly that he ought not to have gone. Only the results and later history suggested it. Here Isaac was explicitly forbidden to go to Egypt. God appeared to him as He had done to Abraham (12.7) just before his descent to Egypt. God reassured Isaac with the knowledge that there was a place to which He would direct him. The language in which this reassurance was couched is close to that used when God directed Abraham (12.1) to leave Ur. Isaac is presented here as the heir to Abraham's spiritual legacy. Indeed this chapter is the most substantial passage in the story of Isaac. Here Isaac himself is observed - not his bride (compare ch.24), nor his sons (compare chs.25 and 27). But in this chapter he is seen more fully than anywhere else as heir to Abraham's blessing by God. Jacob and Esau were vividly introduced in ch.25, in relation to their birth and their interaction over the birthright. Yet here, immediately afterwards, they are totally ignored in the story of Isaac's lapse in Gerar. This seems at first sight very odd. It almost looks as if Isaac's place in the continuation of the story of divine purpose is preserved in this chapter by the exclusion of distractions. It is not necessary to worry about the chronology, for the episodes are not always chronologically arranged.

God not only directed him to stay in Gerar. He also promised to be with him and bless him. This promise to be with him is one which will be seen to be confirmed to Jacob (28.15). This chapter contains echoes of earlier incidents involving Abraham; it also sets up themes which will be taken up again in Jacob's story. God was going to bless him and give him and his descendants "all these lands" (RV), an advance on the promise to Abraham of "this land". God would also establish (RV) with Isaac the oath which He swore to Abraham (22.16-18), in its final form. Moreover, God would multiply his descendants to be as innumerable as the stars. The promise that in his "seed" all the nations of the earth would be blessed repeats God's promise to Abraham (22.18). Verse 5 makes it clear that God had in mind the climax of Abraham's experience of divine promise and blessing, for it refers to Abraham's obedience, which was specially commended in ch.22. The verse contains the first reference in Scripture to laws, using the Hebrew word TORA (8451). Indeed the elaboration of the "commandments, statutes and laws" seems to be intended to emphasise the fullness of Abraham's obedience. As some commentators have put it, his obedience anticipated the kind of demands that God would later make when He gave His law through Moses. God called out Abraham and blessed him, and Abraham responded. He had failures but he was characterised by faith and obedience. The same would be expected of Isaac, and Jacob, and all who in later generations would seek to know God's blessing in their lives.

Verses 6-11: Isaac Repeats Abraham's Failure

When Abraham disowned Sarah in Egypt he anticipated trouble before he even entered the country, and arranged the lie (or half-truth) with Sarah to protect himself from potential threats. That Pharaoh's men had her taken to his harem is proof that Abraham's fear had some grounds. Chapter 20 does not state whether Abraham volunteered the lie when he disowned Sarah as his wife in Gerar, or told it in response to questions. But again, his fears were perhaps well grounded in that she was taken into the palace of Abimelech. In the case of Isaac in ch.26 subsequent events do not show that his fear was fully justified, for he was there a long time (v.8) before his lie was discovered. Admittedly the men of the place asked him about Rebekah, presumably because she was beautiful. Even Isaac's failure, however, is a reminder that he was successor to Abraham. His motives, arising from fear, suggest the link. There was, however, one incidental difference: Abraham's lie was a half-truth, while Isaac's was a whole lie.

The discovery came by accident, one might say. Abimelech looked out through the window and saw Isaac and Rebekah together. Where they were, whether in another building or, as some suggest, a garden, is not important to know. What Abimelech saw showed that they were man and wife. Verse 8 says Isaac was "sporting with" Rebekah. Perhaps this verb should be rendered as "fondling" (Hamilton). At any rate Abimelech was left in no doubt that they were not brother and sister but husband and wife.

Abimelech's reaction to this realisation was one of righteous indignation. Isaac had no excuse except his fear. The form of Abimelech's question, "What is this thou hast done to us?" is normal in legal accusation. It is reminiscent of God's question to Eve (3.13): "What is this that thou hast done?". The substance of the charge is implied in the following statement, that someone might easily have incurred serious guilt by taking Isaac's wife in the mistaken idea that she was his sister. The use of the word "guiltiness" (v.10, ASHAM - 817) introduces the possible notion of religious guilt by violating the holy or touching the forbidden (compare Lev 5.2,3 and many contexts in that book where the word has a sacrificial connotation).[†]

The word "touch" (NAGA - 5060) in v.11 is also common in such contexts. Abimelech accepted full responsibility for guaranteeing the safety and inviolability of Isaac and Rebekah, to the extent of threatening to execute anyone guilty of "touching" them. In such a country, with clear, firm discipline, there was little need for Isaac to be afraid of admitting that Rebekah was his wife. Perhaps, however, the very severity of the king's threat may be an indication that this was an exceptional measure designed to protect these people because they were aliens and not automatically protected by the laws which governed citizens' rights.

In any case, Isaac failed as Abraham failed, and indeed lied more blatantly than Abraham had done. Abimelech's scruples about Isaac's security will be seen to be connected with a growing awareness that this man Isaac enjoyed divine favour. God is still the focus of the action.

Verses 12-22: Isaac's Prosperity Causes Conflict

The next three verses outline Isaac's conspicuous prosperity. Interestingly, he sowed grain and had a bumper crop. The yield of a hundredfold is the highest recorded in the Lord's parable of the sower, even in the best of soil (Mk 4.8). He was the only patriarch who is said to have sown grain. He was gaining a place in the land sufficiently secure to enable him to make this kind of medium-term investment. The sowing of the crop declares that the covenant people have a stake in the promised land. The fruitfulness of his sowing is attributed to God, another sign of His blessing. Verse 13 produces its effect by an accumulation of expressions denoting increase and greatness. His wealth was conspicuous for its steady increase to a formidable level. Verse 14 defines what kind of wealth he had, flocks, herds and a large number of servants. All of this was very visible, and the inevitable result was that "the Philistines envied him". Even today many people envy the Jews their prosperity, and still it is a cause of conflict.

Abraham had arrived at a covenant with the Philistines over water-supply (21.27-32). Evidently they considered that it was a covenant with Abraham and not with his son Isaac, for they filled in the wells which Abraham had dug. Then they told Isaac that he was too successful to stay in the area. His attempts to stop in any part of the valley of Gerar were not acceptable to the Philistines. He was attempting to reactivate his father's water-rights, which they now rejected. This seems to be the intention he had in naming the wells as his father had named them (v.18). The statement that they found a well of "springing (or "living") water" (v.19) suggests symbolically the divine blessing which Isaac enjoyed. But the herdsmen fought, first at the well dug at Esek (Contention), then at Sitnah (Enmity). Isaac, as ever the quiet man of patience and peace, moved on and dug a well at Rehoboth (Room), so named because "the Lord hath made room for us" (v.22). In purely human terms water is the most basic resource. It is the most precious of the natural resources on earth, the one missed most quickly if there is a scarcity. East African tribes still fight to the death over control of wells which stand between a tribe and extinction. Observers of the Middle East predict that water, not oil, will soon be the most hotly disputed resource in the area. Spiritualising the story brings to mind the Lord Jesus calling to people whose celebration of the Feast of Tabernacles had left them empty.

They had had a moving ceremony at the climax of which they poured out water from Siloam to the sounding of trumpets, all calculated to cause joy and exuberance. But He called, "If any man thirst, let him come unto me and drink" (Jn 7.37). The water of religion had failed them. They needed the water which would be in them a well of water springing up unto eternal life (compare Jn 4.14). Isaac was indeed the man of wells, enjoying the blessing and prosperity which only God could give. He experienced what David expresses in Psalm 31.8: "Thou hast set my feet in a large place" (RV).

Verses 23-33: Back to Beersheba

Back then he went to Beer-sheba, a place rich with sacred memories of his father. "And the Lord appeared unto him the same night" (v.24). God's announcement, "I am the God of Abraham thy father," underlines his succession to Abraham's spiritual legacy. God repeated the promises and assurances He had already given him in v.3, and expanded them. Isaac showed himself a true son of his father by his response to the divine encouragement: he built an altar, as Abraham would have done, and called on the name of the Lord. He pitched his tent there, still a sojourner. He placed his own distinctive mark on the experience by having his servants dig a well.

Then he had surprise visitors, Abimelech and his chief men. Isaac was less than courteous to them, for they had forced him out of their area (v.16). His opening question was brusque: "Wherefore come ye to me, seeing ye hate me, and have sent me away from you?". Their reply was conciliatory. They explained that they wanted to enter into a covenant with Isaac, based on an oath, because they had seen how God was prospering him. This would be a covenant of non-aggression, in which each would agree not to harm the other. They were quite correct in saying that they had not "touched" Isaac, and it has been seen that this had overtones of religious scruples in it. It was not quite so accurate to claim that they had done Isaac "nothing but good", in view of their pressure on him to go away. Indeed they resorted to a euphemism when they described their driving him away as sending him "away in peace" - as one would see friends off and wave to them after a social visit! The climax of their conciliatory speech was that he was "now the blessed of the Lord".

Such an approach could hardly be refused. Isaac made a great feast, a sure sign that he was ready to accede to their request for an agreement. The covenant oaths were sworn early the next morning and the visitors went on their way with mutual expressions of goodwill ("in peace"). God set His seal of approval once more on Isaac, for that very day his men found water and called the well Sheba. This was yet another repetition of an experience of Abraham, a covenant with the Philistines and a well called Sheba (compare 21.31-32). If the name of the city near by, Beer-sheba, is differently interpreted in this chapter and in ch.21, this is not abnormal in view of the Hebrew passion for word-play.

Verses 34-35: Esau's Two Wives

This brief note about Esau's two wives belongs, strictly speaking, to ch.27. The search for a suitable wife for Isaac was sufficiently important to merit a very long chapter. She was sought among their own people in Paddan-aram. Esau simply chose two wives for himself, not just one. Both were Hittites, an unacceptable match for someone of the stock of Abraham. His choice reinforces the message that he was not going to be at the centre of the purpose of God for the family of Abraham. Esau's contempt for his birthright matches his disregard for what he must have known were the convictions of his parents about keeping the family free from intermarriage with the Canaanites. One's mind goes back to Noah's family and the curse of Canaan, son of Ham. The sacred record here simply states that the wives were "bitterness of spirit" (literally) to Isaac and Rebekah. Isaac showed inappropriate favouritism toward Esau, but was not so spiritually obtuse as to miss the significance of this choice by his favourite son.

Notes

1 The king of the Philistines, here as in ch.20, is called Abimelech. It is best to take it that he is a later king of the same name. Or perhaps it is a title or quasi-title. The other names repeated here may be similarly explained.

10 The word "guilt" may actually mean "retribution" arising from guilt, in which case the accusation may be more direct than has been suggested above.

GENESIS 27

The Blessing and its Sequel

Verses 1-4: Isaac Plans to Bless Esau

This episode is introduced by a most significant reference to Isaac's dimness of vision due to his advanced years. Its significance is emphasised by the plethora of references in the chapter to the senses - sight, hearing, smell, touch, taste, all feature in the narrative at crucial points. His blindness is perhaps to be contrasted with that of Jacob in ch.48, for there blind Jacob was able to "see" what Joseph could not (48.13-14). Here Isaac is physically and spiritually without the power to distinguish between things that differ. Hence he called Esau, his older son, and prepared to make arrangements to confer on him his formal blessing. There may be something in the suggestion that his intention to keep this ceremony strictly between himself and Esau was abnormal in that his other son was to be excluded from any blessing. The decision to bless Esau in this exclusive way sits awkwardly just after the reference to his unsuitable choice of wives (26.34-35).

Some scholars see in the words, "I know not the day of my death", a formal statement indicating that he was about to make a legally binding disposition of his property. However that may be, he was trying to look ahead and make due preparation against the day of his death. Sadly, his powers of perception were not adequate even to see what was around him in his own house.

Isaac wanted to mark the occasion of the blessing by a celebratory meal with Esau. His weakness for food resurfaces here in the tell-tale "such as I love". His love for Esau, one recalls, was based on Esau's hunting skill which satisfied Isaac's appetite. The details of his request to Esau may also suggest how he viewed him. The quiver and the bow were essentially male equipment: Esau was a real man, a "man's man". He was not, however, God's man, and it is sad to hear old, blind Isaac declare his soul's desire to bless Esau before he died. This was against what God had decreed in the oracle at the boys' birth. So Esau went out to the field to hunt, out to his natural environment.

Verses 5-17: Rebekah Conspires with Jacob

Isaac senses were dull, but Rebekah's were razor-sharp. She overheard Isaac's request to Esau. Isaac had perhaps forgotten the oracle from God which identified Jacob as the son to have the pre-eminence. Rebekah had not forgotten it - was he not her favourite son? It is worth recording that in this episode Jacob is described as Rebekah's son (v.6), while Esau is Isaac's son (v.5).

Always a person of action and initiative, like her brother Laban, Rebekah began to form a counter-plan to Isaac's plan. She briefed Jacob on what she had overheard Isaac say to Esau. She had her plan ready, and all Jacob had to do was obey her (v.8). Let him go to the flock and fetch two good kids, with which she would make a stew just like the one which Isaac enjoyed so much when Esau made it for him. All Jacob had to do was to take the food she had cooked to Isaac, he would eat it, and Jacob would get the blessing. It was entirely Rebekah's plan, devised because Jacob was her favourite - and incidentally, but only incidentally, God's oracle would be honoured. This was another clear case of people in Genesis trying to help God out of a difficulty. Of course God was not in a difficulty, and He did not need crooked devices to help Him carry out His purposes. But Rebekah thought He did.

Jacob had no objection in principle to the plan proposed by his mother. He was happy to deceive Isaac, if he could. But he was not confident that he would succeed in the deception. Isaac could not see, but perhaps he could feel (v.12), and perhaps he would think that Jacob was mocking him and so curse him rather than bless. He does not seem to have had scruples against mocking Isaac so long as Isaac did not find him out. His mother's reply was, "Upon me be thy curse, my son: only obey my voice, and go fetch me them". Her attitude brings into high relief the disunity within this family. Later there is similar disunity in her brother Laban's family (31.15-16). Her energy is impressive, but her mention of a curse is chilling. Something recalls the episode in 1 Kings 21.7 where Jezebel, that wicked woman, said to her husband, "I will give thee the vineyard of Naboth". Like Jezebel, she succeeded in her plan, for she was certainly efficient, but like Jezebel she paid the price.

Jacob obeyed her, as he usually did. Preparations went on apace. The kids were brought, the meal prepared. Then the deviousness of Rebekah's plan emerged. She brought out Esau's robe, kept for special occasions, and dressed Jacob in it. In answer to Jacob's fear that Isaac might detect him by touch, she put goatskin on his neck and forearms. Note how vv.15-17 are full of verbs which detail what Rebekah did, for she was the brains behind the operation as well as the driving force of it. Finally she put the dish, complete with bread, into Jacob's hand, and the play could commence.

There have been previous examples in Genesis of people trying by human ingenuity to bring about what they believed God wanted. It is not clearly stated here that Rebekah made these devious preparations to bring God's plans to pass. It is left to conjecture as to whether she perhaps simply wanted her favourite son to be blessed. It is maybe a reasonable surmise that she placed some value on the fact that if she succeeded in her plan Jacob would gain the blessing, the inheritance, and also the spiritual legacy of Abraham and Isaac. It may be so, but her deviousness is what is emphasised. It should be said at this point that God intended that Jacob would have the blessing and He did not need Rebekah's trickery to achieve that end. How much more interesting if the opportunity had been given to see God at work in His own way rather than to see Him overrule the crookedness of Rebekah. Maybe there is so much of Rebekah in us that we need to see how God can achieve His ends in spite of us, even when it is mistakenly thought that success in using questionable means is a proof of God's approval of our actions.

Verses 18-25: Jacob Deceives Isaac

Jacob's approach to Isaac was appropriately respectful. But almost at once

Jacob was obliged to reinforce his previous steps of deception with an outright lie. It is seldom possible to achieve crooked ends by telling one lie, for lies breed lies. Isaac, surely unwittingly, drove him to it with the simple question, "Who art thou, my son?". His reply was a lie with which he would live for many a year until he learnt to change the claim, "I am ... thy firstborn". In answer to the angel's question (32.27) at Peniel, "What is thy name?" he learned by bitter experience to say, "Jacob". Charades may fool old men whose discernment has gone, but they are of little value when dealing with God.

Jacob quickly passed on from the awkward subject of who he was to the invitation to his father to eat the meal which he had prepared. But Isaac asked another awkward question: "How is it that thou hast found it so quickly, my son?". His reply put his soul in deeper peril, for he brought God into the fiction: "Because the Lord thy God brought it to me". Jacob must have been glad, at that moment, that he had such a resourceful mother, for Isaac asked him to come closer so that he might feel whether he was really Esau. The disguise was good, for Isaac was satisfied with what he felt. Just one point evidently continued to puzzle the old man: the voice was the voice of Jacob. "So he blessed him" (v.23), or, as Allen P. Ross translates it, "and he was about to bless him". The tension and uncertainty are sustained in the narrative in that, at this juncture, the question was repeated: "Art thou my very son Esau?". And again the lie was repeated: "I am". In this vacillating, unsatisfactory way Isaac came to the point where he agreed to eat the apparently real game brought by his apparently real eldest son, in preparation for blessing him.

Verses 26-29: Isaac Blesses Jacob

Evidently now completely satisfied that this was Esau, Isaac invited Jacob to come near and kiss him. This was part of the ceremony of blessing. Again, how Jacob must have rejoiced in his mother's cleverness, when Isaac smelt Esau's cloak with its hint of the open-air life which Esau loved and which provided Isaac with the tasty food which he loved. Everything was *almost* right for Isaac's plan - the touch, the taste, the feel, the smell. Yet he was completely deceived and providentially prevented from going against the purpose of God.

The blessing which he pronounced begins, characteristically of Isaac, with a reference to the evocative smell which he had detected on Esau's cloak. From that rather inauspicious start he moved on to identify correctly the blessing on the field as being from the Lord. Thus he passed on to call down the blessing of God on his son in the form of dew from heaven and abundant crops from the land, corn and wine. The blessing looked forward to more settled occupation of the land in which Isaac had made a first beginning (26.12). Such prosperity, it must be emphasised, was in God's gift. It was mediated through the man who was in the line of men of faith, men whose family line would receive divine promises and learn that God keeps His covenants.

The other side of the blessing was political. First, Isaac's son would enjoy supremacy over peoples and nations. Next, he would enjoy priority over his brothers. The plural here does not necessarily imply that Rebekah had more than two sons. The blessing would be fulfilled in the wider family circle (the more general sense of brothers) as the narrow line(s) of the chosen family took a place of pre-eminence over the rest. The language of the early part of v.29 makes one think inevitably of Joseph, but in ch.49 both Joseph and Judah will be seen as exalted over the other tribes.

The end-piece of the blessing is the familiar curse pronounced on all who would curse God's chosen, and blessing on all who would bless him (compare 12.3).

The blessing was complete. It had been uttered and was irrevocable (compare v.33, "and he shall be blessed"). God had purposed Jacob's blessing and Jacob was blessed. Both Rebekah and Jacob had acted most shamefully to obtain the blessing, and they would spend years reaping what they had sown. Isaac had acted irresponsibly in trying to bless Esau, but God did not need either a responsible Isaac or honourable Rebekah or Jacob to further His purpose. He brought it about in His sovereignty.

Verses 30-37: Esau Returns Too Late

God's timing, as always, was impeccable. Jacob had scarcely left his father's presence with the blessing safely bestowed when Esau came in from hunting. He too brought in a tasty meal made from the game he had caught. He cheerfully invited his father to rise and eat before bestowing on him the promised blessing. Then came the shocking question, "Who art thou?". With sickening apprehension Esau gave almost exactly Jacob's reply, "I am thy son, thy firsborn, Esau". Then it was Isaac's turn to be shocked; "trembling, Isaac trembled fearfully, even to excess" (Spurrell, rendering it almost literally). He managed to stumble out the question about who, then, had brought venison to him before Esau came in, and he added, "and (I) have blessed him? Yea, and he shall be blessed". The pathos of the scene hangs on the irreversibility of what has been said and done.

Esau's reaction is rendered by Spurrell in language similar to that describing Isaac's realisation of what had happened: "...crying aloud, he cried with an exceeding loud and bitter cry, even to excess" (v.34). His plea was, "Bless me, even me also, O my father". But this could not be, for the blessing given to Jacob gave him pre-eminence; it was the blessing designed by Isaac for Esau. Only one of them could be pre-eminent. Jacob had "taken" the blessing. Esau bitterly commented on Jacob's being well named the Supplanter, for he had supplanted him twice, birthright and blessing. Note again, in passing, that Scripture lays the blame for the loss of the birthright on Esau's contempt for it (25.34). Now his anguished question was whether there was not a blessing which Isaac could still bestow. Isaac explained the nature of the blessing he had given to Jacob. The explanation was sufficient to show why that blessing was unique. So what could Isaac do for Esau now?

Verses 38-40: Esau Obtains Less than a Blessing

Esau pleaded for even one blessing. "Bless me, even me also, O my father". Again he wept and cried aloud. But he had made his choice when he despised his birthright, and it was unrealistic to seek the blessing at this late stage. The Genesis narrative at this stage lies behind the comment in Hebrews 12.17: "For ye know that even when he afterward desired to inherit the blessing, he was rejected (for he found no place of repentance), though he sought it diligently with tears" (RV). He sought the blessing in vain, because when the birthright was freely available he despised it for a dish of stew. Of course God was in all of this, because He had sovereignly chosen Jacob, but Esau's choice was free. Our free choices today may preclude us from blessing in years to come.

Isaac must pronounce on Esau what is as near to a blessing as he can come. Most scholars now agree with the RV margin rendering of Isaac's pronouncement in v.39: "Behold, away from the fatness of the earth shall be thy dwelling, and away from the dew of heaven from above". The best has been given to Jacob. Esau must settle for relatively infertile land. He must also be prepared for a life in which he must live by the sword, evidently in an unsettled society surrounded by enemies. He would be in a position of subjection to Jacob, for Jacob had been granted pre-eminence. It is obvious that all of this went far beyond the future of the two young men; it encompassed the national future of their descendants. In this wider context, the best that Esau's descendants, the Edomites, could hope for would be to break, even temporarily, the bondage imposed on them by Jacob's descendants (compare 2 Kings 8.22).

Verses 41-46: The Bitter Aftermath in the Home

Esau's hatred for Jacob because of the blessing was bitter and festering. He felt that Isaac had not long to live and he planned that when Isaac was dead and buried he would kill Jacob. The ugliness of this purpose is underlined by his words, "Then will I slay *my brother*". This recalls ch.4.8 and the first murder of a brother by his brother. Did Esau delay out of respect for his father, or out of fear? The answer is not given, but it has been significant to see how devoted Isaac was to Esau. His expectation of Isaac's death was premature, as events were to prove (compare 35.29).

Esau, however, seemed destined always to be too dull for his sharp-witted mother. She somehow found out what he had in mind. He must have confided in someone what v.41 says was "in his heart". Anyhow, Rebekah again conferred with Jacob. She put the case bluntly: "Esau is taking comfort from the fact that he has a plan to kill you". As he had done when he deceived Isaac, Jacob need only "obey" Rebekah, for she had a plan. He was to go to her brother Laban in Paddan-aram. In "a few days" Esau would cool down and Jacob could come back. Rebekah was usually a very competent manager of people and situations, but here she made a gross miscalculation. This was not a matter of a few days but of twenty years. She would send and fetch him back from there, she said, but in fact she would never see him again. This seems to be the inference to be drawn from the story of later events.

Her fear, she said, was that she would lose both sons in one day. If Esau killed Jacob she would have lost her favourite. But justice would pursue Esau because of blood-guilt, so he too would be killed or exiled. It is worth commenting on the fact that she could safely assume that a man who would murder his brother could no longer live, or at least he would be cut off from the community. This was her appeal to Jacob, to persuade him to flee.[†]

Her approach to Isaac was from a very difficult angle. She could hardly raise, or keep alive, the awkward issue of the hatred between their sons in view of the cause of it. After all, she had been directly to blame for it. Instead she raised a question on which she and Isaac saw eye to eye, the wives of Esau (compare 26.34,35). She referred to them as "the daughters of Heth" to ensure that Isaac would be reminded of how disastrous the match was which Esau had made. Now, she reasoned with Isaac, if Jacob should marry a wife from the same stock, how could she, his mother, bear to live any longer? Rebekah was correct to imply that a repetition of Esau's unwise marriages would be unbearable for Isaac as well as herself. Her arrangement that Jacob should go to Paddan-aram was a sound one. Incidentally, she seems at this stage to have given Isaac no inkling of this plan. Or did she hint at it obliquely? Or did Isaac think of it independently (28.2)? It is interesting to see that, however perturbed she may have been, she had lost none of her initiative or organising flair or deviousness. She was a true sister of Laban.

As in so much of the patriarchal narrative, here is a major character displaying some knowledge of the responsibilities which rest on the people of Abraham, the covenant people of God, while also manifesting features of character which are less than transparently honest. There are no heroes or heroines in the conventional human sense in these stories. There are instead imperfect men and women, acting from mixed motives, but aware of God and ultimately committed to His covenant.

In this chapter the main initiator of action was Rebekah, with Jacob her assistant. Isaac as the heir of Abraham's blessing, bestowed blessing according to the will of God, despite his own efforts to do otherwise. However blind Isaac was, however devious Rebekah's actions were, and however unappealing Jacob seems to be at this stage, God was carrying forward His great plan. Yet the other side of the coin is the truth that the human characters were sowing freely what they would later reap copiously and bitterly.

Notes

45 There is a possibility that when Rebekah said "you both" she meant both Isaac and Jacob. Esau, on this interpretation, would kill Jacob as soon as Isaac was dead; and thus she would lose both her husband and her favourite son in one day.

GENESIS 28

Jacob, Sent from Home, Reaches Bethel

Verses 1-5: Isaac Sends Jacob Off with God's Blessing

So far Jacob has only been seen in his father's home with his family. The manner of his gaining the blessing demanded that he leave home, and Rebekah managed this by raising the vital matter of a suitable wife for him. It was essential, however, that before he left he receive a blessing on his journey from Isaac. The more comprehensive blessing which he had received in the previous chapter was intended, one realises, for Esau.

Isaac, then, called him and charged him not to take a Canaanite wife. It will be remembered that one indication of Esau's unsuitability to be Isaac's spiritual heir was his choice of two Canaanite wives, seemingly without a thought and without any consultation with his parents. Isaac instructed Jacob to go to Paddan-aram to get a wife from among his mother's kinsfolk. It is probable that this instruction was based on the fact that Abraham's servant had obtained a bride for Isaac there. It is not necessary to read into the reference to Jacob's "mother's brother" any oblique, sarcastic suggestion by Isaac that Jacob was Rebekah's favourite son. It may even be that it was considered better for a man to marry a near kinswoman, but on his mother's side rather than his father's. In this case it would be natural to refer to the relationship as Isaac did.

In calling down on Jacob the blessing of "God Almighty" (El Shaddai), Isaac was using the title which God had used in 17.1 when making promises to Abraham of many descendants, indeed many nations as descendants. It is used again by God to Jacob (35.11) when promising him a very similar blessing. To make the implication of this continuity clear Isaac prayed that God would give him the blessing of Abraham, that is the blessing which He had given to Abraham. Not only did he pray for the blessing of God in numerous descendants for Jacob, but he also prayed that Jacob would inherit the land in which he was a sojourner, the land which God had given to Abraham. This was a poignant touch, for not only were all the patriarchs in some sense sojourners, but Jacob was about to embark on a period of movement and insecurity which would last for twenty years. This chapter develops the implications for Jacob of what it meant to have the birthright and the blessing. It also introduces the process of educating Jacob before he could enter on his inheritance in the land. "And Isaac sent away Jacob" (v.5). Then follows a summary description of who precisely would be at journey's end to receive him, namely Laban, Rebekah's brother. Rebekah, it seems, would never see Jacob, her dear son, again. This was the price she must pay for her part in deceiving Isaac. From now on, Jacob would be dealing with Laban, and this would be very different from dealing with Rebekah. She had exercised the guile which was a family feature, but she had exercised it on Jacob's behalf, at others' expense. Now similar guile would be experienced by Jacob, but this time at his own expense. For a time he would succeed in giving as good as he got, but he had to get beyond that method, as he did at Peniel when he again met God.

So many details of this story of Isaac and his family show the tensions of a home divided by parental favouritism. It made Isaac blind to God's rejection of Esau. It made Rebekah willing to resort to unworthy and disastrous subterfuges on behalf of Jacob. It led to the danger of violence and perhaps murder. It blinded both parents to what they should have corrected in their sons. Both parents failed their sons, the favoured one no less than the other. It is a sobering thought for parents to remember the simple words of 25.27: "And the boys grew". As children grow the mistakes made by parents in their relationships with them may become apparent in the directions their lives take and in their ability to relate to each other.

Verses 6-9: Esau Marries a Daughter of Ishmael

Esau had not been very observant. Now he began to take notice. He saw that Isaac sent Jacob away with his blessing to Paddan-aram to get a wife. He noted that Isaac warned Jacob not to take a Canaanite wife. And Jacob had gone away obediently to seek a wife. Esau pondered the meaning of what he had seen and heard. He had two Canaanite wives, and his father did not approve. Was this the first time he had realised how Isaac disapproved of them? Rebekah did not approve either, but Esau was, first and last, Isaac's dear son. To him it was of little importance if Rebekah disapproved.

How then could he improve matters? He could take a third wife, not a Canaanite. His choice was a daughter of Ishmael, who was, he no doubt reasoned, a grand-daughter of Abraham, and therefore presumably acceptable. It can be taken that when v.9 refers to Esau going "unto Ishmael" it means going to the Ishmaelites, for Ishmael himself was by this time dead. That the bride was of a branch of the family which had been removed from the mainstream of the blessings of the promises was something Esau seemed incapable of appreciating.[†]

Verses 10-15: Jacob's Dream

The story returns to Jacob's journey from Beer-sheba to Haran. Most of the journey was unremarkable and is passed over in silence. One night's stopping-place was important, and it receives close attention. At first it is an anonymous place, only of interest, apparently, because it was a convenient stopping-place arrived at around sunset. He "took one of the stones of the place, and put it under his head" (v.11, RV) and settled down to sleep.

In his earlier life Jacob had usually been in conflict, or at best competition, with Esau from the womb until he left home. He had usually had his mother in close attendance to champion his cause and organise his victories over

Esau. This night, however, he had no one with him and no mother to outwit his foes. He was alone and setting out on a journey in which he would reap as he had sown. His stony pillow was a symbol of the way ahead. "And he dreamed". God had previously communicated with Abimelech in a dream (20.3) to warn him, and he would later communicate with Joseph in dreams and also enable Joseph to interpret dreams. Here at last, when others were far away and their influences for better or worse removed, God spoke to Jacob in a dream. It was one of the greatest experiences of his life. Nothing up to this point suggests that he had had dealings with God, and it must be remembered that he was a mature man, not a youth.

Down to v.12 Jacob was in control of his actions. Then, in his dream, the experiences, so vivid, were all in the hands of God. "Behold a ladder ... behold the angels of God ... behold, the Lord stood ... " (vv.12-13). A ladder (or preferably "a stairway") stood on earth, but its top reached to heaven. The grandiose scheme at Babel (11.1-9) was to build a tower which would reach to heaven, but God "came down" even to have a look at it. It fell short of linking earth to heaven, for it was devised on earth and started from earth. This stairway which Jacob saw was divinely ordained, devised in heaven, and it fully spanned the two places. Jacob must learn that the God of heaven has ability to see that His will is done on earth. Much of Jacob's energy had been directed towards seeing that he had his own way on earth. He was confronted with a new concept, that God was in control, however men schemed.

God has His agents who do His will. Angels were engaged in two-way journeys, bearing His instructions and reporting back that His will had been done, or reporting to God what they were observing on earth and returning to earth to make adjustments in accordance with His instructions.

"And, behold, the Lord stood above it". The last two words may be translated "beside him" (as in RV margin) which gives perfectly good sense, but it is perhaps more in keeping with the dramatic, overpowering scene before him to follow the AV and see Jacob lying on the earth and seeing the Lord so plainly in control from heaven. Certainly it was a sight which Jacob would never forget. It was one thing to know about the Lord and the promises and the family destiny, but it was quite different when, that night, he *saw* the Lord.

The voice that spoke to his awe-struck soul had no rebuke for him, only promises. Jacob had a series of stern lessons to learn, but he was starting with a direct communication from the Lord about his privileges and prospects. First he was identified by the Lord as the third in the chosen line, for the Lord was, "the Lord God of Abraham thy father, and the God of Isaac". The inclusion of the descriptor, "thy father", places Jacob firmly in the line. Later in the story of divine purpose there will be heard the frequent refrain, "the God of Abraham, Isaac and Jacob". This night was the introduction to this idea in the personal experience of Jacob.

Earlier in the chapter Isaac had spoken to Jacob of his inheriting the land of his sojournings. This night God promised him the land, on which he lay, for him and his descendants. The description, "whereon thou liest", is poignant in view of the circumstances which caused him to leave home in a hurry to suffer the hardships of this lonely journey. The promise closely follows God's earlier promises to Abraham. Descendants as numerous as the dust echo the divine promise to Abraham in 13.16. That they would spread widely in all directions again echoes the promise to Abraham in 13.14. To him, as to Abraham (12.3), God promised that in him would "all the families of the earth be blessed". The climax of the promises is the most movingly gracious: "Behold, I am with thee, and will keep thee in all places whither thou goest, and will bring thee again into this land" (v.15). Jacob's departure from home was directly occasioned by his cheating Esau, but God was overruling this in His sovereign grace to use the journey to promote Jacob's blessing and education. Jacob would need assurance like this in the next twenty years: God with him, keeping him, until the time came to bring him back. God's work in Jacob, to make him the man he would become, would continue until the process was complete. God would decide when Jacob was ready to return (compare 31.3) and in due course Jacob would have another unforgettable interview with God, at Peniel (32.24). Bethel and Peniel are the twin peaks in the landscape of Jacob's life.

Verses 16-22: Jacob's Vow

When he awoke Jacob assessed his experience soberly. How casually he had chosen this convenient place to spend the night. This place, despite his earlier ignorance, was where he met the Lord. "And he was afraid". Earlier thoughts about the birthright or the blessing or the promises had aroused his interest and ambition, however mixed his motives had been. But this was an experience to inspire fear and awe. Here was the house of God and the gate of heaven. In his father's house paternal authority had been weak and his mother had schemed and planned for him. Here he was in God's house where paternal authority was absolute and only transparent honour could be tolerated. The gate of heaven may connote two things. He had seen God and seen that the angels were busy about God's business on that stairway which did indeed reach heaven's gate. So near was heaven to where he lay. But the gate of heaven may also suggest the other use of the term "gate", not only the entrance but also the place where authority was exercised, for the city magistrates sat in the gate (compare, for example, Ruth 4.1-10). In this sense the gate of heaven and the house of God become virtual synonyms for the place of God's authority. In 1 Timothy 3 Paul refers to "the house of God, which is the church of the living God, the pillar and ground of the truth", and this is in a context where he is stressing the need for disciplined behaviour in the local church. The verse in 1 Timothy 3 alludes to Genesis 28 and also uses the term "house of God" to identify the place of God's authority over His people.

Jacob lost no time. He rose early (and we remember that this was also a feature of his grandfather Abraham's response to God's leading) to mark this event by setting up a memorial. The pillow became a pillar. This was to stand for God's house (v.22), because he was sobered by the thought that he was a man who had God for his God. The pillar, consecrated with anointing oil, declared his waking acceptance of the purport of his dream. And what name could he give the place but "Bethel", the House of God?

Then Jacob vowed a vow, the first recorded in the Bible. The language is formal, as befits a vow. The conditional clauses are not indicative of a grudging attitude by Jacob, as if he were sceptical about whether God would fulfil what He had promised. He soberly itemised the implications of the divine promises given to him personally - and not intended for Esau, this time! Thus the list reads:
- if God will be with me
- and will keep me in this way that I go
- and will give me bread to eat and raiment to put on
- so that I come again to my father's house in peace
- and the Lord will be my God.[†]
His response to God's care will be:
- then this stone ... shall be God's house
- and of all that thou shalt give me I will surely give a tenth unto thee.

First, then, an enumeration of all God's promised supply for him and, by implication, his dependence on God. Home was receding, but had not God promised that He would not leave him? God had indeed promised to bring him back to "this land". Jacob, still smarting from his fear of Esau's possible reprisals, rephrased this as "to my father's house in peace". God would indeed do this, but that was still a very long way off, and Jacob had much reaping to do first.

Then his undertakings. Back in the land after his wanderings, he would return to Bethel to declare his allegiance to God who had met him on this memorable night and spoken so graciously to him. He would also pay tithes to God as a declaration that he was God's man and that he owed all that he had to God's bounty. Jacob had started on the road to a personal appreciation of the God of his father Abraham and of Isaac. He had much to learn yet, but this experience of God at Bethel had put into his soul the seed of an attitude of worship which was previously lacking. It took a sight of God's nearness and interest in him to stir this response. It still takes an experience of God's nearness and interest to stimulate feelings of awe and worship in our hearts. He condescends to grant us such experiences to lead us on to desire a deeper knowledge of Himself. The response of consecration and practical devotion is spontaneous when we meet God personally. If the response is real it expresses itself in ways which are practical and financial - there is nothing so designed to wean us from covetousness as an awareness of the value of our relationship with God. No book of rules about duty and responsibility is a substitute for a personal experience of God.

Notes

9 There are complications about the names of Esau's three wives which need not detain us. Main characters in these stories change their names, or are called by different names from time to time; there is no need to be distracted by such problems among minor characters. Compare also 36.2,3 with footnote there.

21 This last clause is best taken here, as the RV margin takes it, among the conditionals; it is a kind of summary of what has preceded.

GENESIS 29

Jacob Acquires Two Wives and Four Sons

Verses 1-8: Jacob at the Well

Encouraged by his experiences at Bethel, Jacob went on to his destination at Haran. His arrival, like that of Abraham's servant in ch.24, is signalled by his reaching the well, the meeting-place of the people. The importance of this point in the story is emphasised by the double exclamation mark, as it were, in v.2: "behold ... lo" (really the same expression repeated).

The detail in vv.2-3 about accepted conventions at the well is a good preparation for the following story of Jacob's protracted stay with Laban as a shepherd. Attention is drawn to that large stone on the well, for it will feature in the later events in the chapter.

Jacob's polite address to the shepherds as "brothers" comes abruptly, for, although there were three flocks, no mention has yet been made of shepherds. It seems almost as if Jacob arrived at the well, observed by silently suspicious, or perhaps silently curious, shepherds. Contrary to the expectation that strangers will be courteously received, the behaviour of these shepherds seems distinctly cool. Replies were extracted from them with difficulty; they replied when they had to, and were eager to pass the stranger on to Laban's daughter as soon as possible (see v.6). The suggestion that they were much younger than Jacob and shy of a stranger may be a possible interpretation of their behaviour, and more charitable.

The contrast between this scene at the well and that in ch.24 is virtually complete. The servant had arrived at the well with costly gifts borne by his camel train. He had prayed to God on his arrival and, before he had done praying (24.15), Rebekah arrived as a gracious answer to every detail of his prayer. Here Jacob arrived as a virtual fugitive, with no bride-price, and apparently with no camel train, to be met with a reluctance to communicate. He does not appear to pray. Yet under this unpromising surface there was the current of divine purpose flowing. The first people he met were from Haran; they knew Laban, and they drew attention soon to the imminent arrival (signalled again by "behold" in v.6) of Laban's daughter Rachel.

While Rachel was drawing nearer with her father's flock, Jacob commented critically to the shepherds on their arriving so early at the well and thus losing grazing time. Jacob, as will be seen later, was a conscientious and skilful shepherd and this seemed to him bad practice. Their explanation hardly provides an adequate answer to his criticism. If, as the story suggests, Jacob removed the stone single-handed, it scarcely required three of them (there were three flocks already there) to remove it. This is true, even if, as some suggest, they may have been quite young. There may be some merit in the suggestion that they were determined to be there to hear what the stranger would say to Laban's daughter. On the other hand, Jacob might well have preferred to speak to Laban's daughter without an audience of neighbours listening in to his business.

Verses 9-12: Jacob and Rachel Meet

At any rate their conversation was terminated by the arrival of Rachel and her father's flock. If Jacob was telling the simple truth in 30.30 then the flock of which she had charge was small, for in that passage he reminded Laban of how few sheep he had until he (Jacob) took charge of them.

It seems from v.10 that as soon as Rachel arrived Jacob rolled the stone from the well and, putting Rachel at the head of the queue, watered Laban's flock before the others had a chance. Only then did he greet her with a kiss such as a relative might be expected to give. She may well have been taken aback at this time, for she had had no explanation of the behaviour of this stranger, not having been there to hear his conversation with the others. He now explained to her that he was related to her father, being Rebekah's son. His use of the term "brother" of the relationship prompts thoughts about how he may be received. How ought brothers to treat each other? Abraham knew (13.8) when he refused to fight with Lot. It remains to be seen how Laban will view it, bearing in mind the way Jacob treated Esau and how Esau might have treated Jacob if Rebekah had not arranged this long journey for her favourite.

Rachel, then, ran to her father with the news of his arrival.

Verses 13-19: Laban Welcomes Jacob, Who Asks for Rachel's Hand

Laban's response to the news of Jacob's arrival was prompt: he ran to meet him, embraced and kissed him, and brought him to his house. This is now the third house in Jacob's education by God - the first his father's, then God's, now Laban's. This was going to be the most testing experience so far. But at this early stage Laban was very warm in his welcome: "Surely thou art my bone and my flesh". It must have been already clear to Laban that Jacob was not at all so good a financial prospect as Abraham's servant had been all those years ago, with his ready gift of jewels and saddle-bags stored with bride-price. So Jacob stayed with him for a month. At this stage in the story the interest lies in Laban's reception and Jacob's success in arriving at his kinsman's home to a warm welcome. Rachel has so far made little impact; almost nothing is known about her, or her importance. There is (as yet) no description of her, nor any mention made as to whether she was a good worker. In these respects she contrasts with Rebekah at this point in her contact with the family of Abraham.

In one month Laban had ample opportunity to weigh Jacob up. It was time to begin to regularise his status in the house. Laban's address to him in v.15 is interpreted in two different ways by scholars. One interpretation takes words as they appear in the AV and represents Laban as saying, "The fact that you are a close relative does not justify my asking you to work for me without pay. How much wages do you want?". This is understandable, even given Laban's grasping nature, if we accept (with Hamilton, for example) that he is really suggesting that, while Jacob as a relative could hardly expect pay, he would pay him, so reducing him to the level of a hired hand.

An alternative translation would read, "Are you my relative? Should you serve me without pay? How much wages do you want?". The answers to the first two questions would be "No". In other words, they are rhetorical questions. Laban on this reading would be implying to Jacob, "You are not really a sufficiently close relative to be expecting to join the family and entertaining hopes of inheriting property. If you were a close relative you would receive no wages on the understanding that you would inherit. As a hired hand, of course, you will get your wages and that is all".

Whichever way we read the verse, Laban reduced Jacob to a hired man receiving wages. The second way of reading the verse presents a more subtle Laban, edging away from his earlier warm welcome. Either way, it is interesting to reflect that, in a deeper sense, Jacob was about to receive wages for his earlier behaviour. He had worked at deception and fraud and was about to get the wages in kind - deception and fraud from Laban.

Jacob's reply was, at first glance, out of character. But before his answer is made known some background information is necessary. Rachel has already appeared at the scene albeit only momentarily. Laban, however, had another, older, daughter called Leah. The brief description of the two sisters has the word "but" in the middle. Rachel "had beauty both of form and face", as Knox translates it. The "but" which connects her description with that of Leah requires that Leah was otherwise. Tantalisingly, we read only of her eyes, which are described as "tender" (AV, RV, Hamilton), "soft" (Wenham), "weak" (RSV, NIV), "dull" (Knox, REB). The required sense is something which made her less desirable, therefore "weak" or "dull" seems preferable. It is easy therefore to understand why Jacob acted out of character. He had fallen in love with Rachel. Hence his very generous offer of seven years' work for her hand. This is the first time he is seen in the inspired record offering anyone generous terms. In his offer he described her, in formal terms, as Rachel "thy younger daughter". Jacob's tender feelings for Rachel might lead him to make a generous offer. Laban's response was not made under any such softening emotion. It was the measured response of a man making careful calculations, a man avoiding explicit, precise words such as Jacob had used. Where Jacob had said, "Rachel thy younger daughter", Laban in reply said "her". Jacob's proposal was full of thoughts of Rachel, while Laban's reply was along the lines of "better you than some other man", and he clinched the oddly vague bargain with, "abide with me". So Jacob stayed.

Verses 20-30: Jacob, Cheated, Acquires Two Wives

The next seven years passed quickly and happily. Jacob's love for Rachel kept him happy in the hard work he was doing. Laban was happy too, in the knowledge of what he planned to get out of Jacob. Indeed Jacob felt that seven years were just like "a few days". This skilful touch recalls how Rebekah had said to him (27.44), that he should stay with Laban "a few days, until thy brother's fury turn away". The seven years seemed to Jacob a few days. One wonders how long it seemed to Rebekah.

Then came the time for payment. Jacob's demand was urgent and sharp, without polite toning down: "Give me my wife". Laban responded with apparent good will. He made a feast to celebrate the wedding in proper style. Evening came and the bride was brought to her eager bridegroom in bridal veil as custom demanded. The couple went to bed and the marriage was consummated. The bride even had a handmaid allotted to her, Zilpah by name. A very proper day's proceedings was completed. Indeed, an almost real implementation of the deal struck seven years before.

The morning dawned and "behold, it was Leah". Leah of the dull eyes had come to the bed of Jacob of the unseeing eyes. Did Jacob remember, one wonders, that day when his father and his brother realised how Jacob had deceived the old man in his blindness (27.33-34)? Even so had Laban deceived him when his eyes were blinded. Josephus surmises that Laban had dulled Jacob's senses with wine, but it may not be absolutely necessary to imagine any such explanation for Jacob's lack of perception. One can be sure that there was no courtship in the modern sense, no opportunity for Jacob and Rachel to spend time together alone. It would have been improper.

Jacob's outcry keeps echoing that earlier occasion when he had cheated Esau. The blessing pronounced by Isaac had promised (27.29) that peoples, including his brothers, would "serve" him. His outcry against Laban complains how he had "served" with Laban for Rachel and been cheated. "Wherefore", he cried, "hast thou beguiled me?" but in this there is the echo of old Isaac sadly saying, "Thy brother (Jacob) came with guile, and hath taken away thy blessing" (27.35, RV).

Laban's reply was disingenuous: "It must not be so done in our country, to give the younger before the firstborn" (v.26). So that was what he was thinking about when he made the wording of the agreement with Jacob so vague in v.19! But even this reply brings back so sharply to memory the issue of the younger who had so improperly defrauded the firstborn in ch.27. If Laban had intended to deal honourably with Jacob he could have told him this rule at the time when the agreement was reached. The fact that God intended Jacob to have the blessing is not relevant here in this experience of Jacob reaping what he had sown.

But Laban was a capable dealer. Let Jacob fulfil the necessary rituals of the first week of marriage with Leah, said he, and then he could have Rachel as well - and serve a further seven years. So Laban would retain the services of this hardworking and skilful shepherd and incidentally get a suitable marriage for his less marriageable daughter. Laban would gain doubly, a generous offer by Jacob now given a second life. Jacob could not undo the marriage to Leah, and what the daughters would feel about it, favourably or unfavourably, was not seriously considered. It was an offer which Jacob could not refuse. He did love Rachel, and in a week's time he would have her and all would be well, or nearly well. The week passed and Jacob took Rachel also to wife. Laban did the proper thing by her also in providing her with a handmaid, Bilhah by name. It will be seen later why it was important to identify these handmaids. The marriage with Rachel was also consummated.

So Jacob had his two wives, and one of them was the only woman he truly loved, the only woman for whom he would ever have entered upon business arrangement on terms generously in favour of the other party. He loved Rachel "rather than" (REB) Leah. He served a further seven years and, although there is no record of how long it seemed, it cannot have felt like a few days. Jacob would never again be free from tension and strife in his home. His father's home had been divided because of a wrong relationship between conflicting parental roles and sibling rivalry with Jacob taking the initiative. His own family life from the start was torn by rivalries and, later, hatred.

Verses 31-35: Leah Bears Four Sons

Laban had evidently given little thought to his daughters' feelings when he used them as a trading commodity. Jacob may have been consoled with his love of Rachel. Was there no one to feel for Leah - sold by her father, "unloved" (v.31, Wenham) by Jacob? Yes, the Lord saw that Leah was unloved, and He opened her womb. Amazingly, this is the first mention of the Lord since Bethel, though he had assuredly kept His promise to be with Jacob. The purposes of God were more important than the temporary sorrows of Jacob or any other of the human personalities. The line of descendants was of vital importance, and the Lord opened Leah's womb. Rachel was beautiful and was loved, had been loved for well over seven years, had the sense of security which this love gave her, but it was Leah whose womb the Lord opened.

The terse statement, "but Rachel was barren", continues a theme previously visited in Genesis, that of the barren wife. It is God who gives children, insists the sacred record, God the giver of life. In this case the barrenness of Rachel gave rise to jealousy, as it did when Sarah saw Hagar bear a son. It is interesting to reflect that while Rachel is jealous of Leah's fertility there is no mention of Leah being jealous of Rachel's beauty. That she grieved over Jacob's obvious love for Rachel is a different matter.

In vv.32-35 Leah bears four sons to Jacob, yet the story is heavy with the fearful isolation of Leah. She obviously had physical intimacy with Jacob, but there was no tender sharing of feelings of care and love. The names of the children she bore spell this out eloquently. Her comments on the names given to the first two include references to her "affliction" and her being unloved.

Reuben the firstborn should surely have been welcomed by Jacob and Leah with shared joy. However, *she* called him Reuben, and it was she who named two of the others and possibly all three of them, for the naming of Levi is not attributed to anyone in particular. Leah's comments on the names she gave her sons are not to be taken as exercises in etymology so much as plays on names in the common Hebrew tradition. She called her firstborn Reuben and said, in effect, that it reminded her how the Lord "had looked upon (her) affliction". The angel had told Hagar she would have a son saying (16.11), "the Lord hath heard thy affliction", and she had commented (16.13), "Thou God seest me". Leah's sad yearning was that now her husband would be more disposed to love her. It was not to be so.

Her second son was Simeon. Her comment, "The Lord hath heard that I am unloved", gives her reason for calling him Simeon. Again the words recall how the Lord had heard Hagar. The third son, Levi, was so named because she hoped that now at last her husband would be "joined" to her in affection. Her hopes were rising. The fourth son, Judah, brought her hopes of being loved to a climax. How could her husband fail to love her, now that she had borne him four sons? The Lord was to be "praised" for this happy event.

This whole section is full of unfulfilled longing and sorrow, except for the rising hope at the end. Would Jacob be "joined" to her? Praise the Lord, she thought, it must be so! But her confidence appears not to have been justified by a response from Jacob. This was a lonely woman, finding some hope in her God-given fertility, but living in a home in which her husband's affection was given to another woman, her sister. Yet through her fertility God gave her two sons who were the heads of the most important tribes in Israel: Levi whose sons were priests or Levites, and Judah whose sons would be kings and one of them the King of kings.

THE NAMES OF JACOB'S SONS

In Genesis the names given to Jacob's sons have a background in Hebrew from which the final name is derived. The names with these underlying words are listed below.

THE SONS OF LEAH		
REUBEN (7205) 29.32	Behold a son	Because the Lord "had looked on her affliction". From RAA (7200) "see, look at", and BEN (1121) "a son".
SIMEON (8095) 29.33	Hearing	Because the Lord "hath heard". From SHAMA (8085) "to hear".
LEVI (3878) 29.34	Joined	Because now her husband would be joined to her in affection. From LAWA (3867) "to be joined".
JUDAH (3063) 29.35	Praised	Because "now will I praise the Lord". From YADA (3034) "praise, give thanks".
ISSACHAR (3485) 30.18	He is wages	Because of Leah's "wage (hire)" when Rachel paid her for the mandrakes. From SAKAR (7939) "to hire, to be rewarded".
ZEBULUN (2074) 30.20	Wished for habitation	Because Leah said, "Now will my husband dwell with me". From ZEBUL (2082) "habitation, height".
THE SONS OF BILHAH, RACHEL'S MAID		
DAN (1835) 30.6	Judge	Because God "has judged (vindicated) me". From DIN (1777) "to judge".
NAPHTALI (5321) 30.8	My wrestling	Because Rachel had prevailed in her "wrestlings" with Leah. From PATAL (6617) "to wrestle, to twist".
THE SONS OF ZILPAH, LEAH'S MAID		
GAD (1408) 30.11	A troop comes	A play on his name gives "good fortune cometh". From GADAD (1413) "to gather in troops, to cut through".
ASHER (836) 30.13	Happy	Because Leah said, "Happy am I". From ASHAR (833) "to be fortunate".
THE SONS OF RACHEL		
JOSEPH (3130) 30.24	He shall add	In hope that God would "add" another son to Rachel. From YASAP (3254) "to add".
BENJAMIN (1144) 35.18	Son of the right hand	Called this by Jacob despite being called Benoni (1126), "son of my sorrow", by Rachel. From YAMIN (3225) "the right hand".

GENESIS 30

Fertility in Family and Flocks

Verses 1-13: Four Sons by the Handmaidens

The chapter opens with a striking situation. Rachel was filled with envy of Leah because Leah was fertile and she was barren. Yet Leah never, so far as the record goes, envied Rachel her good looks. There may be excessive concern nowadays with physical appearance. The means even exist to alter appearance by plastic ("cosmetic") surgery, but even if the beautician or cosmetic surgeon can beautify, that is no guarantee of happiness or even popularity. Leah did suffer because of Jacob's lack of love for her, and it is well to consider the impact of attitudes to family and friends, including failure at times to notice emotional needs.

There is little indication thus far of what kind of person Rachel was, apart from her physical beauty. Up to this point there is no record of her speech, except that she ran and told her father when Jacob first arrived at the well. Her first recorded words, in v.1, sprang from months and years of pent-up frustration and envy: "Give me children, or else I die". The household of Laban was a place of frustration and sometimes unhappiness. Did not Jacob himself feel the frustration at the end of his seven years' service when he, too, cried to Laban, "Give me my wife"? Now it was his turn to be faced with the pressure of emotional demands. Rachel felt that if she had no children she would die. In the event she bore two sons and, in bearing the second of them, died.

Her demand of Jacob betrays her lack of the understanding which the people of faith had already acquired, that children come from the Lord. The Lord would later give her a son who would save the world from starvation, but, as so often, He would demonstrate that the great purposes at work in the line of Abraham, Isaac and Jacob were the purposes of God. They demanded patience and willingness to suspend judgment when it seemed that God was in difficulties.

Jacob was angry, for he knew that only God could grant what she wanted. It was unreasonable of her to accuse him - unreasonable but understandable. It will be remembered that Sarah, having "given her maid into Abraham's bosom", then railed on him because the maid became too high and mighty when she conceived. Irrational, but very human.

It then becomes clear why the divine record gave the name of Rachel's handmaid, Bilhah. Rachel gave her to Jacob as wife, so that any child born of the union would be Rachel's. This is the meaning of bearing on Rachel's knees; bearing a child which Rachel would rear as her own. When Sarah resorted to this means of getting a child the system failed, for the handmaid became her rival. In Laban's house there was Rachel's fertile sister with her four sons, and there were two handmaids belonging to the two sisters. This was a recipe for confusion and fragmentation, but not the bitter hostility of a sole wife defied by her own handmaid, as in the case of Sarah and Hagar.

Bilhah duly bore Jacob a son, for Rachel. Rachel named the child Dan, for, she said, God "hath judged me", or "vindicated me". She thought God had answered her prayer. Maybe she had begun to pray on the basis of what Jacob had said to her: "God ... hath withheld from thee the fruit of the womb" (v.2). The divine record does not say that God had heard her until v.22 when she herself became pregnant. In the record of God's dealings with His people they are constantly brought into circumstances in which only God can enable them to continue in the path of His will. In many situations His people seem to manage to manipulate their affairs. They sometimes seem to be able to succeed without God, but their devious schemes always go awry. God's answer was seen, not in Rachel's strategy to use her handmaid as surrogate, but in His opening of her own womb. Surrogacy is the human answer to a problem, not the divine answer.

Bilhah conceived again and when a second son was born for Rachel he was named by her Naphtali. She explained that in her mighty wrestlings with her sister she had prevailed. It is worth a thought that neither Dan nor Naphtali became head of an important tribe. Rachel's future fame as a mother in Israel would rest on a later birth.

By this time Leah realised that her own fertility had suffered a setback and she felt challenged to reply to Bilhah's fertility on Rachel's account. Accordingly she gave Zilpah to Jacob as wife. When Zilpah bore a son for Leah, Leah called him Gad, for, she said, "Fortune (or a troop) is come"! Zilpah bore a second son, whom Leah named Asher, "My happiness". She rejoiced that other women (the daughters) would call her happy. This was a matter of enhanced status.

Verses 14-21: Leah Buys Jacob Back

At this juncture one of the next generation appears as a character in his own right. Reuben, by now a young boy of perhaps six years old or thereabouts, went out into the field during wheat harvest and found mandrakes.[†] When he gave the fruit to his mother, Leah, Rachel asked politely if she might have some of them. Rachel, though she was loved, and though she had sons by her handmaid, was frustrated on account of her barrenness. Her request was motivated by a desire to use this herb to give her hope of conceiving. Leah understood quite clearly why her sister was asking for some of the mandrakes. Her resentment at Rachel's position as favourite wife now boiled over and she stormed at her sister as having taken her husband and now trying to take her mandrakes. She herself obviously wanted to use the mandrakes to help her conceive. Her fury was irrational but, in the highly charged atmosphere of competition and baby-counting in Jacob's home, it is understandable. Jacob's behaviour in his father's house had caused sibling rivalry which required that he leave home, but he could not get away from the very thing which he had caused. Jacob was reaping as he had sown.

Rachel at this point shows something of the trading instincts of her father. She made no attempt to argue with Leah. Instead she suggested that they strike a deal: let Leah lie that night with Jacob and Rachel would have the mandrakes. It had become the custom for the men-folk in the family to use the women as a commodity. Now the women were using Jacob, even as Laban had already used him, for their own ends. These are the choppy waves on the surface of the stream of events, but underneath flows the steady current of divine purpose, carried forward with co-operation of the human actors or, just as often, in spite of their activities.

Leah's exuberance in accosting Jacob before he could even get home from the fields jars on our sense of propriety, but it was the frenzied response of a very overwrought woman. "I have hired you," she said. First Laban had turned him into a hired hand on the farm, now Leah claimed him on a similar basis, as if to shame him into loving her. He slept with her and God heard Leah. After the devious experiments with handmaids and the tough trading between sisters, God heard Leah. The son she bore as a result she called Issachar. She connected the name with her having had to give her maid to retain a hold on him.

After this she conceived again and bore Zebulun. In this name, Zebulun, she expressed her growing confidence that Jacob would dwell with her. Her comments in giving this name show a confidence parallel to her earlier buoyant spirits when she named Judah. Here, though, as in Issachar, her attention is more focused on her hold on Jacob than on the goodness of God.

The next verse inserts a bold statement, seemingly out of place in this record of a series of sons. It tells of her later bearing a daughter whom she called Dinah. Later events (ch.34) will show why this daughter is mentioned specially, for there were other daughters whose names, as indeed was normal practice, were not recorded at all (37.35).

Verses 22-24: Rachel at Last Bears a Son

Very simply, and very appropriately, the divine record states how Rachel's deepest desire was met. God "remembered" her, and "hearkened to her, and opened her womb". The mandrakes are not mentioned at this point. Whether she used them or not, the vital factor was that God answered her desires, and He was not dependent on herbal medicine. At any rate she conceived and bore a son, whom she called Joseph.†

Verses 25-43: Jacob's Deal with Laban

The birth of Joseph seems to have prompted Jacob to think more sharply about the future of his family. His opening approach to Laban on this subject was a request that he be released to go back home to Canaan. This was a suitably oblique way to introduce the subject which formed the core of the negotiations which followed. His next request (v.26), that he should take his wives and children, came closer to his real concern. Interestingly, it is another of those key requests made under a strong emotion and beginning "Give me" - in this case "Give me my wives and my children". That a financial settlement is being sought becomes clear when Jacob adds, "for whom I have served thee". Jacob knew that his future did not lie in Haran. His place was Canaan. Had not God promised to bring him back there (28.15)?

Laban's reply, as usual, was devious and smooth. "Please be kind to me", he said, "and stay on, for I have discovered by divination (AV "learned by experience") that my present prosperity is due to the Lord's intervention on your behalf". This was a very positive note to strike, and one calculated to make Jacob more disposed to make a less stringent demand. Laban continued with, "Just name the wage you want" (v.28). If what Jacob said in 31.41 ("thou hast changed my wages ten times") was true, as it probably was, then this opening by Laban was purely tactical, a way of putting Jacob in the position of naming the opening figure in the bargaining. Its modern equivalent is the advertisement of a vacant position for which no salary level is stated, because the salary is "negotiable", which means that the prospective employer will judge the mettle of the applicant by how he or she negotiates for a salary.

Jacob was not to be caught on the wrong foot so easily. He reminded Laban of how faithfully he had served him and how the animals had prospered under his care and management. His reminder of how small Laban's stock had been when he came was a little more pointed. Now, he said, they were very numerous. The Lord had indeed blessed Laban through Jacob, but what about Jacob's family? They still had nothing to call their own. Laban's reply was a terse rephrasing of his earlier invitation: "What shall I give thee?" (v.31).

Instead of naming sums of money Jacob made a complicated proposal. To understand it, it is necessary to realise that sheep would normally, as in our country today, be white, while goats were black or dark brown. Jacob, then, proposed that he would go through the flock and take the abnormally coloured sheep or goats; that is, goats with some white on them or sheep which were black (v.33 gives the clearest picture of this detail). From then on he would have as his own animals the sheep and goats so described.[†] When Jacob mentioned (v.33) his "righteousness" he was saying that the criteria which he was laying down would enable Laban to check that he was keeping to the bargain.

What Jacob was asking was, on the face of it, very little. One would expect the normal colours to predominate. Laban was understandably satisfied with the agreement (v.34). After all, normal goats were black or brown and normal sheep were white. Jacob would have the odd, exceptional animals. But Laban was not content to leave his agreement at the mercy of statistical probability. He did not trust Jacob any more than Jacob trusted him. He felt, therefore, that he must get a head start on him by removing from his care all the animals such as he had described, giving them into his sons' care and sending them a good three days' journey from Jacob to ensure that there would be no cross-breeding (vv.35-36). Jacob was thus left in charge of only animals which gave little prospect of offspring to which he could lay claim.

It is difficult to decipher what precisely Jacob did in his unusual breeding programme. It is impossible to determine how it worked. But then it must be remembered that God was on his side, and, even if he had had no special breeding programme, God could have given him extensive flocks. Jacob had served Laban faithfully and suffered at his hands. This had been his education in the school of God, his time also of reaping what had been sown. But God was over all and would not send His servant home empty to Canaan.

The technique used by Jacob involved peeling strips off rods taken from three kinds of trees, exposing a pattern of white wood under the darker bark.[†] He appears to have placed the rods thus treated in the troughs where the animals were drinking. It was not clear whether this was intended to bring the females into heat or merely influence the colour of the offspring of those which were in heat when they came to drink. At any rate an exceptionally high proportion of animals was born whose colour entitled Jacob to claim them (v.39). These animals he now kept separate (v.40). He also bred selectively by mating the more vigorous animals according to his system and letting the weaker breed outside the system (vv.41-42). Thus the stronger offspring became his and the weaker Laban's. What was happening was that Laban was still getting as good a return from his animals as he would have got by his own inferior breeding methods, but Jacob was getting vastly better returns by his superior methods - or was it by God's intervention?

At any rate Jacob prospered within the agreement which he had with Laban until he had a great number of animals, servants of his own and many baggage animals and mounts. At last he was about to emerge from the crucible of Laban's house. He had suffered greatly, had continued to exercise his natural subtlety in dealing with a subtle master, and would soon learn that there was yet another lesson in God's school, the lesson of knowing when one cannot win by subtlety or skill. Incidentally, Laban was now also beginning to learn that a man reaps as he has sown.

Notes

14 The mandrake has spreading leaves at ground level; it bears violet-coloured flowers and yellow, tomato-like fruit. Its roots, which look like a pair of legs, probably account for its widespread ancient reputation as a fertility herb and an aphrodisiac. Hence its importance in this scene.

23,24 Her comment that God had taken away her reproach is a fairly common kind of statement in such circumstances in Scripture. It does incidentally contain yet another Hebrew pun on the name of the new-born son, for "has taken away" (ASAP-622) contains echoes of the name "Yosep", or Joseph. The name Joseph itself is linked with the verb "may he add" (YASAP - 3254), for her wish was that the Lord would "add" another son.

32-35 The distinction between spotted, speckled and ringstraked ("striped") merely describes comprehensively the bi-coloured animals.

37 The "poplar" of the AV may have been the storax tree, the "hazel" of the AV was the almond tree, and the "chestnut" of the AV was the plane tree.

GENESIS 31

Jacob Starts His Journey Back to Canaan

Verses 1-3: Reasons for Leaving Haran

Jacob's conspicuous success as described at the end of ch.30 could not fail to attract attention. Laban's sons have been mentioned only in passing when Laban entrusted to them the abnormally marked animals so as to prevent Jacob getting his fair share from the deal made between them. Now they resurface because of their resentment of Jacob's success. Their assessment that Jacob had taken away what was their father's was inaccurate if Jacob's account (30.30) of how few animals Laban had until Jacob's superior animal husbandry made him (Laban) prosperous is to be believed. It was not that Laban's property had been taken away from him, but that Jacob, after twenty years working for Laban, had begun at last to exercise his skills on his own account. The result had been that Jacob's property, identifiable as agreed between him and Laban, was vastly increased while Laban's was relatively less.

Their view, that it was from what was their father's that Jacob had got "all this wealth" (RV margin, AV "glory"), overlooked the amount that Laban had owed to Jacob for his diligent work over many years. One recalls that Jacob had agreed to work a very generous seven years for Rachel's hand, had been cheated and had agreed a further seven generous years, because he had no option if he still wanted Rachel. Moral right was on Jacob's side.

But Laban had begun to listen to his sons and he had a poor memory for his own devious acts. Circumstances in the form of Laban's changed attitude to him prompted Jacob to think of leaving. God had by now placed him in a position in which he would not be leaving empty-handed. The time had come for him to go back where he belonged. "And the Lord said unto Jacob, 'Return ...' " (v.3). The covenant-keeping God had not forgotten the promises made to Jacob at Bethel.

This was one of the pivotal moments in Jacob's life. His departure from Canaan had been prompted by Rebekah's voice, "Arise, flee thou to Laban my brother to Haran" (27.43). No doubt God was in control of his going, but Rebekah's proactive style of management provided the visible impetus to set him in motion. His return was mobilised directly by the voice of God. He was to go back to the land of his fathers, by which one understands Abraham and Isaac. Jacob was in the covenant, and of the line which came to its grand climax in Jesus the Christ. He was to go back to his kindred, for he was linked by spiritual inheritance with a people to whom Canaan belonged by divine decree. So God would be with him in his return as He had promised him in 28.15: "I am with thee, and will keep thee in all places whither thou goest, and will bring thee again into this land."

Verses 4-16: Jacob Consults His Wives

Jacob's response to God was both prompt and shrewd. His mind was made up, but he needed to carry his wives' goodwill in his decision, and the home of Laban was a place where distrust made confidences insecure. Therefore he called Rachel and Leah out into the field, where his flock was, so that he could talk to them privately. He told them of their father's changed attitude and contrasted it with the constancy of the support of his own father's God. He was able to call his wives to witness ("ye know") that his service to their father had been whole-hearted. Only God's protection had prevented Laban from harming Jacob materially by his constant changes in the terms of Jacob's service (v.7).

New insights into the recent period of Jacob's service are given in this talk which he had with his wives. Laban had apparently tried to circumvent the effects of Jacob's skilful breeding programme but God had constantly upset his devious plans. So the success of Jacob's breeding methods in producing so many offspring on which Jacob had just claim was due to divine intervention, not just skilful management by Jacob. It was only in this context that Jacob now had claim to offspring which might have been expected to belong to Laban (vv.8-9).

Jacob had been assured that this result was due directly to God's intervention when "the angel of God" spoke to him in a dream. The dream put into picture form what had been happening in the rapid increase in bi-coloured animals. Jacob had been invited by God (for v.13 makes it clear that "the angel" was in fact God Himself) to "Lift up now (his) eyes", to take particular note of a significant sight. The sight of the vigorous breeding of flocks which were his was God's reassurance to him that He had seen all that Laban was doing to him. When God speaks of "seeing" how someone has ill-treated His servant it can be anticipated that the guilty party will be frustrated in his designs.

Jacob's comfort in this reassuring vision was completed by God taking his mind back to Bethel. For twenty years he had worked hard and suffered deceit and trickery. But God had made promises and now Jacob heard that wonderful title to bring back the precious moments during his flight to Canaan: "I am the God of Bethel" (v.13). Jacob was reminded of the pillar he had raised, for his pillars spoke of his real experiences of God. He was to remember also his vow to God. Now the time had come for the transaction between God and Jacob at Bethel to be brought to its successful outcome in his return to Canaan. All of this Jacob related to Rachel and Leah, who had not shared in his Bethel experience, nor yet in his dream and vision in Haran.

Their reaction reveals a great deal about their experience of Laban and his household. They had, they said, no "portion or inheritance" (v.14) in their father's house. Jacob had brought no monetary dowry to their father. If he had brought a dowry their father would have been expected to use at least part of it to ensure their financial security. But the dowry had been paid in kind, by the fourteen years of hard labour, and Laban had not given anything to his daughters in return. Laban had treated them as if he had no responsibility for their future, as if they were foreigners (v.15, AV "strangers"), and had appropriated what might reasonably have been considered to be theirs - "our money" ("the price paid for us" RV margin). They were happy that what God had diverted to Jacob was God's provision for them and their children (v.16). Thus they were happy that Jacob should do what God bade him do. They were with him and he could feel free to act on God's command without family worries.

Verses 17-21: The Journey Begins

Jacob seems to have acted at once. He provided his wives and sons with camels to ride. He undertook also the very onerous task of collecting his flocks and herds and other belongings to begin the journey back to his father in the land of Canaan. Before he left home the prime mover was his mother, but she disappears from the divine record as far as activity is concerned and Jacob's return was to his father.

A question is bound to arise at this point about what Laban was doing while this preparation was afoot. In fact he was so busy about his sheep-shearing that Jacob did not need to worry about him for a little while. News travelled slowly, for Jacob was already three days on his journey before Laban heard that he had gone (v.22). But Jacob, had he but known it, had another cause for concern, for Rachel had stolen her father's teraphim.[†] She may have taken them as a guarantee of a safe journey. There is some ancient evidence of people carrying their teraphim on journeys to bring good luck. Or she may have taken them to spite her father, remembering how he had sabotaged her marriage and cheated her out of her dowry. Or again she may have taken them to prevent her father from tracing her by the magical use of the teraphim. The theory that she took them to give Jacob a claim to an inheritance from Laban is not convincing. While possession of the teraphim often would indicate who would be next head of the family on the death of the father, it would not necessarily ensure inheritance. In any case, if the teraphim were stolen this would surely negate any claim based on a person's possession of them.

In the absence, then, of Laban at sheep-shearing, and accompanied by Rachel with her father's teraphim in her baggage, Jacob set out secretly. It was not an auspicious start to the very important journey home. Yet in a way it was fitting that Laban should be repaid for his crooked dealings, and here he begins to reap what he has sown. After the statement that Rachel stole her father's teraphim (v.19) comes the parallel statement (v.20) that Jacob "stole the heart of Laban the Aramean" (literal translation for AV "stole away unawares to Laban the Syrian"). The description of Laban as "the Aramean" also echoes the Hebrew word for "deceive" (RAMA - 7411, used in 29.25). The deceiver was now being deceived; the one who stole was suffering what he had inflicted. However fitting the details of the event, Jacob's departure was a flight. It took him over the Euphrates (v.21 "the river") towards the mountainous area of Gilead.

Verses 22-25: Laban Takes Up the Pursuit

It seems that Laban set out almost immediately he received word of Jacob's flight. He took kinsmen (literally "brothers") with him presumably with the intention of forcing Jacob to return or hand over at least part of his possessions. Laban had plenty of time to brood over his discomfiture in the seven days which it took him to overtake Jacob's slowly moving train hampered as it was with animals and baggage. He overtook Jacob in the mountainous area of Gilead, but before he could establish contact he had an experience which pulled him up short.

God had already intervened to ensure that Jacob received pay for his years of work. Now He intervened again to protect him from violence or robbery. "God came to Laban the Syrian in a dream by night" (v.24). These words were used in 20.3 when God intervened to prevent Abimelech from touching Sarah. In both cases God intervened at a crucial moment to prevent men from doing anything which would frustrate His purpose. In His warning here to Laban He added that Laban must not speak to Jacob "either good or bad": in other words, he must not undertake to pass judgment on Jacob as if he were acting as head of the house in judging him. This interpretation of "either good or bad" accords with that given at 2.9 and 24.50. The timeliness of this divine intervention is underlined by the immediate statement (v.25) that Laban overtook Jacob. The tension between them is economically expressed by the statement about each of them pitching camp in the same area. It is as if the lines for a verbal battle have been drawn up. The divine intervention would prevent anything more extreme than a battle of words.

Verses 26-30: Laban Makes His Accusation

The meeting of the two men is indicated by Laban's abrupt accusation in the traditionally framed charge, "What hast thou done?". Twice (vv.26, 27) he used the word "steal" in describing Jacob's unannounced departure. His second charge was that Jacob had carried off Laban's two daughters, as if they were captives taken by the sword. The weakness of his case is betrayed by repetition and by misrepresentation - Rachel and Leah had accompanied Jacob voluntarily. Yet a man such as Laban might not realise how low a regard his daughters had of him and he may not have been able to conceive that they would consent to go. It is, perhaps, significant that, many years before, Rebekah too had been quite willing to go from this same house when invited by Abraham's servant (24.58).

Then abruptly Laban changed tack. "I was so disappointed," he said, "that your secret departure prevented me from giving you a farewell party, music and all". This borders on the farcical. It is difficult to conjure up an image of Laban, the genial host, making emotional speeches at a banquet put on at his own expense in honour of the man he had cheated again and again and daughters whom he had deprived of their dowry-money. And then there was the deep emotional trauma of losing his daughters and grandsons without being able to kiss them goodbye! One cannot imagine Laban being overcome with emotion. The tirade peters out with a lame, "Thou hast now done foolishly in so doing" (v.28). It is as if he were saying to Jacob, "How much we have all lost, yourself included, because you have gone and spoilt everything by your lack of consideration!".

His frustration comes out clearly in v.29, where he speaks of his ability to harm Jacob and his two wives - notice the plural "you". The only thing which restrained him was the warning which he had received from God. Godless he may have been, but he recognised the reality and might of the One who had warned him. At various points the narrative shows the irresistible might of God when He intervenes. Laban's accurate reporting of the warning he had received is an indication of how great an impact it had made on him. Beginning to calm down a little he admitted that it was understandable that Jacob would want to go home to his father's house. (It had taken him a long time to realise this, when he was prolonging the service of this efficient servant.) But then his feelings boiled up again, for he remembered that someone had stolen his gods. So he bluntly accused Jacob of the theft.

Verses 31-35: Jacob's Reply and the Search for the Teraphim

Jacob's reply, "Because I was afraid", refers to the early part of the accusation. He had fled secretly because he was afraid that Laban would forcibly restrain his two daughters. As for the theft of the gods, Jacob was indignant that such an accusation should be levelled at him. He expressed his indignation by decreeing, as head of his own house, that if anyone was found with the gods in his or her possession they should be executed. He invited Laban to take anything belonging to him which he found in Jacob's possession. Their relatives who were present would decide if what was found belonged to Laban (v.32).

At this point tension mounts, for we know that Rachel had the teraphim, and Rachel was the one person whom Jacob truly loved. The tension rises further as Laban's search goes from tent to tent - Jacob's, Leah's, the two maidservants', then finally Rachel's. But Rachel was equal to the challenge, true daughter of Laban that she was. She had concealed the teraphim in a camel-saddle pouch and sat on them. In passing, note the indignity suffered by these idols - to be sat on by a woman and possibly polluted! Camel saddles were quite commonly used as seats in tents. Laban "felt" (v.34, AV "searched") about the tent, and the apprehension is palpable, similar to the occasion when Jacob had the goatskin on his neck and arms and Isaac "felt" him and was fooled (27.12, 22). However, this time Jacob was in ignorance. Laban failed to find the teraphim. Rachel meanwhile sat calmly on the gods - who says there is no humour in the Bible? She coolly excused herself for not rising when her father was searching. Her excuse was that she was indisposed because of her menstrual period. And still Laban "found not the images". Whether Rachel was lying about her period or not, it was a tactic to which Laban had no answer, for the possibility of pollution was no doubt real to him.

Verses 36-42: Jacob Defends His Record
Laban's painstaking but fruitless search brought Jacob's pent-up resentment to boiling-over temperature. He angrily rejected Laban's charges. His questions, "What is my crime, what is my offence, that you should hound me?" are his formal rejection of Laban's initial, "What hast thou done?". His indignation about the meticulous search takes up again the verb "felt about" (v.37, AV "searched"), pouring contempt on a man who would rummage about in innocent people's belongings. Let Laban, said he, set out before the family witnesses anything belonging to him which had been found. This was a repetition of his offer in v.32 that the members of the family should judge whether anything found in Jacob's baggage belonged to Laban.

Then his long repressed frustration seized on another issue - his twenty years of faithful service. He detailed how under his care the ewes† and the she-goats were brought to successful delivery of young. Further, he claimed, he had not taken rams from the flock for his necessary food. The modern equivalent would be an employee who refused to claim his subsistence allowance. Moreover, he had personally borne the loss of any animals torn by beasts, by day or by night, for Laban demanded this. In the Mosaic law (Ex 22.10-13) distinctions were later made between losses for which the shepherd might reasonably be held responsible and those which were judged to be beyond his responsibility. Laban evidently had made no such distinctions - Jacob was always liable. All of this brought vividly back to Jacob's mind the fierce thirst as he kept the flocks by day and the piercing frost and wakefulness as he guarded them by night. He had by now forgotten those early, optimistic times when seven years seemed but a few days. He looked back over twenty years and they felt long, so long. His pay had been two wives - he tactfully omitted the marriage night deception and the extra wife foisted upon him - and the flock. Laban had changed his terms of payment to try to reduce the payment due to Jacob. Only the intervention of the God of his fathers had prevented his being sent away empty.† God, he insisted, had taken note of how he had suffered at Laban's hands and how hard he had worked. That was why He had rebuked Laban the previous night in his dream. Those who work for an employer in secular employment would do well to ask whether their record of honest effort at work is as good as Jacob's was.

Chapter 31.43 - 32.2: A Covenant is Made

Laban's reply begins with a statement that the daughters, children and flocks were all his. His subsequent question (v.43) is interpreted in two different ways. Some read it as meaning: "How can I do anything hostile to harm my own flesh and blood?". (Therefore let us make a non-aggression pact.) Others, more appropriately, suggest interpreting it: "What can I do in the present circumstances for my own family, when they are going away and I do not know what will befall them?". (Therefore let us make a covenant so that you will be encouraged to treat them well.) On this reading of Laban's question the heap of witness will serve to constrain Jacob to maintain a positive attitude to Laban and his family.

If Laban wanted to maintain the high moral ground, or the psychological advantage, Jacob's immediate action, with no preliminary talk, snatched the initiative from him. Jacob at key points in life set up pillars as symbols of his worship to God. Here again he set up a pillar. He called the relatives to collect stones and make a heap, or cairn. It is perhaps easiest to explain the erection of both a pillar and a cairn by supposing that the cairn was erected around the pillar and supporting it. In the ensuing narrative they are mentioned together as if they served the same function or were seen as one item with two parts. The two men showed their agreement in making the covenant by eating together at the cairn. Each of them declared his understanding of its significance by naming it "Heap of Witness" in his own language. Jacob had spent twenty years away in Haran, but his own language was still Hebrew, quite distinct from Laban's Aramaic. The cairn was also called Mizpah, "Watchtower", as a sign of its being an appeal to the Lord to take account of any failure to observe the terms of the covenant between the two men. This was Laban's idea to curb any tendency on Jacob's part to be false to an agreement - which was somewhat ironic in view of Laban's record. His concern was to ensure that Jacob would not ill-treat Rachel and Leah when they were in Canaan, and that Jacob would not take new wives to their detriment. Laban's fear is a good example of how people who are themselves crooked cannot trust others.

The cairn also served (vv.51-53) to indicate that neither Laban nor Jacob would pass it to enter the other's territory with hostile intent. Laban was keen to make this agreement as firm as possible, so he swore by the God of Abraham, then seemingly by the god (or gods) of Nahor, and added, confusingly, "the god(s) of their father", which presumably meant the god(s) of Terah. Jacob swore simply by the fear of Isaac (compare v.42 with comment there). Again the agreement was sealed by a sacrifice and a meal eaten together on the mountain.

Early next morning Laban, now satisfied with his agreement with Jacob, bade his family goodbye, blessed them and went home. Thus he ceded all claim to them and to what Jacob now possessed. The intervention of God had weakened his resolve to get even with Jacob.

Jacob also went on his way, "and the angels of God met him" (32.1). The last time he had had a sight of the "angels of God" was at Bethel on his way to Haran. This new encounter marked the start of his re-entry into Canaan as the previous one had marked his exit from it. His previous dream, at Bethel, had filled him with awe at the manifest presence of God and at the realisation that God was so closely involved in what went on upon earth. On this occasion he seems to have been mainly conscious of the power of the angelic host, which appeared to him when he was about to move into an area in which he would be vulnerable. He had felt on the previous occasion that he must name the place to celebrate the occasion; hence the name Bethel. Similarly he felt he must name this place. His name for it, "The Two Camps", may be a reference to the power of the angelic host in welcome contrast to the weakness of his own company - his tiny "host". It was as if one should say, "Even a tiny force is invincible if it is allied to an angelic host". But the interpretation of the encounter is not easy, for little is told about it. At any rate, Jacob was nearing Canaan and God had not forgotten him. Indeed God was taking good care that Jacob would know that the Bethel promises still stood. The echoes of Bethel are clear throughout the description of the encounter. It is good for us to keep in mind that the promises of God still hold, even when we are conscious of much in our lives which may cause us to be aware of our unworthiness of His love and care.

Notes

19 Teraphim were images, whose size might vary from small ones which could be hidden in a saddle (v.34) to large ones which could serve as a dummy to pass muster as a sleeping man (1 Sam 19.13).

38 The reference to "ewes" is poignant, for the Hebrew word is the plural of RACHEL (7353, 7354), the name of Jacob's beloved.

42 There is some doubt about the translation of "fear" (PACHAD - 6343), but it should probably stand. It can be understood as meaning "the God whom Isaac fears" or "the God of Isaac, a God who is to be feared"; the latter is preferable.

GENESIS 32

Jacob is Prepared for Meeting Esau

Verses 3-8: Jacob Sends Messengers to Esau

Jacob had spent over twenty difficult years holding his own in the battle of wits with Laban. He had discovered (31.42) that he would not have come away with any possessions if God had not intervened on his behalf. Now he faced a difficult experience, for he had lived all those years with the memory of the fact that his flight and exile were due to his alienating his brother Esau, and now he was about to meet Esau. God had commanded him to return to the land which He had promised to give him (28.4, 13, 15). But returning to the land involved meeting Esau. Even so in our spiritual experience, if we are to enter upon our spiritual inheritance we find that there come moments when we must face up honestly to the things we have done in the past and come to terms with who we are.

Jacob's instinct still ran along the lines of tactical manoeuvres. He sent messengers ahead to Esau his brother. He must surely have remembered, that his last contact with his brother had been less than fraternal. Their relationship, such as it was, had been broken by Jacob's deception. Tact was now required, and Jacob knew when to be tactful. The phrase "my lord Esau" which he used in instructing his messengers was an address commonly used in polite letters. If Esau was "my lord", then Jacob was "thy servant". One's mind goes back to the blessing given by Isaac (in the belief that it was Esau whom he was blessing): "Be lord over thy brethren, and let thy mother's sons bow down to thee" (27.29). Jacob had not yet reached to full flowering of this blessed state as he bowed low before Esau. He was not yet ready to enter fully upon the blessing, for it had been acquired by deception.

Quickly Jacob's message got down to the facts, how in Haran he had accumulated oxen, asses, flocks, menservants and maidservants. He was hoping, he said, that he might be favourably received by Esau. One presumes that the list of his property had some connection in his mind with the hope of a good reception. This was of course a first line of approach. More was to follow.

The messengers returned to report back. They had found Esau in Seir of Edom. They had no report to make of any response to Jacob's message, except the news that Esau was coming to meet Jacob - with 400 men. It would be difficult to meet Esau, but to meet him with his 400 men, that would be terrifying!

Jacob's terror was overwhelming, but he was a man of action. This was a standard procedure to ensure against complete disaster in the loss of everything. If Esau destroyed one company the other might escape.

Verses 9-12: Jacob Prays

God had been with Jacob, as He had promised. Jacob's mind now turned to prayer, the first recorded prayer by him. His mode of address to God shows him going back to his initial experience of God, at Bethel. All the titles he uses in addressing God come from ch.28 - Yahweh ("the Lord"), God of my father Abraham, God of Isaac - God had used them all in addressing Jacob in that chapter. But he called upon his experience of God since then (31.3,13) as a basis for his present prayer. God had said to him, "Return", and he was returning. He referred to the promise of God, given in 31.3, that He would "be with" him, quoting it in the form, "I will deal with thee" (RV "I will do thee good"). It is good when praying to be able to go back to one's first knowledge of God, better to be able to plead on the basis of subsequent experience of God, perhaps best of all to be able to say to God, "according to Thy word" (compare Num 14.20). God cannot be expected to answer in ways which would be contradictory to His Word, the Bible.

Jacob's growth in grace appears in his acknowledgment of his unworthiness of God's mercies and of the truth which God had shown him. The "mercies" and "truth" are probably to be understood as "covenant kindness" and "faithfulness" and the whole statement should be seen as an acknowledgment that God, in acting with covenant-based kindness, had faithfully performed all that He had promised.

He recalled in his prayer how at the start of his journey to Haran he had nothing but his staff, and now God "had made him" two companies (compare 32.2). A pilgrim character (symbolised by the staff) is a good beginning for a developing experience with God. If the interpretation of the two companies at Mahanaim is correct, the lively realisation of the strength of a weak person closely supported by divine might is a good basis for the development of experience of God.

The burden of his request to God comes in v.11. He was praying for deliverance from his brother Esau, lest he come and strike him and spare not even mothers and children. After all those years he knew that the basic quarrel which had led to his flight to Haran remained unresolved. Would Esau have forgotten? Or become tired of nursing his anger? Or decided that he was happy enough with his lot - after all Jacob had been exiled while he had freedom to live in his chosen area at Mt.Seir in Edom? Jacob had no reason to be confident that any of these things had happened. No message of forgiveness or hope had been sent to him, and conscience, which "makes cowards of us all", was at work reminding him of the way he had deceived Esau.

If Esau attacked and slew the family, what would become of God's promise of descendants as numerous as the grains of sand on the seashore? The final appeal in his prayer is based on the utter reliability of God when he makes a promise. If there is the assurance of a promise from Him there is certainty that it will be fulfilled in His own good time. This is the surest basis for prayer.

Verses 13-21: Presents to Pacify Esau

Jacob's awareness of his vulnerability and of the strength of Esau led him to prepare "a present for Esau his brother". The animals listed in vv.14-15 make up a very substantial present - almost 600 animals, including a good number of camels, which were particularly valuable. To achieve maximum impact for his gifts he divided them into droves. His servants were fully briefed as to how they should address Esau. It could be taken for granted that he would demand an explanation from the servants for these substantial numbers on the move without any owner travelling in person with them. They were to say that the animals belonged to Jacob, "thy servant", and that they were "a present sent unto my lord Esau". Each group of servants was to add, as a most important note at the end of the explanation, that "thy servant Jacob is behind us" (v.20). So the ground was prepared by Jacob for his meeting with Esau.

Jacob's thinking in this carefully orchestrated series of presents is given in loaded language. He sent "a present" (MINCHA - 4503, the word normally used in Leviticus of the meal offering). His hope was to "appease" Esau, literally to "cover his face". The "covering" part of the phrase (KAPAR - 3722) is a root word frequently used in the levitical offerings of "making atonement" for the offerer. Jacob was approaching as an inferior to a superior. His all-consuming desire was to see Esau's "face" directed in favour towards him. He wanted to "cover Esau's face" by means of the presents which went "before his (own) face", then, said he, "afterward I will see his face", and he hoped to be accepted by him. But before he would meet Esau he was to have a life-changing experience at Peniel when he would "see the face of God" (compare v.30).

The encounter with Esau, seeing him face to face after over twenty years' absence, was what filled Jacob with apprehension. In the busy years in between he had been able to suppress his memory of how he had treated Esau. Now he was returning to Canaan and resuming his place among the covenant people. As the bearer of responsibility for carrying on the central line of descent to David and Messiah he must face the consequences of what he had done. He could not hide any longer in exile. He had been sent away for "a few days", as Rebekah had put it, to get a wife and to allow Esau's anger to cool. Now after many, many days he had returned and the issue with Esau had to be faced.

Sometimes Jacob is blamed too harshly for his cowardice in this situation. We should be careful to remember the times when a bad conscience has made *us* cowardly, perhaps even magnifying the danger into which our sins and failures have brought us. Jacob was returning because God told him to return. He was returning because he was at the centre of God's purpose for the line of Abraham and Isaac. He was the man to whom the divine promises had been given. But he must face Esau. Meanwhile he prepared to spend the night in the camp (AV "company").

Verses 22-32: A Man Wrestles with Jacob

Jacob had sent presents to Esau as a preliminary insurance against a hostile reception. He then felt the time had come to send his family and possessions across to Jabbok. He sent the family across the river ford during the night, which may indicate that he was in a state of some agitation despite his presents already sent forward to Esau. It is not entirely clear whether he himself remained north of the Jabbok or whether the bout took place south of the river. In any case there was no sleep for Jacob, for the meeting with Esau was imminent.

What he had not been expecting was that an unknown opponent would come and enter into a struggle with him in the darkness, until the day broke. Jacob did not seek the conflict, but he was not a man to yield easily when challenged. The stranger did not succeed in causing Jacob to succumb to force. He therefore struck (v.25, AV "touched") him in the hollow of the thigh and put an end to any hope Jacob might have had of winning by superior strength. The thighs, or loins, are commonly viewed in Scripture as the seat of virile strength, and Jacob was stricken in the thigh.

There follows a strange conversation between the two combatants. The stranger broke the uncanny silence first. "Let me go," he said, "for the day breaketh". It was time, spiritually, for a new day, and Jacob needed to be ready to enter upon it. Jacob's response, with its urgent request for blessing, indicates his realisation of the superior status of his opponent. It may even show that he knew this to be an angel, or even "the Angel of the Presence" - in other words, a theophany, God visiting in human form. Jacob refused to let Him go unless He blessed him. If the Stranger was sufficiently superior to bestow a blessing on Jacob, was He not sufficiently strong to crush him, claim victory over him and depart at His leisure? This incident involves the mystery of God struggling with a mere man. He came to confront Jacob, to subdue him but not to crush him. The crippling blow on the thigh could have been delivered at the very start, but Jacob was being taught that, however hard he fought, he could not overcome by strength, for God was stronger. The long struggle was a vital learning process for Jacob. At the end of the conflict Jacob could still cling but he could not fail to admit to his weakness against this divine opponent.

Then came the telling question: "What is thy name?" God knew Jacob's name, had known all about him and his lineage when He encountered him at Bethel (28.13). But Jacob did not yet know enough about himself. He had lived for over twenty years with the memory of how he had claimed, twice over (27.19,24), that he was Esau the firstborn of Isaac. Now again the question came, not from blind Isaac but from God: "What is thy name?" Jacob could give only one answer, in one word, "Jacob". As has been seen in the case of Adam (3.9) and Cain (4.9), God asks questions which can cause men to look again at themselves and understand how they stand before Him.

Jacob had asked for a blessing. Instead he was given a new name, as Abram and Sarai were renamed by God Abraham and Sarah (17.5,15). Jacob was given the name Israel, which would for all future generations identify him with the nation sprung from him. So far the divine purpose has been carried forward by one member of each generation - Abraham, Isaac and Jacob. Now the sons of Jacob-Israel were to be the patriarchs of the twelve tribes, so it was appropriate that God's blessing of him should be this new name.[†] He had striven with men and had prevailed. He had struggled with all his guile to gain his ends and (against Laban) to get his rights. But had he prevailed against God? Or was he blessed because, having prevailed against men, he had now struggled (though not prevailed) against God? Hosea (12.3-4) does seem to say that he prevailed against God: "He took his brother by the heel in the womb, and by his strength he had power with God; yea, he had power over the angel, and prevailed: he wept, and made supplication unto him". His divine antagonist could, of course, have crushed him, but this was never the purpose of the struggle. Jacob learned as he wrestled that this was a supernatural opponent and that with his hip out of joint he could not throw that opponent. Yet by this same realisation he was encouraged to gain blessing by clinging to Him when he could not throw Him. So by being in some sense broken he prevailed against God. God would not be bullied into blessing him, but He would never crush a man who clung to him. From the start God set out to bless Jacob and He accomplished His purpose while at the same time teaching Jacob how dependant on God he was. We do not need to make God willing to bless us. We may need traumatic experiences to make us willing to cling to Him in faith and in acknowledgment of our weakness. Blessing comes from His strength, not from our wrestling. The message in this is rather like the message in 2 Corinthians 10-13 where the overall theme is how God's "strength is made perfect in weakness". God does not need supermen, but He can and does use weak men who have learned their own weakness.

Jacob did not gain all that he asked. His request to know the name of his opponent was answered by a question: "Wherefore is it that thou dost ask after my name?". In the almost parallel passage in Judges (13.17-18) Manoah asked the angel of the Lord a similar question and received the answer: "Wherefore askest thou after my name, seeing it is wonderful?" (RV). Jacob obviously had knowledge that this was at least an angel. In one sense it is impossible for mere man to know God fully, for He is infinite. His name is Wonderful. It is well to tread warily in talking about how, even now, God and the Son of God can be known. The Lord Jesus Himself said (Mt 11.27), "…no man knoweth the Son, but the Father; neither knoweth any man the Father, save the Son, and he to whomsoever the Son will reveal him". Jacob could know the blessing of God, for He "blessed him there". He could call the place Peniel, the Face of God, saying, "I have seen God face to face". Yet there is a fullness in God which goes far beyond what the mind can fathom. God could know Jacob through and through, but Jacob, or any other person, can only hope to go on learning God. At least Jacob was learning. The Lord Jesus in the days of His flesh could tell those who met Him with carping criticism and unbelief, "The Father himself, which hath sent me, hath borne witness of me. Ye have neither heard his voice at any time, nor seen his shape. And ye have not his word abiding in you: for whom he hath sent, him ye believe not" (John 5.37).[†] His critics refused opportunities to learn from God's communication, even when it was given in His Son. They insisted in being self-sufficient and secure in their own theories, therefore they could not get to know God. Jacob had faults, but he was quick to identify opportunities to know God, and he had spiritual ambitions.

This was the third time he had experience of angelic ministry, and the third time he felt constrained to rename a place because of the experience. He was awe-struck at Bethel because of the authority and nearness of God revealed. He was reassured at Mahanaim by the realisation that his small company was accompanied by the power of an angelic host. Here again he could say with courage that he had seen the face of God, so that he could now, with life preserved, meet the face of Esau (v.30). He had had an experience of the presence of God with him, the face of God turned towards him. Only then is it recorded that "the sun rose upon him". His new day had dawned, Israel's day. And Israel was a man who could not compel God, yet had gained a blessing from God when he "wept and made supplication unto him" (Hos 12.4).

This was not just a visionary experience, for after it he had a limp (v.31). He had a reminder, how lasting is not told, that his night experience of struggling with the angel showed his weakness. It also showed how weakness can prevail upon God to be strong in one's cause, but, nevertheless, what remained to Jacob and those who saw him walk was his limp, token of his weakness. The episode is closed by an editorial note explaining that the "children of Israel" to this day do not eat of the part of the thigh containing the sciatic nerve. This, explains the sacred record, is in memory of Jacob's night struggle, when God put His mark on him.

In the later story of Jacob he is called, now Jacob, now Israel. The features associated with the name Jacob were not totally eradicated from his character, nor did he ever revert fully to his old crookedness as if he had never had the Peniel experience. Certainly he was never the same again. He could always go back in memory to Peniel, as he had previously gone back, and would continue to go back, to Bethel.

Notes

28 The interpretation of Israel varies. It probably means, "God strives". But if God strove with Jacob, Jacob strove with God, as is stated in v.28.

30 The words "his shape" in this quotation from John 5 correspond to the Greek (LXX) translation of "the face" of God (Peniel) in Genesis 32.30. This verse shows Jacob receiving revelation from God.

GENESIS 33

Jacob Meets Esau

Verses 1-3: Jacob Arranges for the Moment of Meeting

This was going to be a most important day for Jacob, a day to which he had looked forward with apprehension. The moment of meeting is highlighted by the inspired writer by the statement that Jacob "lifted up his eyes, and looked, and, behold, Esau came". We have seen that this form of words ("lifted up his eyes, ... and behold") always heralds a point of crucial importance. And again, as in 32.6, it is recorded that Esau was accompanied by 400 men, presumably his personal retainers (compare Abraham's force of 318 in 14.14).

Previously Jacob had gone to great lengths to keep himself in the background until he would see how Esau was disposed towards him. Now it looks at first as if he were continuing on the same tack. He put the two handmaids and their children in front, then Leah and hers, then finally Rachel and Joseph. Did he want to expose Rachel and his favourite son Joseph to least risk of violence? Or was it a matter of priority, first those of lower status and last the most honoured wife and child? It appears that this second suggestion is to be preferred, for Jacob himself, having placed his family in due order, "passed over before them", which means that he "went on ahead of them". His night struggle with the angel had evidently given him new confidence. Having seen the face of God he need not fear the face of Esau as he had previously done.

Whatever his increase in confidence since a few days ago, he knew that this was a time for most careful diplomacy. He must make it abundantly clear to Esau that he was not reckoning merely on purchasing his favour with gifts. He was also prepared to declare eloquently by his posture that he was the inferior approaching the superior, the offender seeking pardon from the offended. Hence his sevenfold obeisance, bowing prostrate to "his brother". These last two words in v.3 place his abjectly humble approach in the context of the old sibling rivalry and dispute. Jacob had striven with the angel and "seen the face of God", but this did not remove from him the obligation to seek to remedy what he had marred in his relationship with his brother. We too need to understand that we cannot ride roughshod over our brothers because we know ourselves freely forgiven by God. Our acceptance with God through His grace should be a strong incentive to rectify and keep right our relations with each other.

Verses 4-7: Jacob Introduces His Family to Esau

Jacob had done what was required when he approached with deep humility. Esau's response was surely far more positive than Jacob had dared to hope it would be. Esau was older than Jacob and was the offended party but he ran to meet Jacob. He had had no clear apology or statement from Jacob but he embraced him as one embraces a friend or close relative. Then he threw his arms around his neck and kissed him. Jacob had eloquent proof of Esau's pardon. Incidentally, the language of v.4 is remarkably like that used by the Lord Jesus in Luke 15.20: "And he arose, and came to his father. But when he was yet a great way off, his father saw him, and had compassion, and ran, and fell on his neck, and kissed him". The prodigal's father in this parable, grossly offended and sinned against, could read his son's repentance without need for words. His response was prompt and whole-hearted: "(he) ran, and fell on his neck". Time had evidently healed much of Esau's anger and hurt. Jacob was welcomed back with joy. "And they wept". Both had come to a point where they could rejoice in the recovery of brotherly feelings.

Then Esau noticed the women and children behind Jacob. He had the experience, which many have had, of meeting old friends after a long separation and realising that family circumstances have changed radically. Jacob had gone away a single man, with only his staff, and now he came back with wives and children. In answer to Esau's question about who they were Jacob explained that God had graciously given him these children - he did not use the word "blessed", for it was a sensitive term in view of his past deceit. He was establishing the fact that he had enjoyed the favour of God, as evidenced in the numerous children around him. In this chapter the favour of God and the favour of Esau blend in subtle ways. In some sense the situation may illustrate Proverbs 16.7: "When a man's ways please the Lord, he maketh even his enemies to be at peace with him".

The children of the four women must be introduced, in inverse order of their importance in the mind of Jacob. So first came the handmaids and their children, bowing low to Esau, followed by Leah and her children. Finally came "Joseph ... and Rachel"; it does not say Rachel and Joseph. Is this a first foreshadowing of the pre-eminence of Joseph which we shall see before the Genesis record closes? From ch.37 onwards "the generations of Jacob" will consist mainly of the story of the rejection, sufferings and supremacy of Joseph.

Verses 8-11: Esau Receives the Presents

Esau changed the subject quickly to the lavish gifts which had met him as he came - "Quite a 'host' (MACHANEH - 4264) of animals", said he. This was the word Jacob had used to describe the heavenly "host" that met him and encouraged him at Mahanaim. There is surely an irony in the fact that Esau, who was ignorant of the events at Mahanaim, should hit on the same word to express how Jacob had gone in for comprehensive insurance in providing such a lavish "host" of gifts.

"What did it mean?", asked Esau. Jacob could only reply that he was seeking by this means to obtain Esau's favour - "the favour of my lord". Esau's reply was dignified: "I have an abundance, my brother" (Hamilton). It was a courteous reply, and the reply of a man who had no chip on his shoulder. Jacob was courteously deferential ("my lord"); while Esau was courteously reassuring and generous ("my brother"). Let Jacob keep his own property, said he, for there was no need to purchase his favour.

Jacob continued to press the presents on Esau, begging him to accept them as a means of doing a favour to Jacob - "if now I have found grace in thy sight". He used a loaded word in his plea to Esau: he asked him to receive his "present" (MINCHA - 4503) from him. This word was the one used in Leviticus of the offerings of the Lord, especially the meal offering. It was a word which fitted circumstances in which an inferior made a gift to a superior. In the offerings men sought to please God. So Jacob came seeking Esau's favour as from a superior. In this sense Jacob's word must be accepted that he had seen Esau's face "as one seeth" (v.10, RV) the face of God. Esau had looked on him with favour and in this Jacob detected evidence of the favour of God. He pleaded that Esau would accept the gift ("blessing" was his word for it in v.11). It is interesting that he had gained the confidence to use this word "blessing", which he had avoided earlier on because of its unhappy associations for Esau.

God, he explained, had dealt graciously with him and he had all he needed. This was his insistent theme to Esau, how God had dealt bountifully with him. Commentators have seen in his persistent pleading with Esau, and in the lavishness of his gifts, evidence that Jacob was seeking to make amends in some sense to Esau for having cheated him of his blessing. This certainly may have been a factor in the situation, though the text does not make it as clear as that. Finally, in response to his urging, Esau accepted his gifts. The whole episode is marked by oriental courtesy with its insistence on oblique statements which must not be taken strictly at face value. It is a probable that both men were well satisfied with the outcome of the discussion. The spirit in which it was conducted suggests that a reasonable relationship, though not a cordial one, had been established.

Verses 12-17: Esau and Jacob Go Their Separate Ways

Esau's next proposal (v.12) should be understood as an offer to accompany Jacob, to keep pace with him, presumably for his protection. While no doubt happy with the outcome of the discussions so far, Jacob was not yet ready for a prolonged journey with Esau to Seir, outside Canaan. It is probable that he already had plans to go at a gentle pace westwards across the Jordan to Shechem or thereabouts, quite a short distance. The journey to Seir would be much longer and harder. This would explain his language in v.13 about the danger to his children of a hard trek and the danger of overdriving his flocks with their young. His fear that "all" the flocks would die is best taken as an exaggeration. He asked Esau to go on ahead ("pass over before thy servant") and he would follow slowly at a pace suitable for flocks and children. Later on, he was suggesting, he could go to Seir to see Esau. He may well have done so, though Scripture does not tell of such a visit. Even if Jacob did not later go to Seir, the proprieties of the present situation required that such a possibility should not be raised.

The story focuses on Jacob and the purpose of God. Meeting Esau at this stage was an essential part of Jacob's education but later incidental meetings would be outside the scope of the inspired record.

Esau made one more gesture of goodwill before he parted. He offered an escort, which Jacob politely ("let me find grace in the sight of my lord") but firmly refused. Such an escort would put Jacob under pressure to go to Seir before it suited him to go and he had no intention of being put under any pressure now that he had an agreement of peace with Esau. So Esau went back southward to Seir and Jacob went westward to Succoth.

The name of Succoth is connected here with the shelters (AV "booths") which Jacob built for his cattle there. For himself and his family, he built a house. Some commentators say that this really means that he pitched his tent there. Men's homes were often referred to in Scripture as their houses, whatever their structure. It is true, however, that it would be surprising to read of men "building" a house if what they did was to pitch a tent. The suggestion implicit in the statement is that Jacob was intent on staying at Succoth for quite some time despite the divine command to go back to Canaan. It must be remembered that Succoth was east of Jordan, outside Canaan. How long he stayed there is not told, but it can be assumed that a good number of years elapsed between Jacob's departure from Haran and the events of ch.34, for the family grew in the intervening years from childhood to maturity.

Verses 18-20: Jacob at Shechem

Translators do not agree on the rendering of v.18. In the AV it appears as "Jacob came to Shalem, a city of Shechem". The RV rendering would take Shechem as a man's name, presumably the man of that name in the story in ch.34. Whichever way it is taken, there can be identified in v.18 a typical Hebrew comment by means of word-play on the nature of the events: Jacob came in peace to Shechem or came to a city called Peace (Shalem), in Shechem. Then ch.34 tells a story of shame and violence.

One point is made explicit—that he came into Canaan, as God commanded him, completing his journey from Paddan-aram. In later years Shechem came to be associated in a special way with Jacob. For example, John 4.5 speaks of "a city of Samaria which is called Sychar, near to the parcel of ground that Jacob gave to his son Joseph" - this would have been near the Shechem of Genesis (compare also Gen 48.22 and comment thereon). Yet Jacob had first met God at Bethel, and when, once again, after the divine call to leave Haran (31.3), he received divine instruction for his journey, the command was to go to Bethel and dwell there (35.1). So perhaps his journey from Paddan-aram was not complete until he did reach Bethel.

It is disquieting to read that at Shechem he "pitched his tent before the city". The language is rather reminiscent of how Lot "pitched his tent toward Sodom" (13.12). Too close a contact with the people of the land, and city-dwellers at that, would not be the best environment for Jacob, with his family now growing up. His intention of staying there was indicated by his buying the piece of land where his tent was from Hamor, Shechem's father.[†]

Jacob certainly meant to acknowledge God, for he erected an altar there. It is probable that a distinction is being drawn between this occasion and the time when he was told by God to go to Bethel to live (35.1) and was *commanded* to make an altar there. Shechem appears to have been a false start, a well-meaning but perilous venture before he reached the place where God wanted him to be. He made his confession in naming the altar, El-elohe-Israel ("God, the God of Israel"), but he did not reach the place of peace and rest until he got to Bethel and replaced El-elohe-Israel by El-Bethel ("The God of the House of God").

Notes

19 The price is given as 100 "pieces of money" (Q^eSITA - 7192), but the value of the Q^eSITA is not known. The Q^eSITA is mentioned in Job 42.11 in the account of Job being restored to prosperity. His acquaintances came to visit him and "every man also gave him a Q^eSITA". Literally the word means a lamb; presumably the coin had a lamb on it.

GENESIS 34

Dinah, Shechem and a Massacre

Verses 1-4: Shechem Takes Dinah

This incident explains why Dinah's name occurred (30.21) in the list of children born to Jacob by Leah. Her name was associated with the terrible events of this chapter and left a lasting mark on the minds of the people of Israel. In view of the shameful way in which affairs were managed in the chapter it comes as no surprise to us that God is not mentioned in the story; Dinah's brothers did not need God's help to behave as they did.

A superficial reading of v.1 might suggest that the events began with an innocent curiosity on the part of a young girl - she "went out to see the daughters of the land". The verb used here, "went out", recurs in the chapter usually referring to movements by people outside the bounds of their own community (compare vv.6,24,26). In view of the need to preserve the identity of the covenant people casual contract of this kind posed a threat to the young girl's community. The events were, to a considerable extent, due to the ill-advised decision which Jacob had taken to pitch his tent so close to a Canaanite city. Today, also, those who have the heavy responsibility to bring up a family need to remember the strong influences which will be at work to hinder godly parents in establishing moral awareness in their children. Family choices taken merely for financial gain may have disastrous results for the children because they are unnecessarily exposed to evil.

Dinah went to see the girls of the land. No doubt the social life of the Canaanites was interestingly different. Perhaps its lack of inhibitions appealed to her. One might have expected that her parents would have protected her from the risks which were inherent in her adventures into Canaanite society. There have been instances in Genesis of the leading men among peoples outside the covenant expecting that they should have a right to possess women who appealed to them (compare 12.15; 20.2). This was another such incident.

People who are governed by their senses and appetites behave outside the guidelines appropriate for the people of God. Shechem, the prince, "saw ... took ... lay with ... humbled" (AV "defiled", ANA - 6031) Dinah. None of this necessarily indicates violence. The verb "take" (LAQACH - 3947) is used again in this chapter in contexts where wives were to be "taken" in the normal course of weddings arranged and agreed (vv.9,16,21). By the standards of the people of God it was a shameful thing that intercourse took place outside of wedlock. It was the more grievous in that at the time when it occurred there was no immediate prospect of a marriage relationship being established. In this sense Dinah was indeed "humbled". It might be argued that the fact that Shechem was an uncircumcised Canaanite was also a factor in the humbling of Dinah, but the argument does lose some force in view of the other instances (38.2; 41.45) where members of Jacob's family had Gentile marriage partners.

It is fair to understand from v.3 that Shechem became genuinely fond of Dinah, came to love her rather than merely to desire her. Yet the physical acts in which they engaged together are appropriate only inside the marriage relationship. Sex outside marriage is not blessed in Scripture and cannot be condoned in modern times either. A marriage in the christian sense exists only when a man and a woman enter into a formal, permanent contract. To speak, as some do, of a genuine caring, or stable, relationship is to side-step the issue that, in the beginning, God gave the first man a wife in a permanent relationship of marriage. There is no question of a "trial period" of physical intimacy before entering upon a marriage contract. Though Shechem loved Dinah, as she may well have loved him, their relationship was shameful.

Shechem at least acted honourably in seeking to regularise the union. He asked his father to arrange for Dinah to become his wife. It appears from later in the chapter (vv.17, 26) that Dinah remained in Shechem's house pending the outcome of his father's negotiations for a marriage settlement.

Verses 5-7: Reaction from Jacob and His Sons

News of what Shechem had done reached Jacob. To him Shechem's actions amounted to "defiling" (TAME - 2930) Dinah - the word is not the same as the one used in v.2 (ANA - 6031). It seems fair to express the difference by identifying the impropriety of Shechem's action in v.2, while seeing here the uncleanness of it in Jacob's eyes. Years had passed since Jacob settled at Succoth and then Shechem. It seems that he had become less self-assertive, perhaps less sure of his own position in the household. Since his sons were out with the cattle when the news reached him, he waited for their return before he would react to the news about Dinah. His inactivity may also be due in part to the fact that Dinah was Leah's daughter, and Leah was the unloved wife.

Meanwhile Shechem's father Hamor came to Jacob to discuss the matter. Jacob's sons also heard of the events and came in from the field. They were indignant (AV "grieved") and very angry as they thought of the "folly" (NᶜBALA - 5039) which Shechem had wrought. Folly is to be thought of as something wrong, even criminal, which offends the right feelings of the community, something which is "just not done". Shechem had wrought folly "in Israel" in the sense that, though he was not an Israelite, his actions had their effect on Israel as a community. Note the increasing emphasis at this stage on a broad community of people, here called Israel, though a nation of Israel as such did not yet exist. In view of the reckless form assumed by the brothers' revenge it is perhaps justifiable to doubt whether they had much concern about what kind of community God was building. It looks as if they felt that their family, and they themselves in particular, had "lost face". It was a matter of "honour" at dispute between the young men of two families belonging to two different communities.

Verses 8-17: Proposal and Counter-Proposal

Hamor's proposal to Jacob and his sons follows on so closely from the description of the sons' feelings that it looks as if they had burst in while Hamor was actually negotiating with Jacob. At any rate Hamor read the situation shrewdly and made the case for Shechem. He highlighted the fact that this was first and foremost a matter concerning Shechem and Dinah, a young man and the girl he loved. He requested permission from Jacob and his sons (note the plural "you" in v.8) for the young couple to marry.

But then, with a fine sense of diplomacy, he suggested a much more extensive linking of the families. Why not have an understanding, said he, that the families should intermarry? Let the sons of Jacob consider this as their home and feel free also to trade and settle in it. This was a comprehensive alliance which he was proposing. If, as can probably be assumed, the Shechemites were numerically stronger than Jacob and his family, then this looks on the face of it like an attractive offer. Shechem himself backed it up by an offer to pay as a bride-price whatever they asked. This was a positive offer to open financial negotiations. It would appear that he may have expected them to answer along the lines of the sons of Heth (23.15), stating a price as a next phase of the deal. That they should reject his approach probably never occurred to him as a possibility. He would have had no concept of why they should be upset at what he and Dinah had done. The incident in 1 Kings 22 comes to mind in which the ungodly King Ahab of Israel invited Jehoshaphat to join him in a military alliance. Jehoshaphat's mistake is spelt out in his misguided, "I am as thou art, my people as thy people, my horses as thy horses" (v.4). But Jehoshaphat was not like Ahab and Judah was polluted by contact with apostate Israel.

Shechem's lack of understanding of their thinking made him an easy victim of their guile (v.13). They argued that they could not agree to give their sister to an uncircumcised man. They represented this problem as a matter of "reproach", something which would expose them to mockery and ridicule. It is interesting to see here how, though Hamor had come to deal with Jacob, the negotiations by this time were between Jacob's sons on the one side and Hamor and his son on the other. This was basically a young men's dispute. It was being handled on the basis of actions being seen as embarrassing or "shameful", rather than sinful. There is an important difference between shame and guilt.

The solution, the brothers argued (v.15), was that all the males in Shechem should be circumcised. The proposal effectively made the covenant rite of circumcision remote from the spiritual implications of the covenant, for there was no suggestion that they were inviting the

Shechemites to seek admission to covenant privileges and obligations. If the men of Shechem were circumcised, the brothers said, intermarriage could be agreed and a uniting of the two peoples.

If the Shechemites were unhappy with this proposal, the brothers would simply take their "daughter" and go their way. This use of the term, their "daughter", reads very oddly, but one takes it that they were really doing a father's part on behalf of Jacob and presuming to speak for him. In all of this there was no clear indication that they were aware of the necessity for the covenant people to be separate from identification with Canaanite society with its corrupt religion and morals. Their resentment owed more to personal loss of face than to religious scruples or awareness of God.

Verses 18-24: Hamor and Shechem are Deceived

Hamor and Shechem would not have understood Jacob's family's stance if they had explained that they were a different kind of people, belonging to the one true God. They did understand the approach which suggested that a simple ritual operation could overcome obstacles. Shechem in particular (v.19) was well pleased to have such a simple solution which would enable him to marry Dinah, for he was, says the sacred record, infatuated with (AV "had delight in") Jacob's daughter. His eagerness to agree to the proposed terms so that he could marry her was important for the revenge being prepared, for he was held in high esteem in Shechem and could sway the men "in the gate" of the city, the decision-makers.

So Hamor and Shechem put the proposal of Jacob's sons to the men in the gate. This was their case: Jacob and his sons were peaceable people, fit to be accepted as neighbours and to have a place among the local businessmen; there was plenty of space for them; therefore an alliance leading to intermarriage would be a good thing. Admittedly there was the technical detail that the newcomers were demanding that all the local males be circumcised, but the advantages of the expansion of the local economy were obvious. In practical terms the Shechemites would absorb these prosperous and enterprising neighbours (v.23). The proposal was accepted by the local community (v.24) and everything seemed very satisfactory - for two days.

Verses 25-29: Vengeance Falls

The third day brought them to their senses. Their circumcision wounds were now angry, and they were physically in no fit state to defend themselves from attack when Simeon and Levi, full brothers of Dinah, entered the city unopposed (AV "boldly"), sword in hand, and slew all the males. Among those who fell were Hamor and Shechem. Dinah they took from Shechem's house and left the city. Scripture does not say whether Dinah had remained there voluntarily through affection for Shechem, or whether she had been detained there because Shechem was infatuated with her. It may well have been her wish to be there.

The main group of Jacob's sons then descended on the city and plundered it to continue the avenging of their sister's defilement. They took all the animals inside the city or outside, all the valuables, all the wives and children and all the household goods. This grim penalty was exacted on people who could hardly have understood what moved these men to such fury. The sons of Jacob deceived a man and his son, and through them a city, who wished them only good if they posed no threat to the local community. Is it too much to see in their powers of deception something of the character of their father? They had used the divinely-given rite of circumcision as a device to give them military advantage. The events recorded here presage savage and bitter feuds in future days. It has been well said that, while it is not clear that Dinah was raped by Shechem, it is clear that (metaphorically) the sons of Jacob raped the city.

Verses 30-31: Jacob's Remonstrance

Jacob identified Simeon and Levi as the main culprits, presumably because they had carried out the massacre. Their lead role in the massacre was due to the fact that they, like Dinah, were children of Leah. There is no need for subjective impressions of what they had done, for Jacob's initial reaction against it is given here, as is his assessment at the end of his life (49.5-7). His initial reaction was one of fear lest the violence and murder committed by his sons should bring down on all their heads a violent response from their neighbours (v.30). His later assessment, in ch.49, charges them with violence, anger, self-will and wrath, and pronounces on their tribes a sentence of scattering and division. It is interesting that at this point in ch.34, Jacob did not rebuke them for doing evil, only for acting imprudently and in a way which threatened his, and their, security. There can be no doubt that Scripture condemns such savage over-reaction, in the Old Testament as well as in the New. The God of the old covenant is the same God as the Father of our Lord Jesus Christ.

They responded bluntly. Shechem had dealt with Dinah, their sister, "as with an harlot". This was not an accusation of rape, for harlots are not usually raped. It may have been an accusation that his offer to pay a high bride-price and gifts was in effect an attempt to gain what he wanted by payment, as if Dinah were a commodity to be bought. Or again it may have been an expression of their indignation that by seducing Dinah he had placed her outside the normally accepted tradition of parentally arranged marriage as the first step - he had made her an outsider in her own community as if she were a harlot. Whatever their thinking, their violent and unrestrained reaction and their carefully premeditated murder of neighbours left a deep and lasting scar on Jacob's mind, as ch.49 shows.

GENESIS 35

Back to Bethel and Three Deaths

Introductory

This chapter concludes "the generations of Isaac", which began at 25.19. The main character in the section has of course been Jacob, Isaac's son. In the recent narrative, notably in ch.34, he has been seen to lose the initiative to his grown-up sons. While he has ceased to dominate the action, he remains an important figure for the spiritual record in the section (37.1 onwards) headed "the generations of Jacob", in which the main character is Joseph his son. Here in ch.35 he is seen back at Bethel, where he began his spiritual education (ch.28). His return there is in response to a specific divine command (35.1), and it seems that when he reaches there the time has come for the signal that an era has ended, hence the three deaths recorded in the chapter.

Verses 1-8: Jacob Returns to Bethel: Deborah Dies

It was in response to a specific command that Jacob returned from Haran to Canaan (31.3). When, however, he had made his peace with Esau, he spent some time in Succoth and later in Shechem. In the period between his meeting Esau and the start of this chapter the voice of God has fallen silent. Peniel left its mark on Jacob but he lived for years without benefit of fresh experiences of God.

At last came the renewed call of God, a specific command to go to Bethel. It was a journey upward in literal and topographical terms, but also spiritually. He needed a renewing of that awareness of God which he had felt at Bethel at the start of his exile. He was instructed also to stay there long enough to carry out God's other commands. He was told to build an altar at Bethel, not the first altar he had built (compare 33.20), but the first one which God had told him to build. God did not idealise the initial experience of Jacob - it was of "God, that appeared unto thee when thou fleddest from the face of Esau thy brother". The description does not even mention the fact that, in addition, Jacob was going to Haran to seek a wife.

That was the sum total of the instructions he received from God. There was not a word about idols or preparing his people for the pilgrimage to Bethel. Yet his first action was to call upon his family and followers to put away all their foreign (AV "strange") gods. The lesson is that if there is to be sensitivity to the danger of alien spiritual influences, it will most probably come from a sense of the living God rather than a book of rules. While Jacob took the decisions about where he would live the idols could remain among the stuff and no doubt were worshipped by at least some of his people. But when they were under God's orders the idols must go. In this context commentators aptly quote Psalm 24.3,4: "Who shall ascend into the hill of the Lord?

or who shall stand in his holy place? He that hath clean hands, and a pure heart; who hath not lifted up his soul unto vanity (vain idols), nor sworn deceitfully".

The holiness appropriate to the place of God's choice was also stressed in Jacob's command to his people to purify themselves and change their outer garments. Ritual washings and putting on new or clean clothing were a constant practice in approaching God. While not following such rituals to-day, it is always appropriate for believers to avoid slovenliness when engaged in spiritual exercises. The spiritual realities of clean lives symbolised in the rituals are, of course, the prime consideration.

Jacob outlined the plan, that they would go up to Bethel where he would build an altar to God. He made more general the reference to the circumstances in which God had appeared to him by his phrasing it "who answered me in the day of my distress" (v.3), rather than speaking of his fleeing from Esau. He testified to his people that God had been as good as His word in being with him "in the way which (he) went" (v.3, compare 28.15). The people obeyed fully. They gave him all their foreign gods and all their earrings - presumably these earrings had some connection with their idolatry. Jacob buried them under the terebinth tree by Shechem, possibly the same landmark as Abraham had visited in 12.6. Idolatrous people often took their gods with them on journeys in the hope that they would protect them from danger. It may be that in Jacob's company there were some who had misgivings about parting with their teraphim, now buried beneath the terebinth tree. If so, their experience now may have convinced them that the best protection on a journey was to have the blessing of the living God, for "the terror of God was upon the cities that were round about them" (v.5). Thus they travelled, at God's command and under His protection.

Jacob's arrival at Bethel is stated in terms which draw attention to the significance of the journey. Its old name Luz, is recalled as are the facts that it was in Canaan and that its name had been changed to Bethel. All of this recapitulation marks out this coming to Bethel as important in the story of Jacob's experience of God. He understood this too. At Shechem he had given the place of the altar the name El-elohe-Israel (God, the God of Israel), as if staking his claim to relationship with God. Here he was content with God Himself and named the place of the altar again as El-Bethel (God of Bethel, or God of the House of God) - the name starts and finishes with God. It is a new level of spiritual maturity in Jacob. He looked back and traced the meaning of his experience since he left Canaan to the God who made Himself known at Bethel and promised to be with him and bring him safely back. God had gone before him and had also been his rear-guard.

This episode is closed by what seems at first an odd account, namely of the death of Deborah, Rebekah's nurse. Firstly, her name is given here for the first time. Then she was mentioned only once before, in 24.59, and that was a long time ago in the narrative as well as in chronology; she must have been very old. How she came to be at Bethel is not known - perhaps she had come there after Jacob's return to see him before she died. It appears that her death was viewed by Jacob with considerable sorrow, for the oak tree under which she was buried was named by him the Oak of Weeping. Most peculiarly, why was she mentioned here and Rebekah herself passed over? For an answer, it is necessary to go back to Rebekah's management of Jacob's flight. She had explained that he would need to go away to stay with Laban for "a few days" (27.44) until Esau's anger subsided. She obviously expected to see him again soon but it seems that she never did see him again. After Jacob left home Rebekah passes off the page of Scripture, except in relation to her family and her nurse, until it is revealed indirectly (49.31) that she was buried in the cave of Machpelah with Isaac. Her handling of the deceit of Isaac placed her outside the sacred story of how God educated Jacob and carried His purpose towards its goal. Deborah serves as a reminder that seemingly great and important people, such as Rebekah seemed to be, can write themselves out of God's work by their actions. A near parallel is found in the record of David's mighty men. One might have expected the redoubtable hero Joab to feature in the list. Instead Abishai and Asahel (his brothers) are listed, and his armour-bearer(s), but no mention there of Joab (2 Sam 23.18,24,37). He had disqualified himself. So this verse in Genesis 35 about Deborah is God's comment on Rebekah. There is no record of when or in what circumstances she died nor even whether Jacob knew of her death until he returned.

Verses 9-15: Reaffirmation at Bethel

In v.1 it was seen that God spoke again to Jacob to direct him to Bethel. Now in v.9 He spoke to Jacob and reaffirmed His Bethel undertakings to him. First He blessed him, one of the constantly repeated assurances in Genesis - that God blesses those whom His grace takes up to work out His purposes. Then the name-change from Jacob to Israel was repeated. This indicates the divine plan to elevate Jacob, to refine out of his behaviour the old Jacob features. It is not to be taken as a literal statement that he would no longer be called Jacob, for the divine record rings the changes on the two names, even in the same sentence (for instance, in 49.2).

God's declaration to Jacob, "I am God Almighty" (El Shaddai), recalls the two previous occurrences of the title. God had used it in 17.1 when introducing the covenant sign of circumcision. Then Isaac had used it when blessing Jacob (28.3) and calling down on him the blessing of God Almighty. Now God Himself gave a fresh assurance to Jacob using the same title of Himself as He had used in 17.1 when addressing Abraham.

His command to Jacob to be fruitful and multiply seems singularly appropriate in that the chosen line branched out into what would become the twelve tribes when Jacob's wives bore him so many sons. The mention of kings (v.11) coming from his loins promised distinction within the chosen line. There would be kings until a Son of Judah's tribe became pre-eminent (49.10). Of course not all the kings would be of Judah's line - Saul, for example, was of the tribe of Benjamin - but Genesis must be read in the context of Scripture as a whole to understand the prominence given so widely to David and his Son.

Now that Jacob was back in the land it was appropriate that the promise of the land (v.12) should be repeated. While he dwelt in Paddan-aram (as it is called in v.9) attention was focused on a wife or wives, and on children. At this point he owned a small piece of land at Shechem, just as Abraham never owned more than a burial plot, but he was back in the land and God repeated the promise of "the land which I gave Abraham and Isaac". This was no short-term promise, it was to Jacob and his seed - a promise for a chosen people, not for immediate or early fulfilment. It must always be remembered that, while Genesis is a book of promises given and of movement towards fulfilment, it is but the beginning of a long journey started by a people at the invitation of their God towards glory which they could hardly imagine. Even the whole of the five books of Moses leave many deliberate indications of unfinished business. God gave promises, gave tokens of future blessing by present blessings enjoyed, but always there was a sense of waiting for the maturing of much greater plans. Having reassured Jacob and whetted his appetite for the divine blessings, God "went up from him", so ending the appearing.

Jacob saw that this was a significant event and celebrated its importance by setting up a pillar as he had done at Bethel in 28.18. But here he also poured a drink offering on it, the first mention in Scripture of such an offering. Is it too much to see in this some hint of the joy which is sometimes connected with the drink offering (compare Phil 2.17-18)? Andrew Bonar in his commentary on Leviticus says of the drink offering that "it was an expression on the offerer's part of his cheerful and hearty acquiescence in all that was done at the altar". Jacob had recaptured at last something of that sense of wonder which had possessed him in ch.28, and in recognition of it he confirmed the name Bethel. He had placed God rather than Jacob at the centre of his thinking.

Verses 16-20: Rachel Dies and Benjamin is Born

This chapter records a number of journeys: at v.5 Jacob and his people journeyed to Bethel from Shechem; here at v.16 they journeyed from Bethel to the region near Ephrath; then in v.21 they journeyed on beyond Migdal-eder. Each journey introduces a new episode.

At this point, then, they journeyed from Bethel, but some distance before they reached Ephrath (better known as Bethlehem), Rachel, who was pregnant, went into labour. It was a difficult labour, says v.16. When the labour pains were at their most severe (v.17) the midwife spoke to her reassuringly: she must not be afraid, for this was another son. Whether she understood or heeded the message is not known, but as she was dying she named the baby Benoni, "Son of My Sorrow". Jacob was moved by the pessimism of the name to intervene and give the baby an alternative name. This was the only occasion on which he named any of his children. He said, "Not Benoni, but Benjamin", not "Son of My Sorrow", but "Son of the Right Hand" (or perhaps "Son of Good Fortune"). There are some parallels between this story and Luke 1.63, where Zacharias named his son John when the relatives wanted to call him Zacharias. This was Jacob's last child, according to the biblical record. So Rachel died and was buried on the way to Ephrath. She had had her wish, to bear another son, granted after many years, but it cost her her life. Her death made a deep impression on Jacob - he referred to it again at 48.7. He marked its significance by setting up a pillar on her grave. Others also accepted that this was an event of some importance, for the pillar continued to be known and noticed until the time when Genesis was written (v.20).[†]

Verses 21-22: Reuben is Disgraced

They journeyed on with the sorrow of Rachel's death heavy on Jacob, and his youngest son motherless. The next stopping place was Migdal-eder (AV "the Tower of Edar"). At this point Jacob had another sorrow, this time involving his eldest son Reuben who "lay with Bilhah his father's concubine". She was Rachel's handmaid and mother of Dan and Naphtali. In this context Jacob's reaction is not recorded, though it is noted that Israel (that is to say, Jacob) heard of it. But he was deeply shocked and never forgot the insult to himself and the wickedness against God, as 49.4 shows. This offence disqualified Reuben from enjoying the rights of the firstborn. Other incidents show his unsuitability for the position, but in ch.49 Jacob traced his loss of the firstborn's rights to this incident.

What caused Reuben to lie with Bilhah must remain a matter of conjecture, and certainty is difficult to achieve. The most reasonable suggestion is that he was expressing an aspiration to take over leadership from Jacob before Jacob died. Jacob has been seen taking an increasingly low profile in the affairs of his family, inactive when he would have been expected to lead. This may have encouraged Reuben to stake his claim by lying with Bilhah (compare Absalom in 2 Sam 16.21-22). In the absence of anything to suggest that he used force it can be taken that Bilhah consented rather than was raped. Whatever moved Reuben to commit this foul deed, Jacob acted decisively when the time came by announcing the honours to go to the tribes of Judah and Joseph, and making explicit his rejection of Reuben for any place of excellence (49.4a).

Verses 22-26: Jacob's Sons Listed

This has been a chapter of deaths and endings. It marks the end of the section called "the generations of Isaac". Hence the need felt here for a list of Jacob's sons, complete now that Benjamin has been born. The sons are listed under their mothers' names, first Leah's sons, for she was Jacob's first wife. Then follow Rachel's, Bilhah's and Zilpah's sons. The statement that the sons were born to Jacob in Paddan-aram is to be taken as a general statement, for it is obvious that Benjamin was born in Canaan (v.16). There is a poignancy in the fact that, at the head of the list, Reuben is recorded as "Jacob's firstborn". The moral imperative inseparable from the status of Israel as the covenant people cannot ever be lost sight of in Scripture. Reuben may have had legal rights, but these were God's people and no man dare presume to demand rights for which he has no moral fitness.

Verses 27-29: Isaac Dies

This short section brings Jacob back to Isaac. There has been no mention of a previous contact between them since Jacob left home with Isaac's blessing in 28.1-5. In ch.27 it was seen that Isaac's faculties were already failing at that time and it appears possible from the age at which he died that he lived for another eighty years. Certainly he has not featured in the story since ch.28 and it requires no stretch of imagination to realise that, blessing or no blessing, there was no close bond between Isaac and Jacob. However, both Jacob and Esau went to Hebron to him. They performed their filial duty by burying him. He died "being old and full of days".

The traditional expression is used of him, that he "was gathered unto his people". (See at 25.8 for comment on the implications of the idiom.) Right to the very end Isaac remains the least visible of the patriarchs. He always had a low profile, never seeming to do great things for God. He did, however, wait patiently for God to fulfil promises. He also passed on the spiritual torch, which he had received from his father Abraham, to Jacob. He features among the people of faith in Hebrews 11, as the man who by faith "blessed Jacob and Esau concerning things to come" (v.20). He was a man who understood that believing God required a life which took due account of the future in the promises of God. It is sad that Esau failed in precisely this regard, living as he did for the satisfaction of present appetites and disregarding the supreme importance of future blessing from God (Heb 11.15-16).

Notes

19,20 It is difficult to locate Rachel's tomb. In 1 Samuel 10.2 it is referred to as being "in the border of Benjamin", presumably the southern border near Jerusalem. Jeremiah (31.15) refers to the sorrow ("a voice was heard in Ramah, lamentation and bitter weeping") as the children of Rachel were carried into captivity. He speaks of Rachel "weeping for her children ... because they were not". It is attractive to think of this as a reference to Rachel's tomb, somewhere close by where her descendants were marshalled on the border of the Southern Kingdom to be taken away into exile. This passage in Genesis 35 seems to locate the tomb near to Bethlehem, rather farther south. But the precise location is only of secondary importance compared to the pathos of Rachel's death, so deeply felt by Jacob and so touchingly remembered in Israel.

GENESIS 36

The Line of Esau

Introductory

In 25.12-18 "the generations of Ishmael" were recorded, removing him and his line from the main thread of divine purpose. There followed a chapter in which Isaac was the central character, for he was the man in whom God would continue His purpose. So here in ch.36 we have "the generations of Esau", eliminating him and his family from the story of God's purpose. In the following chapters, indeed until the end of Genesis, the main character is Joseph. The record of the generations of Esau is much more detailed than that of Ishmael, possibly because Israel was to have more contact with the Edomites than with the Ishmaelites over the generations to come. Chapter 36 falls into six main sections consisting mainly of lists of names. There is overlap between some sections and it is difficult to see any consistent pattern.

Verses 1-8: Esau and His Family

The first point established in this account of Esau's wives and sons is that Esau is to be identified as ancestor of the Edomites. As commented in the footnote to 28.9 there is confusion in the naming of Esau's wives. While a few people in Scripture appear now under one name and now under another, it does seem that problems have arisen in the textual transmission of the names.[†] The record of Esau's three wives once again shows how completely he was removed from participation in covenant blessings: two of his wives were Canaanite and the third an Ishmaelite. Ironically, while all of Jacob's sons except Benjamin were born in Haran (Paddan-aram), Esau's sons were born in Canaan.

If it is to be understood, as seems inevitable, that the parting of Esau from Jacob (vv.6-7) took place after Jacob's return to Canaan, it is clear from 32.3 and 33.14 that he had earlier links with Seir. What is recorded here would seem to be a subsequent, perhaps more complete, move to Seir. The difficulty which arose when the two very prosperous owners of animals lived in the same area is the same as was seen in ch.13 when Abraham and Lot parted company. The final statement in this section makes sure that the fact that Seir was Esau's true home is not forgotten, for he was the father of the Edomites.

Verses 9-14: Two Generations from Esau

Yet again the record is headed by a reminder that Esau is to be thought of as ancestor of the Edomites, who lived in Seir. As was found earlier in Genesis, a number of the family of Esau gave their names to places, so effectively the family tree was of interest in Israel in later generations as linking certain neighbours outside the covenant with Esau.

Amalek, Esau's grandson, however, receives special attention. Esau's son Eliphaz was father of five sons by his wife, but he also had a concubine called Timna who bore him a son, Amalek. This is a notorious name in Scripture, the name of a nomadic tribe which was perpetually at war with Israel. On the march the Israelites had to guard against surprise Amalekite raids which would characteristically strike at the vulnerable section in the rear (Deut 25.18). Hence the divine instruction that they should "blot out the remembrance of Amalek from under heaven" (Deut 25.19). The Amalekites developed a separate identity from the more settled Edomite descendants of Esau. It is perhaps apt, in view of this separate identity, that Amalek was the only person on this list who was the son of a concubine.

Amalek is usually taken as conveying spiritual lessons about the flesh, the natural propensity to sin, especially by way of self-pleasing and self-indulgence. This enemy attacks at any weak point. It is particularly skilful at nomadic-type raids which wreak havoc, then it retires for a time, until watchfulness is again dropped. No wonder the warfare goes on, even "from generation to generation" (Ex 17.16). How appropriate that Esau, that "profane person" (Heb 12.16), should be ancestor of Amalek. Esau sold lasting blessing for momentary gratification of appetite.

Verses 15-19: Chiefs of Clans Descended from Esau

These verses record very similar data to vv.9-14. Most of the names are identical, but throughout this list the term translated "duke(s)" in the AV recurs. It appears that this list puts the Esauites into their political and military framework.

Perhaps the most significant point of interpretation in the section is the translation of the word "duke" (ALLUP - 441). Some scholars (among them Hamilton) argue that it is best taken as meaning "clan", which gives us a similar emphasis in the section, but arrives at it by a different route. It is probably best to retain the general idea of the AV "duke", but "chief" (Wenham) would be a better word for it. "Duke" has too many modern British overtones to give the true sense.

Verses 20-30: The Children of Seir

The names in this genealogy are those of the descendants of one Seir, a Horite. He gives his name to the area, Seir, where Esau and his family settled after they had displaced native Seirites. His genealogy is also given, partly because Esau married a grand-daughter, Aholibamah, daughter of Anah, son of Seir. Once again "chief" would be a preferable term to the AV "duke".

The peculiar episode related of Anah, son of Zibeon, in v.24 raises insuperable problems for translators. The AV says he found "mules", which is not likely in an area where horses were at that time evidently not in use - mules are of course hybrid offspring of ass and horse (usually he-ass and mare). The Latin Vulgate translates it as hot springs, and this is followed by some modern translations. The Septuagint made no attempt to translate the Hebrew word YEMIM (3222) into Greek. Other translations have given water, or giants, or fish, or a mirage. It is noticeable that a number of the translators come to an interpretation which involves water, which is the more likely in that it is said that he found it, or them (the word is grammatically plural), in the wilderness while feeding his father's asses.

The main function of these verses is to show Esau in the context of the people with whom he was linked by marriage and amongst whom he settled. He was at home in Seir.

Verses 31-39: Kings of Edom

The list contains the names of eight rulers over Edom. Of the line of Esau, they may be taken to be part of the fulfilment of the promise to Abraham (17.16) that descendants of his would be kings.

Unlike the later history of the kings of Israel and Judah, the succession in Edom was not hereditary. This would seem to mean that these men were strong individuals who inspired loyalty, not unlike some of the Israelite "judges".

At first glance the statement that these kings reigned in Edom "before there reigned any king over the children of Israel" reads oddly. Its strangeness, of course, arises from the fact that Israel had no kings for hundreds of years after the time of Moses. It may be easiest to understand it as a reference to the fact that, as Moses knew, kings would reign over Israel, as promised to Jacob (35.11), not just Abraham. The nearness of this reference in ch.35 makes this interpretation the easier to sustain. Moses, then, may be taken to be saying that, while both Abraham and Jacob had received promises of kingly descendants, the descendants of Esau had kingly men among them before such a situation could be experienced in Israel.

Verses 40-43: Chiefs Descended from Esau

This is not a repetition of the names in vv.15-19. A new factor is the arrangement, not by genealogy, but by where they lived. In the absence of time indicators it is not possible to be sure of the relative chronology of the various lists in the chapter. It is probable that this list is given in order to supplement the earlier genealogical data by information about the territory of sections of the line of Esau. It is hazardous to build much on the recurrence of names in view of the tendency for families to perpetuate favoured names in later generations (compare vv.20 and 24, where Anah is a name shared by uncle and nephew).

Notes

2,3 Henry Morris in his commentary "The Genesis Record" does his best to sort out the tangle, but his solution is very involved. His analysis (p. 526) is worth examining. Also worth study is the analysis in Keil and Delitzsch (pp. 321-2 in the 1-vol. edn.).

GENESIS 37

Joseph Dreams, is Rejected and Sold

Introductory

The opening verse of the chapter is a linking statement to return us to the main theme after ch.36. It serves to remind us that the main story is about a family line in a promised land, in the purpose of God. It may also be seen as leading to the next phase (signalled in 47.27) in which "Israel dwelt in the land of Egypt". At v.2 a new main section of Genesis begins. It is "the generations of Jacob", lasting until the end of Genesis. While the main character is Joseph the subject is not so much the spiritual career of Joseph as the development of God's purpose through the sons of Jacob. This is borne out by the important prophetic burden of ch.49, where Jacob looks at the future of the twelve tribes and relates at least some of their future history to the record of their patriarchal heads as recorded in Genesis. When the section is understood in this way, episodes in it which seem to interrupt the Joseph cycle of stories can be seen to be contextually relevant as contributing to an understanding of the broad picture of the origins and future of the tribes.

Verses 1-4: Joseph as Jacob's Favourite

The birth of Joseph had been particularly gratifying to Jacob because he was born to Rachel, Jacob's beloved wife. Yet up to this point, when he was seventeen years of age, nothing has been told of Joseph's boyhood. It was the events related here which determined his future experiences.

This is yet another example of a man whom God would later exalt to greatness but who is first seen in the Scripture record as a shepherd. It is an open question whether "his brethren" in v.2 refers to his brothers generally or only to those four specified, the sons of the handmaids. If he won the enmity of his brothers generally, as he did, it may well be that this refers to his brothers as a whole. He was with the four sons of the handmaids and it seems probable that "the lad was" (v.2) should read as "he served", in the sense that he and those four were being trained as shepherds. Leah's four eldest sons were much older and more experienced men.

Joseph "brought the evil report of them unto their father" (RV). The expression "brought the evil report" has given rise to much comment. It is used elsewhere (Num 13.32 and 14.36,37) of the spies bringing a bad report back from Canaan, and it seems normally to indicate a report that is untrue or biased. A problem about taking this statement in this critical sense is that such a criticism of Joseph here sits uncomfortably with much of what is said of Joseph elsewhere. It is out of character and it is not developed in the context as one would expect if it were intended as a criticism. Yet the words do normally bear this kind of critical sense. If it is difficult to take the words as neutral, meaning that he brought back a report of how badly his brothers behaved; there may yet be a different explanation. One suggestion which has been made is that it means that he reported to Jacob the slanders about him (Joseph) being spread by his brothers. The "bad report of them" would in this reading of it be the false report by them rather than about them.† Whichever way it is taken, the story of Joseph's youth is a story of complete lack of harmony with his brothers.

What is sure is that his father loved him more than his brothers. Jacob was guilty of favouritism, as his own mother had favoured him while his father favoured Esau. It was noted earlier that Jacob's partiality towards Rachel caused grief to Leah. In this series of events the bitterness caused by his partiality towards Rachel's elder son is seen. Joseph was "the son of his old age". He was the son for whom Jacob and Rachel had waited so long, though when he was born Rachel was still not satisfied, for she said, "The Lord shall add to me another son" (30.24). This special rejoicing that Rachel's barrenness had been removed may be adequate explanation for Joseph being called "the son of his old age", in spite of the fact that Benjamin was some fifteen years younger.

Jacob wanted to give a visible, tangible proof of his love for Joseph and he chose to give him a special coat or cloak. Our translation "of many colours" (PASSIM - 6446) derives from the ancient Greek versions, for the word is not common. The word is found in Scripture only in this chapter and in 2 Samuel 13.18,19 where David's daughter Tamar had a similar garment - "for with such robes were the king's daughters that were virgins apparelled". Most modern translators prefer to translate the word as meaning "long" or "long-sleeved". A long, or long-sleeved, robe might mark the favoured son out as being above manual labour. At any rate it would certainly be distinctive. Jacob meant it as a sign of honour, but it merely stirred up hatred and envy. His brothers came to the point where they could not bear to speak to him with common civility.

Verses 5-11: Joseph's Two Dreams

What showed Joseph as different from his brothers was not just his father's attitude or his special cloak. He was also the one who had the dreams.

Jacob was not discreet in his open favouritism towards Joseph. Joseph was equally indiscreet in telling his first dream to his brothers. No doubt his dream came from God, as did others in Genesis (20.3; 31.24; 40.5; 41.1,5). He was naive to tell it to his brothers when he must already have known about their resentment. His sheaf which he was binding in his dream stood upright, while his brothers' sheaves bowed low to it! No wonder they were resentful. They understood the dream perfectly well: he would rule over them.

The second dream confirmed the message of the first (compare 41.32). But it was even more offensive to them. He stood in his dream while the sun, moon and eleven stars bowed down to him. There is a reference in Revelation 12.1 to Israel as a woman "clothed with the sun, and the moon under her feet, and upon her head a crown of twelve stars" to help in identifying the eleven stars as Joseph's brothers, the patriarchs of the twelve tribes. Even without help, both Jacob and his eleven sons could interpret the symbolism. His brothers felt hatred (v.8) and envy (v.11), but Jacob was content merely to rebuke him (v.10). Rachel must have been dead years before this, so the moon in the dream must be taken as Leah, his step-mother, unless we are content to take the moon as included for completeness of the picture. His father, though resentful at Joseph's telling the dream, was provoked to thought and further reflection on it (v.11). There is more than a passing parallel between this incident and the response of Mary to the message of the shepherds at the birth of the Lord Jesus (Lk 2.19) and again after the incident when He was left behind in the Temple at the age of twelve (Lk 2.51).

Verses 12-24: Joseph, Sent to His Brothers, Is Thrown into a Pit

The next incident took place at a location with unpleasant associations for Jacob. His sons went to feed their father's flock at Shechem, where Dinah was seized (ch.34) and where Simeon and Levi started a massacre. This fact may have caused Jacob to be anxious about their welfare (v.14), so he sent Joseph to find out how they were faring. When he reached the area he found that they had moved away. A man who found him wandering about trying to trace them was able to tell him that they had said they were going farther, to Dothan. Having already come some fifty miles he must go a further fourteen.

One must question Jacob's judgment in sending Joseph on this errand. He was still young, his brothers were hostile to him, the journey was long and the Shechemites might well be resentful of the presence of any of the family of Jacob in the area. It does appear that he was confident that Joseph would report truthfully to him, and indeed he may not have had anyone else whom he could so trust. This may help us in interpreting v.2.

His brothers saw him a long way off (v.18) and recognised him. He was recognised early, perhaps, because of "that" robe, which he was wearing. Their immediate plotting to kill him shows how questionable Jacob's judgment was in sending him. The dream episodes still rankled, for they sneeringly referred to him, in their plotting, as "this dream-master". The bitterness and division which we saw in embryo in ch.30 was about to bear bitter and violent fruit. Their first thought was to kill him and throw him into a pit, possibly a water cistern. Their minds raced on: they would say that a wild animal had eaten him. So much for his dreams of grandeur!

But God had a future for Joseph. What was in Reuben's mind when he intervened is not revealed. It seems that he was not involved in the initial plot, for v.21 says that he "heard it". Was Reuben too weak to be a successful man of violence? Simeon and Levi would have been more resolute. Or was

Reuben eager to atone for his earlier offence against Jacob (35.22)? Or had he a conscience which forbade him to shed his brother's blood? At any rate he counselled that no blood be shed. Instead they should put Joseph into a pit unharmed. Doubtless the brothers were intended to understand that they would be free from blood-guiltiness if they simply left him to die of thirst and hunger. Reuben's intention, however, was to come back later and rescue Joseph. All this planning took place before Joseph reached them.

Then he arrived, clad in the hated robe. First of all, it must be removed. They followed Reuben's advice and cast him into the pit near by. It appears that it may have been a water cistern, for the point is made in the narrative that "there was no water in it" (v.24). The story is so terse that it would be easy to miss the reality - a young lad seized by his mature brothers, stripped and thrown into a pit where he would be trapped. His cries for mercy were unheeded, but they rang again in the ears of his captors, years later (42.21), as their consciences were at last stirred: "We are verily guilty concerning our brother, in that we saw the anguish of his soul, when he besought us, and we would not hear".

Verses 25-28: Joseph Sold

At this stage the brothers were untroubled, for "they sat down to eat bread" (v.25) while Joseph lay desolate in the pit. Then they saw something significant ("they lifted up their eyes") and had a new idea. Reuben was not with them (compare v.29) and they were able to agree on a new plan. The new factor in their thinking was the approach of a camel caravan of Ishmaelite traders carrying costly goods to Egypt. They were travelling from Gilead, famous for its balms, with a cargo of such items. Judah, appearing as an active participant in events for the first time, saw a sensible and profitable way forward. There was no profit in killing Joseph - that was certainly true. They should sell him to the traders, unharmed and therefore worth more money! After all he was their brother, so they should not kill him, just sell him as a slave. Strange logic!

The Ishmaelites were, more specifically, Midianites - just as an Englishman might more specifically be a Yorkshireman. They were business men and paid, it would appear, the going rate (compare Lev 27.5), according to the age of the slave. Thus Joseph arrived in due course in Egypt. It may have been during this journey that the words of Psalm 105 were true of him: "His feet they hurt with fetters; he was laid in chains of iron" (v.18, RV). So much, it would appear, for his dreams!

It is good that Psalm 105, brings this to light , for there exists a danger of becoming unduly occupied with the wickedness of Joseph's brothers and with what a pity it was that Reuben once again was missing at the vital moment, when he might have saved Joseph. The story leaves no doubt that Joseph had Someone to care for him who would never be missing at the vital moment. So it was that God "sent a man" before the family of

Jacob (Ps 105.17). The Psalm details the sufferings of Joseph, "until the time came that his word came to pass" (v.19 RV). God had not lost control. If we suffer unjustly while we are serving God faithfully we need to remember that we have no guarantee of exemption from injustice, but we have the example of the Lord Jesus "who, when he was reviled, reviled not again; when he suffered he threatened not; but committed himself to him that judgeth righteously" (1 Pet 2.23). Joseph had no such example to console him, but he was going to the place where, after suffering, he would be exalted by God. The rejection and subsequent exaltation of Joseph are inevitable reminders of the Lord Jesus, rejected by His brothers, sold to death, and exalted by God.

Verses 29-32: The Blood-Stained Coat

Reuben's plans had gone terribly wrong. When he realised that he could not now rescue Joseph he expressed his mourning by rending his clothes. What could he do now? He was the eldest and therefore in some sense particularly to blame for allowing Joseph to be harmed. He had his father to face. His brothers were not concerned about his problem any more than they had been about Joseph's pleas. They took the blood of a goat, dipped the offensive cloak in it and sent or took it to Jacob. They said they had found it and invited Jacob to decide if it was indeed his son's cloak. Later, when they had repented, they confessed (42.21) that Joseph was their brother; now they evidently wanted to wound the old man as deeply as possible, so they spoke of "thy son". The callousness of the brothers as they coolly spun this monstrous tale before Jacob brings into high relief that bitterness which is peculiar to disputes within families.

Jacob may or may not have remembered another day when old Isaac was approached by him in Esau's coat with its familiar smell of the open air, and was deceived by the flesh and the skin of a goat. It is still, however, fresh in the mind of the reader. Jacob continued to reap what he had sown. So the division and strife which was established in this family continued to dog their steps.

Verses 33-35: Jacob Mourns

The callous young men, who had planned to blame a wild beast for killing Joseph, did not even need to make this suggestion for Jacob spoke first to draw that conclusion. They had sinned in planning to tell that hideously cruel lie but they were saved by his cry from the further sin of telling the lie.

All Jacob's hopes for Joseph seemed dashed. He could only mourn the disaster, while his older sons looked on. His mourning was no routine ritual as prescribed by custom; it was the outpouring of a heart broken because a favourite son, the special darling son of Jacob's dear wife, was gone and had died, it seemed, so cruelly. The family, of course, gathered around to offer comfort. Those who had so cruelly deceived him joined in with hollow consolation. Jacob absolutely refused to be comforted. Only death would end his mourning, he said, and death would reunite him with Joseph. What a home that was, with young men who had come within an ace of murdering their own brother, who had actually sold him into slavery, who now pretended to comfort their old father. We should surely fear lest we fall into the sin of envy, for it could lead us into we know not what further sins.

Verse 36: Joseph's Destination

The trading caravan reached its destination with its precious consignment intact. The good-looking (compare 39.6) young Hebrew slave was easy to dispose of. He had also, as later events showed, the potential to become a good organiser. Whoever bought him would surely get good value for money. His purchaser was an official at the court of Pharaoh, Potiphar the "captain of the guard". There is some disagreement among scholars about the correct translation of Potiphar's title. Some maintain that he was "chief steward". He was evidently in charge of the prison to which offending officials were consigned (40.3), so perhaps the AV rendering is near the mark. All things considered, Joseph could have been worse off, except that he had had those dreams and now they seemed light years away from fulfilment. He could not know yet that God had brought him there, but later he would know (compare 45.5-9): "God did send me before you to preserve life" (RV).

It is important to realise that God may use adversity to bring his people to the place where He will use them. There are many lessons in the attitude of Paul the apostle to his imprisonment: "I want you to understand that the progress of the gospel has actually been helped by what has happened to me. It has become common knowledge throughout the imperial guard, and indeed among the public at large, that my imprisonment is in Christ's cause" (Phil 1.12-13 REB). If God chooses to take Paul to Rome in chains He can still produce the results which Paul desired in Rome as easily as if Paul had travelled there in style. This is a wonderful thing to contemplate, but at the beginning of his experiences in Egypt it would have been hard for Joseph to begin to think like this. His experiences may still bring great comfort to God's faithful servants when they are subjected to injustice and persecution.

Notes

2 See "Note on Gen 37:2" by J. Peck, in Expository Times Vol 82 pp342-3 for an unpacking of this interpretation.

GENESIS 38

Judah and His Family

Introductory

Viewed superficially this chapter interrupts the Joseph story. It must be seen as comment on Judah, who not only had a significant impact on the experience of Joseph (compare 37.26; 43.8-10; 44.18-34), but also begins to emerge in this section of Genesis as a person of significance for the future history of the family and nation. In these chapters there is interplay between Joseph and either Reuben or Judah, for Reuben the firstborn was to lose kingly glory to Judah (49.10) and the firstborn's double portion of the inheritance to Joseph (Num 1.32-35). In view of this destiny for the tribe of Judah the question of his descendants was of the utmost importance, and that question is dealt with in this chapter, which ends significantly with the identification of Pharez (Perez) as Judah's heir (compare genealogies such as Mt 1.3). In this connection it is relevant to remark on the honoured place which Tamar holds in the genealogy of the Lord Jesus through her association with Judah (Mt 1.3), a shining example of how the grace of God works.

It is worth referring to the judgment of Griffith Thomas on this chapter's place in the Genesis record. He identifies Joseph as the instrument of the transfer of Jacob's family to Egypt, the divine power as the cause of the transfer, and the moral condition of Judah, as evidenced in ch.38, as indicating the need of the Egyptian experience. God was removing His people from the corrupt influence of Canaan.

Verses 1-5: Judah's Marriage and Three Sons

So far the sons of Jacob have been seen together as a group, with Joseph alone, "separate from his brethren" (49.26). At this point Judah also moved out of the group to live among the Adullamites, in particular to be neighbour to Hirah. It appears that Hirah also became a confidant, for Judah sent him on a delicate mission in v.20 (also compare v.12). Relations between the family of Abraham and the tribes of Canaan were much easier than when the nation of Israel later came out of Egypt. Abraham was seen to be an ally of Amorites (14.13) and here Judah was the friendly neighbour of Adullamites.[†]

But Judah took a further step which went beyond what was proper. Chapter 24 related that when Abraham wanted a wife for Isaac he sent to Paddan-aram to his own people. Similarly Rebekah sent Jacob to Paddan-aram for a wife. Esau, who was not alert to such values, married unsuitable wives. So now did Judah. There seems to be a danger sign indicated in the statement that he "saw there" a daughter of a Canaanite. The phrase echoes that in Judges (14.1) about how Samson "saw a woman in Timnath", who turned out to be a snare to him. These suspicions about the unsuitability of Judah's wife are confirmed by the fact that her name is not given - she had no place amongst the people of faith.[†]

The family life of Judah is not reassuring. There is nothing to suggest love or affection or personal relationships. He saw, he took in marriage, he consummated the marriage, she conceived and bore a son, he called his name Er. Then there followed Onan and Shelah, after the same pattern. She was at Chezib when she bore Shelah. The record is bare and stark.

Judah had proposed to his brothers that since Joseph was their brother they should not kill him but rather sell him into slavery (37.26-27). Perhaps it is more expedient to sell one's brother than to kill him, but neither is right. Judah was going to go through experiences which would challenge his approach to life and cause him to value people more highly. So far his brother's cries and his father's mourning seem not to have moved him, but in time he mellowed and before the end of Genesis there was a more human face on the man who had always had "leadership potential".

Meanwhile his marriage was doomed to be plagued by problems. Mothers mould their children more than anyone else, and Judah's sons always laboured under this handicap, for handicap it was in their case. There is still a vital message in this for a christian man, that the influence which will be exerted on his children by his wife is a paramount consideration when he thinks of marrying. There is also a message for a christian woman, that if she contemplates marriage and becoming a mother the influence which she will exert for God on her children is probably the most significant that she will ever have on anyone during her life. The refrain in Kings and Chronicles, "and his mother's name was ...", has very significant implications; it deserves some research in a concordance.

Verses 6-11: Judah's Sons and Tamar

It was very important that the eldest son should have a wife and that she should bear sons. So Judah took a wife called Tamar for his eldest son, Er. Nothing is said about Tamar's origins but it is usually assumed that she was a Canaanite. However that may be, Judah's plans for Er went awry, for Er was cut off prematurely by the Lord because of his wickedness. No individual in Genesis so far has had this written of him or her. Masses of people were wiped out by the flood and in Sodom and Gomorrah, but individuals have not been said to have been singled out for summary divine judgment.

This created a problem, for Tamar had not conceived; hence there was no heir. In Bible times the normal solution to this problem was for the dead man's brother to beget a son on the widow. This is usually referred to as levirate marriage. The son of this union would be counted as the son of the dead man and so the name of the dead would be perpetuated in his inheritance. It seems that unless the widow had children in this way her late husband's inheritance would pass to his brothers (Num 27.8-11) rather than to her.[†]

The responsibility of seeking to produce a son for Er fell on Onan as second son of Judah. Onan pretended to fulfil his obligation, but on each occasion when he had sexual intercourse with Tamar (this is the meaning of the words used) he ensured that she would not conceive, for he practised what is normally called coitus interruptus. His repetition of the offence proves that it was not accidental and that he kept pretending to do his duty to his deceased brother. Thus he sought to prevent Er from having a son who would share in Judah's inheritance along with him and Shelah. The matter at issue was purely one of the name and inheritance of Er and Tamar's place in it. So serious was his sin in this matter that the Lord removed him also. If Onan had openly refused to do his duty by his dead brother it would have devolved on Judah to act, and possibly Onan could have been subjected to disgrace of the kind involved in the ceremony of the removal of the shoe. This ceremony appears later (compare Deut 25.7-10; Ruth 4.7-8) as an institution in Israel.

As the theme of family succession is followed, a point of great tension is now reached. Judah had a wife and two grown-up sons, both of whom he had now lost. All depended on the young son, still immature, surviving to produce a son himself. It is not now merely a son for Er but a grandson for Judah that is at stake. The survival of the line of Judah is in the balance. But Judah feared that Shelah might share the fate of Er and Onan if he had contact with Tamar. It seems almost as if he feared that the problem lay with her rather than the wickedness of his sons. To preserve the life of Shelah he distanced him from Tamar by sending her back to her father's house, "till Shelah my son be grown". Thus Judah was left at home with his wife and young Shelah, while Tamar was safely back, as Judah thought, with her father.

Verses 12-26: Tamar and Judah

After some time had passed Judah's wife died. This removed the possibility of Judah having more sons through her. Sheep-shearing time came round and Judah went with his friend Hirah to the sheep-shearing at Timnath. When Tamar heard this she devised a plan to get her due from Judah. Shelah was evidently now fully mature (v.14) yet Judah was keeping her separate from him. She realised that Judah had no intention of giving her her levirate rights (compare v.11).

Her plan involved the removal of her widow's clothing and the wearing of a veil to prevent Jacob from recognising her. She sat at a place where she knew she could attract Judah's notice, "in the gate of Enaim" (RV translation, where the AV gives "in an open place"), on the way to Timnath. She obviously dressed as a prostitute to draw Judah's attention. Judah saw her sit there and drew the conclusion which she had intended he should draw. He thought she was a prostitute. Since she was veiled he did not recognise her. He approached her with a view to purchasing her services. She asked what price he would pay. On being offered a kid she said she would need security to guarantee payment, for obviously Judah would not be carrying a kid around. He allowed her to chose what security she wanted and she asked, in effect, for his identity card. His seal (AV "signet") would likely have been a cylinder with his personal mark on it. The cylinder would hang around his neck on the cord, and the third item, his staff, would also be of his personal design. Her intention was, of course, not to ensure that the kid was paid, for she could not be found to receive it, but to identify the father of the child which she hoped would be born from their union. So he handed over his pledge, his security, and had intercourse with her and she conceived.

Later on, the law of Moses (Lev 20.12) specified that if a man had sexual intercourse with his daughter-in-law both should be put to death for "working confusion". It is clear from the words used in this chapter of Genesis that Tamar was considered to be Judah's daughter-in-law in view of her being engaged to Shelah (vv.16,24). This happened, of course, before the law was given to Moses, but it was still confusion. Judah admittedly did not know that she was his daughter-in-law.

Tamar viewed this as an isolated incident, arranged to highlight the injustice done to her. When it was over "she arose, and went away, and laid by her veil from her, and put on the garments of her widowhood" (v.19). For Judah it was not yet over, for he must pay his fee. But it was less embarrassing to send it through an agent, so he sent it "by the hand of his friend the Adullamite", that is, Hirah (compare v.12). More important for Judah than the payment of his fee was the retrieval of his seal, cord and staff.

There was, however, a difficulty: Hirah could not find the supposed prostitute. He made enquiries about her whereabouts. The word he used for prostitute in vv.21-22 raises an interesting question. Hirah in his enquiries called her a cult-prostitute (QADESH - 6948, literally "devotee") and this was also the term used in the replies to his questions to the locals. Tamar may have taken advantage of the fact that in Canaan those who practised heathen fertility rites included the use of devotees who were cult-prostitutes.

This would be particularly prevalent during festivals such as sheep-shearing. Perhaps more probably, Hirah may have felt more comfortable to raise (as he supposed) a mere financial transaction onto a more religious level by using the cult word in his enquiries. Judah was content to suffer the loss of his property to prevent his becoming a laughing-stock. He had tried to pay the fee and had failed, so he would let the subject die there (v.23).

All went well until, after three months, a disturbing report was brought to Judah that his daughter-in-law Tamar was pregnant. It was clear that she must have "played the harlot" and this could not be tolerated. In the law of Moses (Deut 22.21) a woman who, upon marriage, was found to have been sexually immoral was condemned to die by stoning. If a betrothed woman committed adultery with a man in the city both of them, under Moses' law (Deut 22.23-24), must be stoned; if however the event took place in the field it was assumed that the woman had not consented and only the man was to be stoned (Deut 22.25-27). This legislation of course was still in the future, but it shows how serious a view was taken in Israel of such offences.

Judah decreed that she should be burnt. The only other place where this penalty was laid down for such an offence was in Leviticus 21.9, where a priest's daughter found guilty of "playing the whore" was condemned to this fate. Judah was very indignant about conduct of this kind, which fell so far short of what was expected in his family circle. Evidently it was not considered so serious for a man to consort with prostitutes. The whole story exemplifies the double standards which often operated in ancient times, and often still operate in modern society. Men commit what are considered to be excusable pecadillos when they engage in sexual sin, whereas women are despised for similar behaviour.

"Bring her forth," said Judah, "and let her be burnt". Then, as Tamar was "being brought forth" for the punishment to be exacted, she suddenly sprang the trap. She sent a message to "her father-in-law" (note the term used) disclosing that she was pregnant by the man whose seal, bracelets (or cord) and staff she now produced. Judah could only admit that he was indeed the owner of the articles and therefore the guilty man. Immediately he was aware of why she had acted as she had done, "because that I gave her not to Shelah my son" (v.26). So she was pardoned. Nothing at all was said, it would appear, about how inappropriate it might be for Judah to seek the services of a prostitute. As to his having had sexual intercourse with his daughter-in-law, he did not know, of course, that that was who it was. If he had known who she was, this would later be seen (Lev 20.12) in a serious light, indeed as a capital offence. Only the unanswerable force of Tamar's case saved her.

Judah found it relatively easy to sidle out of the situation, making the interesting concession, "She hath been more righteous than I" (v.26). At least he had the integrity to admit his guilt, for "he knew her again no more". Jacob's discomfiture when confronted by the evidence of his guilt reminds us of David's embarrassment in the matter of Uriah's wife. When Nathan told David in parabolic form of the man who took the other man's pet ewe, David decreed that the man must die. Then Nathan said, "Thou art the man". David's indignation at the wickedness perpetrated at once dissolved. It took months of agony to bring David through the repentance and restoration so movingly sobbed out in Psalm 51.

It is interesting at this point to reflect on the education of Judah which had now begun. He had been deceived by Tamar's clothing, just as he and his brothers had deceived Jacob by the use of Joseph's coat (37.32). He was reaping something of what he had sown, but the reaping was far from over yet. There were changes in Judah as the gracious discipline of God refined him in the years that followed this incident.

Verses 27-30: Tamar's Twins

When Tamar came to the bringing forth of her baby it is suddenly recorded ("behold") that it was twins. It might be thought that these twins would make up numerically for the loss of Er and Onan. But the divine record is seldom concerned about making up numbers, as has been seen in earlier chapters when one or two people were the only survivors carrying on the chosen line. It must be kept in mind that God had spoken of innumerable progeny of the line of Abraham leading to blessing for the world.

It was clear, even before the twins were born, that they were to be rivals, or at least alternatives, rather than complements to each other. Importance was placed by the midwife on who was born first, so when one baby put out his hand she marked it by a scarlet thread, but the baby withdrew the hand and the other baby was born first. He appears to have been born quickly, for the midwife exclaimed, "What a breach you have made for yourself!" (v.29, Hamilton). This explains why he was called Pharez, which means "Breach". Only then was the other baby born, and he was called Zarah.

The double birth, with its struggle for priority, echoes the story in ch.25 of the birth of Jacob and Esau. On that occasion Esau was born first, but with Jacob grasping his heel. Here Pharez was fully born after Zarah had staked his claim to priority by putting forth his hand. In the event it would be Pharez who would carry the line of Judah towards its destined goal (compare 46.12; Ruth 4.12,18; Mt 1.3). It is only when the later Scripture references to Pharez and his line are considered that the reason for all the detail of this birth narrative is understood. Once again the child who was technically the firstborn had to cede priority to one born after him. The divine record does not follow human rules on people's rights. God is sovereign, and He takes up one or another as He pleases.

God was going to exalt the tribe of Judah to unparalleled honour. How little the beginnings of that story owe to human effort or human excellence! Judah acted unjustly towards Tamar. Tamar took revenge by exacting from him the due denied her through Shelah. Thus she started, through her younger twin, a line which reached to King David and on to the Christ. This was the line of Judah, but what an unpromising start it had, with sons cut off for their godlessness and a covert deal between the Patriarch and someone whom he thought to be a prostitute! Truly God works out His purposes more often despite the demerits of His servants than through their virtues.

Notes

1 Adullam lay in the valley of Elah, in the lower hills (Shephelah) south-west from Bethlehem, north-west from Hebron and north-east from Lachish.

2 In 1 Chronicles 2.3 Jacob's wife appears in the AV as "the daughter of Shua the Canaanitess", in other translations (RV for instance) as "Bath-shua the Canaanitess". But Bath-shua in any case simply means "daughter of Shua".

7,8 Scholars are not agreed as to whether the brother of a childless deceased man was originally required to marry the widow or whether he was merely required to seek to produce an heir. His obligation was later codified in Deuteronomy 25.5-10, where v.5 does explicitly mention marriage.

GENESIS 39

Joseph Goes from Slavery to Prison

Introductory
   The career of Joseph may be conveniently divided into his experience in four houses. Previous to this chapter he was in his father's house; here he is in Potiphar's house, then in prison; in 41.40 he will be promoted to the palace. Chapter 37 ended with a very bare statement of his being sold to Potiphar, so this chapter recapitulates in v.1.

Verses 1-6: Joseph's Rapid Promotion in Potiphar's Service
   In the record of Joseph's being purchased, Potiphar is described (v.1) as "an officer" (SARIS-5631), which strictly means a eunuch. It is not necessary, however, to take the word in its strict sense of a castrated man, for it had come by extension to mean any officer in a great house. Certain officers who served in the inner rooms of a palace would certainly be eunuchs but others would probably not.
   Joseph quickly caught his master's eye. The reason given is that "the Lord was with him". The story of Joseph emphasises the truth that if a man is in the purpose of God and remains faithful to God he will be brought through whatever circumstances arise to the appointed goal, which may be a place of exaltation. But before the goal is reached there may be years of suffering and apparent loss. So it was to prove with Joseph.
   Meanwhile he enjoyed the favour of Potiphar, for "he was a prosperous man" and "he was in the house" of Potiphar. This last statement probably indicates his rapid appointment to perform indoor work of a type done by reliable and favoured slaves. Then, remarkably, Potiphar concluded from Joseph's extraordinary skill that the Lord was with him. Perhaps it can be understood from this that Joseph had been explaining why he was the kind of man that he was: he was a worshipper of the Lord, the God whom his fathers, Abraham, Isaac and Jacob, had served. In any case Potiphar sensed that he had a bargain in this slave and he made him a close personal servant ("served him", v.4, or "became his attendant", REB), with responsibility in his house. The term "overseer in his house" is like expressions used in Egypt at this period for people raised to high office, but here the context is the house (broadly understood) of Potiphar. The extent of Joseph's responsibility is seen in that "all that he had he put into his hand". That last phrase "into his hand", meaning "in his power", will be echoed in a sinister way very soon.
   The result of Joseph's promotion was the Lord's blessing on Potiphar's house "for Joseph's sake". The theme is being repeated that "I will bless them that bless thee" (12.3), the promise of God to Abraham. Indeed the

comprehensiveness of God's blessing on Potiphar is expressed by the formula "in the house, and in the field" (v.5), that is, throughout his possessions. At the end of Genesis the theme of blessing comes again prominently into focus, with particular emphasis on the blessings experienced in Egypt through Joseph and his family coming there. God was fulfilling His promise to bless the descendants of Abraham. He was also making them a blessing to Egypt, first Potiphar, then Pharaoh and all the land.

Potiphar had learnt that Joseph was not only efficient but also entirely trustworthy, for he "concerned himself with nothing but the food he ate" (v.6b REB). In other words, Joseph ran the household and Potiphar could simply concern himself with his personal affairs and rest easy. If Joseph had known the exhortation which would be given to slaves almost two millennia later by Paul, he could not have followed it more faithfully: "Servants/slaves, obey in all things your masters according to the flesh; not with eye service as men-pleasers; but in singleness of heart, fearing God ... for ye serve the Lord Christ" (Col 3.22-24). A servant of God who is faithful to God and works for an earthly master can hardly fail to bring blessing to his master. In serving the master well the servant serves God well.

The end of v.6 describes how Joseph, like his mother Rachel, was handsome in face and figure (compare 29.17). Almost immediately this fact was to deprive him of his comfortable position and put him in deadly peril.

Verses 7-12: Joseph Is Tempted but Stands Firm

It was his beauty which caught the fancy of Potiphar's wife - she "cast her eyes upon Joseph". How much may have been communicated to him of her interest by the way she looked at him is not told, but when she spoke there could be no mistaking the nature of her intent: "Lie with me". Similar abrupt demands have been met, in 29.21, when Jacob demanded of Laban, "Give me my wife", and in 30.1, when Rachel cried to Jacob, "Give me children, or else I die". All of these are instances in which tension has built up and finally bursts forth in abrupt demands. Lust had seethed within Potiphar's wife, and now it boiled over in this crude, blunt demand.

"But he refused" (v.8). Her demand was clear-cut, and so was his response. Would that the believer's responses to clearly evil proposals were always so incisive! He had two loyalties which sustained him: he appreciated the trust placed in him by Potiphar and he understood his obligation to God. His relationship with God underpinned his moral integrity. He knew, and of course Potiphar's wife knew, that there was no question of Joseph's yielding to her without base treachery to his master. The ethics of his job demanded that he refuse her. But sound ethics are always strengthened by an understanding that sin against one's fellow-man is primarily sin against God (compare Ps 51.4 - "against thee, thee only, have I sinned"). This would be sin against God in that she was another man's wife. It would be adultery, and God hates adultery.

So far so good. But the harder part of Joseph's test was that she refused to accept his rejection of her demands. She was accustomed to being obeyed, and her insistence continued "day by day". Joseph was being required to show that his first rejection of her was not just a matter of his inhibitions. It was a matter of principle. The statement (v.10) that he refused "to lie with her" is not exactly the same as in v.7. It may imply here that she invited him simply to lie beside her and engage in pleasant, "harmless" flirtation. Joseph rejected this proposal too, and indeed he sought to avoid even her very presence.

The matter came to a head one day when his work took him into the house at a time when only Potiphar's wife was there. She was now determined to have her desire. She caught him by his clothing, repeating her demand. But Joseph, still firm, "left his garment in her hand" and fled outside. Paul has apt comment on the situation (2 Tim 2.22): "Flee also youthful lusts: but follow righteousness, faith, charity, peace ...". Here is the echo of Potiphar leaving all his affairs in Joseph's hand, under Joseph's control. To preserve his integrity and to honour the trust placed in him by Potiphar, Joseph had to leave his garment "in her hand". She had Joseph's future in the household in her control, for she could use his garment to make an accusation against him. It has been previously seen in Genesis how clothing could be used to deceive others. Jacob wore kid-skin and Esau's robe to deceive blind Isaac (27.15-16), and Joseph's brothers took his special coat and dipped it in blood to deceive old Jacob (37.31-32).

Joseph could easily have rationalised his situation and persuaded himself that he had to give in. He might have argued that the situation was impossible. One could hardly be expected to lose all the things with which God had blessed one when one's owner's wife made demands which may well have been common enough in that corrupt society. But Joseph believed that his standards must come from God, not from society. He believed that, whether his master would ever learn about the adultery or not, he owed loyalty to him, for that was implicit in the trust placed in him by Potiphar. Such men are needed today in the corruptions of business and social life. Loyalty to one's master or, more vitally, to one's wife or husband, is not so valued today as it was a generation ago. Current fashions may depart from scriptural standards, but the godly will be guided by Scripture, not fashion.

Verses 13-20: Joseph Is Falsely Accused and Imprisoned

Potiphar's wife reacted quickly to Joseph's rejection of her advances. It was now clear to her that he could not be seduced. That being the case she would destroy him, and in her grasp she held the means to do so. He was, it would appear, in her power.

First of all she made preparations by calling in the other male servants to see that she had Joseph's coat in her hand. She bade them come as witnesses to the outrage offered to her by the Hebrew (therefore a foreigner) whom her husband had brought in to insult and mock the household. Her insinuations cast a slur on foreigners, on her husband, on Joseph, on anyone but herself. She believed that the best means of defence was attack. She said that she had cried out loudly because Joseph had attempted to rape her. She said he had left his garment behind in his haste to escape detection. Then she carefully laid the garment by her to meet her husband when he would return.

On his return Potiphar was met by a torrent of well-rehearsed words. It does not say that Potiphar believed her, merely that he became angry. Nor does it say that he became angry with Joseph; his anger may have been because he was put in an impossible situation, in which he was bound to lose the services of the best man he had. He had shrewdly weighed up Joseph and decided that he was totally trustworthy. It does seem possible that he would have reservations about the integrity of a woman so brazenly unfaithful and dishonest as she was. Whether he believed her or not he could not side with a slave against her - that would be socially unthinkable. He must punish Joseph. The fact that Joseph was imprisoned, not executed, suggests that Potiphar was not totally convinced of his guilt. Whatever was going on in Potiphar's mind, the end result for Joseph was that "he was there in the prison".

Verses 21-23: Joseph Again Prospers

Surely it was a terrible thing for the man destined by God for greatness to be in a prison. Perhaps, but the next statement gives reassurance; "The Lord was with Joseph, and shewed him mercy". If Joseph had been weighing up the cost of submitting to Potiphar's wife against the cost of refusing her, the equation that was before him is now clear. He could remain in Potiphar's house enjoying her "favours", constantly risking exposure and, above all, having lost the smile of the Lord. Now he was out of his privileged place in Potiphar's service, he was in the prison with all its discomforts - and the Lord was with him. He had infinitely the better deal. He had proved his integrity and his moral fitness to be exalted in the service of God. Young men need to take note of the implications of hard decisions whose repercussions go on into the future and effect fitness for future service for God. If God has important work for a person to do He will test that person to prove his or her suitability for the task ahead.

The direct result of the Lord's favour to Joseph was that he found favour with the jailer. This led, after an unspecified time, to his being given a place of a trust, with extensive oversight over other prisoners. In this position of responsibility Joseph again proved so reliable that the jailer ceased to have to check on what he did, because everything within his remit went so smoothly. This was the third house in which Joseph had proved himself worthy of trust - his father's house, Potiphar's house and now the prison. All of this was due to the favour of the Lord and Joseph's consistent living in the light of that favour.

But, as in so many places in Genesis, godliness and divine favour did not necessarily mean that all would go easily for Joseph and that he would be vindicated and released. The reward for faithfulness was to come only after a long and anguished delay, and this will be the subject of the next chapter.

GENESIS 40

Joseph Interprets Two Prisoner's Dreams

Verses 1-8: Joseph Joined by Two Officials, who Dream

The point in Joseph's imprisonment at which the king's chief butler and chief baker joined him is not given. The expression "after these things" merely indicates that some time passed. It is known that Joseph was seventeen years old (37.2) when he came into conflict with his brothers on account of their misbehaviour, and that he was thirty when he first stood before Pharaoh (41.46). It would appear that most of the intervening period of thirteen years was spent in prison and most of the rest of it in slavery.

The two men who now appeared in prison were palace officials. The chief "butler" (AV) would more precisely be described as cupbearer. He would, as chief cupbearer, have the great responsibility of ensuring that all the drink offered to Pharaoh was both good and safe to drink. If his utter loyalty and efficiency were called in question he could not function in his role as cupbearer, for this could endanger Pharaoh's life. The chief baker also had a responsible role, not only in being in charge of the preparation of Pharaoh's bread but also, in all probability, having responsibility for bread used in religious ceremonies. The making of dozens of kinds of bread and fancy confections was a complex tradition in Egypt, and many of these were used in offerings to the gods.

The two men, then, found themselves in the same prison as Joseph, and Joseph was soon allocated the task of serving them (v.4) as he had served Potiphar (compare 39.4). It must be kept in mind that this is a story of God's activity on behalf of His people. In His providence He brought these two palace officials in contact with Joseph when he was in prison on a trumped-up charge. At this stage a speedy vindication of Joseph might be expected but this would be premature. If Joseph is to be prepared for greatness he must go through the tempering process of suffering.

At v.5 there is a reminder that Joseph had experience of dreams in his early life, for the other two men had dreams, both on the same night. The expression used here, "each man according to the interpretation of his dream", means "each with its own meaning"; that is, they both had separate dreams in one night, but the dreams had different meanings. The laboured detail of the verse emphasises the importance of the dreams by these two prominent men who were palace officials of Pharaoh.

In the morning Joseph came in to where they were to serve them as usual. Despite his own problems he noticed how "sad" (AV) they were.[†] Like most people in ancient times they took dreams very seriously but would not necessarily be upset at having a dream. In prison, however, they had no access to the professional interpreters who were so plentiful in court. This difficulty over interpretation was worrying them (v.8).

Joseph gave them an answer which was completely in character. He had resisted Potiphar's wife because he lived in the consciousness of his relationship with God. Here again he reacted to this problem by referring to God, as he would do again in 41.16 before Pharaoh. The Egyptians looked to experts in dreams for interpretations; Joseph directed men to God as the infallible source of true interpretations. God who made all and who judges all also knows the future as easily as the past (compare Is 46.10; Dan 2.27-28). The story at this point is beginning to bring God and Pharaoh and Joseph together, but the process is not yet complete.

Verses 9-13: The Chief Cupbearer's Dream Told and Interpreted

Joseph's testimony to the ability of God to give interpretations was accepted by the chief cupbearer. In his dream he saw a vine around which features and events are grouped in quick-moving patterns of three - three branches, three processes of growth, three activities by the chief cupbearer in achieving the transition from grapes on the vine to a full cup in Pharaoh's hand. The events in the dream concerned things related to his job, but some would normally have been his personal activities as chief cupbearer. Joseph gave the interpretation promptly: the threes represented three days before the fulfilment of the dream, and in three days he would be back in favour in the old way. The speed and ease with which events followed each other without any untoward features made it easy for the chief cupbearer to give the details and expect a good interpretation. Joseph found it easy to give him what he expected.

Verses 14-15: Joseph's Appeal to the Chief Cupbearer

So confident was Joseph of the accuracy of his interpretation that he quickly saw and seized his opportunity to ask for the cupbearer's help when the dream came true. He asked first that the cupbearer would remember (AV "think on") him and show kindness to him by putting in a plea to Pharaoh for his release.† He explained that he had been stolen out of the land of the Hebrews, and broadly this is what had happened if his brothers' stripping of him is combined with their selling him to the Midianites, who sold him on to Potiphar. The climax of his plea was that he had also been unjustly imprisoned here in Egypt, here in this dungeon. If it can be taken that the cupbearer was innocent of any crime one might expect that a fellow-feeling would incline him to take up Joseph's cause on his release.

Verses 16-19: The Chief Baker's Dream Told and Interpreted

Having heard the encouraging content of Joseph's interpretation of his fellow-prisoner's dream the chief baker was the more ready to tell his own dream. He too had been engaged (in his dream) in activity linked to his own skills. He had been carrying three baskets of white bread (see RV of v.16) on his head. Perhaps the activity would have been a little unlikely for the chief baker; it would probably have fallen to an underling to carry the results of the baking. Events in the chief cupbearer's dream had progressed rapidly and effortlessly to their intended goal, but the chief baker evidently had not noticed a fatal drawback in his dream. This was the role played by the fowls of the air which ate out of the top basket containing food specially baked for Pharaoh. In many scriptural contexts the fowls are predators or even scavengers. They feature in many OT descriptions of the horrors of wars which go wrong, for example in Deuteronomy 28.26, in 1 Samuel 17.44 (in Goliath's threat) and in Psalm 79.2. It is odd that the chief baker had missed such a point, but perhaps it was because he was an Egyptian. Another feature of the dream which differed from the chief cupbearer's was that, while in the other's dream there was emphasis on his hands serving the king, in the chief baker's the focus was on his head, where the birds landed.

Joseph again had little hesitation in giving the true interpretation. Once again the three days before the fulfilment had been symbolised in the three baskets. The emphasis on his head was important for Pharaoh would lift his head off him in execution. His corpse would be exposed hanging on a tree for the birds to land on him and eat his flesh.

Joseph had fulfilled his promise that God would give true interpretations. He had faithfully relayed to his fellow-prisoners what God had showed him. He was a faithful witness. As such he was glad to give the good news, but also courageous enough not to shrink from giving the bad. There are lessons here for those who preach the gospel and teach God's Word.

Verses 20-23: The Dreams Come True, Leaving Joseph in Prison

On the third day, as the dreams had foretold, Pharaoh acted. It was his birthday and he celebrated by releasing the chief cupbearer and restoring him to his former status, but he hanged the chief baker. The linking of the action with Pharaoh's birthday suggests that he acted on whim rather than on evidence. Great kings, it appears, celebrated their birthdays for their own pleasure, but the birthdays brought danger for other people. The release of the one officer and the execution of the other seem to have been equally irrational acts. It is a sobering reflection that in Scripture the only other king's birthday recorded is that of Herod (Mt 14.6-11; Mk 6.21-28). On that occasion John the Baptist was the victim of a royal whim which opened the way for the vengeance of a wicked woman called Herodias upon that great man of God. It is a constant joy to believers in God that He can be a just God and a Saviour (Is 45.21). He does not act on whim and does not need the attentions of a crowd of court flatterers to boost a flagging ego. He who has forgiven all the believer's sins and who has promised not to remember them again always keeps His promises and acts on a basis of strict justice. Calvary has provided Him with a comprehensive basis for rich forgiving grace.

Whether justice was done or not in the case of the two officials, the chief cupbearer did not treat Joseph justly, for he promptly forgot him completely. Joseph had now suffered being rejected and sold by his brothers, falsely accused by Potiphar's wife and imprisoned by Potiphar, and forgotten by his fellow-prisoner whom he had helped. Surely after all that God would intervene and vindicate him. Or would he perhaps grant him a dream as the chief cupbearer had had a dream? The economy of the divine record is most eloquent, for ch.41 opens with a bleak reference to the passing of a further silent, empty two years before any light of hope was given to Joseph. How Joseph emerges from this severe trial is seen when he first speaks in ch. 41 (v.16).

Notes

6 Wenham translates this word "sad" (ZA'AP - 2196) as "ill" and compares Daniel 1.10 where it occurs again in a similar context, translated in the AV as "worse liking", (Newberry margin, "sadder"). "Sadly" in v.7 in Joseph's question to the men is a different word - RA' (7451).

14 Some commentators see in the language of Joseph's appeal an echo of God's statement in Exodus 20.2 about how He had brought Israel "out of the house of bondage" at the exodus from Egypt. The echo may well be deliberate.

GENESIS 41

Pharaoh Dreams and Joseph is Exalted

Introductory

In this chapter Joseph is exalted in a heathen nation. Pharaoh is taught that God lives and speaks, that He has power even in countries where He is not acknowledged. The parallels between Joseph interpreting Pharaoh's dreams and Daniel interpreting Nebuchadnezzar's (Dan 2.27-45) are striking. In this part of Genesis the family of Jacob are to be taken from Canaan in time of famine to dwell in Egypt under Pharaoh later to return to the land. This to some degree parallels the situation in which Daniel found himself as one of those carried away to Babylon from Canaan under Nebuchadnezzar after Israel lost their land through their unfaithfulness to God. In both situations God made it known that He ruled in the kingdom of men and gave it to whomsoever He would (Dan 4.17). God had not lost control, nor had He handed over the reins of earthly government to men who refused to acknowledge Him.

Verses 1-7: Pharaoh has Two Dreams

Two full years (literally "two years of days") had passed since the cupbearer had gone back to his post without a thought for the insignificant Hebrew slave with whom he had shared a prison. But while he had no thought for Joseph, God had, therefore He showed Pharaoh in a dream what He was going to do (v.28), and Joseph would be needed to interpret the dream. This would bring Joseph into a situation in which the early dream-promises of exaltation would be fulfilled. The helplessness of Pharaoh and his experts to interpret also took the initiative from him and showed that not he but God was in control.[†]

The first of his two dreams found him observing seven beautiful, fat cows feeding among the reeds along the Nile. Then a second seven cows, ugly and emaciated, came up out of the river, stood by the fat cows and ate them. He awoke, fell asleep and dreamt again. This time it was seven ears of corn, blasted by the wind, which sprang up after seven full, fat ears and ate them. Again Pharaoh awoke and considered these two strange dreams.

Verses 8-13: The Interpreters are Baffled and Joseph is Mentioned

It takes little imagination to see why Pharaoh was troubled after these strange and sinister dreams. Cannibalism is barely conceivable among cows and certainly inconceivable among ears of corn. Egypt was a famous supplier of corn to other countries, thanks to the fertility induced by the annual flooding of the Nile. The cow was one of the main animals associated with religion in Egypt, and animal-gods were the norm there. Blasted ears of corn eating full ears was economically alarming, but the cattle brought in a deeper note of menace on a religious level.

The experts were called in, but none could give him an answer which carried conviction. Perhaps they were out of their depth because on this occasion there was something more than Pharaoh's psychological condition behind the dreaming: God was intervening, and they had no knowledge of God.

At this point the chief cupbearer, first met in ch.40, spoke up to Pharaoh. He recalled his earlier period of temporary disgrace, told the story of his own dream and that of the baker, and mentioned (after all this time!) Potiphar's young Hebrew slave who had interpreted accurately for them.

Verses 14-24: Pharaoh Summons Joseph and Relates His Dreams

Pharaoh responded quickly. Joseph was called and prepared with all speed for an interview with him. Anyone appearing before Pharaoh had to be scrupulously clean, and this required that a man be shaved. Prison clothing had to be replaced with something more suitable, though even if he had been well clothed Joseph would probably have been required to change his clothes before being presented at court. The sense of urgency continues in v.15 where Pharaoh presents to Joseph an explanation for why he has been summoned.

He had heard, he said, that Joseph could interpret dreams. Joseph's reply shows us that the awareness of God in all circumstances did not desert him when he was greeted with this flattering description. "It is not in me", he explained. The answer would be from God. Joseph's answer was plain and lacked the finer points of court flattery, but it was courteous - note how he constantly said "Pharaoh" rather than "you", out of deference to the king. Men of God seldom engage in empty flattery, but they can be expected to be courteous to rulers, for they "fear God" and "honour the king" (1 Pet 2.17; compare Rom 13.7).

Pharaoh was satisfied with this reply, for he immediately launched out into his account of the two dreams. In keeping with the more vivid language of direct, firsthand narrative the story has a couple of telling points of variance from the narrative in vv.1-7. He was moved in the telling of the dreams to exclaim that the ugly, lean cows were "such as I never saw in all the land of Egypt for badness" (v.19). Plainly the interpretation will require a meaning full of menace. The second variant added that after the ugly cows had eaten the fat ones "it could not be known that they had eaten them; but they were still ill favoured, as at the beginning". Again the menace is unmistakable. Yet, he complained, his experts could not interpret it.

Verses 25-32: Joseph Interprets the Dreams

Joseph's interpretation was a masterpiece of clear, incisive analysis. The two dreams carried the same message, they were one. God was informing Pharaoh what He was about to do.

The sevens in the dreams told of seven-year periods, first of bountiful harvests, then of famine. Evidently such prolonged periods of failure of crops were recorded on occasion in Egyptian history. This imminent famine, after seven years of plenty, would be so severe, said Joseph, that "all the plenty shall be forgotten in the land of Egypt" (v.30). In the manner of normal OT narrative and direct speech the details are repeated with telling force. Just as Pharaoh had laid emphasis on how ugly and bad the destructive forces in his dreams were, so Joseph laboured the point that the dreams were a warning of very extreme emergency during the famine to come.

The dream, he explained, had been given in two forms ("doubled") to show that the events were sure to happen ("established") and that they were imminent. Note the deliberate repetition of "God" in v.32. Pharaoh must be made to see that God, not Pharaoh, was in control in Egypt as in Canaan or anywhere else.

Verses 33-36: Joseph's Advice

Joseph did not stop short at explaining what was going to happen. He was completely confident in the accuracy of his interpretation, for God had shown him the meaning of the dreams. That being so, and since God's word is always reliable, the immediate question was what should be done to take advantage of God's warning.

First, said Joseph, Pharaoh needed a man to oversee the emergency preparations for the famine and also, later on, the system of distribution of corn. He required a man capable of seeing the precise nature of the task, a man of vision and discernment, a man who could analyse the problem, an "ideas man". This kind of picture seems to be conjured up in "discreet" (AV), "intelligent" (Hamilton, Wenham), "a man of vision" (REB). But he must also be a man with organising ability, who could see that what needed to be done was actually carried out. This was the "wise" (AV) man.

In addition to this key figure they needed "officers" (AV v.34, "overseers", RV, "commissioners", REB) to take charge in the regions of the country. The task would be to gather produce from the land during the seven years of plenty. In v.34 the AV has "take up the fifth part of the land of Egypt" and most translators understand the Hebrew verb CHAMASH (2567) in this way. Hamilton understands it as "divide into five districts", taking it as an administrative arrangement. Wenham and others take it to mean, more generally, "organise". A 20% tax was levied, on the evidence of 47.24, whether this verse is interpreted as saying so or not.

The corn should be gathered from the land and stored in the cities during the years of plenty. This would be a sensible procedure by way of centralising stocks and keeping them in secure stores. It was important to prepare against the time when food would be less plentiful, people would be desperate and it would be essential to ensure that supplies were generally available.

Verses 37-46: Joseph Appointed and Exalted to Honour

Once again, as in previous, less favourable circumstances, Joseph gained favour. Both Pharaoh and his officials recognised the wisdom in his interpretation and proposals. The one question in Pharaoh's mind was where to find a man to organise the project. He would need to be a man possessed of the kind of wisdom which betokened his being under the influence of God's Spirit. Joseph had said that the interpretation was from God. Pharaoh's conclusion about the qualification needed in a master-organiser led him to the man who described the organisation needed, Joseph (v.39). Joseph would be "over my (Pharaoh's) house". This may mean that he would be vizier, the rough equivalent of prime minister. It may just possibly be an Egyptian term for a lesser office, still powerful but below the vizier. In his work, at any rate, Joseph would be answerable directly to Pharaoh, and all must obey him (v.40). His responsibilities included all of Egypt (vv.41,43).

In vv.41-43 the investiture is described. First came the formal pronouncement: "See, I have set thee over all the land of Egypt". To perform his duties Joseph needed the royal seal, a signet ring. His dignity was made visible by his official clothing of fine linen and his gold chain of office around his neck. In one way this shows Joseph recovering special status, albeit in a new setting, for he had in early life been distinguished by that special coat of honour (37.3). To ensure that people had opportunity to identify the new appointee he was paraded in a chariot less splendid only than Pharaoh's own. Officials accompanied his progress crying out, "Bow the knee", if indeed that is the meaning of the obscure Hebrew word ABREK (86). Another suggestion is that the word means, "Make way".

To make certainty double sure, Pharaoh confirmed to Joseph that, with the full authority of himself, Pharaoh, Joseph had power over all kinds of activity (lifting hand or foot) in all Egypt (v.44). His new status would be signalled by a new name, Zaphnath-paaneah. Many meanings have been suggested for this obscure name. Scripture does not say what meaning the name had in Pharaoh's mind or Joseph's. Perhaps the most reasonable suggestion that has been made is "God speaks and lives" or something along those lines. The name is given here but hereafter is ignored in the sacred record.

A further honour bestowed on Joseph was a nobly born Egyptian wife. She was Asenath, daughter of Poti-phera priest (or "prince") of On. The better known name for On was Heliopolis, the City of the Sun. Poti-phera must not be confused with Potiphar, Joseph's former owner. Joseph, of course, had no choice in regard to marrying Asenath. She was Pharaoh's gift and one did not refuse his gifts.

It is emphasised (vv.45,46) that Joseph "went throughout all the land of Egypt". His responsibilities gave him Pharaoh's authority everywhere, and they also required that he survey the area which would be affected by his project. This new status came to him when he was thirty years of age, almost thirteen years since he had lost his liberty when his brothers sold him as a slave.

Verses 47-53: Seven Fruitful Years

Joseph implemented his plan and gathered corn throughout the seven years of plenty. It was stored, as planned, in the cities, each city collecting from its surrounding area. There was, as he had said, a rich abundance, so that they reached a point where they could no longer be sure of precisely how much they had (v.49). The fruitfulness of Egypt at this time is expressed as "corn as the sand of the sea", a figure used (22.17) of the fruitfulness of Abraham's descendants.

During these seven years Asenath bore him two sons. In the Genesis story this is of more importance than figures about amounts of corn. His first son he called Manasseh, because he wanted to acknowledge that God had made him to "forget" (NASHA - 5382) his toil and his father's house. This may mean the toil or trouble associated with his father's house, that is his rejection and consequent slavery and suffering. Or it may mean his toil as a slave and prisoner in Egypt, and his father's house with its strife and rejection. The difference is slight. Perhaps most important in this naming is his continuing lively perception of the place God must have in his life. It is sometimes easier to cry to God for help in trouble than to recognise His hand with us in blessing when we are in prosperity. "Give me neither poverty nor riches", prayed the wise man (Prov 30.8-9), "... lest I be full, and deny thee, and say, Who is the Lord?". Joseph stood the test of prosperity.

The second son he called Ephraim, "fruitful". God had not only preserved him through bad times but had brought him through to great material prosperity. Fruitfulness is associated elsewhere also with Joseph, as for instance in 49.22: "Joseph is a fruitful bough". He was not only personally prosperous but he also brought prosperity to others through his wisdom and foresight. As before, he attributed this fruitfulness to God: "God hath caused me to be fruitful in the land of my affliction" (v.52). Incidentally this description of Egypt as the land of his affliction is echoed later in the affliction of the family of Jacob in Egypt. The future greatness of the tribe of Ephraim must be attributed to God's continued grace to the son whom old Jacob would later prophetically see as greater than Manasseh (48.19). Ephraim was a large tribe, powerful among the twelve tribes. Indeed, when the kingdom was divided, many centuries later, the larger northern kingdom was often referred to as Ephraim because of the dominance of that tribe.

This expression of the fruitfulness of Joseph closes the record of the seven years of plenty. The wisdom and efficiency of Joseph were about to be manifested in the testing time of famine.

Verses 54-57: Seven Years of Famine

Then followed the seven years of famine, "according as Joseph had said". Famines were more frequent in many surrounding countries than in Egypt. On this occasion the famine was general, and other countries looked, as they often had to, to Egypt for help. There was corn for them to buy despite the fact that famine had struck Egypt as well, because Joseph had alerted Pharaoh and mounted a rescue operation.

In Egypt itself the people appealed to Pharaoh when their private stores ran out. His direction to them is the focal point of the narrative: "Go unto Joseph; what he saith to you, do" (v.55). As had happened before during his years as a slave and a prisoner, Joseph now again enjoyed the complete confidence of his master and was given full authority. Is it an accident that at His first miracle (Jn 2.5) Mary the mother of the Lord Jesus used almost identical words to those who had no wine for their wedding - "Whatsoever he saith unto you, do it"? The honours heaped on good men often suggest in a limited way the honour which God delights to see accorded to His Son.

In this son of Abraham there was fulfilled to some degree what had been promised to Abraham: I will bless thee, and make thy name great; and thou shalt be a blessing" (12.2). It begins at this point to be seen why God had sent Joseph through the long years of suffering. He had been preparing him through suffering for glory and to be saviour of others. The principle of suffering before glory, which conspicuously refers to the Lord Jesus (compare Lk 24.26), is seen in the experience of Joseph also. He lived for a further eighty years after he was first summoned to appear before Pharaoh. The early years of suffering must often have seemed to him, in retrospect, to have been short, though they were bitter while they lasted. For the godly the years of suffering are "but for a moment" when measured against eternal glory, and the affliction is light compared with the weight of glory to come (compare 2 Cor 4.17).

Notes

1 See Allen P. Ross "Creation and Blessing" p637.

GENESIS 42

Joseph's Brothers go to Egypt for Corn

Introductory

Chapter 37 opened with a reference to Jacob dwelling in Canaan and closed with Joseph sold to an Egyptian officer, in Egypt. Much of the narrative since then has followed the experiences of Joseph in Egypt. The time has now come to show how Joseph's brothers came to follow him there. They will all go there and finally, in ch.46, God will direct Jacob also to go. The focus of God's dealings with the house of Jacob is now moving firmly towards Egypt, where He will transform them at the exodus into a nation, referring to them as "my people", as, for example, in Exodus 3.7.

Verses 1-5: Jacob Sends His Sons to Buy Corn

The chapter opens with Jacob and his sons back in Canaan, but most of the action will take place in Egypt and the conversation in Canaan will concern mainly who should go or not go to Egypt to buy corn. Canaan was not exempt from the famine and somebody had to go to get corn for Jacob's family.

The question of Jacob in v.1, "Why do ye look one upon another?" appears in the Septuagint as, "Why are you idle?", and this does appear to be the import of his question. He ordered them to go and buy corn. It may be a deliberate hint of the drama to come that in v.3 it is not "Jacob's sons" but "Joseph's brethren" who are referred to. In the following chapters the relationships between Joseph and his brothers will be crucial. At this point, however, Jacob is still in control, even if his orders are somewhat petulant.

Jacob was willing to send his sons on what might be a dangerous mission in this time of general crisis. He was not willing, however, to allow Benjamin to go with them. Benjamin was by this time fully grown, but he was, as far as Jacob knew, the only surviving son borne to him by his beloved Rachel. He had previously sent Joseph on a dangerous mission and something, it seemed, had happened to him. He would not make the same mistake again. Thus ten sons of Jacob, who were brothers of Joseph, came to Egypt to buy corn.

Verses 6-17: Joseph's Brothers Appear Before Him

The story of the reception which Joseph's brothers received from him opens with a restatement of his position of authority in Egypt in relation to selling corn. This explains why, when they came into his presence, they prostrated themselves before him as befitted starving suppliants begging to be allowed to buy corn. Now can be seen how Joseph's early dreams were being fulfilled. Those dreams had involved sheaves of corn, theirs bowing down to his; and this situation in which they now found themselves had been presaged by a dream of Pharaoh about ears of corn. The symbolism in the dreams was devised by the God who knew from the start what would happen and could provide a most appropriate set of pictures to express it.

The very restraint in the statement that "Joseph saw his brethren, and he knew them", is poignant. The last time he had seen them was all those years ago when he was being carried off in distress by the Midianites while his brothers stood watching. Joseph must have wondered what was in their heart, whether they remembered him as well as he remembered them, what their feelings would be if they were reminded of their shameful treatment of him. They were at his mercy, but he did not seek revenge. Instead he began to test them; he pretended not to recognise them and spoke harshly to them. First he wanted to know where they came from. They replied and added that they came to buy food. It is not surprising that they failed to recognise him. He had of course matured, but he was also clean-shaven in the Egyptian style (while they wore beards), dressed as an Egyptian and spoke Egyptian, using an interpreter when he conversed with them. Then, as he stood there and watched them bow low before him, he remembered his dreams, "which he dreamed of them" (v.9). He must test them. So he accused them of coming as spies to see Egypt's nakedness (that is, weakness). They protested their innocence and good faith. They had come, they said, to buy food; they were one man's sons (unlikely if they were spies); they were true men. Again he accused them. This time they were prompted to add circumstantial details; how they were indeed one man's sons; how there were twelve of them; how the youngest was at home with their father and "one is not". Thus for the first time they admit the former existence of a twelfth brother, Joseph. He was not prepared to let the matter drop. At least he now knew that Benjamin, his only full brother, was safe at home with Jacob (v.13). He explained that he was going to test their story by having one of them fetch their youngest brother while the rest of them stayed imprisoned in Egypt. He swore by the life of Pharaoh - which must have had a chilling authenticity to these demoralised men - that if they could not pass the test they were in deep trouble. Then, to give them time to digest the seriousness of their plight, he put them in prison for three days (compare the comment above on 22.4 about three-day ordeals). They were beginning to suffer as their cruelty had made him suffer. But their suffering was not yet over.

Verses 18-26: The Brothers Leave Simeon in Prison

After three days Joseph sounded more conciliatory towards his brothers. He had a humane proposal for them, as befitted, said he, a man who feared God. He just might be able to spare their lives if they proved their good faith. His proposal was that one brother stay in prison in Egypt while the others took the corn which they would buy back home to Canaan. Undoubtedly he wanted to ensure that there would be enough men to escort an adequate caravan of baggage donkeys to provide for old Jacob and the others at home. One thing he insisted on, that they must bring their youngest brother to him.

All of this was harrowing for the brothers - the imprisonment of Simeon (chosen by Joseph to stay), the threat to Benjamin, the still present fear for their own lives, the thought of how Jacob would take this latest development. In their distress they let their minds go back over twenty years, to the distress of their other brother, the one who now "was not". They remembered his cries for mercy (v.21), "and we would not hear". Their present predicament was stirring emotion, but it was also awakening conscience. Their conscience reminded them that the lad whom they had sold was "our brother" (v.21). Yet when they had carried the blood-stained coat to Jacob they had said, not "our brother's coat", but "your son's coat". They confessed, "We are verily guilty concerning our brother", and concluded, "therefore is this distress come upon us". So sins can be brought back to memory, even after many years, and short-term evil gains can be shown to have been in reality horribly bad bargains.

At this point Reuben interjected a typically impractical plaint. In effect he said, "You should have listened to me. I told you so". His statement that "his blood is required" may be another indication that his brothers had never really fully explained to Reuben what they had done to Joseph. Remember that he was not present when they sold Joseph.

All this while, as they poured out these cries of distress and recrimination, Joseph listened and understood. Had he been marked by their kind of spirit he might have gloated at their discomfiture. Instead he turned away from them and wept. They had hated him, reviled and sold him, but there were signs that now at last they had begun to realise that it was their brother whom they had cast out. He had true humanity in his heart even if they had not. But he soon regained his composure, for the task of restoring his brothers to a proper relationship was not complete. He bound Simeon as they looked on. His humane proposal was going ahead as planned.

One thing they did not see was what happened as their sacks were filled with corn. The amount they had bought was filled into the sacks, then was added an extra amount for their journey, then into each sack went the silver they had paid for the contents. When they had received the twenty pieces of silver for Joseph there had been no money given back to anyone. It is difficult to decide exactly why Joseph returned their money - to show kindness, to confuse them, to punish them by a reminder of their earlier preference for money rather than their brother, or simply psychological pressure? It certainly would cause consternation. But for the present the nine brothers loaded their donkeys and went their way in ignorance of this latest twist in their circumstances, while Simeon lay in an Egyptian prison.

Verses 27-38: The Journey Home and Jacob's Sorrow

All went well on the journey home until the overnight lodging place was reached and the donkeys had to be fed. One of the brothers opened his sack to feed his donkey (and probably those of the others) and there in the mouth of the sack was his money. His call to his brothers telling them what he had found caused dismay and fear. Their immediate reaction was, "What is this that God hath done unto us?" This may once more indicate how active their guilty consciences were. They had old memories of wrongs done, quite apart from the selling of Joseph or the conspiracy to murder him.

On their return to Canaan they reported to Jacob. Their description of Joseph as "the man, who is the lord of the land" is telling in its acknowledgment of the real power wielded by him. There are some differences between what they reported and what had happened. They reported how they had told "the man" of the twelve brothers, of whom one "was not", and the youngest was with their father in Canaan. This reverses the order in which Joseph and Benjamin were mentioned by them to Joseph. Perhaps the postponement of Benjamin to the end of the sentence here serves to lead on to the burning issue of whether he would go back to Egypt with them. This issue is raised only two verses later (v.34). When telling how they had been forced to leave Simeon behind they omitted the graphic detail of Joseph having bound him before their eyes. They also softened the threat in Joseph's demand, "This do, and live" (v.18), by quoting him as saying, "So will I deliver your brother, and ye shall traffick (AV, RV; "travel freely", Wenham) in the land" (v.34). The negative promise, that they would not be killed, had become a positive promise that they would have freedom of movement in the land.

Their consternation was roused further by the discovery, when they opened their packs, that everyone's money had been returned, not just that of the first man to open his pack. If, as seemed likely to them, this return of the money was sinister, they were all in trouble. Jacob's fear may need further explanation. He cried out bitterly (v.36) that they had bereaved him of his children. First Joseph had disappeared, presumably eaten by a wild beast. Then Simeon failed to return. Now there was a threat to take Benjamin away, probably never to be seen again. Could circumstances get any worse? Jacob's depression is understandable, but was as unjustified as it was possible to be. Things were just becoming very good indeed, for he was about to be reunited with both his "lost" sons.

There is a line of interpretation of Jacob's fear which merits mention. Some commentators suggest that in blaming his sons for bereaving him Jacob may have been suggesting that he had suspicions about their earlier explanation about the disappearance of Joseph. They had come back from Dothan without Joseph but with his blood-stained coat in their hands and with money which they had not had when they left home. Now they were home from Egypt with the corn they had bought, without Simeon, and with mysterious money in their sacks. Had they sold Simeon as they had presumably sold Joseph? Would they sell Benjamin next? This may be excessively melodramatic, and it is not really required to make sense of the story, but it is an interesting possibility.

Reuben again spoke up, and again his lack of appreciation of reality shines clearly through his dramatic gesture. He would guarantee the safe return of Benjamin. But then he had been absent when Joseph was sold, so why should he be trusted with Benjamin? He offered his two sons to be slain if he failed. But what benefit would it be to Jacob to add the loss of two grandsons to the loss of Benjamin if he did fail to return? Jacob ignored the gesture. He would not allow Benjamin to go. In referring to Benjamin as "my son" and to Joseph as "his brother" Jacob was continuing his habit of seeing the sons of Rachel as separate from his sons by other women, whether Leah or the two handmaids. Benjamin's brother was dead, he said, and only Benjamin was left. That is of course true if only Rachel's sons are taken into account. If mischief befell Benjamin, Jacob would die of sorrow and this would be the outcome for the surviving brothers as they mourned him.

GENESIS 43

Second Visit to Egypt - with Benjamin

Introductory
This chapter begins the story of the second visit of Joseph's brothers to Egypt to buy corn. This visit was more complicated than the first, requiring chs. 43-45 to complete the story. The first important new factor this time was that Judah was now the undisputed leader of the brothers (compare 43.3,8 and 44.14,18), and, as events unfold, will display the characteristics which made him a leader. Secondly, the presence of Benjamin also made a great impact on the course of events. When they met Joseph and bowed in his presence (43.28) there were eleven brothers prostrate before him, as his dream had said.

Verses 1-14: Jacob is Persuaded to Let Benjamin go to Egypt
In the opening scene of ch.42, Jacob was incisive and urgent in his exhortations to his sons to go quickly and get corn. Here, in ch.43, the situation was at least as critical and the need as pressing. Yet Jacob's call to his sons to go to Egypt was calmer and almost tentative - "buy us a little food". Perhaps he spoke with reluctance because he knew that if they went they must take Benjamin with them.

Judah acted as spokesman in reply. His growth in moral stature in this section is notable, exemplified particularly in his moving and eloquent pleading with Joseph in 44.18-34. Here his task was to make the reality of their position unmistakably clear to Jacob. "The man" had insisted to them that unless Benjamin were with them they would achieve nothing ("ye shall not see my face"). Jacob, then, had a choice; he could send Benjamin with them, in which case they would go; or he could refuse to send him, and they would stay in Canaan. He was still reluctant to yield. What, he wanted to know, had possessed them to disclose to "the man" that they had another brother? It then emerged that they had told Joseph the details given in 42.13 in answer to detailed questions. Joseph, of course, could ask very pertinent questions in this one-sided game of cat-and-mice, for he knew many of the answers before he asked the questions. And how were they to know, complained Judah, that "the man" would demand that they bring down Benjamin?

The decisive point in the discussion came when (v.8) Judah undertook personally to be responsible for "the lad" - his use of the term "the lad" may spontaneously reveal some affection in his heart for Benjamin. He argued first that the survival of the whole extended family was at stake. His personal guarantee for Benjamin's safety was impressively solemn: "of my hand shalt thou require him", and, "let me bear the blame for ever". This time it was Judah who expressed the urgency of getting on with the mission (v.10), which was being delayed by Jacob's reluctance to agree to Benjamin's going.

Once persuaded Jacob decided quickly on suitable preparations. They must send "the man" an appropriate present.† In addition to balm, storax (AV "spices") and myrrh (ladanum), which (see 37.25) were the Midianites' stock in trade, they were to take honey, pistachio nuts and almonds. While these were not perhaps very luxurious gifts to be presented to so great a man in wealthy Egypt they were refined gifts, expressing respect.

As to the money, there might have been some mistake about it, so they should take back what had been put in their packs and a further supply of money to pay for the next consignment of corn. Then, at last, he told them to take Benjamin, their brother. One notices in this phase of the story how tellingly terms of relationship bring in the suggestion of the healing of ruptures in the family. The one exception in most of this narrative is Joseph, who remains "the man", until the wonderful day of his self-revelation to his brothers. Having finally made up his mind to let Benjamin go, Jacob was ready to send them all off at once: "and arise, go again unto the man" (v.13).

His parting prayer for his sons called upon El Shaddai (God Almighty), the God who had confirmed His covenant with Abraham (17.1), whose blessing Isaac had called down on Jacob when he first left home (28.3), who had spoken to Jacob (35.11) as He sent him back to Bethel. All of these were momentous events in the lives of the participants. The prayer included the release of Simeon, mentioned as "your other brother", but most urgently was on behalf of Benjamin. If Benjamin were to be taken from him, then he must accept that it was his lot to be bereaved of his children. It is almost as if the sons of his other wives did not exist, for the crucial problem for Jacob was that Benjamin was, to the best of Jacob's knowledge, the sole surviving son of Rachel. The prayer shows by its formal nature how solemn the occasion was for Jacob.

Verses 15-25: Joseph's Steward Receives the Brothers Kindly

The brothers set out as agreed, with double money and Benjamin. In due course they reached Egypt. Evidently Joseph saw them before they saw him, and he noticed that Benjamin was with them, for there were ten of them. He instructed his chief steward to bring them to his own house, kill an animal and make food ready for a banquet at noon. This would have been an unusual time of day for a banquet, the more usual time being the evening, around sunset. Evidently, however, the very rich occasionally entertained guests to what was in effect a late breakfast, perhaps what might now be called "brunch", at about noon.†

So "the men" (as the brothers are referred to in these verses) were brought to Joseph's house. This was to them a most sinister development. They would have preferred to have gone quietly about the purchase of food, returning the mysterious money and getting out of Egypt, along with Simeon, as soon as possible. Was this invitation connected with the appearing of the money in their packs? Was he going about deviously to accuse them and reduce them to slavery? They must approach the steward and try to make the best of their situation by explaining to him, before they went in, what exactly had happened.

They outlined carefully to him in what circumstances they had found the money. Their account of this does not tally exactly with what happened (compare v.21 with 42.27-28,35), but their story did make the point it was intended to make, that the return of the money was a complete mystery to them. Anyway, they had brought the money back (v.21), and they had brought further money to pay for what they wanted to buy now.

The steward responded reassuringly. They should not worry. It must have been their God, their father's God, who had put the money in the bags, for he had received their payment in full. To reinforce his reassurance he released Simeon to them, brought all eleven of them into the house and extended to them the usual courtesy of water for foot-washing after their journey. He also fed their donkeys. And so preparations went on apace for Joseph to receive his honoured guests at noon. What a contrast to the first visit with its accusations of spying!

Verses 26-34: Joseph Entertains the Eleven Men

On Joseph's return to his house they went into his presence with their gift and, in presenting it, bowed to the earth. So the eleven sheaves bowed to his sheaf. He calmly enquired after their health and the health of their father, "the old man of whom ye spake" (v.27). Still nervous, they replied as courtesy demanded, but with care. And again they bowed low.

A forward movement of the action is signalled in the narrative by the statement that Joseph "lifted up his eyes" (compare 13.10 and 22.4, for example). What he saw (and what a moment that was!) was Benjamin, "his brother...his mother's son". Though Rachel was long dead her shadow still fell over this family. Was this, he asked, their youngest brother, of whom they had spoken? He graciously called down God's blessing on Benjamin. On the surface this was a perfectly normal event, a high official receiving foreign guests whom he had decided to honour, and everyone being very proper and polite.

But Joseph had to get this diplomatic prelude concluded, for he was overcome with emotion to be so close to his only full brother, who had been only a child when Joseph was sold into slavery. He had to withdraw to weep in his private quarters. After all those years, to be reunited with Benjamin and to know that all was well with Jacob! But he soon collected himself, washed his tear-marks away and came out to call for the meal to be served.

Egyptians did not like to eat with foreigners, as other ancient writers testify. Herodotus and other Greek historians also refer to this fact. The Jews were not the only race to have food taboos. So Joseph ate by himself, as the dignitary that he was, while the Egyptian officials ate at their table and the sons of Jacob at theirs.

Earlier apprehension may have been somewhat allayed by the time they sat down, but this was either reawakened or replaced by amazement when they discovered that "the man" had seated them in exact order of their ages. The narrative still skilfully refers to the brothers as "the men" (v.33), for the disclosure of their relationship to Joseph was still to come. There was a testing still to be carried out.

As they ate, Joseph sent pieces of food from his table to his guests as a token of the honour he wished to bestow. This is still a practice in some oriental countries, where the host may give an honoured guest a special delicacy, such as the head of the chicken or fish, or perhaps the tail of the sheep, by putting it on the guest's plate. The titbits were duly presented to the guests, but a distinct feature of the exercise was that Benjamin, though youngest, was singled out for conspicuous honour by receiving five times as much as any of the rest in this distribution of delicacies. Many years before, when Jacob had honoured young Joseph above the others there had been an unholy row. But these were now beaten men, subdued by fear and worn down by anxiety and insecurity. They had no leisure to indulge in envy of Benjamin. Anyway, they were learning that they must survive together rather than by competition. Their reception by "the man" depended on Benjamin for some reason which they could not fathom. They showed that the old envy had now no place in their hearts. They had passed their first test. Humanity was beginning to win in their relationships.

So they ate and drank enough to induce euphoria. Wine made glad the heart of man. They felt secure and relaxed. It appeared that their troubles were over and that the man was genuinely well disposed to them and they would all get home safely with the second consignment of food.

Notes

11 The word for present (MINCHA - 4503) is that used in ch.32 of the present carried by Jacob to his estranged brother Esau. It was appropriate for a present from an inferior to a superior.

16 See Everyday Life in the Holy Land, by James Neil, page 80.

GENESIS 44

The Cup in the Sack

Verses 1-13: Joseph's Cup Placed, then Found, in Benjamin's Sack

The banquet was over and Jacob's eleven sons were happy, and unaware of preparations being made by Joseph. He had his steward fill the brothers' sacks as full as they could be, replace the money in each as before and put Joseph's silver cup in the sack of the youngest brother. It was surely a baffled steward who obeyed, for the whole episode so far had been increasingly complicated. Morning came and the brothers made an early start. But they had only got clear of the city when Joseph sent his steward after them with questions which were obviously calculated to mystify them and cause greater alarm than ever.

His opening question to them was an accusation. They had abused Joseph's hospitality, and had "rewarded evil for good". He made a baffling reference to his master drinking from "it" and divining by "it".[†]

No mention had been made to them about the cup, but they must have deduced that he was talking about a cup. Of course his questions were based on the pretended assumption that they had the cup and therefore knew well enough what he was talking about. They protested that they had no knowledge of whatever it was they were accused of stealing. They reasoned with him that, since they had returned the money found in their sacks, they had shown themselves honest men. And would they now steal valuables from his lord's house? So confident were they of their innocence that they volunteered that anyone found in possession of whatever "it" was should die, and for good measure all the others would go to slavery. The brotherly solidarity in the family is becoming steadily stronger - they will survive or perish together. The search for stolen goods in baggage is reminiscent of the time Rachel stole the teraphim from Laban (ch.31). On that occasion too there was the agreement that whoever had stolen the goods should die, only then the teraphim were not found, whereas on this occasion the person at risk was Rachel's son Benjamin, and the supposedly stolen goods were found.

The steward softened the terms to be exacted of them if "it" were found: the one in whose sack it was found would become a slave and the others would go free. This reply was a further test of their solidarity, their loyalty to each other. So they quickly took down their sacks and began, conscious of their innocence, to open them. The search began at the eldest and continued to the youngest. Thus the climax came at the very end of a prolonged search, when "it", the cup, was found in Benjamin's sack.

The other brothers could have abandoned Benjamin to his fate, as they had abandoned Joseph in the pit and then to the tender mercies of the slave-dealer. The steward had deliberately left them this opening, for his brief was to bring back Benjamin to his master. But they refused this solution. When Joseph was sold the only person who rent his clothes in mourning (37.34) was old Jacob. Now all the brothers, faced with the prospect of losing Benjamin, rent their clothes and returned promptly to the city. This section of Genesis has much in it about searches, but under the searches of baggage there was also a deeper search going on, for Joseph's brothers were being searched as to their motives and values and loyalties. They are now beginning to emerge from this deeper search as men whom God has searched and found true to their family and its values, true in some sense to God's intention for His covenant people.

Verses 14-34: Judah Pleads for Benjamin

In this episode Judah emerges spiritually head and shoulders above his brothers. It was "Judah and his brethren" who came to Joseph's house, Judah who was spokesman. It had been he who had proposed that they sell Joseph (37.26,27), admittedly as the alternative to the deeper crime of murdering him. The intervening period of some twenty-two years had changed and refined the man. God had been at work in his heart.

They found Joseph still there. Of course he was still there, yearning for the moment when he could see the old breach healed and embrace his own flesh and blood, and Benjamin in particular. And again they fell on their faces before him, this time in abject appeal.

Joseph repeated the accusation in general terms: "What deed is this that ye have done?". Surely they were foolish, he suggested, to think that such a man as he was could not detect their guilt. Judah exclaimed that they could hardly find words to plead their cause or protest their innocence. God had found them out. God had not found them guilty of spying in Egypt, or stealing Joseph's silver cup, for these were mere figments of Joseph's strategy to break them down. But God had found them out in the one thing that was at issue - whether or not they had repented of their hatred of Joseph, selling him into slavery and breaking their own father's heart by suggestions of wild beasts eating Joseph. They had given up hope of making sense of the details of the present accusations or receiving justice on these new charges, but they were deeply conscious of the awful possibility that God was now visiting upon them that old crime which they had thought had passed unnoticed.

Judah presented himself and his brothers to go into slavery, along with Benjamin. What a contrast to the day (37.25) when they sat down calmly to eat, impervious to the cries of young Joseph in the pit! But Joseph refused their offer. He was going to put their loyalty to Benjamin to the test. He insisted that his only quarrel was with the "guilty" man, and Benjamin must become his slave. Let the rest of them go home to their father with his goodwill (literally "in peace").

It seems as if the reference to going home to their father opened up a floodgate in Judah's heart. He remembered Jacob's broken-hearted lament when they had callously presented to him the blood-stained coat with the invitation, "Know now whether it be thy son's coat or no" (37.32). He remembered Jacob's cry, "Joseph is not, and Simeon is not, and ye will take Benjamin away" (42.36). Judah's eloquent plea which follows is full of genuine concern for his old father. The plea is not simply that Joseph take pity on Benjamin. It is above all else a plea for Jacob. Whatever else Joseph's testing of his brothers had done, it had caused Judah, and probably the others, to begin to see that they needed at last to feel some compassion and natural affection for their father. Judah's appeal contains the word "father" some fifteen times. If he had known all the facts he could hardly have chosen a plea more calculated to touch Joseph, who had now seen all his brothers and longed to be reunited with his beloved father. The appeal is marked also by careful courtesy in Judah's address to "the man" and in his begging for a patient hearing (v.18) from a man who was "even as Pharaoh". Presumably this last plea was intended to say that, even as Pharaoh had the power to grant petitions, Joseph had the power to grant this plea. The brothers and also Jacob were constantly referred to by Judah as "thy servants", while Joseph was addressed as "my lord".

In vv.19-23 Judah reminded Joseph of the questions Joseph had asked on their first visit, of their answers and of his insistence, despite their reluctance, that their youngest brother should be brought to Egypt. Otherwise they would "see his face" no more. It is important to notice the touch in his narrative about the youngest brother not being able to come because without him their father would die. This keeps the emphasis on Jacob's feelings rather than Benjamin's.

In vv.24-29 he told Joseph of the exchanges between them and their father when they had come to the time when they needed to return to Egypt for more food. Their discussion had revolved around whether Benjamin could go to Egypt. Joseph must have listened with deep feeling to the narration of Jacob's lament, especially the fact that he had spoken of Rachel as "my wife", as if he had only one, and of "two sons", as though only Joseph and Benjamin mattered to him. What must he have felt when Judah, unwittingly powerful in his plea, spoke of Jacob's heart-broken cry that one son had gone out from him and was presumably torn in pieces? Of this story, fabricated by the brothers, the reader is already aware, but Joseph had not heard it. Judah had had many years to recall, as he must often have done, his father's pathetic cry about going down mourning to the grave. This cry was first uttered in 37.35 when Joseph did not return and was developed in 42.38 when it was proposed to take Benjamin away to Egypt. The fact that Judah's eloquence on this point sprang from his now awakened sense of affection for his father must not be overlooked.

It was now time for Judah to apply the argument based on these narratives. Judah was about to return to his father. If the youngest brother (note again the affectionate term "the lad") were not with them Jacob would die, so closely was Jacob's soul knit with Benjamin's, as the Hebrew literally expresses it (v.30). It may not be too fanciful to see a graphic touch in Judah's words "when he seeth that the lad is not with us"; Jacob would be watching as they returned, counting the heads, looking for the specially loved youngest son. So, Judah argued, they would have the sorrowful task of burying their old father.

Judah pressed another argument. He had personally gone surety with Jacob for Benjamin's safe return and he related faithfully to Joseph the solemn undertaking into which he had entered with Jacob to bring Benjamin back. This was a good reason, he pleaded, why he himself should stay a slave in Egypt for ever so that Benjamin might go back home to Canaan. His plea reached its climax in the memorable question, "How shall I go up to my father, and the lad be not with me?". Earlier Reuben had unrealistically pleaded in effect with Jacob, "Here am I, take my two sons as victims". Here Judah, with powerful realism and wonderful self-sacrifice says, "Here am I, accept me as Benjamin's sacrifice". And this was the man who had said to his brothers, "Come, and let us sell him (Joseph) to the Ishmaelites" (37.27). Joseph had come a long way since that day of bitter betrayal by his own flesh and blood. But so had the brothers, especially Judah. Jacob's present favouritism towards Benjamin moved Judah, not to envy but to compassion for Jacob and therefore sacrificial loyalty to Benjamin. A relationship with God can cost us dearly, but it can transform us in the process from greedy, envious, callous people into those who will sacrifice all for those whom we love, and for those whom they in turn love.

The tests were complete. His brothers had shown that the old hatred and animosity had been abandoned for a new spirit of affection within the family. They had demonstrated by their very confusion when disaster struck (42.21) that they had feelings of repentance for rejecting and selling Joseph. But Joseph changed his face towards his brothers at this point because he could contain his deep emotion no longer. Judah's obvious compassion for Jacob's suffering brought back to Joseph's own mind the memory of how dearly he had been loved by Jacob and how dearly he had loved Jacob in return.

Notes

5 It need not be supposed that Joseph actually engaged in divination by means of liquid in a cup. This was part of the fabricated evidence against the brothers, given a non-Hebrew flavour for authenticity. Such practices were later forbidden in Israel. Whether at this time they were current in Egypt is somewhat beside the point.

GENESIS 45

Joseph Reveals Himself to His Brothers

Verses 1-15: I Am Joseph Your Brother

Previously when Joseph had been overcome by emotion during his questioning of his brothers he had had to withdraw to weep. Now that they had been fully tested he could weep in their presence. But the reconciliation was too sacred an event for Egyptians to be allowed to witness it. Therefore the first thing was to send all the Egyptians out of the room.

The suddenness of this order to all the officials to leave must have caused his brothers to wonder what was coming next. Was this another alarming turnabout? But then come the wonderfully poignant words, "Joseph made himself known unto his brethren". The verses that follow are liberally sprinkled with terms denoting relationship. He was no longer "the man", feared and unpredictable. They were no longer merely "the men".

All the emotion which had been bottled up since they, and especially Benjamin, first came, now burst forth and Joseph wept so loudly that those in the rest of the house could hear him. Not only they, but also those in Pharaoh's house, seemingly close by, could hear the loud weeping. What could this new behaviour by the man mean?

His words were simple, their meaning obvious. But how could his brothers take in the message - "I am Joseph"? Joseph went on talking and explaining and reassuring his brothers, but no word from them is recorded until v.26, where they reported to Jacob this most amazing revelation, though v.15 does say that they spoke to Joseph. After his initial statement his first thought was for his father's welfare. Was he, could he still be, alive and well? Could it be true? But they were so struck dumb with amazement and perhaps fear that they could not answer.

He had to reassure them by inviting them to come near. Up to this point they had had to keep their distance from the great man; now they must come near to their brother. He repeated, "I am Joseph your brother", a reassuring thought, but he must add an authenticating statement which in itself was unnerving for them - "whom ye sold into Egypt" (v.4). But immediately he followed this with an exhortation to them not to reproach themselves for having sold him, for God had been in the selling: "God did send me before you to preserve life". Joseph's mind was in the great work which God had sent him to do. As he had taken a lively awareness of God into his menial place in Potiphar's house and into the prison, so now he saw God in his present ability to save lives.

He explained what they did not know, that the past two years of famine were only the beginning of a seven-year famine. For a further five years, then, there would be no ploughing (AV "earing") nor harvest; in other words, cultivation as a whole would be at a standstill. Hence the importance of the work he was doing, to save lives by a careful distribution of the garnered treasure of corn. In the first place, and most importantly, God had sent him to ensure the survival of a posterity (RV "remnant") for the house of Jacob. Most translators render the end of v.7 (which the AV gives as "and to save your lives by a great deliverance") by "and to preserve for you a great number of survivors" (Wenham) or similar words. The salvation would not be limited and partial but on a grand scale.

God, he repeated, had sent him to Egypt. God made him "a father to Pharaoh", an Egyptian title of great honour. He had made Joseph lord of all Pharaoh's house (personal estate) and ruler throughout all Egypt, so wide did his authority run. Let them go with all speed to Jacob and tell him that Joseph had sent a message to him, Joseph whom God had now made lord of all Egypt. Let them urge Jacob to come to him as quickly as possible. He would have a home in Goshen, in the eastern part of the Nile delta. There with all his family and possessions he would be near Joseph, and Joseph would take special care of him during the remaining years of famine. Let them tell his father of all his glory in Egypt, all that they themselves had seen. Had they not, he said, seen him face to face and heard him speak? And Benjamin, his brother (again that special relationship of those two), had seen and heard him. At which he and Benjamin embraced each other warmly and wept for joy. Then he kissed all his other brothers too and wept and they "talked with him". What a conversation that must have been!

There are features of Joseph's experience which recall the Lord Jesus. He was loved by his father, envied by his brothers, sold by those close to him, steadfast in temptation and rejection, in various circumstances aware of God with him, glorified while still rejected by his brothers. Now after his glorification he is reconciled to his brothers and brings blessing not only to his own brothers but also to the world. So the Lord Jesus will, in a future day, be made known to His own people Israel, they will repent of their rejection of Him, He will reveal Himself to them in a time of suffering for them and bring unprecedented blessing to both them and the world at large.

Verses 16-24: Joseph's Brothers Sent Home Enriched

It was soon common knowledge in the palace that Joseph's brothers had come, and both Pharaoh and his officials rejoiced on his behalf. Pharaoh's goodwill expressed itself very practically. He bade the brothers load up their baggage animals and go to Canaan to fetch their father and the rest of the household. He would give them the best of everything. It must be remembered that the famine had almost five years still to run, so this command from Pharaoh was very timely. To make sure that they would be able to bring all that they wanted from Canaan, Pharaoh told them to take wagons to carry their wives, children and possessions. As to their possessions, they should not worry unduly about what they brought to Egypt, for he would supply the best of everything (v.20). They were happy to obey and went off under Joseph's personal providing, with ample provision for their journeys. To honour them he gave them clothes, but made a special gift of money and clothing to Benjamin. There is no doubt an echo of Joseph's early days when his special coat was a mark of his father's favouritism towards him. This time there was no envy. Ten donkeys and ten she-donkeys were needed to carry the special gifts for Jacob, including food to see him safely back to Joseph in Egypt.

In most translations v.24 ends with the exhortation, "See that ye fall not out by the way", or some other form of words to encourage them not to quarrel. Wenham, among others, prefers to give the verb RAGAZ (7264) the meaning "to be stirred up", which he understands, in the negative command, as an exhortation not to be apprehensive or afraid, though he does not rule out the sense of quarrelling or recrimination. If the verb is limited to quarrelling or recrimination it does come rather abruptly. If it was a word of reassurance this may match the odd fact that at no point in all this section of this episode is there any record of anything that the brothers said. They must still have been in a virtual state of shock and in need of some such reassurance.

Verses 25-28: The Brothers Carry the News to Jacob

The bare statement of v.25 might easily have been a graphic description of hustle and bustle as the groaning wagons set out for Canaan. It would have been such a narrative if this had been a human story told for emotional effect. But the inspired record is economical of details which have mere human interest. Yet it must have been a wonderful caravan.

The brothers gave an accurate report when they arrived. They started with the most important matter: Joseph was alive and was ruler over all Egypt. And, wonderful to relate, they were able to tell this without any suggestion of envy or regret. But Jacob could not take it in. He was stunned at the news, for he had had no hint of it before. He just could not believe that the news could be so good, so different from what he had feared. He had seen Joseph go away and not return, then Simeon, then Benjamin if his fears should be realised, but now Simeon and Benjamin were both back safe and sound, and Joseph was alive and exalted. After all those years!

He listened in a daze while they told him all that Joseph had said, and how well they remembered those amazing words, "I am Joseph your brother"! Then he looked at the wagons laden with goods beyond his imagining, realised that it must be true and his spirit "revived". Commentators point out that in v.28, after a long period of being called Jacob, he is referred to again as Israel. He realised that all was not against him as he had supposed (42.36). He knew now that all had been carefully brought together for his good by the God whom he had met at Bethel and Peniel, and he was Israel, safe in the hands of God when his cleverness failed him and he could only cling to God.

His cry of exultation is triumphant: "It is enough; Joseph my son is yet alive: I will go and see him before I die". Not a word of the wealth or glory or security or friendship of Pharaoh. His heart was full of Joseph, so loved and so mourned for and so long lost to him. He must go and see him. This would be fulness of joy, even if it were the last thing he did - "I will go and see him before I die". He now had the courage to accept Pharaoh's invitation, and he had the motivation to go. But this is an inspired narrative of the covenant people and there was more to this journey to Egypt than that. It would be inaugurated with full divine approval, as the early verses of ch.46 show.

GENESIS 46

Jacob Goes to Egypt

Verses 1-7: Encouraged by God, Jacob Goes to Egypt

It may be significant that at this stage in the narrative Jacob is frequently (though not always) called Israel, for the move by all the family and possessions to Egypt is the prelude to the formation of the national community later referred to as "the children of Israel". The emphasis in many of the details of this narrative is on the fact that Jacob and all his family took all their possessions down to Egypt. It was a full family migration, not merely a temporary visit to escape famine.

The first step of the journey took them to Beersheba, the last settlement before the southern border of the land. It was a place which had sacred associations for the family, for Abraham had planted a tamarisk tree there (21.33) and called on the name of the Lord, and Isaac had built an altar there (26.25). Jacob viewed the passing of Beersheba as an event of deep significance, for he offered sacrifices there. The only other place where this precise expression (using the Hebrew word ZABAH (2076) for sacrifice) is used in Genesis is in 31.54. On that occasion Jacob was at Mizpah, at his Rubicon on his return from Laban's home to Canaan with his two wives. Here again a vital transition was upon him at Beersheba, as he left Canaan for Egypt. The last time Jacob was engaged in building an altar and making offerings was (35.1-7,14) when, on his return from Laban's home, he finally completed the journey by going at God's command to Bethel, another transition which was important to him. It was appropriate here that he call upon the God of his father Isaac at a place where Isaac had built an altar.

So far Jacob had acted in response to the story of Joseph's survival and exaltation, and the fact that he had a pressing invitation to come to Egypt. But God did not leave him to depend merely on circumstances in making this momentous decision to quit the promised land for Egypt. God spoke to him in night visions with the urgent double call, "Jacob, Jacob".

The vision was a formal endorsement by God of his decision to go to Joseph in Egypt. As such it was introduced as a statement from God that He was indeed God, the God of Isaac. It was identified as a positive message by the encouragement in it that he should not be afraid. The substance of the message was a four-fold promise.

First, God promised that He would make of Jacob a great nation. This was a repetition of the promise to Abraham (12.2) and to Jacob himself (35.11); a similar promise had also been given to Ishmael (21.18). In this context Jacob, on his way down to Egypt to begin the long exile foretold to Abraham (15.13-14), was understandably given no explicit accompanying assurance regarding possession of the land. The experiences of Jacob's family in Egypt were going to be formative in the process of moulding them into a people for God.

The second promise was encouraging for Jacob: he would not be going down to Egypt to make his own way, for God would go down with him. This has already been prefigured in the repeated assertion that, in the vicissitudes of Joseph's early years in Egypt, God was with him (39.2,21,23). When Joseph recalled at that time the dreams of the greatness which God had given him he might well have wondered how his sufferings tallied with them. In future years the family of Jacob might wonder in Egypt about promises to their fathers of a land of their own as God's gift to them, but it was only later on that they were to learn how God had taken note of their sufferings and heard their cries: "I have surely seen the affliction of my people ..... I know their sorrows ... I am come down to deliver ... " (Ex 3.7,8). Between this initial assurance and the later word to Moses there lay years and generations in which it was difficult to see the light of promise. Nevertheless there was a promise, and God's promises are reliable.

The third promise in the visions to Jacob related to that future deliverance: "I will also surely bring thee up again". The promise seems, on a superficial reading, to apply to Jacob personally, but it must obviously apply to his family who "came out of (his) loins". The second promise had also been applicable to the generations who would live in Egypt between Jacob and Moses. It is of great importance that in this story of God's dealings with His covenant people the moment of their leaving Canaan for Egypt is marked by a solemn undertaking by God that He would bring them back to the land. The promise of possession of the land is in some sense implicit in this third promise to Jacob at this point when he was leaving Canaan. Possession of the land as such, however, is not explicitly mentioned here.

The fourth promise was God's answer to Jacob's years of suffering and depression. He had more than once referred to the probability or even the inevitability of a death without consolation, bereft of those who meant most to him (37.35; 42.38). Now the promise was that Joseph would put his hand on Jacob's eyes; that is, Joseph would close his eyes when he died. Joseph would be in attendance personally to perform gently and tenderly this last act of respect for his father.

Thus encouraged, Jacob and his train set out from Beersheba. Those who needed to be carried in vehicles were carried in comfort in the wagons provided by Pharaoh. It is emphasised that he took all his possessions and all his descendants with him. It was a folk migration. The Canaan phase of the story is closing for hundreds of years until it is reopened in the book of Joshua in God's exhortation to him, "Now therefore arise, go over this Jordan, thou, and all this people, unto the land which I do give to them, even to the children of Israel" (Josh 1.2). It was a momentous event when they "came into Egypt" (v.6).

Verses 8-27: The Catalogue of the Family of Jacob

This section lists "the names of the children of Israel, which came into Egypt, Jacob and his sons". It is the first genealogical list since "the generations of Esau" in ch.36, and the only systematised list of the descendants of Jacob in Genesis. In a sense it is another step in the progression towards the history of the people later to be called "the children of Israel", and away from the stories of relationships between members of a single family group, whether the family of Abraham, Isaac or Jacob.

It is beyond the scope of this commentary to attempt to unravel the complexities of the list and its relation to the lists in Numbers 26 and the early chapters of 1 Chronicles. The list is designed to indicate that all the descendants of Jacob went down to Egypt (compare vv.6,7), so they are listed. The total comes to seventy, which was a figure that indicated comprehensiveness, as, for instance, there were seventy nations listed in ch.10 comprising the nations sprung from Noah (10.32). Note that in Luke 10.1 the Lord sent out seventy witnesses ahead of Him to Israel. The Sanhedrin of Jewish elders also numbered seventy.[†]

The list does include the names of some who did not go down to Egypt at this time, for instance, Er and Onan, who died under God's judgment. It includes the names of some not yet born, who may be taken to have gone down to Egypt in the person of their father; among these would be the sons of Pharez (v.12) and probably some at least of the sons of Benjamin, who was rather young to have ten sons at this time.[†] One may doubt whether there were as few girls in the families as are listed. The children listed were those of significance in the record of the people of Israel. Mention can be made in this connection of Pharez's son Hezron, who features in the genealogy of our Lord Jesus Christ as Esrom (Mt 1.3); and Kohath (whom some translators spell Kehat), son of Levi, who was an ancestor of Moses Num 26.58-59).

There are patterns discernible in the numbers in each sub-group. Leah's children, if Jacob is excluded from the count, number thirty-two while her handmaid Zilpah's number sixteen. Rachel's children as listed number fourteen, while those of her handmaid Bilhah number seven. The children of the wife in each case are twice as numerous as those of the handmaid. If the children of Leah are taken as thirty-three (v.15; presumably Jacob is included because he went down and Leah was his first wife, so he was counted in at this point) and Zilpah's as sixteen the total comes to forty-nine. Compare this with Rachel's fourteen and Bilhah's seven, and there is another pattern of multiples of seven. There is clearly some kind of symbolism in the numbers given, as well as a record of a total migration of the extended family (comapare v.27).

Verses 28-34: Joseph Plans for the Occupation of Goshen

Jacob sent one son ahead to plan for the arrival, and by this time it was obvious that the person to take on a responsible task of this kind was Judah. Goshen in the east Nile delta zone was the area in which they would settle. It was an ideal choice because it contained good pasture land, it was within easy reach of Joseph, it was near the border closest to Canaan, and it enabled them to remain a separate community from the native Egyptians. As befitted a person of great consequence, Joseph made formal preparations to receive the family. He "made ready his chariot", a detail which highlights the importance of what was about to happen. Then the meeting took place, a prolonged mutual embrace between Jacob and Joseph with tears of joy. Jacob's exclamation, "Now let me die" (AV) is perhaps better rendered by something like, "Now I am ready to die", or even Knox's, "I can die happy". Jacob's great joy was simply to see Joseph again and embrace him. Nothing more was needed to make his cup of joy in life full.[†]

Joseph still had work to do. He must make an official statement to Pharaoh about their arrival. He outlined to Jacob and his brothers the line he would adopt in his report. They were and always had been herdsmen, keepers of sheep and cattle. They had brought all their flocks and herds and possessions with them, obviously in the hope of being able to continue their traditional occupation. Later, when they would be presented to Pharaoh, they would be asked about their occupation. This would be an apt question, for no country wants refugees who will be a dead burden on the state. Joseph guided his family to make a careful point of their traditional devotion to the pastoral life. Thus it would be easy for him to lead Pharaoh's thinking towards allocating Goshen to them.

The final mention of the Egyptian aversion to shepherds has been variously interpreted. One suggestion is that it was a matter of their resenting foreign nomads coming in, but the passage does not make a point about their being foreigners, merely referring to shepherds. This interpretation is also close to the one which uses this as evidence pointing to the rule of the Hyksos kings (the "Shepherd Kings") in Egypt, but the connection is not firmly established, nor is it clear what it would indicate if it were established. It may be that in a general way the more mobile life of shepherds led to friction between them and cultivators, like the traditional friction between cowboys and cultivators in North America. Possibly men who lived by plunder would roam about under the pretence of being shepherds, or more generally nomads. Joseph, with bitter memories of the corruptions in Egyptian city life, may have been intent on ensuring that his people would, with Pharaoh's blessing, be able to live a life apart, follow their own morality and worship their own God. If this was Joseph's motive in managing that they should be located in Goshen, it did not succeed in the long term, for Joshua had occasion (Josh 24.14) to exhort Israel, "Now therefore fear the Lord, and serve him in sincerity and in truth: and put away the gods which your fathers served beyond the River, and in Egypt; and serve ye the Lord" (RV).

Notes

8 If we read with the Hebrew Masoretic text in Deuteronomy 32.8, "He set the bounds of the peoples (RV) according to the number of the children of Israel", we have the connection between Genesis 10 and Genesis 46 made explicit. The picture is less neat when we know that (a) the LXX and a Hebrew text found at Qumran read in Deuteronomy 32.8 "the angels of God", for "the children of Israel", (b) the LXX here (in v.20) gives Joseph seven sons in Egypt , not two and (c) the LXX gives a total of seventy-five, not seventy. In Acts 7 Stephen seems to be following the LXX (v.14) when he says that seventy-five went down to Egypt. This figure may be arrived at by including Joseph's grandchildren born in Egypt.

21 The picture with regard to the sons of Benjamin is complicated by the fact that (among other things) two or more of those described here as his sons are listed in Numbers 26 as his grandsons, namely Naaman and Ard.

30 Jacob's "I am ready to die" has been well compared with Simeon's joyful exclamation (Lk 2.29) when he held the infant Jesus in his arms and exclaimed, "Lord, now lettest thou thy servant depart in peace ...". Like Jacob, Simeon was saying that now he could die happy (or "in peace") since his dearest wish was fulfilled, and, in relation to Simeon, God's promise had been fulfilled. Neither of them was praying that he might die. In Simeon's case this would have required the form, "Now let (not "lettest") thou thy servant depart...". "Lettest" makes a statement, where "let" would make a request.

GENESIS 47

Jacob, in Goshen, Blesses Pharaoh and Plans His Own Burial

Verses 1-6: Pharaoh Agrees to Jacob Settling in Goshen

Joseph went to Pharaoh, as had been planned, and told him that his father and brothers had arrived with their animals and all their possessions and were in Goshen. He took five of his brothers with him and presented them before Pharaoh. As Joseph had foretold, Pharaoh asked them their occupation, and they replied as they had planned. Their request to be allowed to settle in Goshen was backed up by their explanation to Pharaoh that the severe famine in Canaan had left the land without pasture for their flocks. This served to emphasise to Pharaoh the importance of their flocks to them.

Pharaoh gave his answer to Joseph, for they were being received for Joseph's sake. The suppliants were Joseph's father and brothers, so they could choose, said Pharaoh, anywhere in Egypt, even the best land. No doubt this was diplomatic language and not to be taken as more than an opening statement to indicate that he was about to agree to their request, as he did in the next clause, "in the land of Goshen let them dwell" (v.6). He even suggested that if some of the brothers were expert herdsmen they might be given official charge of some of Pharaoh's cattle. This would give them a privileged position as Pharaoh's servants and, if they were remotely like Joseph in their skills, energy and initiative, Pharaoh would also gain from the arrangement. The suggestion may indicate that Pharaoh by now had realised that there was blessing and prosperity in befriending these Hebrews, as the whole Genesis story shows.

Verses 7-10: Jacob, Presented to Pharaoh, Blesses Him

After the initial exploratory presentation of his brothers Joseph proceeded to the central business of bringing in Jacob. On arrival before Pharaoh and just before his departure (v.10) Jacob blessed him. Commentators have noticed the progress in Jacob's status: he who had himself cheated to obtain a blessing (ch.27) from his own father had so far advanced as to be the one to pronounce a blessing on the mightiest man on earth. No doubt he called down God's blessing on Pharaoh, and probably such a blessing might be understood as a conventional greeting at the start or end of an encounter. In the context of Genesis, however, with its repeated instance on God's blessing falling upon those who befriended the covenant people, this is indeed a pregnant moment in which Jacob came to the highest point in his experience so far.

Pharaoh, impressed by this patriarchal figure, enquired how old he was. People usually ask such questions of the very young and the obviously old. Pharaoh had asked about "the days of the years of (Jacob's) life" (RV), but Jacob answered about "the days of the years of (his) pilgrimage" (RV margin - "sojournings")†. Whether Pharaoh picked up the modification or not, the reader's mind goes to Hebrews 11.9,13 where it is stressed that, even in the promised land, Abraham, Isaac and Jacob were foreigners and sojourners (AV "strangers and pilgrims", v.13). These were men whom God had claimed for Himself, in His covenant, and they could not view the course of their lives as other men would. They "looked for a city".

Jacob went on to comment on how short his life had been, compared with his ancestors' lives, in their "sojournings". This was, quite simply, a matter of fact. In some ways the statement is ominous, for one would not usually make such a comparison until the end of one's life. His life, he said, had been a troubled one, and so it had been. He had had to leave home because of strife, for which he and his mother were largely responsible. He had left home with few possessions. He had been cheated of wages and in connection with wedding arrangements by Laban. He had finally had to slip away from Laban. He had had a nerve-racking meeting with Esau. His home had been thrown into turmoil by his wives' rivalry and his sons' jealousies. He had lost his favourite son for over twenty years and had thought him torn asunder by a wild beast. His family had often grieved him by their bad behaviour. The catalogue had been long. The interview of Jacob with Pharaoh serves to give Jacob an occasion to give this summary of his life - "few and evil". Jacob had been refined and polished in a demanding school, for he had had many defects of character which needed to be smoothed off, to make him the man of faith that he had now become. So he blessed Pharaoh and left his presence.

Verses 11-17: Joseph Provides for His Own and the Egyptians

Having now obtained the approval of Pharaoh which his diplomatic management of the request had ensured, Joseph was able to place his father and brothers "in the best of the land", literally in accordance with Pharaoh's promise. The naming of Goshen here as "the land of Rameses" has caused some scholars difficulties. The problem arises partly because the best known Pharaoh called Rameses did not live until over a century after the traditional date of the exodus from Egypt, which of course was itself long after this settlement of the household of Jacob in the area. It seems best to take it that in this context Moses gave the place a name which was current in his day, not based on the well known Pharaoh but either on a previous Egyptian of the name or perhaps not connected with a man of that name at all. If one were to say that St Patrick tended sheep or pigs near the town of Kells in N.Ireland it would be understood that the modern place name was being used in the interest of clarity, and one would be unlikely to look for evidence of a contemporary of St Patrick by the name of Kells.

More important is the account of the care shown by Joseph to provide adequate food for his own, who are given the extended description (v.12) of, "his father, and his brethren, and all his father's household (contrast, for example, v.11). Provision was carefully judged according to the size of each family, so there was a detailed rationing system to ensure adequate supplies.

The famine was biting deeper, even among the Egyptians. Both Egypt and Canaan "fainted" because of it. This section serves to emphasise how well Joseph cared for his own people, against the backcloth of general need. First Joseph ensured that the Egyptians and Canaanites paid money for corn, while their money lasted, thus filling Pharaoh's coffers. Then the Egyptians came again and pleaded that, though their money had run out, they should still get corn. Joseph's solution was to transfer ownership of their cattle and other animals (vv.16,17) to Pharaoh in return for corn. In practical terms they must have continued to look after the animals, for it would not have been sensible to herd them all into government pens. The difference from now on was that the ownership passed to Pharaoh and any benefit they gained from the animals they gained at Pharaoh's discretion, not as of right.

Verses 18-26: The Egyptians Give Themselves and Lands for Corn

The next year the Egyptians' need was deeper still. They had no money and no animals which they could call their own. They made the proposal that they would forfeit their liberty and their land ownership to Pharaoh for food to keep body and soul together. They pleaded that their land should not be allowed to become desolate, so their proposal involved their continuing cultivation of the land after ownership of it passed to Pharaoh.

If this passage is interpreted as saying that Joseph accepted the offer made by the Egyptians, then v.21 needs to be understood in a way which accords with this. The removal of the people completely off the land, thus preventing them from caring for it, would turn them into displaced persons and receivers of handouts. What they had asked for was to be granted the status of serfs, presumably on the land which used to be theirs but was now Pharaoh's. Reading v.21 as the AV does, following the Hebrew Masoretic text, one might interpret it still as meaning that they were moved about Egypt to facilitate distribution of aid, but it is difficult to see how this would save the land from becoming desolate, as they feared it would if their proposal were not accepted.

Ancient translations (LXX and Latin Vulgate) and the Samaritan Pentateuch text read slightly differently. According to these three versions v.21 would read something like this: "The people he reduced to servitude, from one end of Egypt to the other" (Hamilton). This variant is recorded in the RV margin and it does make very good sense. It is easy to see how the variation in the text could have arisen, and it does eliminate a problem in interpreting the passage.

The one group of Egyptians excluded from this arrangement were the priests. Since they received their allowance from Pharaoh they retained possession of their lands. This suggests that they constituted a formidable power group in Egypt, a kind of established "church".

The most obvious explanation of v.23 is that the people were still on the lands which they had now passed into Pharaoh's possession. But they could not exercise their obligations as serfs unless they grew crops, so they needed seed. Joseph provided them with the required seed. By using irrigation they could do some sowing near the Nile even in famine conditions. Joseph spelt out to the people the implications of their new status as serfs of Pharaoh. They must pay a tax of 20% on their harvest. His description of the amount still left to them, the 80%, would indicate to them Joseph's care for them as people. The needs of the hungry families had not been forgotten. Both in the ancient world and even in modern times people in their position in many countries could expect to pay as much as 50% to those in a position to dictate financial terms. The Egyptians were content with a situation in which, whatever they had lost, they still at least had their lives, thanks to Joseph. The editorial note on the arrangement (v.26) explains that the Egyptians continued technically in this relationship with Pharaoh, "unto this day".

Verses 27-31: Israel in Egypt, but Jacob to Be Buried in Canaan

"Israel", we read, "dwelt in the land of Egypt". Earlier in the narrative this would have referred to Jacob personally, but the verse continues with "they had possessions", so there is a transition here from Israel the man to Israel the people. The family settled down in Goshen, the famine passed and they were "fruitful (RV; AV "grew") and multiplied exceedingly". At last the promises of God that Abraham, Isaac and Jacob would have many descendants were being visibly fulfilled. Notice again the theme of fruitfulness which was taken up in relation to Joseph while he was prospering in Egypt (41.52), but this time it is used about Israel as a whole. The prosperity of Joseph was spreading to the rest of the extended family.

Jacob, who had been content to die once he had seen Joseph, lived a further seventeen years in Egypt. Almost nothing is said about his experiences during that time. The emphasis now is on Jacob in relation to his descendants rather than Jacob in the school of God. He who had thought he would die a heartbroken man bereft of his favourite sons lived these years in peace, every need richly met by Joseph. More importantly, the promises of God about descendants were beginning to be seen coming to pass. The "few and evil" (v.9) description is less relevant to his life when the final seventeen years are included in it.

So Jacob came to the end of his appointed lifespan, at 147 years. Once again the figure seems to have a symbolism, being the square of seven multiplied by three. He had "finished his course". Knowing this to be so he called Joseph and begged him to show his loyalty and good faith (AV "kindly and truly") by taking an oath. This would take the form of that sworn by Abraham's servant to him in ch.24 before he went away to get a wife for Isaac, "putting the hand under the thigh".

The oath related to the future, for Joseph had to swear not to bury Jacob in Egypt. He must take him out of Egypt and bury him with his fathers. Joseph promised to do this and accordingly took the oath. Satisfied, Jacob bowed in reverence to God upon the bed's head.[†]

For the writer to the Hebrews (11.21) this was the highlight of Jacob's experience, the event which, along with his blessing of the sons of Joseph, showed him to be a man of faith. In what sense is this true? Jacob had now been blessed with the restoration of his "lost" sons, he had been provided for and his family was prospering and multiplying. What more could he want? He could die happy, even as he had said seventeen years before.

But he was God's man in the covenant, and there were promises relating to the land of Canaan and the place which his descendants would occupy. Therefore there were two matters to which he must attend. In ch.48 he will be seen dealing with the matter of Joseph's part in the inheritance, in Ephraim and Manasseh (in that order). This was an important question in relation to the descendants and their relative places in the family. But first, here in ch.47, he dealt with the question of how he could make a statement at his death about the land of Canaan. Though he was well provided for and in prosperity, he was looking to the future and the past. He was only a link in the chain of covenant-men who expected in God's good time to possess the land promised to them. His fathers were buried in Canaan, in the only patch owned by Abraham. Jacob waited for the fulfilment of God's promise to give them the land, therefore his place was with them there. He was not a man of faith because he had ethereal ideas divorcing him from reality, or enabling him to believe fantastic myths which lesser men found incredible. His faith was a sober confidence in what God had said about inheriting the land. God had said simple things, which Jacob believed. Therefore he deemed it inappropriate that he should be content to be buried in Egypt away from where his fathers were buried in Canaan. He did not think it unimportant where or how he was buried. He wanted his burial to be a statement of his faith in the living God, a statement that promises about the land would one day be fulfilled. Faith depends on a word from God, believes it as being factually true, and acts accordingly.

Notes

31 The LXX reads "the top of his staff", where the Hebrew Masoretic texts reads "the top of his bed". The difference between "bed" and "staff" in Hebrew is very slight. The writer of the Hebrew Epistle (11.21) refers to this incident and says he "worshipped, leaning upon the top of his staff"; he was following the LXX as he normally did. No doctrinal truth is involved, and the matter needs no further elaboration here. Either reading will give expositors scope for useful comment.

GENESIS 48

Jacob Blesses Ephraim and Manasseh

Introductory

The words "after these things" serve to move the narrative on to the closing scenes of Jacob's life. The final verses of ch.47 (vv.28-31) have already begun the theme, but they were mainly occupied with Jacob making advance preparations for his burial in Canaan. Chapters 48-50 progress on to the future of Jacob's people; the double inheritance of Joseph (ch.48), the prophetic "testament of Jacob" concerning the twelve tribes and his death (ch.49), and the burial of Jacob and later death of Joseph (ch.50). This will leave a story which is obviously unfinished. After so much of divine promise in Genesis regarding a great national future and a promised land for the line of Abraham, Isaac and Jacob, the book concludes at 50.26 with "a coffin in Egypt".

Verses 1-7: Jacob Gives Joseph a Double Portion

The action opens with an unnamed messenger, presumably a servant of Joseph, bearing to him the message that his father was sick. The message relates, not just to a sickness in general, but a condition which required the presence of Joseph. Those who translate it as "failing", that is in decline rather than just sick, may have established this emphasis correctly. It was the beginning of the end of Jacob's life, his final decline.

Thus understood, the narrative does not need to explain why Joseph took with him his two sons, Manasseh and Ephraim. They were visiting a dying patriarch and he would have a final message for them, in the normal tradition. Someone alerted Jacob to the arrival of Joseph and he summoned up his reserves of strength (AV "strengthened himself", REB "gathered his strength") to sit up in the bed. In view of the solemn import of what was about to take place it is easy to see why he is referred to here as Israel, the man of God, acting as patriarch of the covenant people.

Jacob's first words as recorded in the episode were a review of the past. He recalled the first time God appeared to him (ch.28), at Bethel. His use of the title "God Almighty" (El Shaddai) in v.3 was no doubt in memory of his father's parting blessing to him (28.3) before he set out on that long journey via Luz/Bethel to Paddan-aram. Now Jacob was about to give his parting blessings to his sons. The blessings sequence goes back, of course, to Abraham, to whom God had said, "I am the Almighty God; walk before me and be thou perfect" (17.1). Jacob recalled how God had appeared to him at Bethel and the blessing he had received there. God had promised him that he would have many descendants. The phrase he used here, "a multitude of people" (AV, perhaps better as RV "a company of peoples", or NIV "a community of peoples"), may in this context refer to the rapidly developing group of families who would become the twelve tribes. It should, however, be noted that a similar expression is used of Ephraim, so too much cannot be built on the phrase. God had also promised him, he recalled, the land of Canaan "for an everlasting possession". This immediately sets up a tension in the narrative, for Jacob and his family had possessions now in Egypt, yet this was not to be mistaken for God's provision of "an everlasting possession" in Canaan.

Having looked back with gratitude for the blessings of God experienced in his past life and linking him with Abraham and Isaac, Jacob now introduced the subject of Joseph's sons born in Egypt, Ephraim and Manasseh. The inversion of the order of their names, compared with v.1 must be noticed, for soon the subject of priority between them would be crucial. For the moment Jacob was content to state that both would be his. This was a formulaic statement of his intention to adopt them formally as his own sons. This is expressed by his statement in clarification, that they were his, "even as Reuben and Simeon" (RV). Presumably he chose these two names as being the names of his two eldest sons. To make the terms of the adoption precise Jacob explained that he was adopting only these two eldest sons of Joseph; other later sons would be Joseph's sons, not Jacob's. The tribe of Joseph would by this adoption process become effectively two tribes, Ephraim and Manasseh replacing Joseph as tribal patriarchs. Thus any later sons of Joseph (there is no record of any) would have to be members of one or other of these two tribes.

Thus Rachel, who bore only two sons to Jacob, would be ancestor of three tribes, Ephraim, Manasseh and Benjamin. No doubt this explains the abrupt reference (v.7) to the death of Rachel. Jacob's affection and loyalty were still reserved primarily for Rachel. His special concern for Joseph and Benjamin in the earlier chapters was due mainly to this affection for Rachel. Here he recalled her death with emotion, remembering the occasion, the journey and the place in Canaan where she died and was buried. The phrase "by me" in v.7 should probably be translated "to my sorrow" (as RV margin), and is what students of Classical Greek would call the "dative of disadvantage". The present adoption of Ephraim and Manasseh would be her lasting memorial in Israel, like her tomb in the area which would be occupied in later centuries by the tribe of Benjamin (compare v.7). Even if Jacob's actions in this context are attributable to his consistent determination to love Rachel and give Leah scant consideration, his arrangements still demonstrate the overruling and guiding hand of God.

Verses 8-22: Jacob Blesses Joseph's Sons and Puts Ephraim First

It should be noted first of all that, as he set about the solemn task of blessing Joseph's sons, Jacob is once again called Israel, for he was acting as the patriarch and man of faith. His sight was dim (v.10, Heb "heavy"), but there is no reason to suppose that he was completely blind. Nor is there cause to think that when he asked, "Who are these?" he either had not noticed them until this moment or did not know who they were. He was about to perform a ritual act of blessing and he began with the question which would identify the recipients of the blessing. Hamilton's comment is apt. He compares the question asked at a wedding, "Who giveth this woman to this man?", though it is already obvious to everyone who is giving away the bride. The question shows that the occasion is formal and follows the ritual.

Joseph's reply gives the glory to God. It was God who gave him these sons in Egypt. Alone of all the tribal patriarchs they were born in Egypt. The position of the tribes which would descend from them must be spelt out, and this incident gives them the credentials - adoption as Jacob's sons and blessed by him in person.

Jacob bade Joseph bring them close to him so that he could bless them. He kissed them and embraced them. Then emotion welled up in the old man and he exclaimed how kind God had been to him, for he had thought at one time he would never see Joseph again (compare 37.35) and now God had allowed him to see Joseph's sons also. To Jacob it was of great importance that there would be descendants from Rachel. Now he had grandsons, young men fully grown, who were of Rachel's stock.

Joseph brought his two sons from their place by Jacob's knees, so that they stood, or more probably knelt, before the old man to receive his official blessing. As this was an official patriarchal blessing Joseph bowed himself low in respect before his father. Then, to facilitate the old man's blessing, he placed the sons so that Manasseh, the older, was at Jacob's right hand and Ephraim at his left.

But Jacob, though dim of sight, was sharp in spiritual insight. He crossed his hands to lay his right hand on Ephraim and his left on Manasseh. The expression rendered "guiding his hands wittingly" in the AV is usually now taken to mean "crossing his hands", as the RV margin translates it. He blessed Joseph, who must have been taken aback at the crossed hands and for the moment unable to protest about the inverting of the order of the two lads.

Jacob continued in his formal blessing by a formal invocation of God. It was triple blessing, based on a threefold reference to God, bringing to mind the blessing to be pronounced by Aaronic priests (Num 6.24-26): "The Lord bless thee, and keep thee: the Lord make his face shine upon thee, and be gracious unto thee: the Lord lift up his countenance upon thee, and give thee peace". This may adumbrate the later revelation of the Holy Trinity, or it may be a way of giving the blessing a ring of completeness by its triple form. First, then, he called upon God as the God before whom his fathers Abraham and Isaac walked (compare 17.1 and 24.40). This formed the essential link with Jacob's fathers and placed his blessing of the two grandsons in the covenant context. Second, he called upon God who had been his shepherd (AV "fed me") all his life. This refers back to when God first appeared to him, at Bethel (28.13-15), when he looked forward to the fulfilment of God's promises (28.20-22). Now he looked back and saw that God had indeed fulfilled His promises, richly and abundantly. This faithful, promise-keeping God would take care of the rising generation. Third, he called on the Angel who had redeemed (or rescued) him from all evil. This is without question one of those occasions when the Angel stands for the Angel of the Presence, the very person of God Himself, active in the affairs of life on behalf of His own. This God was He whose blessing he called down.

The triple blessing was now complete. Then he confirmed his adoption of the lads. "Let my name be named on them" means, "Let them be known as Ephraim son of Jacob and Manasseh son of Jacob". They were to carry the rank of tribal heads as sons of Jacob in the covenant line from Abraham and Isaac. So, when the tribal strengths were declared, the descendants of Ephraim and Manasseh would be declared.

Only now did Joseph expostulate. He tried to correct the "mistake" by moving Jacob's hands. He explained that Jacob had put his right hand on Ephraim as if he were the firstborn. But Jacob had made no mistake. His calm reply was, "I know it, my son, I know it". Both sons were blessed and both would be great, but Ephraim would be the greater. This was yet another instance of God acting in sovereignty to give the younger precedence over the older. Spiritual blessings are not given in accordance with human norms, nor even according to personal merit. Ephraim would become a great tribe, so great that when the kingdom was divided in the days of Rehoboam the larger (northern) kingdom would come to be called Ephraim though it comprised nine tribes. Furthermore, when Israel moved in to occupy Canaan they were led by an Ephraimite, Joshua. The climax of the blessing was the statement that when the Israelites wanted to bless each other they would say, "May God make you like Ephraim and Manasseh".

Then Jacob announced to Joseph that he was dying. He would die in Egypt but God would take his family back to the land of their fathers. This whole context places these men in the framework of God's past promises and future actions on behalf of His people. When they did go back to Canaan, said Jacob, Joseph would inherit an extra portion of the land. This looks forward to the settlement in the land, when the bones of Joseph, which had been brought up out of Egypt, were buried in Shechem (Josh 24.32). The term used for "portion" (v.22 AV) is the Hebrew word SHᶜKEM, (7926), a shoulder or mountain slope. The piece of land seems to be that referred to also in John 4.5. There is, however, a slight problem, for the Joshua passage refers to Jacob buying it from the sons of Hamor, while Genesis 48 refers to his taking land from the Amorites with sword and bow. The existence of two distinct pieces of land can be suggested or other solutions offered, but certainty is difficult to achieve. What is quite clear is that Jacob made sure that Joseph, in the persons of his sons Ephraim and Manasseh, had a double portion of the land and evidently this extra piece as well. In the allocation of land to the tribes Joseph had the firstborn's double portion.

GENESIS 49

Jacob Blesses His Sons

Introductory

Even a casual reading of vv.2-27 of this chapter would establish that it is a different kind of writing from that used in the surrounding narrative. Most translations make the difference clearer by setting the passage out as verse, and indeed that is why it is different. To select some of the more obvious features of it: (i) there is constant use of parallelism, the repetition of an idea with variation, for example in v.2 itself; (ii) there is at least one example of a threefold statement for emphasis, in v.4, best identified by noting the three verbs - "wentest up", "defiledst" and "went up"; (iii) figures of speech abound, best exemplified by the sons of Jacob being referred to usually as animals, but also as things - Reuben like water, Judah the lion, Isaachar the donkey, Dan the serpent, Joseph the fruitful bough and Benjamin the wolf. The use of verse form tends to make the momentous pronouncements stick in the memory. These are solemn last words of a great patriarch, meant to be treated as unusually weighty. In a sense they are Jacob's last will and testament, spiritually speaking. Scholars, therefore, often refer to the passage as the "Testament of Jacob".

Certainly Jacob's utterance is to be taken basically as a pronouncement of blessing, for v.28 says, "every one according to his blessing he blessed them". This brings to a climax the blessing theme in Genesis, and here it is blessing officially pronounced by the patriarch. Verse 28 leaves no doubt that it is not just an estimate of the sons' lives and relationships. It is also a blessing of "the twelve tribes of Israel". This expression, "the tribes of Israel" occurs for the first time in v.16, where the tribe of Dan is included as one of the tribes of Israel, and it is used again in v.28. The blessing looks back, but also forward to the future tribal histories. There is, then, an element of prophecy in the blessings.

There have been previous brief passages of verse in which aging men have blessed their families: Noah (9.25-27) blessed Shem and Japheth (and cursed Canaan, son of Ham), Isaac (27.27-29) blessed Jacob, thinking he was Esau, and later (27.39-40) gave Esau a limited blessing. In Deuteronomy 33.2-29 Moses will bless "the children of Israel". This passage of verse in Genesis 49 stands out as the great blessing which rounds off the book and looks forward to the future outworking of the prominence or obscurity of each tribe ("every one according to his blessing").

Some commentators, who do not accept the possibility of Jacob (or anyone else) knowing the future by divine revelation, have great difficulty understanding the chapter. Some of them even seek for hidden meanings which would turn the most clear blessings into adverse comments - their interpretation of the blessing of Judah is an outstanding example of this perversity. However, accepting the reality of divine revelation and having no need to rationalise prediction away, the blessings can be taken in their natural sense and in them be seen the outworking of a great scriptural principle, that "judgment must begin at the house of God" (1 Pet 4.17). Scripture insists that to be one of God's people places on one an awesome responsibility: "Be ye holy; for I am holy" (Lev 11.44 RV, quoted in 1 Pet 1.16).

Verses 1-4: Introduction and Reuben

This was a family gathering, not a series of meetings with individual sons. Jacob was going to tell all of them about their future. The expression "in the last days" (AV) is rendered "in the latter days" by the RV. It is usually an expression denoting the end times when the prophetic purpose of God will be seen coming into fruition. Part of this chapter does look forward to such times (see v.10 with comment there) if the words are taken in their most probable sense. Most of the blessings, however, while relating to the future, do not deal specifically with "the end times" as that phrase is used in relation to prophetic truth.

The form of v.2 indicates the formal, almost oracular, style of Jacob's speech. The verse is an appeal to all present to listen carefully because what follows is of great importance.

Reuben's blessing is a good illustration of how the positive and negative blend in some of these pronouncements. In v.3 Jacob gives all the positive advantages of Reuben, the dignity of the firstborn, who had been his father's pride as his first son. Where the AV has "the beginning of my strength" Wenham translates "the first fruit of my virility". All this was his privilege, but v.4 tells the sad story of how he had failed to live up to his privilege, how he had abused his place. In a community in which succession and the promise of numerous progeny were so important, what could be worse than a firstborn son who had a forbidden relationship with his father's concubine? He could not have the dignity of the firstborn while his life was shameful, and the double use of "excellency" in v.3 is cancelled by the statement "Thou shalt not excel" in v.4.

Much interest centres, in this assessment of Reuben, on the meaning of "unstable as water" (AV, v.4). Most scholars now seem to be agreed that the sense of "unstable" (PACHAZ - 6349) lies somewhere in the realm of "seething" (Leupold), "uncontrollable" (Hamilton, REB), "turbulent" (NIV), or "frothy" (Wenham). Davis refers to water "boiling over".[†] What this adds up to is that Jacob was not referring to Reuben's weakness so much as to his recklessness and lack of self-control. This was not the yieldingness of water but its destructive power when out of control (compare Is 57.20). The reference is to the single event recorded in 35.22, where Jacob's reaction is not recorded. That single event was evidence of the bent of Reuben's character, and now Jacob gives his assessment.

The later history of the tribe of Reuben reflects this adverse assessment. The tribe produced no great leader in Israel. In the rebellion of Korah, Dathan and Abiram (Num 16) both Dathan and Abiram were Reubenites. The tribe chose, with Gad, to settle east of Jordan (Num 32) where they later took a less prominent role than Gad. In the heroic struggle of Deborah and Barak against Sisera the Reubenites were indecisive and gave no help (Judg 5.15-16). As a tribe they "did not excel". Moses' blessing of Reuben in Deuteronomy 33 deals with the survival of the tribe, but translators are divided about whether the second part of Moses' blessing expects them to become numerous or few.

Verses 5-7: Simeon and Levi

Simeon and Levi are taken together because their record is so similar. They had acted together on an occasion when they had so grievously offended Jacob (34.25-31) in the episode involving the avenging of Dinah. That episode explains the bitterness in Jacob's address to these two in this context.

He describes them first as brothers. They were literally full brothers, sons of Leah, but the meaning probably goes beyond that to their similar characters. They were true brothers. They are denounced here for their anger and cruelty.

So much is clear, but the last clause of v.5 has been a notable problem for translators. Where the AV has "instruments of cruelty" most translators have something like "weapons of violence". In the other part of this clause the AV has "are in their habitations", but this translation is far from commonly agreed. The RV renders this as "are their swords". Since ancient times the translators have varied widely in representing this Hebrew word M^cKEROTEHEM (4380). The rendering "swords" or similar ideas makes the statement somewhat bland - men usually commit violence with such things as swords, and Jacob would surely be unlikely in this highly wrought poetry to state the obvious. If the difficult word is rendered in a neutral way as "tools" (Leupold) or "are equipped with" (Wenham) the statement at least establishes that Simeon and Levi tend to go about whatever they do in a violent way, and this may be the best option.[†]

Jacob's exclamation in the first half of v.6 shows his abhorrence of becoming linked in any way with the bitter anger and conspiracy of which they had been guilty. They had slain a man or men (second half of v.6). This presumably refers to the slaughter of Shechem or Hamor or the men of the city in general. But then occurs the second part of this half-verse, rendered by the AV as "and in their selfwill they digged down a wall", and by the RV as "and in their selfwill they houghed (hamstrung) an ox". The latter seems the correct translation, but then what does it mean? Their sin consisted in their treatment of people, the men of Shechem, so this could refer to butchering strong men (referred to in this interpretation as "an ox") or perhaps the young man Shechem himself, or his father Hamor (whose name means "donkey", thus causing very confused images if this is to be the reference). Thus far, interpretations of the half-verse have been examined on the assumption that it is a case of straight parallelism, both clauses referring to basically the same fact. But it would be possible to take the two clauses as referring to the same event but to different dimensions of it. A suggestion which merits consideration is that "hamstrung an ox" refers to their leaving Jacob helplessly exposed (like a hamstrung ox) among the Canaanites whom they had offended by their cruel vengeance on the Shechemites. This, of course, was Jacob's main complaint in response to the massacre (34.30). One weakness of this interpretation in this context is that here Jacob's emphasis is on the cruelty which they had perpetrated rather than on their embarrassment of him. They had acted in selfwill rather than indiscretion. While the suggestion has some attraction it may be better on balance to refer the hamstringing to their butchery of the men of Shechem.

This is the only time in this chapter that Jacob pronounced a curse. Remember that Jacob was speaking oracularly as patriarch and pre-eminently as man of the covenant. Such blind anger as the brothers had shown was unsuitable in God's people. God's character was the same then as it is now. In later years David's loyal but ruthless follower Joab failed to attain to the highest honour, even though his armour bearer did. He sacrificed the honour on the same basis as Simeon and Levi lost out in the blessing, for ruthless cruelty in contrast to the merciful dealings of David.

The sentence on Simeon and Levi was that they would be divided in Jacob and scattered in Israel. Both clauses suggest a weakening by dispersal. The first may mean that the two tribes would be prevented from making common cause by being separated from each other. The second would most naturally be understood, in the case of Levi, as a reference to their not having tribal territory in one place. As the priestly tribe they had provision made for them throughout Israel, but they had no integrated tribal land allocated to them. Simeon grew weaker in number, from 59,300 in Numbers 1.23 to 22,200 in Numbers 26.14. They did, however, have tribal land, an enclave in Judah (Josh 19.1). When in the land they had little separate influence and were effectively absorbed in Judah.

Both, then, were scattered, but in different senses. Simeon became weak and of no great significance. In the blessing of the tribes by Moses in Deuteronomy 33 Simeon is omitted completely. They did have one episode of glory in the days of Hezekiah (1 Chr 4.41-43) when 500 Simeonites went to Mt Seir and won a glorious victory over Amalekites there. This was, however, far from typical.

Levi on the other hand, while having no territory, had a place of special privilege in Israel as the priestly tribe. Moses, it is explained, gave them no inheritance because "the sacrifices of the Lord God of Israel made by fire are their inheritance" (Josh 13.14). Again in Joshua 13.33 it is explained, "The Lord God of Israel was their inheritance, as he said unto them". This was high privilege indeed.

The turning point in the history of Levi was the incident in Exodus 32.26-28 when they answered the call of Moses to take sides with God against the idolatry of their own people. This glorious vindication of their dedication to God features in the very different blessing by Moses on Levi in Deuteronomy 33.8-11, especially v.9: "Who said unto his father and to his mother, I have not seen him; neither did he acknowledge his brethren, nor knew his own children: for they have observed thy word, and kept thy covenant". So the goodness and grace of God were seen in the rehabilitation of Levi, His severity in the eclipse of Simeon. Yet Simeon does appear in Revelation 7.7 among the twelve tribes from whom the 144,000 will be made up in a future day, sealed as servants of God.

Verses 8-12: Judah

Judah and Joseph come in for most praise and together take up almost half of the space in this series of blessings. Judah was promised power and plenty. It should be observed that attention is given to his relations with his brothers (v.8), for he held the sceptre (v.10). This pre-eminence of Judah is foreshadowed in the responsibility which he began to hold personally in the later chapters of Genesis, as has been already noted.

First of all, then, there is the play on his name, Judah (Praise), for his brothers would praise him. He would be honoured by them, presumably, for his victories over his enemies and theirs (v.8). He would be like the lordly lion whom one would hesitate to disturb when it had its prey (v.9).

Then follows (v.10) the reference to Judah's sceptre and ruler's staff (see the RV of v.10, which reads "the ruler's staff" where the AV has "a lawgiver"). The picture of the ruler sitting in state with his staff securely in his grasp and resting between his feet is adequate to do justice to the words used. Judah personally was the son of Jacob who most conspicuously was changed from harshness (he proposed that Joseph be sold) to nobility (compare 44.18-34, that wonderful plea on Jacob's behalf). But in this passage in which Jacob sees the future glory of Judah's tribe, is it too much to see a hint of a former less glorious episode in which Judah's staff became a pledge to a supposed prostitute (38.18)? Other sons were blessed in ways which suggest a similar ambivalence, which may encourage the belief that this hint of contrast with past failure is intended. If this is accepted, the manifestation of the grace of God in Judah is the more glorious.

So far so good. The one detail, however, on which it is difficult to feel confident of the translation is the next clause, "until Shiloh come" (AV). The clause which immediately follows this implies that the sentence is messianic: "unto him shall the gathering of the people be" (AV), or perhaps more precisely, "unto him shall the obedience of the peoples (plural) be" (RV). The verse refers to a coming king who will rule over the nations. Ultimately it must be seen as a promise of Messiah, the Lord Jesus Christ. There is evidence at Qumran that this messianic interpretation was in vogue among the community based there, though their judgment need not necessarily warrant much confidence. This leaves the difficult expression, "until Shiloh come". There is of course, the option of taking Shiloh as a messianic title and staying with the AV (as the NKJV does). Other renderings depend on technical details of language but they leave the messianic message unaffected. For example, the NIV and RSV render it, "until he comes to whom it belongs"; the REB (and Hamilton effectively) gives, "until he receives what is his due"; Wenham prefers to translate it as, "until tribute is brought to him". With minor variations these indicate that Judah or his messianic descendant will hold sway over nations as he deserves, or will receive the tribute which they are forced to give him. The

NIV/RSV version may receive some support from Ezekiel 21.27: "I will overturn, overturn, overturn, it: and it shall be no more, until he come whose right it is; and I will give it him". Translators generally agree on the meaning of the Ezekiel reference.

Some commentators make amazingly heavy weather of vv.11-12. After v.10 further comments would be expected on his power or prosperity, and that is what is found here. The dominant theme in the two verses is plenty, as symbolised by wine and milk. Wine will be so plentiful that he can casually tie his donkey to a vine, even a choice vine. Usually one would not do this because the donkey would destroy the vine, but if wine is so plentiful, why worry? The reference to his donkey and his vine may also speak of peace, for the donkey is the mount used in peace and tending one's vines is a peacetime occupation. The man who can afford to wash his garments in wine (v.11) must have more than he knows how to use. His glowing health and prosperity shine from his eyes and his teeth: "Darker than wine are his eyes, whiter than milk his teeth" (REB and many other versions ancient and modern). The descendants of Judah will not only have power, but they will include Messiah and have great prosperity.

The later history of Judah did, of course, bear this prophecy out. Judah came to prominence. David was raised up by God as His chosen king over Israel, taken from Judah. The Lord Jesus, who will sit on the throne in His messianic kingdom, is of Judah. In the later chapters of Genesis this future glory is foreshadowed in the growing influence of Judah the man.

Verses 13-15: Zebulun and Issachar

These were Leah's last two sons. In Deuteronomy 33 Moses blessed them together and their tribal territories adjoined each other. Their order of birth is inverted here and also in Deuteronomy 33. The territory of Zebulun did not extend right to the Mediterranean coast, and some commentators suggest that "near" or "towards" would give better sense than "at" the seashore. Zidon was the main Phoenician city in the region in the early history of Israel and no doubt its name stands for the Phoenicians generally. Zebulun was obviously a trading tribe, hence the references to ships, the sea and the great trading race, the Phoenicians. Zebulun, Naphtali and Issachar together controlled the south-west shores of the Sea of Galilee.

Historically, Zebulun had a distinguished military record during the period of the judges, both in valour under Deborah and Barak (Judg 4-6) and in providing a judge called Elon (Judg 12.11). The tribe supported David both militarily and with supplies (1 Chr 12), acting along with Issachar and Naphtali.

Though little is said about Zebulun the impression gained is of a tribe successful in trade and prosperous. No hint is given here of any criticism.

Issachar is described as a strong donkey (literally "a donkey of bone"), the idea perhaps being well represented by Wenham as "a strong-boned ass". The donkey was viewed in Scripture as an admirably durable and useful animal. It was extensively used in times of peace to carry its owner or do various types of hard work. But this donkey is lying down, whether "between two burdens" (AV) or "between the sheepfolds" (RV). The impression given is of a tribe with unrealised potential.

In v.15 he is seen resting and enjoying it, satisfied with his fertile territory, but so given over to material things as to become a drudge (a servant "unto tribute" AV; "under taskwork" RV; under "forced labour" NIV). The distinguished service of the tribe under Deborah and Barak must have been uncharacteristic. They did produce one judge, Tola (Judg 10.1). Their land and experience had similarities with those of Zebulun, but they seem to have made less of their opportunities.

It is sobering to reflect on the relative obscurity of two tribes which enjoyed material prosperity yet failed to make a mark on the spiritual history of the nation. Today many of the countries in which God is most signally honouring His Word and blessing the witness of His people are countries in which poverty and even injustice are endemic. Spiritual prosperity never was synonymous with a life of ease and plenty. Should it be felt that this is distinct from OT times in which material possessions were more obviously connected with the blessing of God than they are today, remember the word to Israel in Deuteronomy 32.15: "But Jeshurun waxed fat, and kicked: thou art waxen fat, thou art grown thick, thou art covered with fatness." The word of Agur in Proverbs 30.8-9 is most apposite: "Give me neither poverty nor riches; feed me with food convenient for me: lest I be full and deny thee, and say, Who is the Lord?". The NT version of this principle is the charge of Paul in 1 Timothy 6.17, "Charge them that are rich in this world, that they be not highminded, nor trust in uncertain riches, but in the living God, who giveth us richly all things to enjoy".

Verses 16-18: Dan

The opening comment on Dan is a play on his name (He judged). Rachel had given Dan this name at his birth because, as she said, God had judged her, that is, had taken up her cause by giving her a son through her handmaid Bilhah. Now Jacob, in a play on the name, says Dan shall judge his people, that is, shall have control over, or vindicate, his own people. Dan would be counted as a tribe, with full tribal rights, though the tribal head had been a concubine's son. But the reference to judging his own people may well extend to his championing the nation of Israel, not just the tribe of Dan.

Dan would never be a strong tribe. They occupied the most northerly territory, exposed to attack from outside Israel. They were relatively slow to clear and settle in their territory, as the incident in Judges 18 illustrates. If they were going to survive it would not be as the lordly lion whom people would be reluctant to rouse (compare v.9) but rather as the serpent making surprise attacks on its enemies.

But this would be a formidable serpent, in fact a horned viper (AV "adder"). Historically, Samson was a Danite at a time when the tribe still dwelt in the south, among Ephraim, Benjamin and Judah. Samson judged Israel (Judg 14-

16) and wrought great deliverance from the Philistines. The stories associated with him in Judges illustrate his guile as he repeatedly outwitted the Philistines. Yet it must be said that Samson was a flawed hero, one who failed to make the most of his God-given strength and who ended his life a sad, blind man mocked by his enemies. Even in his death, however, he made a flank attack on his enemies and slew more in his death than he had ever done in his life (Judg 16.30).

Dan was always a tribe about which there was some factor which marred the record. They were the first tribe in Israel in which idolatry appeared, as the story of Judges 18 recounts. Later, when Jeroboam set up the rebel kingdom of Israel in defiance of Rehoboam (1 Kings 12), he set up idolatrous altars at Bethel and Dan, the latter (located in the north) being the main centre of the tribe of Dan by that time. The tribe does not feature at all in Revelation 7 as contributing a contingent to those sealed as servants of God in the period preparatory to the future Millennium. Yet in Ezekiel 48 the tribe does receive an inheritance in the Millennial kingdom.

Maybe this last positive detail is a suitable introduction to Jacob's outburst at this point: "I have waited for thy salvation, O Lord". It comes abruptly into the blessing on Dan, as if Jacob felt that this weak and inconsistent tribe called for an admission that Israel must trust God rather than men in hoping for deliverance from their enemies. It is inevitable that this is seen as in some sense messianic. It is the first occurrence in Scripture of this word "salvation" (Y^{e}SHUA - 3444) and we note that it is "*thy* salvation, O Lord". It will recur in Scripture in memorable contexts: Exodus 15.2, "he is become my salvation"; Psalm 116.13, "the cup of salvation"; Isaiah 12.3, "with joy shall ye draw water out of the wells of salvation"; Isaiah 49.8, "in a day of salvation have I helped thee"; Isaiah 52.7, "How beautiful…are the feet of him…that publisheth salvation". In the midst of blessings which mingle references to the failures and weaknesses of the sons and tribes of Israel with hints of their strengths, this is a reminder that the Lord alone can be depended on, for He never fails.

Verse 19: Gad

Gad inauspiciously chose to settle east of Jordan when Israel was going in to possess Canaan. This decision had obvious implications for them. They were constantly exposed to the attacks of their enemies and their tenuous topographical links with the other tribes rendered them vulnerable. It would indeed be true that "a troop shall press upon him" (RV).

Yet all was not gloom and despondency, for the next clause reassures Gad: "But he shall press upon their heel" (RV, for AV "but he shall overcome at the last"). Exposed they might be, for the desert-dwellers to the east had ready access to their territory, but they would fight gamely. In view of their weakness their tactics would be flank or rear attacks on the enemy. The kind of attacks to which they would be exposed were likely to be from marauding desert tribes. The sense is perhaps most neatly represented by the REB: "Gad is raided by raiders, and he will raid them from the rear".

If we choose to live on the fringes of christian testimony the best we can hope for is to win minor victories as we are constantly subjected to the attacks of our vigilant enemy. If we are the Lord's, some victories can assuredly be won, but our choice to live on the fringe is ill-advised nevertheless. We must remember that Gad failed to support Deborah (Judg 5.17, referred to there as "Gilead"; compare Josh 13.24-25). They survived, but they limited their usefulness to God by the initial choice which they made.

Verse 20: Asher

This was the "happy" tribe, as the name Asher suggests. The tribal territory stretched northwards along the Mediterranean coast from Mt Carmel, lying, therefore, west of Zebulun and Naphtali. This was fertile land and it also bordered on the Phoenician trading posts. All this led to material prosperity and encouraged the production of luxury goods ("royal dainties") for the readily available markets. It appears also from Deuteronomy 33 that the tribe enjoyed security - "thy bars (RV) shall be iron and brass". The blessing of Moses there also contains that familiar promise, "As thy days so shall thy strength be".

All of this sounds favourable and comfortable. One contrary indication has to be mentioned, which may suggest that there was a deeper sense in which Asher was less blessed and less prosperous. Judges 1.31-32 records the many cities from which Asher did not dislodge the original inhabitants. Their policy, according to v.32 of that chapter, was to co-exist with the Canaanites; they "dwelt among the Canaanites". Is this yet another indication of the difficulty of thorough-going devotion to God while seeking to enjoy and be deeply involved in accumulating material possessions? In this chapter, however, no hint is given of any such reservation.

Verse 21: Naphtali

The blessing of Naphtali contains two clauses and the translation, especially of the second clause, is problematical. First comes the statement, "Naphtali is a hind let loose" (AV and RV). The great majority of translators and commentators give renderings which vary little from this translation. The "let loose" part of it is variously understood, but the idea seems to be that Naphtali has a freedom of action which reminds one of a graceful wild deer, hence Wenham's "a free-running doe".

The second clause is understood in one of two ways by those who take the first clause as above. Some translate similarly to the AV's "He giveth goodly words". Variants within this translation include "beautiful words" (NKJV, NIV footnote) and "a message of gladness" (Knox). A problem about this rendering is the abruptness with which a concept remote from a free-running hind is introduced. The main historical context suggested for the beautiful words is the Deborah-Barak episode and the message of victory which followed (Judg 4-5). Barak (Judg 4.6) was of Naphtali and the tribe distinguished itself in the fight against Sisera. Even so, the transition is abrupt.

A number of translators render the clause in some way like the RSV, "that bears comely fawns"; these include the NIV and Hamilton. Wenham includes an interesting element in his translation - "she gives birth to fawns of the fold". This variant is based on taking the word rendered by others as "beautiful" (SHEPER - 8233) to be a version of a word SHAPPARU in Akkadian, meaning a sheepfold. The linguistic basis of the link with Akkadian may not be strong enough to give any certainty. If it is accepted, it introduces one of those ambivalences which have occurred before in the chapter between a promising picture of vigour and liberty on the one hand, and on the other a contrary picture in this case of tameness and constraint - a wild animal in a sheepfold. Despite the questions about the linguistic basis for it, this rendering is most attractive.

Naphtali was a prosperous tribe materially, enjoying fertile land and good relations with neighbouring tribes. They did suffer from their nearness to marauding outsiders from the north. They did not completely subdue the Canaanites in their allotted territory. The assessment here by Jacob may contain some negative overtones, but it probably has a broadly positive message.†

Verses 22-26: Joseph

The blessing of Joseph is a story mainly of fruitfulness, but also of struggle and victory. Judah was distinguished by his royal destiny, Joseph had the pre-eminence in respect of the double inheritance of the firstborn. His descendant Ephraim would head the leading northern tribe and would produce Joshua, who would lead Israel into the land. Judah was the focus of the power of David, but Ephraim was reluctant to follow David. When the kingdom was divided it is not surprising that the southern part became known as Judah and the northern, breakaway part was called Ephraim (remember that Ephraim was son of Joseph). Jeremiah 31 is a passage in which the restoration of Israel is prophesied, and in that chapter (v.9) the Lord says, "I am a father to Israel, and Ephraim is my firstborn". It is a sobering reflection that, when Israel was divided, these two great tribes, Judah and Ephraim, became the leaders of the two sides. Religiously it was Israel (Ephraim), the northern kingdom, which was astray from the orthodox practice of worship, but it was Rehoboam's folly which drove them away in the first place. Rehoboam, King of Israel, following the advice of his young men, rejected crudely the complaints of citizens who felt that his father, King Solomon, had treated them harshly. When they asked for some alleviation of the demands made on them his reply was that he would be even more demanding (1 Kings 12). So Jeroboam's stirring up of discontent was met by Rehoboam's harsh reply, and it was the kingdom which suffered, and the people. If only we could learn from this example!

But an attempt must be made to sift out the details of this most detailed blessing of Joseph. If it is translated more or less as the AV does Joseph is described first as a fruitful bough (literally "son of fruitfulness") by a fountain. This is readily understood, for the godly are occasionally described (for example in Ps 1.3; Jer 17.8) as trees planted by streams (usually irrigation channels), prosperous and fruitful. His branches (literally "daughters") luxuriantly spread over the nearby wall. Then abruptly (v.23) Joseph's persecution is introduced.

The threefold, repetitive description of the attack in that verse ("grieved…shot at…persecuted", RV) serves to emphasise its bitterness. But Joseph would be steadfast under pressure, his hands strong upon his bow, thanks to the power of the Mighty God of Jacob, the Shepherd, the Stone of Israel, the God of his father, the Almighty.[†]

Another line of translation, which at least merits mention, takes some of the difficult expressions very differently, but it must be said that the final message is not all that different. First is the understanding of the "son of fruitfulness". Doubt arises about the traditional rendering which describes Joseph as a bough. No other blessing describes any son of Jacob as a plant, unless the alternative rendering of the blessing of Naphtali is accepted. The description of Reuben as being "as turbulent as water" is not quite the same inasmuch as it is a simile rather than a metaphor. The other sons were said to be animals if such imagery was introduced. A slight adjustment of the vowels in the word "fruitfulness" (PARA - 6509) can produce a word for "a wild ass" (PERE - 6501). The wild ass was seen as an animal of splendid vigour, so the imagery would be suitable. On this understanding the theme of fruitfulness would be delayed until later. The "branches" (literally "daughters") would then be daughters of the figurative wild ass. The transition to the attacking enemy might be easier with this understanding of the opening figure. However, the overall message remains substantially the same.[†]

In view of the trend already noted a play on the name of Joseph or Ephraim might be expected in the early part of the blessing. Ephraim as we have seen was so named by Joseph (41.52) because God had made Joseph fruitful. It would therefore perhaps be better to follow the line of interpretation which preserves the early reference to fruitfulness in this blessing. There are technical difficulties with the language in this interpretation, but they appear not to be so great as to outweigh the benefits of retaining the play on Ephraim/fruitful.

The next point of interest in translation is in the first half of v.24, where the AV makes it refer to Joseph's hands being firm and steady. The alternative is to understand the first half of that verse as referring to Joseph's enemy. The translation would then read, "His bow remained firm (that is, the enemy's bow remained rigid, unbent) and his hands and arms were agile" (that is, though he actively sought to shoot). The lines contain a word-play on Joseph's name and it is perhaps better to preserve in the translation the reference to Joseph's self-defence with his bow, though he has not been mentioned in the previous clauses as defending himself in this way.[†]

The NIV translation of vv.24-25 merits quotation in full:
"But his bow remained steady,
his strong hands stayed supple,
because of the hand of the Mighty One of Jacob,
because of the Shepherd, the Rock of Israel,
because of your father's God, who helps you,
because of the Almighty, who blesses you…".

However the details are translated, Joseph is seen as being attacked by his enemies and protected by God's power. This was true in his personal life. Then his defence was his personal integrity which, after suffering, brought him through to inevitable glory, for God was with him, and God was real to him. This would be true later of Ephraim, the tribe, for they were strong and enabled by God to excel, despite opposition.

The last verse and a half of Joseph's blessing is an elaboration of the many facets of his blessedness and fruitfulness. He would be blessed by the Almighty (Shaddai). Blessing would come up from the deep from lakes and springs. The wombs of the tribe would be fertile and the breasts would have milk to feed the babies born. The opposite to this last blessing would have been the judgment described in Hosea 9.14: "Give them, O Lord: what wilt thou give? give them a miscarrying womb and dry breasts".

Translating the first half of v.26 as in the AV gives a sense something like this; "Your father has been blessed more than his forefathers, with blessings which extend throughout the land, even to the age-old hills".[†]

Many modern scholars interpret the verse along the lines which Wenham follows: "The blessings of your father surpass the blessings of the eternal mountains, the bounty of the everlasting hills". This would tie in with the thought of Joseph's fruitfulness, beyond even the bountiful fruitfulness of the blessed hills of the land.

Whichever way the verse is taken, the general sense is similar. God had blessed Jacob abundantly and he was now, in the second half of v.26, praying that the blessing would be continued in Joseph and his tribes. He prayed that this abundance of blessing would be "on the head of Joseph…him that was separate from his brethren". The word "separate" (NAZIR - 5139) is rendered "prince" by many translators.[†]

The story of the man Joseph is a story of one who was always separate from his brothers, not involved in their wrongdoing and later living far from them. It is also the story of one who was marked out by dreams to be separate from them in his exaltation, a forecast which was fulfilled in Egypt when he saw them bow before him. Both senses blend into one. The tribe perhaps could be seen as manifesting princely power over the others more than moral or spiritual superiority. At any rate, in this blessing Joseph is marked out for special distinction.

Verse 27: Benjamin

Most of what has been read of Benjamin thus far has given the thought of him as the sole surviving son (it seemed) of Rachel. It was surprising to find such a long list of sons of Benjamin recorded (46.21) as going down to Egypt. Benjamin was a fertile branch of the family and would be a virile tribe. He would be fully capable of hunting to support his offspring, to take up the metaphor used here. His night's hunting would provide a morning feast which would last until evening.

In Judges the Benjamites distinguished themselves on two occasions. Ehud, a member of the tribe, killed Eglon king of Moab and, having thus delivered Israel from Moabite rule, judged Israel (Judg 3). In a later grievous quarrel with the rest of Israel the tribe proved very competent warriors (Judg 20). King Saul, the first monarch of Israel, was of Benjamin (1 Sam 9.1) and the tribe was noted for its prowess in that period (1 Chr 12.2, for example). Queen Esther (Est 2.5) was of the tribe, as was Saul of Tarsus (Paul the Apostle, Rom 11.1). They had, then, a record of military might, marred here and there by ferocity beyond the accepted level. The wolf imagery fits the history.

Having linked Benjamin's success in conflict with the natural ferocity of the people, it is interesting to read the blessing of the tribe by Moses in Deuteronomy 33.12. There the emphasis is firmly placed on the divine protection of the tribe. It seems that ferocity in itself is not enough. Maybe God preserves those who are most determined in championing their own cause in spite of their ferocity rather than because of it. He will bring about that which is best for us in accordance with His will. If that result seems to us to be success He does not need us to act belligerently to achieve it; indeed our activity may hinder His gracious intervention on our behalf. God saw to it that Isaac blessed Jacob, not Esau. He would have done that without Rebekah's "help".

Verses 28-33: Having Arranged for His Burial Jacob Dies

Having thus delivered his blessing and his spiritual legacy Jacob began to arrange for his burial, for he knew he was dying. He instructed his sons to bury him in the cave of Machpelah. He gave them a commentary on the place, which serves as a reminder that the destiny of the line of Abraham is closely bound up with the land of Canaan (compare v.30); the site of this tomb was available because Abraham bought it (the only land he owned in Canaan) and Abraham, Sarah, Isaac, Rebekah and lastly Leah were buried there. It is interesting to note that Jacob once again was speaking here as patriarch, and Leah's burial is mentioned without reference at all to Rachel though she was Jacob's loved wife. Leah was of course Jacob's first wife and mother of more children than any of the others. Jacob's memory of the past helps us here to see this moment in its historical context. Abraham, Isaac and Jacob will soon all be together, but the God of these three men is the God of their future descendants, so this is a transition:

> God of our fathers, be the God
> Of their succeeding race.

His orders were then complete and he could die in peace. The last days of his life had been occupied in blessing his descendants, recalling how God had dealt with his fathers and looking forward to how He would deal with his sons. He "died in faith" (Heb 11.13), the future as promised by God just as real to him as the past in which God had proved faithful to His promises. So he deliberately drew up his feet into his bed, expired and "was gathered unto his people". This was just one point, albeit an important one, in an unbroken continuum in the dealings of God with the line of Abraham.

Notes

4 The root word occurs also in Judges 9.4 and Zephaniah 3.4, where the AV renders it "light" and modern translators give "reckless".

5 An attractive, but somewhat speculative suggestion is made by D. Young in an article in JBL, 1981; 100, 335-342. He connects the word MᶜKEROTEHEM with "kirru-vessels" through an Akkadian word. These vessels were used in marriage feasts as an essential part of any valid wedding. The sense then would be that Simeon and Levi proposed that Shechem and Dinah be properly married (complete with a feast), but in reality they used the occasion for violence.

21 It is worth recording a different translation of the blessing, as exemplified in the REB: "Naphtali is a spreading terebinth putting forth lovely boughs". This rendering is based on slight textual emendations of the words for "hind" and "words". The translation in the LXX may be rendered into English as "Naphtali is a spreading stem, bestowing beauty on its fruit", but is should be admitted that the word rendered here as "fruit" is usually used of the offspring of animals. The reading is hardly necessary and should probably be noticed but rejected.

22 This line of translation is followed by Stigers, Wenham and Hamilton.

24 This line of translation is retained by the NIV, NKJV, REB and RSV.

24 The Hebrew for "were agile" (WAYYAPOZZU) is said to echo the name YOSEP – see Wenham Vol 2, p.480.

26 The word translated "progenitors" (HARA - 2029) is not elsewhere so rendered; it is connected with the verb "to conceive". The LXX translated the word as "the steadfast mountains", evidently reading the Hebrew as (HAR - 2022). This would point forward to the next clause with its "everlasting (age-old) hills". An old Jewish interpretation (Targum Yerushalmi), as quoted by Hamilton, gives the meaning as, "May the blessings of your father's (sic) be added to the blessings wherewith your fathers, Abraham and Isaac, who are like mountains, blessed you". This suggests that they saw the word forefathers/mountains as deliberately ambiguous. This may well be the true interpretation.

26 The use of NAZIR prompts the thought of Joseph as a prototype Nazarite. The Nazarite in Israel (see Num 6) was a man who vowed to remain for a longer or shorter period marked out as a man dedicated to God. His vow involved his scrupulously avoiding any corruption. The application of the principle to Joseph is clear.

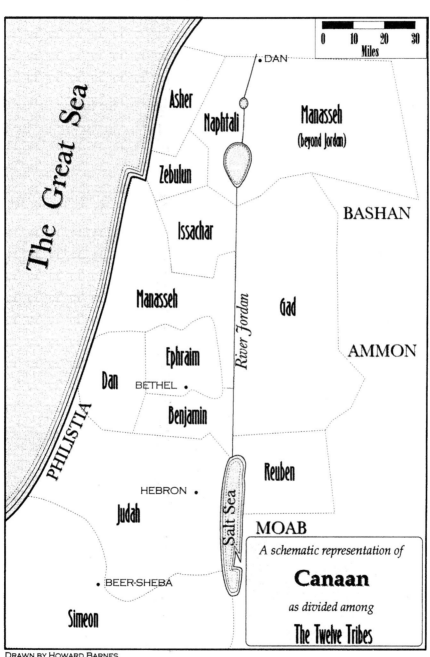

A schematic representation of

Canaan

as divided among

The Twelve Tribes

DRAWN BY HOWARD BARNES

GENESIS 50

Burial of Jacob in Canaan, Death of Joseph in Egypt

Verses 1-3: Jacob Is Embalmed and Officially Mourned

Since the end of ch.46 none of Joseph's brothers has been mentioned by name except in the blessings by Jacob in ch.49. Jacob had expressed his confidence in Judah in 46.28 and had given him and his tribe a special blessing. In the rest of these last four chapters Jacob and Joseph are the main actors. Thus in 50.1, though all the sons doubtless mourned Jacob and expressed their grief, Joseph is the only one mentioned as he "fell upon his father's face, and wept upon him, and kissed him". Joseph did, then, perform the final act of respect by closing his father's eyes in death (compare 46.4).

Joseph also had the authority and resources to make the necessary preparations for Jacob's burial. If Jacob was going to be buried in Canaan his body must be preserved for the time needed for the long period of mourning followed by the journey there. Joseph had physicians available to perform the elaborate preparation of the body through embalming. It is perhaps reading too much into the word physician to suggest, as Davis does, that Joseph avoided using the professional embalmers because of idolatrous practices normally associated with the process of embalming. Embalming was a distinctively Egyptian practice, mentioned in no other context in Scripture except this chapter. The embalming of Jacob was a complete treatment, for it took the normal period of forty days (v.3). The official mourning period of seventy days probably included the forty days taken up with embalming.

Verses 4-13: Jacob Is Buried in Canaan

Having completed the proper period of official mourning which was required by Egyptian custom for such a great man as Jacob, Joseph began preparation for the burial. He tactfully approached Pharaoh through intermediaries to ask for his approval of a burial in Canaan. He used a plea which was difficult to refuse: Jacob had bound him by an oath to bury him at Machpelah (47.31).[†]

Pharaoh could hardly refuse this request. Joseph promised that if approval were given he would return after the funeral. Pharaoh gave his approval in the simple form of a command, "Go up, and bury thy father".

Attention is drawn by commentators to the repeated use of the verb "go up" (ALA - 5927) in this chapter (vv.5,6,7,9,14). The same verb is also represented in the AV by something like "carry up" (vv.24,25). It was also used in 46.4, where God spoke to Jacob and promised, "I will also surely bring thee up again". It is used again in Exodus 1.10, where the Egyptians decided that they must deal subtly with the Israelites lest they "get them up out of the land". Though this is the last chapter of Genesis it contains features which point forward to part of the story still to be told.

So it was that Joseph, with Pharaoh's approval, "went up" to bury Jacob. With him went a great number of officials of different ranks, for he was a mighty man among them and must be honoured. Wenham points out that vv.7-9 contain a great number of phrases which will be repeated in the Exodus story (chs.10-14) describing those who will leave Egypt, both people and animals, though in Exodus they will go without Pharaoh's approval and his servants and troops will there be opposing the movement rather than, as here, escorting the Israelites. It was here a great procession, engaged to all appearances in an Egyptian ceremony, with Pharaoh's authority behind it. Yet when they halted to hold a ceremony of loud lamentation for a further seven days they halted at a threshing-floor, a traditional location for mourning such as this among Semitic peoples like the Hebrews.

The local Canaanites were bemused by this lamentation. The inspired writer refers to their naming the place in memory of the event, but the reference contains a characteristic Hebrew play on words. It can probably be taken that the people knew this place as Abel-Mizraim, "the Meadow of the Egyptians". But into this has been woven the other version Ebel-Mizraim, "the Mourning of the Egyptians". The location of Abel-Mizraim seems to have been on the east bank of Jordan ("beyond Jordan"). From there, after the seven days, Jacob's sons carried him, in accordance with his command, into the land of Canaan. Every detail is spelt out: "Canaan...cave of the field...Machpelah...Abraham bought with the field...of Ephron the Hittite, before Mamre". Jacob's commands had been obeyed to the letter and the record was set down for future generations.

Verses 14-21: Joseph's Brothers Plead for Forgiveness

In v.14 there is repeated reference to the fact that Jacob was now buried. But then Joseph's brothers awoke to the realisation that his death might have sinister implications for them. What if Joseph had not really forgiven them, but only withheld his judgment of them so as not to upset Jacob? No doubt they looked back on their earlier family life, as one does after the death of a parent. What they remembered was not reassuring.

They had no doubt about the enormity of their guilt, but they had never asked Joseph to forgive them, nor indeed had they heard him say in so many words that he forgave them. They had only his words of reassurance (45.5) and his evident goodwill towards them. It seems quite possible, but there is no certainty, that they had discussed the matter with Jacob and been advised as they alleged here that they had been. They may, on the other hand, have just made up the story of the advice which they said Jacob had given them.

Anyhow, they discreetly sent an intermediary to tell Joseph what Jacob had said to them. They gave a threefold confession of what they had done ("trespass", "sin" and "evil") and prayed him to forgive them. They described themselves as servants of the God of Joseph's father, drawing on their father's name to add to the poignancy of the plea. When they went in before Joseph they added further that they were his servants. It was an abject and emotional plea.

Confronted with their confession and plea, Joseph wept. Had he not forgiven them already (45.15)? Had he not explained that God was in it all (45.5-8)? So he repeated his reassurance that they need not fear (v.19). The precise meaning of his rhetorical question, "Am I in the place of God?" is not immediately clear. It seems to mean that God had turned their evil-doing into a happy outcome, namely "to save much people alive"; therefore God had made it clear that Joseph should not harbour bitter feelings and so go against God's will. The "much people" saved must have included his own family, the Egyptians and people of other nations who had come during the famine to buy corn. Joseph had not much difficulty forgiving his brothers because in all his circumstances he sought to find God and in all the high points and low points of his experience God was with him. Why then should he worry about getting his own back? The lessons here are clear.

He repeated his exhortation that they should not fear, for he would "nourish" ("provide for", REB) them and their families. So he "spoke to their hearts" as the Hebrew idiom so beautifully puts it (AV, "spake kindly unto them").

Verses 22-26: Joseph Dies and Is Embalmed in Egypt

After v.21 there is a time gap of fifty-four years before the death of Joseph, which is the next event related. The story of divine purpose for this embryonic race does not require any detail of that period. There have been hints already in this chapter that the real story will soon address the "going up" from Egypt to Canaan. Meanwhile "Joseph dwelt in Egypt, he, and his father's house".

His life-span was 110 years, which various writers have identified as being regarded by Egyptians as a full age. It was shorter than his ancestors, but still he "died in a good old age". His happiness is seen in that he saw his grandchildren and great-grandchildren. This has special importance because of the central interest among the covenant people in the perpetuation of the family line.

The final scene finds Joseph bringing his relatives, literally "brethren", together and announcing his impending death. His message was, however, one of hope. God would "visit" them (compare Ex 3.8) and bring them out into the promised land, as He had sworn to Abraham, Isaac and Jacob (compare 15.16 and later confirmations of this promise). This is another reminder that the covenant still stood and God would be faithful to it.

Joseph also required an undertaking from his people. They had to swear an oath that, when God did visit them as He had promised, they would carry his bones up to be buried in Canaan with his people. This oath their descendants honoured as is recorded in Exodus 13.19. Incidentally, Joseph's solemn insistence on this matter marks him out yet again as a man of faith, making preparation against the day when the promises of God would be fulfilled. Had not God sworn? He would assuredly do what He had said. This whole context has close links with the later history. Genesis, as has frequently been obvious, is not a complete story. It is phase one of a developing record of God's gracious, sovereign dealings with His people Israel.

The final verse, coming after this forward-looking oath ceremony, rounds off the Genesis phase. After the death of Joseph the trend sets in towards enslavement and then the exodus. The enslavement will be heralded in Exodus 1.8-11, where the new Pharaoh who "knew not Joseph" decided to "deal wisely" with the Hebrews, that is to manipulate them by oppression. Here it is simply recorded that "Joseph died, being an hundred and ten years old". Like Jacob, he was embalmed. Like Jacob he would be buried in the promised land, but only after a very long time.

In the meantime he was put in a coffin in Egypt, the only person in the OT who is said to have been treated so. No doubt the fact is connected with his having been mummified. This would normally be followed by the mummy being put in a mummy casket. Ancient Jewish scholars were interested in that fact that the word "coffin" (ARON - 727) was normally used in the OT for the ark of the covenant. They asked why the Israelites carried on their journeyings in the exodus two boxes, one containing the bones of a dead man, the other the covenant (that is, the law) of the living God. Their resolution of this question was typically Jewish in its symbolism: the dead man had in his life exemplified the principles of the law of God. It is at least an interesting idea. For the moment, however, the book which began with the sublime record of God bringing light and life into existence, ends with a man in a coffin. What must not be missed is the fact that he was in the coffin because he believed that God would fulfil His promises and bring His people back into their own land, as it were bringing life out of death.

Notes

5 One detail of what Jacob is reported as having said calls for comment. His words, "which I have digged for me", are most simply taken to refer to the fact that in the cave of Machpelah he would have hewn out a niche for Leah and one for himself at the time of her burial.

AFTERWORD

Genesis is the first instalment of the divinely inspired revelation. It lays the foundation for the story of God's dealings with His chosen people. Through His chosen people He has promised to bless the world, specifically through a promised deliverer. But Genesis ends with the Israelites in Egypt and Joseph's remains in a coffin there. The story is seemingly halted for the time being, with only a hint and a promise of divine activity to reactivate it.

How, then, has the story developed so far? Everything begins with God: "In the beginning God created…" He brings light and life into being. He blesses what He has made (1.22; 1.28; 2.3), for He sees that it is good. Then comes man's declaration of a false independence, the fall of the human race. Quickly God curses the serpent (3.14), the ground (3.17) and the first murderer (4.11). Humanity deteriorates so grievously that God decides to destroy the earth with all living beings on it by means of a flood. The flood purges the earth and God restores it with a blessing on Noah and his sons, the sole human survivors (9.1).

A most significant step forward is taken in 12.1 when God calls one Abram from Ur to a place of privilege and blessing (12.2). Abram travels from Ur to Haran and from Haran to Canaan, and from then onwards Canaan remains the focus of geographical interest, the land of promise. Abraham, as he had by then been renamed, bought a burial plot in Canaan (23.20), a token of the future possession of the entire land. He was uniquely privileged in that God entered into a covenant relationship with him.

Famine led to Jacob, Abraham's grandson, relocating his entire family in Egypt. The lengthy list of descendants who went down with him to Egypt serves as a reminder that after the issue of a promised land there is an equally vital issue of a promised line of descendants. This is particularly important because of the repeated hints and promises of an individual deliverer to come. Until Jacob, it had not been obvious how God would fulfil the promise of numerous descendants within the covenant made with Abraham, for Abraham and Isaac had only a handful of descendants who were included in covenant blessings. Jacob, however, was not just the father of one son, but of many, and they the fathers of tribes. Chapter 49 spells this out in detail.

Jacob's transfer to Egypt was at God's direct command. It was also preceded by Joseph being located there to prepare the way for the whole extended family. The later chapters of Genesis have been seen to contain hints that these people were not to stay in Egypt. After a long delay (compare 15.16) they would return to Canaan. Meanwhile Joseph in Egypt had been a blessing to the Egyptians and indeed, through his famine relief programme, had been in some sense saviour of the world. As Abraham's purchase of a small plot of land was a token of future possession of the whole land, so Joseph's saving work during the famine was a token of how God will bless mankind through the line of Abraham. At each stage where this is seen it becomes clear that the final blessing is still to come. So the Genesis story ends with Joseph mummified and in a coffin in Egypt. It is worth repeating that he was mummified because he anticipated a future return to Canaan and his burial with his people there. The bigger story of God's purpose is unfinished.

The sense of the story being unfinished and of each book of the biblical story being only a part of a bigger whole continues throughout the five books of Moses, as D.J.A. Clines has so powerfully shown.[†]

In Genesis the story points forward with the promise, "God will surely visit you, and ye shall carry up my bones from hence" (50.25). In Exodus the Lord makes His presence known in the Tabernacle at the end of the book, but it is emphasised (Ex 40.36-38) that this relates to their journeyings, for the Tabernacle is a movable sanctuary. They have not finally arrived. In Leviticus we have "the commandments, which the Lord commanded Moses for the children of Israel *in mount Sinai*" (27.34). Numbers carries the story forward with "the commandments and the judgments, which the Lord commanded by the hand of Moses unto the children of Israel *in the plains of Moab* by Jordan near Jericho" (36.13). Deuteronomy moves a stage further with "the statutes and judgments, which ye shall observe to do *in the land*, which the Lord God of thy fathers giveth thee to possess it, all the days that ye live upon the earth" (12.1). Yet at the end of Deuteronomy the story is incomplete, for Moses is dead and Joshua has still not been proved as commander-in-chief, nor has the land of promise been occupied.

Even the OT ends with a promise about the future, a promise to send "Elijah the prophet before the great and terrible day of the Lord come" (Mal 4.5 RV). The NT opens with hope in that "the way of the Lord" is being prepared by John the Baptist who came in "the spirit and power of Elijah" (Lk 1.17). But the One whom John introduced, while bringing blessing and salvation, did not finally set up His kingdom on earth. Hence the "mystery" phase of His kingdom is introduced (Mt 13.11) in His kingdom parables. His coming in manifest glory is still future. It is prophesied in Revelation. Expectation is built up in that book and climaxes in the promise, "Surely I come quickly" (Rev 22.20). The story begun in Genesis is not yet complete. The final fulfilment of the promises of God will undoubtedly be far beyond our imagining, even with the full revelation in our hands. Clines writes of the "overspill" of divine fulfilment going beyond what we thought God had promised because God is infinite. He does not fail in His promises, but we must not be surprised if the fulfilment is infinitely more grand and glorious than we had expected. For the present, we join faithful Abraham in looking for "the city which hath the foundations, whose builder and maker is God" (Heb 11.10 RV). This is revealed to John in the closing phases of the book of Revelation, but for the coming of the day of fulfilment we all still wait.

Notes

David J.A. Clines: The Theme of the Pentateuch (JSOT SS No 10, Dept of Biblical Studies, University of Sheffield 1978, reprinted frequently).